Managing Financial Services Marketing

Managing Financial Services Marketing

J R Marsh FCIB
Branch Manager with Lloyds Bank plc
Examiner in Marketing for the Chartered Institute of Bankers

PITMAN PUBLISHING
128 Long Acre, London WC2E 9AN

A Division of Longman Group UK Limited

First published in 1988
Reprinted 1991, 1992

A CIP catalogue record for this book is available from the
British Library

ISBN 0-273-03700-5

Printed in England by Clays Ltd, St Ives plc

Contents

Preface

The Chartered Institute of Bankers' subject, Marketing of Financial Services is designed to test a candidate's understanding of marketing as an attitude to business generally, its integral relationship with planning and strategy and its application in the various markets for financial services. This book sets out to assist those studying for this challenging examination. However, it is hoped that the contents will also prove beneficial to others, qualified or not, who are engaged in any aspect of marketing financial services. Although written by a banker, this book addresses many of the issues and problems associated with the retail marketing of services which will be common to a number of organisations operating in the busy high street. As such, the staff of building societies, estate agencies, insurance companies and other less well-known financial institutions should benefit from reading this book.

Marketing activity, and markets are an ever-changing scenario. But the basic philosophy and theory of marketing remains fairly constant. However, no book which covers the special factors of retail sales would be complete without including some of the current services on offer, their features, benefits and how they can be sold. The emphasis is on retail banking, so some of the 'wholesale' services are not included. Moreover, although it is written to cover an examination syllabus, the author has included many facets related to the sale of financial services that may not strictly be required by the curriculum. The objective has been to produce a complete work and the main criterion on content has been the degree of relevance in today's competitive climate.

The book is compiled in three sections. The first deals with the philosophy and basic understanding of what marketing is. In the second section how marketing is undertaken at various levels in an organisation is considered; this is the management science of marketing. Finally, the book looks in detail at how financial services can be sold through a branch network and highlights some of the likely characteristics of some key market segments. It is stressed that this book aims to help those bankers working in branches who are now expected, without much formal training, to sell more aggressively.

Some case studies and revision questions are taken from the Chartered Institute of Bankers' past examination papers and their published model answers to questions posed in the Financial Studies Diploma examination subject. The author is deeply grateful to the Chartered Institute of Bankers for allowing unfettered use of this valuable material and their ready agreement to release copyright.

In conclusion, whether readers are experienced marketeers or not, candidates for the Chartered Institute of Bankers' various examinations which have a marketing element, or just searching for a greater understanding of this important management skill, it is hoped that they will all enjoy this book. The marketing of financial services is a complex subject and one which will continue to change. This book should also provide readers with sufficient basic information of the current philosophy, theory and practice so that they will recognise and appreciate the reasons for changes as they occur.

Acknowledgements

Although this book has been written by a single author it would not have been possible for me to complete the task without support and guidance from many people. I owe a debt of gratitude to those long-suffering colleagues who helped and educated me during the years I worked in my bank's marketing and planning department. These colleagues were a mixture of domestic bankers like myself and marketing specialists – too many to mention by name – and I believe this rather unique mixture of people, and this period in my banking experience, gave me a valued combination of management skills.

I must also express deep gratitude to the Chartered Institute of Bankers, especially the encouragement from Mr Brian Rawle, for allowing me to use, in any way I pleased, past examination papers and the matching model answers for The Financial Studies Diploma Marketing of Financial Services examination. The model answers were especially important and have been widely used in the text of some chapters and as case studies.

Other people have made a more direct contribution to the production of this book. Miss Patricia Tennant deserves special commendation for quickly and skilfully producing a typed manuscript from my written draft. Her ability to read my writing, correct spelling errors and generally polish the grammar can only be described as masterly. Mr Chris Farrance kindly agreed to examine the content of the book in detail, bringing to bear his expertise and knowledge of the subject to ensure that the content is factual and readable. He has also written the foreword. Mr Farrance has my thanks for conducting his moderating role so diligently.

Part 1
Understanding
Marketing

Chapter 1
Philosophy and Role of Marketing in Banking

The marketing evolution

Marketing in the banking industry of the style and intensity we see today is a comparatively recent development. It owes much to the creation of a mass production and mass consumption society which in turn has stimulated competition by creating greater selling opportunities and rewards.

This changing environment and increasing competition has spread the banking habit throughout the social classes. Now, the vast majority of the adult population has some form of banking account if one includes customers of the National Giro and the building societies. Free banking, if in credit, became a widespread fact of life in 1985 and the abolition of the ancient Truck Acts towards the end of 1986 also encouraged more people and employers to use the facilities offered by various financial institutions.

Among the business fraternity this wind of change has been no less marked. New services, flowing from a greater appreciation of business needs, have helped the bank's corporate customers to grow. Government schemes to support new businesses have been linked into the services provided by banks. Although the numbers of start-up enterprises which do not survive more than a year or so is still very high, the numbers of small businesses being formed has expanded dramatically in recent years.

Against this background of growing markets for financial services, increasing competition and an improving level of financial awareness and sophistication by the end users, both personal and corporate, the banks have had to develop their marketing skills to at least maintain their market share and profitability levels.

The first professionally undertaken market research study, which is the most vital forerunner of effective marketing, dates back to the 1920s. This early research in the UK banking industry saw for the first time the use of statistical sampling methods. So, in approximately 65 years, market research and marketing in the banking industry we have today, developed from an embryo to their current high level of worldwide importance. This is a truly remarkable rate of evolution when one considers that a world war took place in the middle of that period.

More recently, mainly in the last decade, this evolution has quickened. Growing pains or pains created by cultural changes in the way bankers are expected to operate have appeared. The fiduciary dilemma, which will be discussed more fully later in this chapter, has created soul searching and cries that banking and selling do not mix. Most banks have been 'paper factories' or processing operations and have had little time for marketing. The eradication of paper and a reduction in the clerical processes is a primary goal of many banks, so that more staff time is available to develop the business. If this marketing time is to be used effectively, staff must be trained and co-ordinated in a way that will make maximum impact in the marketplace. All activity will need to be planned and this planning process is covered in detail later in this book. The marketing plan is the very core of successful marketing activity.

The selling and fiduciary dilemmas

The selling role

Before considering what we mean by marketing and its role in banking, it is important first to overcome a major attitudinal obstacle, namely that banking and selling do not mix.

Banking in this context probably refers to an old-fashioned view of what a banker is and should be doing – a pillar of society, running a bank where there is little competition, no touting and a national cartel covering the price of bank services. In this environment, business comes to the bank rather than the manager actively seeking new business as is now the widely accepted role. The reputation for propriety, honesty and efficiency is still paramount, coupled with convenience of location, for these factors are the very platform on which high street marketing activity is built. But more is required of expensive scarce resources as bankers now find themselves in a rapidly changing world which is very competitive. Nevertheless, habits and attitudes die hard and even today some older bankers may not accept or understand the need for change, yet playing 'lip service' to their employer's marketing requirements.

'I wasn't trained to sell', 'I must remain dispassionate', 'my fiduciary responsibilities are more important', 'selling my own bank investment services can cause problems if they do not perform very well'. Many readers will have heard these comments and can also sympathise with the dilemma in the minds of those who make them. Fiduciary responsibilities are important, as is the integrity and image of the branch manager. However, these 'resistance to change' comments are a defensive ploy arising from a lack of understanding of marketing and particularly of the more emotive role of selling.

In banking we are not expecting branch managers without any training or skill to go from door to door like a brush or double-glazing salesman. This is the cold sell. Nor are we expecting them to force services upon customers where no need is perceived. This is the hard sell.

Selling in banking today is that part of marketing concerned with demonstrating to the customer that the service is right for him or her. It is, therefore, one aspect of the marketing process of promotion. If the other elements are conducted properly, advertising, audience selection, identifying and matching the service benefits to customers' needs, competitive pricing and so on, then the final selling act should follow quite naturally.

Therefore, in a marketing orientated bank, the final selling act is a culmination of many other activities all designed to create the sales opportunity. For this reason one cannot say that banking and selling do not mix, especially when considering the enormous range of profit-structured services offered by the clearing banks. These services exist to be sold. Some will sell themselves; they are generic or synonymous with the everyday needs of living and trading – for example, paying in and drawing out cash. Other services need to be more overtly sold.

The growing need to sell (more consciously and effectively) stems from many of the rapid changes taking place in the traditional and the new banking markets. Competition is reducing the numbers of the unbanked, and persuasive marketing in the financial sector of industry is undermining previous high levels of customer loyalty to one particular bank. Cross-selling services to customers makes the decision by customers to change banks more difficult. There is also the need to overcome financial lethargy – customers try not to make decisions, such as making a will, until they are pressed to do so. To expand market share and profitability, 'active' rather than 'passive' marketing is now required.

Research into the corporate market clearly shows that business people would welcome bank managers calling on them and evidencing a closer interest in their trading problems. In the process, bankers would gain a more sympathetic and understanding image, rather than a remote image, only interested in past performance. Getting out and about is just one aspect of the marketing process with the ultimate aim of selling services.

The statement that selling and banking do not mix will remain while hostility, based upon fears of inadequacy to handle market demands, continues. Customer resistance to banks' selling activity will also grow where marketing is not carefully planned, properly executed, and services matched with customer needs.

Fiduciary responsibilities in perspective

When giving advice on financial requirements, the perceived need for impartiality takes on an added dimension. Two main considerations influence the comparison of similar financial services – price and benefits provided. It is a fact that the suppliers of food or consumer durables also sell on the basis of price and benefits, but the perceived need for impartiality does not seem to occur so strongly.

Return business comes from satisfied customers and this is important in banking. A chain of shops, with a heavy passing trade, may not need to place the same emphasis on customer satisfaction and return business. Moreover, financial services have to be more actively sold than food or consumer durables – one has to buy food and clothing to keep alive or remain decent and thus less persuasion is apparent or necessary.

The fiduciary dilemma stems from the need for bankers to gain commitment from customers to buy their services, which generally do not immediately appear to have life or death connotations, or affect the quality of life of the purchasers as, for instance, a washing machine would. Fiduciary responsibilities are also related to the image of bankers as impartial advisers. In this role there is a special need to ensure that this trust and the customer's expectation of objectivity from his/her banker are not misplaced. The 1986 Financial Services Act (Big Bang) has enforced on all advisers this hitherto naturally accepted need by bankers to exercise objectivity. The Act introduced 'polarisation' rules (see Chapter 15) making all investment advisers choose between exclusively selling their own company's services or being independent brokers or intermediaries only selling other companies' investment services. In this way, the public are protected because they now know the extent of their adviser's allegiances.

When customers look to bankers for financial advice, because those customers are unwilling or unable to make their own judgements, then issues such as price and service characteristics, when recommending one service rather than another, take on special complexities. Customer trust is very important in financial matters and the bank manager is obliged to pay attention to achieving the right balance between the commercial and fiduciary issues.

The commercial considerations, mainly the need for profit, should come first. This will invariably favour the sale of the bank's own service rather than that of a competitor. But the effects of the sale of a 'house product' on long-term profit earnings must also be assessed to ensure a short-term gain is not, in the longer term, a much greater loss. If customers feel the bank has not exercised impartiality when it should do so, return business will go elsewhere.

Customers' views of what is expensive, or what the benefits of a service are worth to them, vary widely. It is not for the banker to make these value judgements – it is first and foremost for the customers to decide what service they prefer. The banker's job is to pitch prices and benefits at levels which accord with corporate and marketing objectives and are in line with what he or she thinks the market will be attracted by and pay.

The basis of successful marketing

Marketing starts in the marketplace, but the speed and direction of marketing activity stems initially from a bank's corporate objectives. These two basic features of trading are the main starting points for developing and practising the management skills of marketing.

The needs of customers, and prospective customers, cannot be ignored by any trading company, and banks are no exception. Relying merely on selling only those services that are already available is, at best, a short-term expedient. Market attitudes, preferences, technology and environmental factors are constantly changing. Trading success against this background depends on identifying and reacting to these changes. Moreover, whenever possible, efforts should be made to anticipate market changes. Selling the financial services that are available, rather than the services required by chosen markets was perhaps a feasible strategy prior to 1971. That year saw the end of the clearing bank cartel and the start of a new era of increasing competition both from within the banking industry and from without.

It was the publication of the Bank of England's discussion paper 'Competition and Credit Control' in 1971 which led to greater competition among the banks. However, competitive pressures had been increasing for several years due partially to the activities of the Office of Fair Trading reviewing the trading practices of a wide spectrum of financial institutions. Although market needs are important, a bank must strike a balance between meeting these requirements and the associated costs of providing new services. Making the best use of expensive resources, such as labour, machinery, buildings and time, is a major task for a clearing bank with a large network of branches.

For a bank to survive, profits must be earned, and part of this process involves the containment of costs when seeking the most profitable markets to exploit. Therefore, bank resources must be channelled towards the potentially more profitable trading areas, and this, in turn, necessitates making a choice. It is the identification of these chosen markets and the allocation of the right balance of resources which calls for the marketing skills of research, planning and assessment. A bank's corporate aspirations – its plans for its future size and profit/volume levels compared with its current size and profitability – are the basis on which marketing plans are compiled.

Balancing the use of resources against the market opportunities entails managing the business. This active management of the business of banking, to a greater or lesser extent, should take place at every level of the bank and be co-ordinated to avoid diffusion of effort.

Management of marketing

Thus it is clear that marketing is a management science and not an end in itself. It is a tool of a manager's trade and as such can be used skilfully or badly. Marketing is also a much wider activity than selling, and if defining the role of marketing is carried to the ultimate limit then it is not a specialised activity at all. It encompasses the whole business. If this is so, as it certainly ought to be in a marketing-orientated bank, then what distinguishes those who are simply engaged in marketing activity and those whose job it is to manage that activity? The answer is that those who are engaged in the planning, organising, directing and evaluation of marketing activity within the bank, are actually managing the marketing process. It is the task and responsibility of marketing management to provide 'a disciplined analysis of the needs, wants, perceptions and preferences of target and intermediary markets as the basis for effective product, design, pricing, communications and dis- tribution' (Kotler: *Marketing Management – Analysis Planning and Control*). This process may be thought of as continuous and dynamic. The first stage, planning, leads on to implementation followed by evaluation which in turn relates back to the overall plan.

The organisational structure of the marketing management process in a bank will reflect its importance as well as determining its precise role. McIver and Naylor have related the management function to both the 'unitary' and the 'multiple' organisation. The first uses the marketing department either in a line management or else in a central advisory 'staff' role, and the second contains both 'staff' and line management functions at different levels throughout the organisation.

A third type of organisation using 'product management' gives the marketing responsibility for specific products to individual product managers. These managers can usually call upon the expertise of other central functions such as research or advertising, though they may well be organisationally divorced from the line functions below them.

Finally, beyond product management, the marketing function may be organised around 'market management'. This allows the bank to identify more closely with the needs of selected customer groupings.

The ideal marketing-orientated bank brings together both its central and line-related functions to create a complete marketing management process that is practical as well as theoretically sound.

Marketing concepts and philosophy

The theory and philosophy which lie behind marketing action must be fully understood. This basic knowledge will enhance appreciation of the later chapters which cover the practical issues of selling services, as well as recognising or creating sales opportunities.

What is marketing? A good definition for a financial institution, and there are many versions, should demonstrate marketing concepts in a service selling environment. We are indebted to Derek Vander Weyer, formerly of Barclays Bank, for his definition which highlights many of the practical aspects of marketing financial services:

'Marketing is identifying the most profitable markets now and in the future, and assessing the present and future needs of customers. It involves setting business goals, making plans to meet them and managing services in such a way that these plans are achieved. It also necessitates adapting to a changing environment in the market place.'

This definition highlights the sophisticated world we now live in, but going back to J W Gilbart's preface to the 1849 edition of his *Practical Treatise on Banking* it states: 'The practical end of banking, as of all other trades and professions is to get money'. The importance of profit has not diminished or increased over the years. There are many other definitions of marketing including that put forward by Geoffrey Naylor when presenting the Gilbart Lectures in 1982: 'Marketing is profitable selling and buying now and in the future'.

Whichever definition is used, there are some key elements for financial service institutions:

(a) *Profit and customer satisfaction*   The need to balance corporate goals with customer requirements has already been considered. A high profit, at the expense of customer satisfaction, is likely to adversely affect the potential of future growth through return business. Equally, a low profit or no profit at all may provide customer satisfaction but is not the best longer-term use of resources and reduces the level of funding of new services. There are reasons for marketing loss-making services, but only when the total account relationship can be made profitable immediately or in the medium term.

(b) *Customer requirements and future needs*   Meeting customer needs is at the heart of all marketing activity, and the life-blood of marketing is adapting or introducing services as customers' requirements alter. It has been said that the only constant factor of marketing is its propensity for constant change.

(c) *Setting objectives as a cornerstone of managing the business*   Planning is important, and without the disciplines of systematic planning, marketing successes are less likely. However, more than planning is required; the whole organisation needs to believe in and be harnessed to achieving goals that are clearly defined and accepted as right. To achieve this happy state, good communications, control, flexibility and a host of other man-management functions are crucial requirements.

Our chosen definition highlights the main trading objectives of a business but there are also three important organisational aims encompassed within the philosophy of marketing which are well worth remembering:

(1) *planned pursuit of profit* or profitable volume;
(2) *customer orientation* in all matters and at all levels;
(3) *co-ordination* of all activity towards *common goals*.

Co-ordination of activity through a planned marketing approach is covered fully in Chapters 9 and 10 but a few words on profit and customer care will reinforce these two elements of the marketing philosophy.

The importance of profit

Recent developments in banking have reinforced the importance of profit. Rising operating costs from conducting business through a network of branches has necessitated many banks finding new ways of generating profit. Profit requirements have also stimulated the very nature of the banking industry to change as it seeks higher margins and revenue growth to support expansion and to counter inflation. Longer-term lending is now commonplace, whereas ten years ago the likelihood of banks undertaking mortgage lending, and owning subsidiaries such as estate agents, would have been considered remote. Today, both are a reality and this expansion of banking into less traditional financial operations will surely continue.

Over the next decade, new technology will also have a major influence on the way banks do business and endeavour to meet customers' increasingly sophisticated financial requirements. New electronic payment systems within the United Kingdom and worldwide, together with computer-based treasury management information services for larger corporate customers, are expensive to create and maintain.

Improving profit through realistic pricing policies and entrée into new markets is required to pay for these developments. Profit is also necessary to fund longer-term lending commitments as the level of gratuitous credit balances, hitherto held on current accounts, decline because of improved public financial awareness, partially caused by aggressive competitive advertising.

Profit, and profitability appraisal, will touch virtually every aspect of marketing and is the thread which runs right through the corporate and marketing planning process. Areas of regular appraisal for profit contribution include the following:

(a) *Services* Analysis will cover profitability of each service, comparisons with competitors, gaps in the service range and a cost analysis of providing each service.

(b) *Markets* Research to establish priority market groups, existing customer profiles, and future profit potential of sub-segments of the total market.

(c) *Service developments* This will include a cost/profit analysis of all new services set against the information gleaned from target market research.

(d) *Resource allocation* The way in which a business is managed impacts ultimately on profit levels. Utilisation of personnel and premises, together with the way the organisation's assets/liabilities are managed are important appraisal areas. Analysis of organisation methods, operational systems and attitudes will provide a useful appreciation of the efficiency of the business. The well-structured marketing approach will take these strengths and weaknesses as part of developing marketing activity to determine overall profit capability, and set goals accordingly.

Customer care

Growth of business in most service industries is built up on a reputation for providing customer satisfaction by giving a good standard of attention and care. This is closely associated with exercising fiduciary responsibilities. Retail or high street banking is no exception, and this desire to give good service does not conflict with profit objectives.

Customer care is as fundamental to marketing as the development and launch of a new financial facility. Unfortunately, the marketing benefits of providing a high standard of customer care cannot be quantified very easily. As a result, it is often regarded as an operational rather than a marketing function. Once again, the delicate balance required when utilising resources can be seen. For example, too much effort in trying to gain new business may undermine the efforts made to look after existing business. Gaining new business whilst losing existing accounts through poor service is self-defeating and highlights resource allocation weaknesses which should have been overcome by careful corporate and marketing planning.

Different markets require different styles

It is a fallacy to think that there is only one marketing process shaped in such a way that it will cover any problem or set of circumstances. The marketplace is constantly changing and it is probably true to say that the only constant facet of marketing is its need to change constantly. In Chapter 10 the need to tailor the shape and content of a marketing plan to meet the specific requirements of the marketplace and circumstances is stressed. This requirement of flexibility remains largely true for all other aspects of marketing, not least when communicating with chosen market segments.

We are all individuals, and although many groups of people have broadly similar needs, and can be approached in similar ways, there will always be an individual with requirements for financial services which fall outside the norm or usual parameters. In later chapters, customer groups are considered in some detail. Who are they, what do they want, how are priority markets selected, how are they reached and with what? These are questions which lie at the heart of an operation which pumps the marketing effort. Without customers there is no bank.

In the very broadest terms there are two markets – personal customers and corporate customers. The latter market sector spans from the 'one-man band' through to the multinational companies. The corporate market could also include clubs, societies and charities for often they are run like a business, despite being ostensibly non-profit-making.

Marketing opportunities among personal customers can occur in the following ways:

(a) *At an interview* where the need for a particular service arises in the conversation seeking advice, resolving a problem, or requesting one service which identifies a potential need for another, e.g. request for travellers cheques reveals a requirement for travel insurance.

(b) *Through marketing campaigns* where, because of the lifestyle or circumstances of a group of customers, financial needs are similar and the benefits of a service or services might well match with customers' needs.

Marketing campaigns are now an accepted and necessary part of banking. Managers meet relatively few of their customers and research shows that public knowledge of bank services is very low. Mass marketing activity increases awareness of services. Where needs are correctly recognised and the benefits of suitable services carefully explained, campaign type marketing is effective.

In the corporate market, there are fewer broad areas of similarity in customer requirements. They do exist and some mass marketing activity, especially for specialist services, can be used effectively as a 'softening-up' process. However, most marketing will rely upon 'one-to-one' contact when individual trading needs can be accurately determined and the advice and services tailored more specifically to individual corporate customer circumstances.

Marketing financial services compared with industrial products

The added weight or importance of being a banker with fiduciary responsibilities when selling financial services, compared for instance with those selling sweets, has already been highlighted. In most other respects the differences between selling services and products are more apparent than real. Certainly the marketing principles are similar, although there will be differences in how the elements of the marketing mix – price, promotion, distribution, etc. – are applied in practice.

Nevertheless these marketing mix differences between a financial institution, and a company selling sweets, stem from an understanding of the marketplace, the needs and wants of customers and the buying process used by those customers. In other words, the way in which buyers are made aware of products or services and the means used to distribute them is dictated by the requirements of the buyers in the marketplace and not by the requirements of the sellers.

However, when progressing beyond this basic marketing philosophy of catering or being driven by the basic needs of the marketplace, there are differences, especially between consumer, or retail operations, and industrial marketing. For example, the demand for products or components produced by an industrial process derives from the demand stimulated by the retail operation. There can also be some intermediary demand levels including wholesalers and agents which generally are not found in the financial services arena. Therefore, the nature of demand for a product or component stems from several sources and is often linked to the demand for many other products. Demand for financial services is not derived in the same way through intermediaries or affected to the same extent by other financial facilities except where a bank makes a conscious effort to package or group related services together.

Moreover, financial services have no taste or smell; they cannot be stored nor can they claim they could make the difference between life and death. As has been said earlier in this chapter, clothes are necessary to keep us warm or within the laws of decency; food is required or we will die. Consequently there is a steady demand for both, and it is only the choice of which clothes or food that matters. Wrapping and packaging forms a vital part in influencing this consumer choice. Financial services are not seen as 'life or death requirements' and it is very difficult to 'package' an executor and trustee service in a way that is attractive and will stimulate demand.

The price mechanism as a marketing tool is also more flexible and influential when marketing products than when selling financial services. Local price variations can stimulate sales of a company's baked beans or motor cars in particular areas where competition is fierce or where new markets are being sought. Brand image is important and it is an accepted fact that the average buyer is a creature of habit. Once the consumer is persuaded to buy a certain brand, modest weight and price variations can often be ignored.

This ability constantly to fine tune nationally, and within regional areas, the marketing mix elements of price and promotion by product providers is not yet possible for institutions selling financial services.

Services have a much longer 'life' than a tin of baked beans, and adjustments to prices, especially downwards, to stimulate demand can have a disastrous effect on existing users. The choice of promotional methods also differs, especially when salespeople are used to market products, and when the desire is to stimulate immediate demand for products that are seasonal or decay quickly. 'Sell-by dates' have not encroached upon financial services as yet. It should also be appreciated that many products have a very wide appeal, and advertising activity need not be aimed as selectively for products as for financial services. This is why the major companies selling products and food, which have a natural 'popular' demand, have brand managers whose role is to differentiate and promote one product. Marketing bank services, especially in a high street branch environment, is less simplistic, although there is a case for brand managers to take responsibility for the bank's development and marketing of individual key financial services at a head office level.

There are other ways in which the marketing of products may differ from the marketing of financial services. In recent years these variations have become narrower as the banks have sought to learn from the knowledge and experience of their industrial counterparts. Many marketing methods used by financial institutions including 'give aways' would have been unacceptable only a few years ago. In Chapter 7 the growing trend towards telephone selling, cold calling, and merchandising generally is considered in some depth.

Case study

Are there any circumstances which should cause a branch manager to recommend a competitor's services rather than similar services of his or her own bank?

The most obvious example is to suggest that a customer should try a competitor when a decision is made not to advance a loan. For instance, if the reason for decline is lack of security, the proposition may be acceptable to a hire-purchase company which will have statutory rights over the goods purchased. A bank loan does not embody similar statutory cover.

However, the question presupposes that the manager is happy to make his or her own bank services available, and thus a greater depth of analysis of circumstances is required.

Competition

Competition comes in many guises but in the broadest terms any two organisations which market similar services in a free market do so in competition. The most obvious competition for a bank is another bank. Building societies, investment companies, hire-purchase companies and even local authorities all have common aims – to attract or lend funds. Some have tax concessions (the Post Office for example) which, depending upon the customer's own financial position, provide a commercial trading advantage. Where this, or a high degree of special expertise exists, the number of occasions when the bank's own service is preferable could well diminish.

Buying considerations

Ease of availability, price and perceived service benefits all bear upon the ultimate choice made by the potential buyer. However, in practice many bank customers rely upon their bank manager to make this choice for them. Financial sophistication is growing, but the image of the banker as an adviser still persists. Awareness of this image can lead the banker to recommend a proven service from a competitor rather than his or her own bank's service especially in the earlier stages of the service life cycle when the likely performance is uncertain in the absence of an historic track record – a policy of play safe.

This type of fiduciary dilemma does not seem to apply to traditional services such as a current account or a personal loan. Generally the customer has already made the buying decision. Conflict in the mind of a banker is most likely to occur where investment and savings services are concerned, especially, if in the early life of the service, an in-house service lacks the credibility that comes from a successful track record.

Before analysing the special factors affecting a banker's decision to recommend a competitor's service it is worth looking at the various elements which feature in the buying process. All services are usually compared by price, benefits offered, potential benefits, and past record. When looking at these facets, buyers and sellers may well see them differently and give them different value weightings.

For example, what may be considered too high a price to pay by one customer may be perfectly acceptable to another. The seller's skill involves pitching the price at a level that the targeted market is likely to bear, or at a figure which may be designed to create exclusivity, or restrict or control the demands upon scarce resources. Therefore, it is first and foremost for the customer to assess the benefits and to decide which of the services available in the marketplace he prefers.

Banker recommendations

When customers look to the banker for advice, because they are unwilling or unable to make up their own minds, then the issues of price and potential benefits, take on a further set of complexities. At this stage customer trust becomes more important and bankers are obliged to pay more attention to the commercial and fiduciary issues. In doing so they should examine the commercial aspects first. Moreover, as a guide, it is generally safe to assume on balance that by recommending the service most suitable for the customer, whether an in-house service or not, a banker is probably also acting in the best longer-term interest of the bank.

Therefore, bankers must assess the effects of their recommendations on longer-term profit. In their choice of service they will consider the likelihood of alienating return business, particularly if there is a possibility of customers perceiving an element of bias, or the house product is not reasonably competitive (as opposed to the best on the market).

They will also take into account that satisfied customers can be a powerful salesforce for the bank. The commercial benefits from this, and a good reputation generally, cannot be quantified.

Summary

This chapter has covered a diverse number of philosophical, theoretical and practical marketing issues which can arise in a branch going about its day-to-day business. They are, and will continue to be, key talking-points as the rapid evolution of marketing in banking continues to cause some growing pains. Old habits and attitudes – banking and marketing do not mix, some say – need to be laid to rest. The reality of the current commercial environment, which includes vigorous competition, growing customer financial sophistication, the need to improve profit to cover increasing costs, inflation and expansion, is gradually bringing about a widespread appreciation of the need for marketing. It is only by planning and managing resources correctly that a bank will meet the challenges it now confronts.

Remember –

Marketing is the science of judging the market and providing for it. It follows therefore that consumers' wants, desires, tastes and attitudes are at the heart of any marketing philosophy – marketing starts in the marketplace.

Selling is the culmination of effective marketing activity. If the marketing process is correctly applied, customers will buy.

Customer trust is very important for a bank which constantly strives for 'return business'. When recommending financial services a bank manager must pay attention to achieving the right balance between the commercial and fiduciary issues. The perceived value of a service in the eyes of the customer should not be prejudged by a banker. In circumstances where a customer is unwilling to choose between one service or another and looks to the banker for guidance, the fiduciary responsibilities of a banker will increase with the consequent need for socially responsible attitudes when giving advice.

Marketing is much wider than selling. It should encompass all the functions of business with the ultimate goal of achieving customer satisfaction and profitability.

Customers and customer groups have individual needs. Although customers can be segmented into groups with similar needs for campaign marketing purposes, their needs as individuals should not be forgotten.

The requirements of marketing financial services are similar to marketing products, but the ways in which the marketing mix elements are applied – price, promotion, distribution – will differ appreciably.

Revision questions

1 Describe why and how marketing has developed in the last decade. What have been the main forces for changing the ways in which banks sell services?
2 Banking and selling do not mix. Discuss.
3 Bankers cannot use marketing techniques similar to those applied to selling products. Discuss and illustrate your views with reference to various elements of the marketing mix.
4 Explain how and why marketing is regarded as a managerial process.
5 How does the concept of 'servicing a market' differ from selling the services we've got'? What factors would make one route more profitable than the other for a bank?

Chapter 2
Marketing Research

Why use marketing research?

Arguably market research is the most important function in the whole marketing process. If marketing is to be carried out successfully then obtaining the best possible information, on which to base management's marketing decisions, is paramount. This chapter will concentrate on marketing research as a marketing tool, its role, and the various ways in which research can be undertaken. In those chapters which follow, covering the marketing mix elements of price, promotion and distribution, the practical application of marketing research will be illustrated in much greater detail.

Marketing research is the means by which companies keep themselves in touch with the needs and attitudes of those who buy their goods or services. It can also establish why others buy the goods or services from a competitor organisation. To find out this information, marketing research will need to answer a number of fundamental questions. The way in which the information is gathered, and in a format that can be accurately interpreted, is the basic skill required by all those engaged in marketing research.

Even today there is still some scepticism among senior managers in the major banks about the importance of the contribution that can be made by marketing research. These views generally stem from a lack of appreciation of what it can do and a disbelief that this type of research can widen horizons and improve the quality of decision making. Intuition is cheaper than using structured research methods only when the intuitively-based decisions prove to be the right ones. So marketing research can help to tell you what you do not know but it will also confirm that intuitive views are not misguided.

Moreover, it should not be overlooked that this research should be a continuous process; after all, the marketing environment is constantly changing. Marketing research programmes should be sufficiently dynamic to give the bank up-to-date information to improve the effectiveness of its ongoing activities. Even so, the most comprehensive research can only be an aid to decision making. There is seldom an unequivocal answer to issues and problems, so it can only complement management's judgement and experience. This knowledge and experience derived especially at a branch level, is important, and can be used to supplement and support findings from structured research programmes, so adding another dimension to help improve the accuracy of information and the quality of the resultant corporate decisions that are taken. For a large organisation, such as a high street bank, the communication system upwards needs to be good enough to allow information to come forward in an unfiltered way. Local knowledge can make an important contribution to the marketing research effort provided it is gathered systematically and in sufficient quantity to neutralise the effect of emotive attitudes and personal experiences which may undermine objective thinking.

The main role of market research

A formal definition of market research is as follows:

'The process of defining the problem then systematically collecting, refining, analysing and summarising all information which relates to the problem affecting the bank going about its business generally'.

Most textbooks refer to six steps involved in conducting a marketing research programme:

(1) Understanding the problem
(2) Identifying when and where the research should be undertaken
(3) Refining the way in which the research will be conducted (questionnaire design etc.)
(4) Actually collecting and collating the information
(5) Analysing the findings
(6) Summarising and reporting the results.

Like many other aspects of marketing the outcome of research, as we have said, will largely depend upon the skill of those responsible for the task in selecting the right programme of events and using the best methods available to find solutions to the particular problem being researched. Knowing what to do is only half the solution: knowing how to do it is also vital.

Forces of change

The definition used above is very sweeping and by itself does not highlight the multitude of complex areas that impact on the marketing effort. There are many external and internal forces exercising their influences on the marketplace and a bank's capabilities to respond. The influence of these forces will vary from place to place and affect differing organisations in various ways. Which forces are considered more important than others and which can be neutralised or harnessed to support the marketing effort will be a question of judgement. Nevertheless knowing what areas to research is crucial and the grids below

Table 2.1   Major external market forces

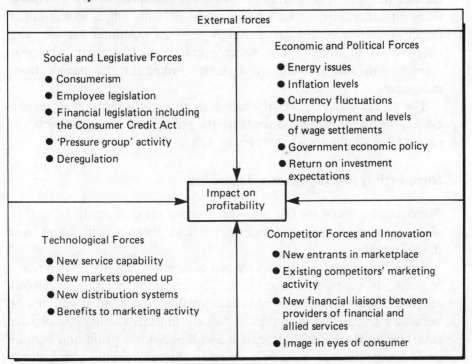

Table 2.2   Major internal market forces

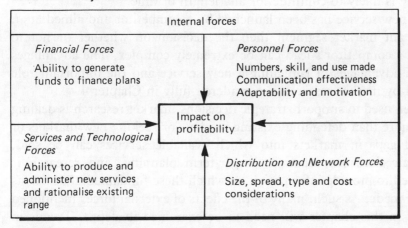

illustrate some of the main external and internal forces which could influence a bank's marketing activity.

Any of these internal and external forces could influence the ways in which a bank goes about its business. The marketing facets which are most likely to be affected in the short term are the marketing elements of price, promotion and the reallocation of services which are considered as priorities for promotion. In the longer term, the fundamental structure of the retail bank operation could be affected. This could include network spread, numbers of staff, reshaping of branch operations into alternatives which range from specialist offices looking after larger corporate customers, through personal customer service sales shops, down to 'lobby' banks which provide mainly mechanical money transmission and information facilities linked to the bank's main computer.

The technological pace of change is already beginning to revolutionise the way in which banks serve the public and this is probably the major force of change at the present time.

Supporting management decisions

Management decisions fall into three broad areas; namely tactical or short term, strategic or longer term and those which cover new developments.

Tactical decisions often occur when competitor activity is such that a response is considered necessary. This type of decision is largely reactive but nevertheless some research will be required. It will first be necessary to assess the impact, or likely impact, of this competitive insertion on the bank's immediate and longer-term profit and volume growth expectations. Research aimed in this way should also indicate whether the competitor's manoeuvre is proving effective and if the activity is likely to continue for any length of time.

If a new service has been launched by a competitor and aimed at an important market segment then the decision on whether or not to follow a competitor's lead can be extremely complex. The advantages and disadvantages of launching a new service and the important role played by market research is considered fully in Chapter 4.

When used to support strategic decisions, market research is dealing with more than defending existing markets or seeking new markets or indeed gaps in markets into which available services can be sold. Strategic decisions relate to longer-term planning, and research is required to provide information on which these fundamental decisions can be made. As such, many of the effects of external forces mentioned earlier in this chapter will need to be examined in depth. Trends in technological progress, environmental, legal and social changes together with the directions being taken by competitors, both new and traditional, will be important research areas. Medium to long-term planning is crucial to the ongoing success of a bank. Poor decisions, based perhaps on inadequate research, or misguided judgement, can set a bank back many years. The most recent example was the Midland Bank's purchase in the USA of Crocker Bank which was subsequently sold. The losses sustained on the sale had a massive adverse effect on City confidence and on the morale of customers and staff. It also impacted on the financial strength of the Midland Bank when compared with the other major clearers.

Finally, development decisions aim to help the banks keep pace with market requirements and, whenever possible, anticipate them. Whether or not to launch a new service or modify an existing one is just one area of development decisions. Others can affect the very heart of the banking process and include whether or not to expand or contract numbers of outlets, buy a stockbroker arm, a chain of estate agents or any other institution that would give additional corporate and trading strength compared with competitors.

The research to provide the information to support development decisions is generally a longer-term programme. As such, the methods that would be used to assist tactical decisions, compared with development decisions, could differ substantially. Critical factors in all research and choice of research methods are: time available, cost, choice of sources available, methods that can be used to gather information and lastly the skill of interpretation. For example, a 'back to the drawing-board' research programme takes many months and would be inappropriate to management required to make a quick decision on whether or not to react to a competitive 'cut price' ploy.

This example shows the need to tailor the research, and the cost of it, to the given circumstances which in the first place created the need for research. The link between cost and perceived benefits must be stressed even though the perceived benefits are sometimes difficult to quantify. Lack of hard facts is not an excuse for management to ignore the cost/benefit relationships of research or for any other marketing activity. Prompt action will invariably call for skilful management and judgement, not just in interpreting the research data but also in deciding what research should be undertaken at the outset.

Using market research

In global terms the chief executives of a retail bank will continually be asking the following questions:

> What sort of bank are we running?
> What sort of bank do we want?
> How do we create that sort of bank?

Answering these questions requires a continuous research programme, and the information collated will be fed into the bank's corporate and marketing planning process (Chapters 9 and 10). As a priority the research will concentrate on regularly obtaining information on:

(a) The chosen markets in which the retail bank is operating and other potential markets and geographical areas.

(b) The quality and demographic (age, sex, wealth, etc.) profile of its personal customer base.

(c) The quality and spread of its business customers.

(d) Its competitive positions in the marketplace in terms of financial performance, share of business and quality potential of its customer profile.

In summary, retail banking is about customers, quality of business and market share. These issues will provide the main framework for research which is undertaken to aid the ongoing development and strategic decisions. To research all these areas the questions starting with 'who', 'what', 'when', 'where', 'how', and 'why' will be the ones most likely to reveal the answers. 'Know your customer and the marketplace' is a remarkably sound adage. But how many organisations really know, or take the trouble to find out, the major characteristics and requirements of their customers and potential customers? Without accurate answers to these and other pertinent questions, business decisions become highly subjective and risky. Thus, research aims to reduce the trading risks inherent in any business.

Contribution to the marketing mix

Marketing research is necessary within the four major business activities which make up the marketing mix – price, promotion, services and distribution. The role of research in these four important areas of marketing activity is to assess the likely effects and implications of possible alternative decisions or strategies and to measure the effectiveness after a decision has been taken and implemented.

How this research contributes in practice is covered more fully in later chapters which look very closely at the marketing mix elements and how they can be utilised by a bank to support its marketing objectives. As a basic platform to develop the understanding of how marketing research can be used in the day-to-day business of banking the next few pages highlight some of the underlying theory of research, the ways it can be undertaken and some of the sources that can be used to provide relevant information.

(a) Price

Price is one of the most flexible elements of marketing and where services are price sensitive one of the most dynamic influences on sales and profitability.

Marketing research can contribute to the bank's pricing decisions by carrying out surveys among financial service users to obtain reactions to different price levels for different services. Perceived service quality among user groups, both customers and non-customers, will also influence what they are prepared to pay for a financial service. Therefore value data is an integral part of any research into pricing and pricing alternatives.

Information about competitor pricing policies and comparisons with the bank's own services which have similar features and benefits is another important contribution that research can make.

Having gauged user views on pricing, and analysed competitor pricing policies, the last area of research will be to ascertain the effects of changes in pricing on likely demand generally, market share ultimately and profitability. Nowadays more and more institutions and banks are competing on price. Discount schemes and special offers are becoming commonplace and perhaps in the not too distant future it will be possible for regional or even branch managers to meet localised competition by exercising tactical pricing options that are not universally followed throughout the bank. The need for good quality market research at least at regional as well as head office level in the future seems to be emerging. Some banks have area marketing teams and this trend will continue as the banks strive to meet more specific customer requirements which have, in turn, been influenced by the type of area in which they are domiciled.

(b) Promotion

A bank has three key audiences to whom promotional activity in all its various forms is aimed. These are, firstly, the government and public at large to whom it wishes to create an image of propriety, soundness and social responsibility. The second audience is its shareholders, many of whom are also staff, and the objectives of promotional activity will be to reassure them that the bank's business is expanding in the right way, is profitable and long-term prospects for their jobs or investment are good. Finally, and arguably the most important group, are those segments of the public who are already users or regarded as potentially profitable users of the bank's services.

Within these three broad groups of people there are a considerable number of sub-groups each with its own characteristics in terms of beliefs, attitudes and financial requirements. So it can be readily appreciated that advertising and promotion in all its forms is a vast area to be researched. In simplistic terms, the overall aims of promotion as a vehicle of communication will point researchers in the right direction. The basic steps in the communication process are to attract attention, gain interest, convey information clearly and accurately, and finally to create impact and persuade the recipient to take favourable action. Each and every step can be researched in order to ascertain whether or not the message, means and timing of the promotion are proving cost effective.

Marketing research will be interested in the impact of the bank's advertising and promotional efforts in different chosen markets and the effectiveness of the various channels of communication being used. This testing of the recipient's awareness of the promotional activity will be followed up by research into the levels of demand or degree of shift in attitude that has been achieved. There is grave danger in assuming that sales levels of a bank service are a fair indication of the effectiveness of promotion, especially of advertising. But if the marketing effort is co-ordinated and applied correctly, advertising is only one factor and other elements, not least price and availability, also influence take-up levels. Therefore it is important to stress that measuring the effectiveness of an individual advertisement or promotion needs to be carried out long before sales figures are known. Otherwise a considerable sum could be spent on communicating with target audiences in a way that makes little or no impact.

(c) Services

Marketing research will carry out a continuous review of existing services to establish the point they have reached in their life cycle. The service life cycle concept is explained fully in Chapter 4 but briefly it recognises that services over a period of time go through four main stages from evolution to ultimate decline – introduction, growth, maturity and demise. Each stage is marked by a sales curve, and the growth and maturity periods when sales are at their highest can be extended by massaging the features of the service, and the way it is promoted. However, to appreciate what stage a service has reached necessitates ongoing and careful research. It would be wasteful to spend considerable sums on promotion in the decline stage when this money might be better spent on developing a replacement service. Knowing how and when to extend the sales life of a service is one contribution that research can make, but its role and contribution extend well beyond this support function. Research is used to review regularly the features of services, the use of packaging with other associated services and demand trends in the marketplace. Competitor services and the effects of these also require continuous research as do the changes in consumer preferences so that new or modified services can be introduced to meet anticipated changes in demand and consumer requirements.

Finally, the contribution that research can make to the development and launch of a new service is enormous. It is very costly to create and market new financial services, and a continuous process of evaluating and testing is necessary to keep costs to a minimum yet ensure the most profitable outcome. The requirements for developing and launching new services are also outlined in Chapter 4.

(d) Distribution channels

The ways in which a retail bank distributes its services have expanded rapidly in recent years. Plastic cards are now widely used and whether these are charge cards, debit cards, credit cards or automatic teller dispenser cards each provides a service distribution channel for the provider.

Home banking using television or telephone networks, Prestel facilities and more recently computer terminal links with the bank's own computers on corporate treasurers' own desks are other examples of how the access to financial services has widened from a situation a few years ago when the only distribution system available was across the counter of a branch of the bank.

The latest distribution development by the major clearers is the introduction of a type of travelling salespeople, usually described as account executives, servicing the larger corporate market sector. For many years the top companies' financial affairs have been administered through specialised departments of the banks. This process has now been extended to include the medium to large businesses (turnover in excess of £0·5–£1 m) with regional or area sales teams making regular calls.

Costs of most distribution systems are high and any major changes in the way banks distribute services will require very careful research. The need to change distribution methods, the cost/benefits conclusions and the likely reactions of account holders and competitors are all areas for exploration before crucial decisions on distribution are taken.

(e) Contribution to planning

Marketing research is the starting point for the planning process, as it attempts to review past performance, assess the current situation and indicate future trends. This review, analysis and assumptions stage, based on information gathered by research is, in a summarised format, the basis for setting future objectives for the short, medium and longer term.

Prior to setting objectives, market opportunities will need to be placed in some order of preference and here again researched information will play an important role in the decision-making process. Having set objectives, the progress made in achieving them will need to be monitored and any significant deviation from the plan investigated. These investigations will need to indicate what changes should be made to improve performance or indeed amend the original objectives upwards or downwards to ensure the goal remains challenging yet attainable.

At virtually every step of the creation and implementation of both corporate and marketing plans, research will be required.

Types of research

Marketing research is either qualitatively or quantitatively based. Qualitative research, sometimes called primary research, is used for exploratory or diagnostic purposes and is particularly appropriate when a more flexible approach is needed than is offered by a structured questionnaire. It is impressionistic and its role is to provide an understanding of, and an insight into, processes rather than to draw definitive conclusions about issues. Qualitative techniques are used in both consumer and trade research for a number of purposes including

(1) to provide background information and the basis for an analytical framework where nothing is known about the issue or product/service field in question;

(2) to identify and examine behavioural patterns, beliefs, opinions and motivations;

(3) to explore reactions and attitudes to concepts.

Qualitative or primary research

Qualitative research projects are often used to provide the raw material to input to subsequent quantitative (or secondary) studies. Information about beliefs, attitudes and motivations can be developed into statements of quantification and analysed by multivariate techniques. Then a hypothesis can be developed for further investigation or quantification.

Sample sizes in qualitative research are usually small, tens rather than hundreds, and may represent different categories of people attitudinally or in geographic/demographic terms, but are usually selected on a judgemental basis.

Two major techniques of qualitative research are the individual 'depth' interviews and group discussions. The individual interviews of qualitative research may be either focused or non-directive. If the former, they will cover a predetermined list of topics, though the respondent or interviewee can reply freely. Alternatively, if the research is non-directive the respondent can move from topic to topic at will, provided he or she keeps within the general subject-matter.

Group discussions consist of a number of respondents gathered together under the direction of a group leader or moderator. The members of the group are encouraged to give their own views about the subject-matter and to discuss among themselves their different experiences, opinions and beliefs. The group discussion often generates new perspectives on a situation, provides greater spontaneity than an individual interview and offers insight into the dynamics of attitudes and opinions.

The choice of technique – individual interviews or group discussions – depends on the type of service and the complexity of the subject-matter and whether innovative ideas are sought. Sometimes both can be used effectively within a project to examine different facets of a topic being researched.

The success of qualitative research depends not only on the skills of eliciting information but also on analytical and interpretative skills. A high level of trust and understanding is also needed between the researcher and the client who commissioned the research because in some cases actions based on the research will have profound trading implications. Any lack of appreciation of the client's true position on the part of the researcher could impact on the quality of the research results.

Quantitative or secondary research

The most familiar type of market research is quantitative research. It is concerned with the collection, analysis and interpretation of data from samples representative of a universe. The data is quantified to indicate the proportion of sample numbers in different response categories. Based upon statistical significance theory and known margins of sampling error, the conclusions of the research are extended to the universe from which the sample was selected.

Quantitative research has a wide variety of marketing applications. Some of its major uses are to establish market size and structures for forecasting and estimations of market potential, to assist with the design, development and testing of new products, to describe consumer characteristics and buying patterns and to evaluate the effectiveness of promotional and distribution methods. Few marketing-orientated companies can operate without any quantitative research and its scope and sophistication are increasing steadily.

Purpose-designed quantitative research uses three methods of data collection – observation, experiments and surveys. Some examples of observational techniques used are retail audits and traffic counts in retail centres whilst television set meters provide data for audience research. Experiments include testing variations in distribution methods or a 'split-run' test for advertisements. Probably the most elaborate use of experiments in marketing is the test marketing concept.

Surveys are the backbone of commercial quantitative research, using a questionnaire to collect data directly from respondents. Questionnaires need careful development and testing to ensure that misleading and inaccurate responses are avoided. Many include a mixture of open-ended questions which allow respondents to answer in their own words, and closed questions involving a list of answers from which respondents make their choice. Questionnaires can be mailed to respondents for self-completion or completed by interviewers in face-to-face situations or by telephone interviewing.

Sample design and structure are vital elements of quantitative research surveys. Samples can be selected on a probability basis with each unit of the population having an equal chance of being selected, or on a judgemental basis when the criteria for inclusion are specified subjectively.

Quantitative surveys can be carried out as and when needed – *ad hoc* surveys – or fieldwork can be conducted continuously. The most familiar types of continuous surveys are panel research and omnibus surveys.

Panels can consist of individuals, households or even companies, and data is collected from them at regular intervals. They are particularly valuable in studying behavioural or attitudinal changes and panels are set up to monitor consumer purchases and service (product) usage.

An omnibus survey is a series of short questionnaires on behalf of several clients who share the costs of interviewing. Most omnibus surveys are based upon national samples of adults, though some cover groups such as motorists, investors, bank borrowers and so on. Speed and economy are the major benefits of omnibus research, which is especially suitable for mass-market products and services which lend themselves to analysis using simple question formats.

Computerised analysis techniques in quantitative research range from straightforward tabulations to sophisticated multivariate analyses. The usefulness of the data depends on the researchers' skill in identifying and interpreting the significant findings and in consideration of the implications for marketing action.

The art of sampling

Sampling techniques can be classified under six separate headings.

(a) Systematic sampling

The first unit of the sample is selected at random but all other subsequent units are then selected in relation to the first unit by a fixed interval, say every fourth item. Systematic sampling is based on the assumption that all the elements of the sample population are arranged in an order which represents the total population. By controlling the intervals between the items in the sample population, the cost of conducting the survey can be kept down. Thus, instead of calling to interview people at every second house, the market research interviewer may be instructed to call at every sixth house only.

(b) Stratified sampling

This method of gathering primary data is often used where there is evidence that some section of the population is more significant for the purpose of the survey than another section. For example, a market research organisation investigating the likely market for pension-savings might have good reason to believe that factors such as age, income and professional status were significantly related to sales. Stratified sampling would give a weighting to the answers supplied by the respondent, corresponding to the selected age, income bracket and professional status which were considered to be of critical importance. A greater degree of weighting would be attached to the answers of a respondent earning £15 000 per annum, than to the answers supplied by a 20 year-old accountant earning £4500 per annum.

(c) Quota sampling

An interviewer might be asked to collect data from a predetermined percentage of a given group or population. Care must be taken to ensure that the selected group is truly representative of the remainder and that the sample population or group is a random sample.

(d) Cluster and area sampling

Costs of gathering data are increased if the individuals in the selected sample are spread over a wide geographical area. In order to reduce costs, the survey is conducted in a particular area only, but once again each individual in the sample must be selected at random.

(e) Multi-stage sampling

This is a process for collecting qualitative or primary information based on cluster sampling. A large sample area is first selected (a town or city) and in-depth interviews are conducted in randomly selected areas or districts of the chosen town or city.

(f) Sequential sampling

This is a mathematical technique where the ultimate size of the sample is not fixed in advance but is dictated according to the mathematical principles, as the collection of the data proceeds. It is a method often used in research where it is difficult to determine initially the size of the population to be investigated. This is because it may not be possible, at first, to tell how many people meet the investigation's criteria. The aims of sequential sampling are to keep costs to a minimum whilst determining the smallest possible sample that will yield the minimum acceptable margin of error.

'Sample' research results can be surprisingly accurate provided the rules relating to random selection and careful correlation of the sample group with the characteristics of the target population are observed. The art is to get the best possible information for the least cost in terms of money, effort and time. There is a trade-off between the upper percentage levels of accuracy and the costs involved in acquiring this extra degree of reassurance. Once again a management decision is required to keep an acceptable balance between the input of resources and the output in terms of accuracy and quality of information.

Desk research

This is a major way of compiling information of a quantitative nature and as the expression indicates involves extracting data from published information.

There is an abundance of material published by Her Majesty's Stationery Office. Also there are national survey documents produced by the many and varied market research organisations; and the clearing banks also compile statistical and market information collectively through IBRO (Interbank Research Organisation) and the Banks' Information Service.

Publications that are likely to prove useful to the banks' research programmes include the following:

(1) *Monthly Digest of Statistics* covering population trends, employ-ment, energy usage, manufacturing output, shipping statistics and inland transportation information
(2) *Employment and Productivity Gazette* which gives information on employment, wage levels, average earnings and the index of retail prices.
(3) *Census of Population, Production and Distribution*
(4) *Statistics of Income, Prices, Employment and Production* published quarterly by the Department of Industry.
(5) *Trade and Industry*, a publication which covers the export and import trade and index of wholesale prices.

There are many other sources of information for desk research not least trade association publications, various year-books, credit reference agencies such as Dun & Bradstreet, Acorn and internal information produced by the banks.

Strengths and weaknesses

In general terms, the relative strengths and weaknesses of qualitative and quantitative research systems can be compared, and the grid (Table 2.3) on page 34 shows the main advantages and disadvantages. However, it should not be forgotten that the circumstances of the problem or situation being researched may also constrain the research that can be undertaken and how it can be carried out. When taking into

Table 2.3

(Strengths) Qualitative	Quantitative
● Relatively fast ● Can be cheaper than quantitative as small scale ● Can be simpler to undertake ● Useful for obtaining overview or market trends ● Helpful information as a forerunner to quantitative research ● Overall when used skilfully is good value for money	● Higher level of accuracy ● Provides factual information ● Results more significant and focused, both as to information gathered and target audience used ● Can establish within significant margin of error facts about a given population

(Weaknesses) Qualitative	Quantitative
● Findings more subjective, calling for higher level of interpretative skill ● Smaller sample sizes reducing statistical accuracy levels ● Greater chance of bias from respondent and through interpretation	● Slower than qualitative ● Can be more expensive ● Not so simple to undertake ● Often requires computer analysis facility ● Problems of low response rates so large sample sizes required to get good results ● Some risk of bias

account these situations, the strengths and weaknesses of the various types of research available may take on further complexities.

Effectiveness of research in corporate markets

Compared with the personal market, it is more difficult to interview business people in sufficient numbers. Apart from being numerically smaller, these people are also more diverse by type. Thus the results of any particular issue being researched will be based on smaller samples. General interpretation will also be more difficult because of the lack of sufficient numbers of similar types representing corporate sectors readily available for interviews.

Corporate market segments do not lend themselves to research by means of questionnaires. It is not simply that segments are smaller than personal markets but that their financial requirements are more complex and that they would prefer to keep much of what they do confidential. Nevertheless there are benefits in using qualitative research, especially for establishing image and quality aspects. However, because of the smaller samples there is a danger of reading too much into the findings.

The cost of researching corporate markets will be substantially higher than for the personal market because of the difficulty of identifying who should be interviewed and of getting hold of them. This cost should be considered in relation to the likely benefits before embarking on research in the corporate market. This nature of the information required will also influence the final management decision on whether or not to use quantitative or qualitative research methods in this important marketplace.

Research models

Types of model and their usefulness is a complex subject, as they vary from the diagrammatic (exemplified by consumer behaviour models and decision trees–if the answer is 'yes' or 'no, what next?') to sophisticated computer-based models.

When building computer models, certain disciplines are involved, the most important being the written construction of a rigorous specification. Moreover, the construction of the data base, against which sensitivities to variations of given elements of the samples can be tested, must be as representative as possible. Thus, if the specification and or sample is suspect, then the findings from the model will also lack validity. Where the model is properly established it allows many different options and courses of action to be explored rapidly and cheaply. Probably the most common model is one used to predict the effects of changes in revenue from the bank tariffs when various elements of a tariff are altered in the model. Again these models, as we saw with sampling, require the input of a representative but random sample of 'real' customer information.

Other types of models include flow models, where time is an essential factor, and decision trees. The latter follow a logical pattern showing all the decisions that could be made on a step-by-step basis. At the end of the process will be the likelihood of any given outcome of a set of decisions when probabilities have been assigned to the intermediate steps. Models can assist a bank's marketing efforts in several different ways by:

(1) Measuring changes when applying a given set of variables;
(2) Providing a more sensitive scaling;

(3) Enabling the inclusion of an 'ideal' factor as a measure of change for better or worse;
(4) Being able to predict outcome and providing a quantitative evaluations against other measurable factors;
(5) Providing a facility to test likely effectiveness of any change of marketing activity.

Case study

How can a bank make the best use of its market research capabilities in general, and with regard to the corporate customer profile in particular?

Many market research departments have wider responsibilities than their title would appear to claim. In a strict definition, market research is the provision of information related to markets, their customers and the provision of services by competitive organisations. Marketing research is the wider acquisition and use of the information for marketing decision-making purposes and would cover information related to all aspects of marketing strategy and planning. It has been defined as 'the systematic design, collection, analysis and reporting of data and findings relevant to a specific marketing situation facing the company'. Increasingly, it is in this broader area that bank market research departments work, providing a significant contribution to the overall marketing information system, and this type of role would be the one sought by a forward-looking marketing department.

The purpose of conducting research is to narrow the area of risk inherent in decision-making activity. By providing guidance as to the outcome of a particular course of action, marketing research is a foundation for marketing planning and this influences both the direction and implementation of marketing programmes. Owing to the often strategic importance of decisions based upon research findings, great care and attention must be paid to the structuring of a research study, to the quality of information gathered and, perhaps most important of all, to the interpretation of findings.

Prime areas of information provided by a bank's market research department include

– Market structures showing market share split by characteristics such as demographic or buying behaviour
– The bank's own customer profile and comparisons with competitor customer profiles for each key service

– Analysis of markets by their needs for various financial services and why certain sub-segments buy one service rather than another
– Estimates of market potential/demand for new services and packaging concepts
– Reactions of consumers to advertising and sales promotion and advertising tracking studies

The format, cost and time-scale involved in a research study are dependent upon the complexity of the situation to be assessed and the importance of the decisions to be taken based upon the resultant information.

The major stages in a research study can be outlined as follows:

(1) The definition of the situation to be examined or assessed, including an indication of the scope and format of information required for meaningful decision making. Inadequate or incorrect definition of the situation will produce reliable or relevant information only by chance.

(2) The identification of information sources relevant to the situation assessment. Information sources can be of two types – primary and secondary data. Secondary data is that gained by seeking information collected for a separate purpose and may be internal or external to the organisation. Secondary data requires careful interpretation since the issues it was designed to tackle may not wholly coincide with those currently under consideration.

(3) The development of a research programme structure involving decisions as to techniques such as quantitative and/or qualitative research, methodologies and the preparation of data collection material such as questionnaires, interview guidelines or traffic counters. The data collection materials should be comprehensive and free from interviewer or respondent bias to ensure meaningful and valid results.

(4) Designing the sample or a decision to study the total relevant population via a census. In most cases it will be neither feasible nor cost-justifiable to undertake a full census so that issues affecting the sample design and structure are to be considered. The key attributes of a sample are that the resultant information is representative of the universe and that the size of the sample is sufficient to enable the error inherent in the resultant information to be calculated with an acceptable level of statistical reliability.

(5) The collection of the information in a format suitable for analysis purposes. Clearly efforts should be made to minimise any data

omissions, since these together with sources of bias will reduce the effectiveness of the data for decision-making purposes.

(6) Methods of analysing the data are dependent on its quality, complexity and the sophistication of statistical and analytical techniques required. Whilst many quantitative surveys are analysed by computer for purposes of speed and sophistication of analyses, some simple manual tabulations can identify areas for further concentration in the main analyses. Qualitative research requires skilled and experienced analysis and interpretation to act as the basis of the generation of hypotheses and realistic decision making.

(7) The interpretation and reporting of results should be conducted in terms of the situation definition outlined in stage 1. Conclusions and implications should ideally be clear, concise and actionable.

Corporate market research

Market research in the corporate sector of a bank's business differs from that in the personal sector in several ways: for example, in the methods used to describe market characteristics and to establish the financial service needs of particular segments. Corporate sector market research activity is frequently concerned with fewer customers but, as the value of the customer relationship is often much greater than that for the majority of personal customers, an examination of needs in greater depth is required so that individual tailoring of services can be considered where justified and the construction of individual pricing policies undertaken.

The market research department would be involved in analysing the bank's existing corporate customers' profiles, comparing these with the general market profile and information available from market intelligence sources regarding competitor corporate customer profiles within the same categories.

The characteristics of corporate customers can be analysed in terms of types of organisation: for example, private and publicly owned companies, government agencies, trade unions, clubs and societies; they can also be analysed by industrial or commercial activity such as manufacturing, distribution, agriculture, professional practice; by industrial category such as food processing, chemicals, or engineering; by geographical area or by evaluation of risk for lending purposes.

A major area of research beyond the establishment of customer profiles is the analysis and interpretation of existing and prospective corporate customers' financial service requirements, their current patterns of usage of bank services and the identification of target prospects for additional service utilisation.

Summary

The importance of research as a management tool to support marketing decisions by reducing the areas of unknown facts cannot be overstated. It will tell you what you do not know and also confirm what you do.

Marketing research is an integral element of the cyclical process of marketing. A problem or task is identified; research and analysis tries to establish the facts; a plan is formulated which includes objectives; action takes place to achieve the stated goals and this is monitored. Results are then researched and analysed and the whole process is repeated all over again.

A research programme includes understanding the problem, identifying when, where and how the information should be collected, actually collecting the data, then analysing, summarising and reporting the results.

Research can be used to support the three main areas in which management's marketing decisions fall, namely tactical strategic and development situations.

Marketing research has an especially important part to play in all decisions relating to the use and changes in the market mix elements of price, promotion, services and distribution. It also supports most facets of any planning process. Research falls into two broad categories: qualitative and quantitative. Qualitative research involves live group discussions and in-depth interviews, whereas quantitative research mainly entails the collection, analysis and interpretation of data from samples of a universe from a wider audience by means of sampling, questionnaire surveys and desk research. The data is quantified to show degrees of significance or uniformity.

Sampling techniques are an important part of quantitative and qualitative research where the chosen respondents must be representative of the universe yet remain a random selection.

Revision questions

1   What are the main tasks of marketing research?
2   How can marketing research help management in making development, strategic and tactical decisions? Give examples of each of

these management issues and by using the situations chosen as examples show how market research can help.

3 What is meant by a marketing orientated business? Explain the main marketing aspects that can be assisted by marketing research.

4 Your branch managers have replied to proposals for marketing research in their locations by stating that they know most of the answers already. How would you respond to their comments?

5 Demonstrate you understand how qualitative and quantitative research could be used when trying to decide whether or not to introduce a Personal Equity Plan investment service.

Chapter 3
Understanding and Identifying Buyers

Without customers there can be no retail bank. So recognising that customers are important, and that they differ from each other in terms of their needs and wants, is the starting point for examining how customer requirements can be satisfied. A bank would not wish to satisfy *all* the needs of customers. Choosing which needs, and which customers should potentially prove the most profitable for a bank, calls for marketing skill and managerial judgement, especially in markets for financial services that are highly competitive.

There is no substitute for selling financial services across the banker's desk, but in practice branch managers and senior staff see only a very small proportion of their total customers. To reach wider audiences other ways have to be found and this in turn means groups of customers must be distinguished from each other – a process called segmentation. Customers can be grouped together in many different ways but only those factors which relate in some way to buyer behaviour will prove important to marketing activity.

This chapter looks first at consumerism and buyer behaviour in order to establish a basic understanding of why people do what they do. Then, with this appreciation, market segmentation including the methods used and benefits derived will be examined in greater detail.

Consumerism and its challenge

Consumerism offers many challenges to a bank. It is a marketeer's task to decide whether or not to meet these challenges by appropriate adjustments to banking practice or seek to deflect them and protect the bank from their consequences. The underlying choice is simply where customer requirements conflict with the bank's own interests whether the bank should meet the customers' needs or try in some way to balance the outcome.

The term 'consumerism' can be described as 'a movement by those in society who wish to augment their rights and power as buyers over sellers'. Traditionally, pricing, distribution and promotional policies, as well as the nature of the service have been the prerogative of the retail banks. In recent years, however, there has been a growing recognition that the customer also has rights and in some cases these customer rights might conflict with those of the bank.

Consumerism has reinforced the traditional customers' rights of not having to buy a service which is offered for sale and of expecting the service to be safe and live up to expectations. This social movement has also given rise to demands for additional rights:

(1) that customers are entitled to adequate information about the service;
(2) that customers have the right to increased protection against questionable marketing practices;
(3) that customers have the right to influence directly the features of services and the way they are sold if these adjustments are likely generally to increase their quality of life.

These 'rights' have widened the scope and role of the seller's responsibilities and consumer protection has been reinforced recently by statutes such as the Consumer Credit Act. As a result, bank marketing has become more complex and selling techniques more sophisticated and pervasive. It is no longer simply the service that is in question but the whole corporate image, and the advertising and public relations functions that are under scrutiny. The challenge of consumerism is such that banks must show a far greater responsiveness, not just to individual customers, but also to the wider market and, ultimately, to the whole of society.

Responding to consumerism

A failure on the part of a bank to protect its own interests or to deflect some degree of consumer demand would be an abdication of its right to state its own case and maintain an appropriate degree of control over its affairs. On the other hand, the consequences of a failure to respond at all to the challenges of consumerism could prove to be equally serious. Confrontation with consumers would lead to stricter regulation and legislation. Moreover, market share, income growth and profitability would suffer.

Avoidance of loss of business and an increase in restrictive controls are sound reasons for adapting to some consumer demands. However, this is a negative stance, and banks should adopt a more positive role of considering consumerism as an opportunity to generate marketing techniques, services and ultimately profit by being in tune with customers' real interests where these can be provided profitably.

If this positive approach is adopted then some internal monitoring of customer reaction to any adaptation of policies or services is required. In practice, this monitoring can be effectively undertaken in a number of ways and the information will enable marketing activity to be improved. Areas of interest will include

(1) Complaints which should be monitored in a way that allows the bank to gauge at an early stage, which consumer groups are primarily responsible for the pressure. The source of consumer complaints is often assumed to be the better educated, more sophisticated, higher income groups and the younger rather than the older, but this situation is rapidly changing. Consumerism is now well spread throughout society.

(2) The nature of complaints and opinions should be analysed to assess the true extent of the problem. Repetitious complaints over a period of time may require major changes to policies or services offered.

Banks must attempt to anticipate consumerist demands, so that rather than always reacting to problems, its services and their promotion are already matched as closely as possible to the customers' real interests. Moreover, the banks will need to try to educate their customers and potential customers by explaining and justifying their policies and service features. This is an important part of the public relations role and one where there should be no relaxation.

Buyer motivation and behaviour

An understanding of customers' buying behaviour is of central importance to the formulation of a bank's marketing strategy. If we can understand how our customers buy and which of them buy, we are then in a better position to sell them services, This understanding is a prerequisite for marketing success. The ways in which the marketing mix elements are used and blended, especially 'price' and 'promotion', will be influenced by an appreciation of why customers buy or do not buy a service, or why they accept or reject individual aspects of a service. What motivates people to do something, including buying a bank service, stems from an unsatisfied need. The buying act is merely the culmination of a motivation process which can be a simple chain of events or a highly complex set of decision-making situations. Figure 3.1 shows the motivation process.

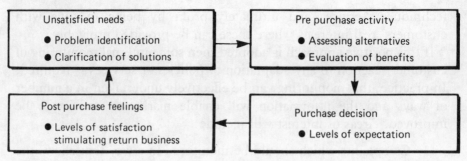

Fig. 3.1

Although the precise reasons for a customer's considering that he or she has an unsatisfied need may be obscure or subconscious, the desire when recognised by a banker should be stimulated. Unsatisfied need is the starting point to buyer activity and it follows that identifying that need and providing information on appropriate services is fundamental to successful selling. Equally, at each stage in the illustrated buyer motivation process, bankers will have an opportunity to influence customer behaviour through their promotional strategy.

Even the post-purchase stage, in which the customer may feel anxiety about the choice of service and benefits derived, gives the banker an opportunity to communicate and reassure. This will strengthen the bank's relationship with its customer and hopefully lead to return business. Banks do not enjoy the same passing trade benefits as a candy floss stall on the pier; long-term relationships are crucial to creating continuous opportunities to sell a wide range of services which change in relation to people's financial circumstances and life cycle.

One of the challenges to bank marketing is that each customer possesses a unique set of perceptions and attitudes that influence his or her behaviour – earlier in this chapter the advantages of one-to-one selling were mentioned. Nevertheless, in general terms, common ground exists enabling these factors to be grouped into four main categories: social, cultural, personal and psychological. Grouping in this way is the basis of the segmentation methods which are discussed later in this chapter.

The most important social factors which impact on buyer behaviour are the family background and individuals' perception of their role and status – we have all heard of the expression 'keeping up with the Joneses'. The main cultural factors, on the other hand, are the prevailing culture norms, sub-culture and social class.

Psychological factors comprise learning, beliefs and attitudes whereas the personal factors which affect the buyer are life cycle, lifestyle, occupation, economic situation, personality and individual concept of self.

It is clear from these four groups that the first two categories comprise external factors whereas the latter two are formed of those which influence the consumer from within. Personal and psychological factors in particular may be utilised as the basis of a psychographic analysis of behaviour. This approach allows consumer markets to be segmented on the basis of lifestyle, personality trait or attitude rather than the more usual demographic segmentation by age, sex or occupation.

All this may prove confusing and irrelevant to the banker selling services across the counter. It is true that once a need has been appreciated by a buyer the real point at issue is the degree of, and the urgency to satisfy, that need. For example, a low-paid weekly worker may need private transportation. A similar need also exists among the wealthy. Social, cultural and personal influences will not affect the basic need but they will dictate the amount spent on a motor vehicle, the sort of motor vehicle purchased, how much customers may need to borrow and indeed from whom they should obtain the finance and the car. Twin-tone horns on a vehicle may be an attraction to one type of person but not to another, and this will be largely influenced by individual backgrounds and attitudes. Bankers should be able to recognise these market characteristics especially if catering for people from all walks of life. They would also have to demonstrate their understanding of them and of their effect on customer requirements in order to convince a prospective buyer that he or she should purchase services from the bank. Stressing the right features to the right prospective buyer demands a degree of appreciation and skill in weighing up the background circumstances of the buyer in the first place.

Before leaving the subject of buyer motivation and behaviour it should be stressed that there are differences between the buyer behaviour of organisations and that of individuals. The buying process for organisations commences with the identification of a need and moves through the establishment of objectives, the identification and evaluation of buying alternatives and, finally, the selection of the supplier. Determinants of organisational buying requirements and who actually has the power will be influenced by organisational and policy considerations. Nevertheless, the role, and therefore the motivation, of the individual even in the largest organisation, remains a major factor in the way his or her organisation evaluates and buys bank services and products.

Segmenting markets

What is segmentation?

Market segmentation is 'the subdividing of a market into homogeneous subsets of customers, where any subset may conceivably be selected as a market target to be reached with a distinct marketing mix'. This approach can be likened to using a rifle (aim for selected targets) instead of a shotgun (aim at all targets at once).

A segment describes a class or group of buyers with a broad set of requirements or susceptibilities which, for marketing purposes, can be distinguished from those of other groups or classes.

Relationship with marketing activity

Before proceeding with segmentation, the question of what markets a bank is in must be answered. In practice this is a difficult and fundamental question to answer.

Once defined, a market can be exploited by mass marketing and advertising methods, but usually this is not a cost-effective approach. Further analysis will reveal a number of market segments within a broad generic market.

Dividing a market into segments is a relatively recent concept in banking philosophy. It arose out of the realisation that people buy similar services for different reasons: that it is usually possible to discern patterns in buying motivation and behaviour, and to group existing and potential purchasers into segments, each characterised by a set of similar buying characteristics and requirements. Each segment can also be differentiated by a degree of buying loyalty ranging from total to nil.

Once these segments have been identified it is possible to develop a distinct marketing strategy to reach the selected segment(s) and achieve minimum conflict of image and maximum profitability.

Thus, despite intense competition, a bank may prosper through creatively serving specific market sectors whose needs are not fully met by competitors.

However, segmentation is not carried out in isolation or in a vacuum, for it remains part of the overall marketing activity. Invariably segmentation research takes a lead from the main corporate planning process which constantly asks the questions:

(1) What markets is the bank serving?
(2) Will servicing those markets achieve the profit/volume growth targets?

(3) If not, then which markets should be included in the bank's marketing activity?

From these self-analysing questions it is clear that markets and market segments fall into two broad categories – customer and non-customer groups. Segmentation of both of these market groups will be an important aspect of the initial review, analysis and assumptions stage of any structured planning process. In practice, some basic research is a fundamental prerequisite to the segmentation process and ultimately to the effective promotion of financial services. It will include analysing, in broad bands, existing and potential customers' profiles, both by type and potential profitability, then comparing the results with an assessment of selling opportunities in the marketplace as a whole. Note that profit or potential profit is the main criterion for determining desirability. Once this research has been completed, the needs of smaller more selected customer segments can be more accurately identified. This rather presumptive or pre-emptive approach speeds up the process of segmentation, channels effort and resources into areas that are most likely to match with corporate aspirations, and very importantly keeps costs of segmentation to a prudent minimum. In summary, segmenting markets should not be a random process and there are commercial advantages in aiming it at areas considered most likely to be pertinent to the bank's main corporate and marketing aspirations.

Segmentation variables

However the market is segmented, each group must exhibit three distinct characteristics if it is to be useful in consumer marketing. Firstly the groups must be measurable in some way, secondly they must be accessible once identified and, thirdly, they must be substantial enough to warrant the costs of their identification and subsequent pursuit.

There are many single variables appropriate to consumer markets, and these may be usefully grouped under four general headings: geographic, demographic, psychographic and behaviouristic. The similarity and overlap with buyer behaviour considered earlier in this chapter should not be overlooked. Even geographic segmentation is interrelated in a wider sense with social, cultural and personal influences on buyer attitudes and motivation.

(a) *Geographic segmentation* divides the market according to location. In its broadest application, this will encompass different countries and states, but within a single country, divisions may be made on the basis of regions, states, counties or even areas of a city or town. Later in this chapter two of the latest computerised aids to segmentation – Acorn and Finpin – are covered as examples of how even branch catchment areas can be easily segmented.

The size of cities and towns may also be used as well as the density of population. For example, urban, suburban and rural.

Geographic segmentation has the advantage of assisting the seller to position retail outlets in the most appropriate locations as well as simply identifying the needs on the basis of the consumers' own location.

(b) *Demographic segmentation* involves division of the market on the basis of age, sex, income, occupation, education, religion, race or nationality, social class, family size and life cycle. This last demographic feature recognises that a person's wants will change depending on whether he or she is single, young, married, with children, pensioned or a solitary survivor.

(c) *Psychographic segmentation* is a form of segmentation that was developed to overcome the general inadequacy of demographics in the identification of attitudes and living styles. The principal variables under this heading are lifestyle and personality.

Consumers' lifestyles are derived from their activities, interests and opinions, whereas personality is based on self-images and self-concepts. Social class, which is explained more fully shortly, is now increasingly utilised as a psychographic variable following research which has shown that there is a significant correlation between a consumer's class and his or her attitude to financial services, and to the banks generally.

(d) *Behaviouristic segmentation* divides customers into groups based on their knowledge, attitude or behaviour towards a product or service and its attributes. This may involve differentiation by purchase-occasion, by user status (i.e. non-user, ex-user, first-time user), usage rate and benefits sought.

Particular importance is now attached to benefit segmentation, in the light of research on consumer perceptions in relation to bank service features. When behaviouristic or benefit segmentation follows on from an initial geographic, demographic and psychographic segmentation process, the outcome is often regarded as the most effective starting point for the sale of financial services.

Benefits derived

There are other ways to refine target audiences by further segmentation of a market. These include segmenting by volume through distinguishing between small, medium and large potential groups and by marketing factor; dividing the segment into subsets responsive to different marketing features such as price levels. Whichever method or combination of methods is used, the benefits to a bank are considerable and are as follows:

(1) they enable a bank to select the potentially most profitable segments;
(2) they enable a bank to concentrate resources on the segments chosen;
(3) this focusing of activity should be more productive and less wasteful;
(4) the analysis gives a bank the opportunity to review developments and anticipate change in its chosen segment from competitive activity, legal/political changes, redistribution of wealth and many other social and environmental factors.

On looking at the benefits in greater detail, it is clear that considerable savings are made if the right services are aimed at the right segments. This saving occurs not just from the better use of labour but also because expensive items such as advertising are made more effective. Promotional messages have more impact when the medium used is correctly matched with the viewing or reading habits of the chosen segment. Equally, sales opportunities are more likely to be effectively and fully exploited by staff when the target audience is properly defined. Above all, effective segmentation should increase sales performance.

Reducing wastage of effort and resources should lead to lower unit costs, a benefit which both bank and customers can enjoy. Other customer benefits derived from the segmentation process are

(1) more apposite services;
(2) prices tailored to customers' lifestyles;
(3) improved levels of service both in terms of sophistication and general standards, based on knowing exactly what customers require. This is particularly true when providing services to the segmented sectors of the total corporate market. Business customer requirements are often more complex, and exact matching of service benefits with needs is therefore very important.

Areas of marketing activity to benefit

Marketing as has already been defined is about getting the right services to the right audiences at the right price and at the most appropriate time and place. If these criteria are achieved then the outcome should be customer satisfaction and profit to the bank.

The ways in which services are presented to the chosen market segments is the main key to success. Figure 3.2 highlights the variety of ways a bank can present services and also the need to ensure that all the elements used at any one time should have a common and supportive focus.

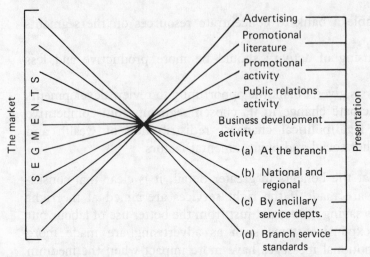

Fig. 3.2 Focusing the presentation variables

Apart from enabling all the presentation variables to be co-ordinated, there are other marketing planning benefits which can be derived from segmenting markets:

(1) By allowing sellers to predict consumers' needs and behaviour as well as take a more sophisticated view of existing needs and behaviour, segmentation allows decisions to be made about the resources that should be allocated to service testing and development, pricing, distribution and promotion, as well as their format and role within the marketing mix.

(2) Redundant services can be dropped and new ones developed but, equally important, accurate segmentation may provide opportunities for the fine tuning and repackaging of existing services (services as well as markets can be segmented).

(3) The impact of pricing decisions can be predicted more accurately through segmentation, and the relative importance of existing customer groups as revenue sources, established.

(4) Segmentation of the existing customer base may in turn lead to segmentation of the branch network and the services provided at each outlet. Similarly, it will enable evaluation to be made of the likely acceptance of alternative delivery channels. (See Chapter 8.)

(5) Finally, through segmentation, the promotional mix can be adjusted for different consumer groups, depending on their susceptibility to each of the component media.

Segmentation is particularly important in niche markets but in more general terms the advantages to the banks from adopting it are as follows:

(1) Small numbers of people can be identified and their financial needs accurately determined. Marketing efforts, based on segmentation should be more cost-effective not least because there will be a higher 'strike rate'.

(2) Selling to chosen segments allows the banks to consider profitability objectives and higher margin services selected for preferential targeted activity.

(3) A degree of staff specialisation is necessary, and this knowledge can be focused on chosen audiences backed up by appropriate promotion and messages. In this way the more complex services will be sold and customer confidence in the bank's professional image enhanced, so encouraging 'repeat' business.

Further selection factors

No bank has unlimited resources and those it has must be co-ordinated, directed and controlled in the best possible way. This is why there is a corporate plan with short, medium and longer-term objectives. When choosing segments these stated corporate goals should be considered. If a bank's aspiration is to improve the quality of its personal customer profile or attract customers of higher net worth, marketing among low educated weekly paid younger age groups will not conform to corporate objectives.

Although compatibility with corporate goals is crucial when selecting the main segments, there are other factors to consider if the chosen audience is still too wide. For example, competitor presence and activity may be stronger in one segment than another and the costs of matching this competition in a particular segment may preclude its ultimate selection.

However, market research will play a key role in this refinement process and information will need to be gathered on the following aspects:

(1) Do the segments initially selected have characteristics which offer marketing opportunities? If so, can the segment be further subdivided in order to allow 'fine tuning' of the marketing mix to create the best possible impact?

(2) Are these characteristics appropriate for the service(s) being promoted or will it be advantageous to modify service benefits to match target audience needs more closely?

(3) How stable are the segments over time? Creating or amending services and promotional activity is expensive – if in the shorter term the market characteristics are likely to change, this will influence the final choice. Overall, the strengths and weaknesses of each segment will need to be evaluated and relative stability is just one facet of this analysis.

(4) There is a close link between risk levels (cost of marketing, activity) and return. When selecting the segments the ease of accessibility of the audience and the effect of this on the cost of the media considered likely to be most effective will need to be borne in mind. So too will be the cost of media in relation to numbers reached and the profitability of the service being sold. Thus, when selecting segments, there is a need to assess the likely revenue return of marketing to particular audiences against the estimated cost and utilisation of scarce resources.

In summary, a chosen segment would need to offer profit potential at a level which was acceptable to the bank and justified the use of required resources. Those segments that are clearly identifiable by their individualistic characteristics, including size, and offer potential for selling services which, in turn, support the stated corporate goals, are most likely to be chosen. Segments will also need to be reachable in a cost-effective manner with a market mix that is effective and can be sustained over time.

Socio-economic groupings

Socio-economic or social class groupings are used extensively by research organisations and consequently are the main classifications for markets in nationally available market data and government statistics. This is another form of segmentation, and is helpful for tracking

Table 3.1 Social class groups

Social class		Type of occupation
A	Upper middle class	Higher managerial, administrative or professional
B	Middle class	Intermediate managerial, administrative or professional
C1	Lower middle class	Supervisor or clerical and junior managerial, administrative or professional
C2	Skilled working class	Skilled manual workers
D	Working class	Semi- and unskilled manual workers
E	Those at the lowest level of subsistence	State pensioners, unemployed people and those with no other earnings

changes in the financial needs and attitudes of the large numbers who fall into the social class groups AB, C1, C2, and DE. However, for a bank wishing to undertake more selective promotions they are clearly far too broad and do not relate particularly accurately to likely present or future financial needs.

Nevertheless these social groups provide a starting point for further refinement, and using the researched information in them can give useful leads as to the way further segmentation should go.

Socio-economic or social class groups can be roughly transcribed into types by occupation as shown in Table 3.1.

Recent computer-based segmentation systems

The need for banks to improve their marketing skills was quickly recognised by others who in turn saw the banks' deficiencies as a market opportunity.

Consultants are now widely used by the banks to provide marketing education for staff, and incentive schemes for customers and staff, as well as advertising and other facets of the promotional mix. Market research companies have also studied the banks' requirements in depth and have come up with new ways to identify and classify segments of the population with similar characteristics. These systems (e.g. Acorn, Finpin and Mosaic) use postcodes and credit-scoring techniques, and are computer-based for ease of use.

(a) Segmenting by credit scoring

Credit scoring is a system of analysing information for making lending decisions. Each possible answer to a number of questions about an applicant's personal characteristics is allocated a number of points representing the 'weight' of the answer. The sum of the points is the credit score, and indicates the degree of risk of the applicant's seeking to borrow money. (It can also be regarded as a delivery system.)

The bank then selects a cut-off score below which the lending decision would be 'no'. Above that figure the answer would be 'yes'. This system is quantifying the odds on making a successful loan to an applicant, and the cut-off score can be moved up or down to extend or reduce the number of loans granted and the degree of risk.

Each system has to be tailored to a particular bank's customer profile and is partially based upon past experience. For example, personal loan applicants are segmented into creditworthy or not creditworthy by using credit scoring. The criteria used for credit-scoring mortgage applications compared with personal loans will differ, as the customer segment profile, circumstances and service features will not be similar. There are a number of marketing advantages for the bank and customer benefits in segmenting using credit scoring. These include:

(1) Unbiased consideration of applications. This is a significant factor for a bank trying to comply with legislation dealing with equal opportunities and consumer protection.

(2) Conformity of decisions, which could also lead to increased growth in lending as the risk is systematically quantified removing the onus for loss from the banker.

(3) Other business development opportunities should follow from the ability to identify and isolate good credit risks.

(4) More effective communication and implementation of lending policy and criteria.

(5) Shorter lending interviews and therefore more time to cross sell other bank services.

(b) ACORN

Acorn stands for '*a* *c*lassification *o*f *r*esidential *n*eighbourhoods'. It is a marketing segmentation system which enables consumers to be classified according to the type of residential area in which they live. It was developed by a company called CACI Market Analysis.

The segmentation system derives from applying published census statistics, and classifies areas of about 150 households into 38 different neighbourhood types. This ACORN classification takes into account 40 different variables encompassing demographic, housing and employment characteristics. The 38 neighbourhood types themselves aggregate up to 11 neighbourhood groups.

Because the ACORN system is based on census data, it is not only able to assign a neighbourhood type to each local area, but is further able to give precise population totals for those areas.

ACORN is linked to postal geography thereby permitting users and survey respondents to be assigned to their appropriate ACORN types simply by analysing postcodes. In this way markets can be analysed by ACORN, and by relating market analysis back to the ACORN profiles of various areas, local market estimates can be derived and further 'market modelling' also becomes possible.

(1) *Examples of ACORN groups*
Agricultural areas
Modern family housing/higher incomes
Older housing/intermediate status
Better-off council estates
Less well-off council estates
Multi-racial areas
Affluent suburban housing.

(2) *Examples of ACORN neighbourhood types*
Agricultural villages
Recent private housing – young families
Modern private housing – older children
New detached houses – young families
Mixed owner-occupied and council estates
Older private housing – skilled workers
Unimproved terraces with older people
Pre-1914 terraces – low income families
Tenement flats lacking amenities
Council estates – well-off older workers
Council estates – well-off younger workers
Council housing for the elderly.

These are only samples of the total segmentation variables but demonstrate the depth and variety available to users wishing to research opportunities in their localities.

(c) Finpin (Pinpoint Analysis Limited)

This is a combination of census data/postcodes from Pinpoint and financial data from Financial Research Services (FRS). As such, this computer-based system also offers a geographic/demographic segmentation facility by classifying people by residential area. It then makes the assumption that people live with others similar to themselves in terms of both their demographic characteristics and their financial habits. Once again, postcodes provide the basis of the analysis.

Examples of the main Finpin types include:

Financially active
Financially informed
Financially conscious
Financially passive.

Each of these four main groups is then broken down into smaller segments. Using 'financially active' as an example, the subsets are as follows:

(a) Most active – Wealthy families with older children
Wealthy families
Families with young children and two adult workers
Wealthy families with students and older children
Families with growing children and two adult workers

(b) Financially wealthy empty nesters
Secure wealthy retired
Savers.

There are 40 subsets making up the four main groups, ranging down the social structures to crowded council tenants and ethnic populations.

Benefits of computerised postcode-based segmentation

ACORN and Finpin are better-known examples of commercially sold segmentation packages. There are others which may vary cosmetically from the two systems which have been described. Most, if not all, offer the following benefits:

(1) For marketing – customer location, identification, classification, direct mail list creation and competitive evaluation;

(2) For branch planning – catchment area analysis and local media targeting;

(3) For service evaluation – market position testing, market opportunity analysis;

(4) For modelling – budgetary control, response analysis, sampling and market planning benefits generally through sales forecasting and performance monitoring.

Gap analysis

'Gap analysis' can best be described as a process which aims to seek out differences between what the market wants and what is actually being supplied – the gap. Effective 'gap analysis' requires comprehensive market research and this in turn involves a wide use of segmentation. Potential purchasers can be divided in several ways but the aim is to try and find new wants of the already identified major subsets.

With this continual creative and exploratory approach, gaps where market needs for existing services are not being fulfilled can be identified. So too can other needs where perhaps no service currently exists. It should be borne in mind that the market and demand levels for services constantly change. These factors will either cause a service to become less desirable or increase demand for it. When considering penetration levels of a service, growth rate in usage, and the growth rate in the overall potential of the market segment, must be considered together. Where market growth is outstripping the rate of usage or penetration, the 'gap' for more marketing activity can be seen.

Profitability, from trying to fill the gaps in the marketplace, will be a decisive factor when formulating the bank's marketing strategy. Other influences will include the longer-term profit potential and the position in the marketplace enjoyed by a bank and its services. A bank wishing to foster an exclusive image is hardly likely to be keen to meet the needs of low-paid workers or the unemployed.

Case study

Financial institutions are increasingly segmenting their markets and delivery systems. Explain:

(a) what segmentation means and how it can be achieved and,
(b) how you would expect segmentation to affect the profit performance of a financial institution.

(a) There are three issues posed. They are, firstly, what is segmentation? Secondly, how is segmentation accomplished, and finally what would you expect from it? Segmentation is the division of a market into distinct groups according to pre-defined characteristics. People in the same market segment will thus have broadly similar needs. If the outcome of the process of segmenting the market is to be relevant to marketing activity, each segment must have certain definable qualities. It must be measurable and thus clearly identifiable, it must be reachable and finally there must be sufficient business opportunity within the segment to make marketing activity worth while. There are various methods that can be used to segment the market.

The first, *geographic segmentation*, is a means of differentiating a market by place. This can be broad or narrow depending upon circumstances. A large company might separate overseas markets from home buyers as the elements of the marketing mix will need to be used in different ways. For example, when operating overseas, price, advertising, promotion and distribution may well be different from those encountered in the UK.

Equally, a bank cannot operate everywhere, so it will need to segment by areas and concentrate on those locations that appear to offer the best profit opportunities.

Acorn is a relatively new method of segmentation based on census data and the use of postcodes. By this method it is now possible to classify areas into neighbourhood groups. This grouping is based on family size, income, ownership of consumer durables, and the amenities available.

Demographic segmentation is a method which categorises the market in terms of age, sex, income, occupation, race, family size or religion.

Demographic factors are those most commonly used by banks in market analysis, as they match well with many financial services. It is a fact that financial needs are closely related to lifestyle aspects. Groups of people are readily identifiable and their needs can be matched easily with service features and benefits.

This method also equates with the life cycle concept, a well-tried basis for matching needs of customers with services. For example, a young married couple will need to set up home, obtain labour-saving consumer durables, and save towards a mortgage and house purchase or for starting a family. All these pose financial requirements which a retail bank's range of services can provide.

Psychographic segmentation is an attempt to categorise buyers according to lifestyle and psychological type.

Socio-economic groupings are used by market researchers to assist segmentation – A, B, C1, C2, D, E equate with social grades of people. A is regarded as senior management, B middle management, C1 clerical and administrative people, C2 skilled workers, D semi- or unskilled workers and E the unemployed or low-income retired.

Volume segmentation is a way in which the researcher attempts to distinguish between heavy, medium and light users of a service. In this way the research will indicate whether the needs or wants differ in demographic or other ways.

Institutional segmentation involves grouping business by size and individual types.

Benefit segmentation categorises the market in terms of the main product or service-related benefits sought by particular groups. This includes use of the other segmentation methods, but then goes a stage further by dividing the already segmented market into sub-segments in terms of the different benefits sought.

There are other ways to segment a market. Whichever method is adopted, the research and analysis should ultimately identify where attractive market opportunities exist, the characteristics within the market opportunity, and the needs that are not being met.

Expectation

(b) To understand fully how segmentation can affect the profit performance of a financial institution, the effect of segmentation needs to be considered. If segmentation is carefully undertaken the resultant information will allow an organisation to focus on those market areas which are accessible and offer the best or most profitable business development opportunities. Thus new market opportunities are revealed, any likely constraints to business development recognised, and this information then provides the raw material for setting business growth objectives. Moreover, by segmenting the market, data which leads to the setting of objectives can also be re-examined if targets are not met in key market areas. For it is the segmentation information which enables an evaluation of the markets and assists management to make the final choice of markets in which to operate.

Segmentation has other advantages, apart from improving sales, through better targeting and a sharper focus on identified needs of customer groups. Resources can be effectively utilised and thus misuse of money and effort minimised. Methods and channels of advertising and sales promotion can all be adjusted in such a way that individual groups of target customers can be reached with high impact from relevant sales messages. We should use the so-called rifle rather than the shotgun approach, as that would only reach a generalised market with sales messages lacking in clarity and distinctive qualities.

This sharp sense of focus and purpose, that segmentation allows, will also improve staff understanding of what is required of them and thus raise their level of effort in support of the business goals.

Summary

Consumerism is a growing force and should not be ignored. Customers have rights and expectations, and will endeavour to force these upon sellers. The bank's role is to monitor and anticipate consumerism and if there is no conflict with its own interests adapt policies and services to meet the challenge.

Failure to consider consumerism and avoid confrontation would ultimately lead to stricter regulations and legislation to control the bank's activities. Also market share, income growth and profitability would suffer.

Buyers go through various stages of motivational feelings and activity, starting with unsatisfied need before continuing through pre-purchase activity, the purchase decision and finally post-purchase feelings.

Market segmentation is 'the subdividing of a market into homogeneous subsets of customers with each group having a broad set of similar needs or susceptibilities that can be distinguished. Each segment must also be measurable and reachable so that distinctive market strategies can be focused successfully.

The various ways of segmenting markets should be understood and how each method can be used in practice also appreciated.

Segmentation enables a bank to select the most profitable segments, concentrate resources on these segments, minimise waste of effort and keep up to date or even ahead of any changes which would impact on marketing activity in these segments.

There are wider benefits to marketing activity generally from segmentation. Marketing mix elements, price, promotion, distribution and services can be constantly reviewed and adjusted from the deeper appreciation of influences on the target markets and the effect these have on their financial requirements.

Credit scoring is a type of segmentation and benefits both customers and the banks.

Revision questions

1 Consumerism offers many challenges to the banks. Should the marketing response be to meet those challenges by appropriate adjustments to banking practices or rather seek to deflect them and protect the banks from their consequences? Discuss.
2 What are the major segmentation variables for consumer markets? Why are they important and how would you use them?

3 What do you understand by consumer motivation and buying behaviour?
4 Describe how your branch segments its customer profile. What do you think are the weaknesses inherent in your branch segmentation methods? If weaknesses exist how could these be overcome?
5 In what ways is computer technology being used to provide better segmentation systems and improve marketing activity? Illustrate your answer with reference to credit scoring and ACORN.

Chapter 4
The Marketing Mix – Services

Introducing the marketing mix

The marketing mix is often described as the blending or combining of the four key elements of all market activity, namely the services, the price, the promotion and finally the distribution systems in such a way that the combination is likely to prove attractive to chosen customer market segments. If the mix is right, people will decide to buy and there is no need for further persuasion and the use of hard-sell techniques.

Each element of the marketing mix will be covered separately in the next four chapters. In practice, however, decisions concerning the ways in which each individual element used is closely linked or interrelated with the others and cannot be isolated. The precise mix of the four is what requires marketing skill and judgement, and the success or otherwise of the 'blend' should be constantly examined and when necessary adjusted to improve sales results.

Arguably, the most important element of the four which make up the marketing mix is the features and benefits of the services being provided by the bank. These service characteristics will influence price, promotion and distribution strategies. Furthermore, financial services differ from products, and this factor also impacts on the way services are promoted and distributed. In particular they are intangible in the sense that they often cannot be separated from the person of the seller. Also they may not be uniform; for example, standards of service can vary from branch to branch.

The way most bank services are developed and sold is related either to a group of services with similar benefits — money transmission, holiday services, lending facilities for home owners, and so on — or to their actual life cycle. The former include expanding or contracting the service mix by altering, positioning or introducing new services and thereby often altering the choice of market segments.

Life cycle influences, which are covered fully in this chapter, relate to a particular stage in the service's existence; either its introduction, growth, maturity or decline. There are ways of using the other elements of the marketing mix to extend the maturity period and ward off decline. This activity of prolonging the life cycle is important to revenue/profit growth. Recognising the various stages is also crucial to the ways in which the marketing mix is applied and also for taking decisions about new service development programmes.

Services compared with products

Generally speaking, the term 'product' can cover goods and services and often textbooks and marketing publications refer to bank products rather than bank services. This tendency to refer to services as products could stem from the desire to relate marketing in banking closely with marketing in industry. Bank marketing is a comparatively recent explosion and many of the ways in which it is currently carried out have striking similarities with its manufacturing and retail counterparts. By referring to a service as a product, the links between the industrial and retail sector marketing systems and financial institutions are forged, especially in the minds of younger bankers, and the word 'product' is now widely used as part of their marketing jargon.

More specifically a product is anything that you can see, eat, smell or physically handle. Some financial services may have facets which can be seen and handled; a cheque book, credit card or even a will document. However, these are not the service; they are merely the means of access to the service or the end result of a service which is an activity, benefit or satisfaction. The main differences between products and services which create special marketing challenges for banks are as follows:

(1) *Intangibility* As services cannot be felt, seen, tasted or touched, the benefits they offer take on greater significance and need special promotional treatment. The benefits of a through-the-wall cash dispenser card is that it provides cash outside normal banking hours and can save the holder from queuing at a busy bank counter. Clean notes and lower charges may also be regarded as benefits by the customer.

(2) *Inseparability* The sale of most bank services largely depends upon the banker's explaining the benefits and completing the formalities. The relationship therefore between buyer and seller is similar to that between doctor and patient.

Because of the financial costs of selling services in this way, new methods of selling services are being introduced which undermine this 'inseparability' characteristic. Nevertheless some services – especially where expertise or financial counselling is required – will continue to have a high degree of buyer and seller personal contact.

(3) *Heterogeneity* Services are not uniform between branches. Standards will vary and so will the level of benefits and satisfaction. A tin of baked beans from one manufacturer will be standard across a wide range of suppliers, so every buyer will get exactly the same product.

   Therefore it is even more important for a bank to pay particular attention to standards of service and to the inputs that are designed to ensure that the banking operation consistently achieves a high standard.

(4) *Perishability and fluctuating demand* Food, especially fresh fruit, has a relatively short shelf life. Similar concerns could be expressed about some specialised services where competition has undermined the sales of a bank's now outdated facility. However, generally bank services enjoy a long shelf life but some are subject to seasonal demand influences. For example, levels of demand for loans for people wishing to buy cars or holidays tend to be seasonal. Even new current account acquisition is not evenly spread, as the main influx is now July to October when teenagers leave school to start work or go on to higher education.

Influences affecting service policies and strategies

Before examining the theory of the service life cycle and the various marketing strategies available to a bank – and these range from modifying services to developing new ones and changing the mix and packaging of services – the market influences affecting these areas should be appreciated.

(a) The speed of change

Research will play a key role in ascertaining what market influences are important and whether or not changes should be made to the existing range of services, the chosen markets and the ways in which they are promoted. However, constant changes to the service range could be counter-productive as they would cause confusion in the minds of sellers and buyers and indeed may well upset existing service users who now find their facility withdrawn or at best out of date.

Thus stability is an important characteristic of bank services; fortunately the major markets served tend to change slowly and new services have time to evolve naturally with the changing market. Nevertheless, constant modifications to existing services and the development of new ones to meet changes in customer requirements need to continue, for this is what the marketing process is all about.

Meeting customer requirements is one side of the equation; on the other side is the bank's desire to supply services that can utilise existing resources and skills and that can be produced profitably. No bank will wish to satisfy customer needs at a loss, unless there are major 'spin-off' reasons for doing so.

Moreover, the bank will also have a choice of what services to produce. The return on capital employed for each service or range of services will influence production as will the amount of money available to market the services. Therefore it can be readily seen that some form of 'service policy' is desirable that has allowed for the various factors that influence decisions on the range of services offered.

(b) Main general influences

The main external influences on the 'service policy' of a bank will include the strength and activities of its competitors, the economic outlook and the trading climate generally. Government legislation and other controls may also restrict the nature and direction of marketing activities generally and therefore indirectly the services which are promoted.

Internally there are a further set of influences. These include the bank's ability to produce new services or modify existing facilities, the skills of its management and the quality of staff and branch operations. If the bank is not in the right shape to sell new services, it would be a waste of effort to introduce them. The state of morale, pay levels, educational facilities, communication effectiveness and many other aspects of banking life will need to be considered alongside 'service policy'.

Equally important is the bank's research and monitoring capability. Without information on performance, competitor activity and current and future needs of customers, a 'service policy' will have little chance of proving successful.

Service policy will also be closely aligned with the desired corporate image. Lloyds Bank sees itself as a quality bank in the high street and needs to ensure that its range of services and standards of customer care supports this quality goal. New markets which offer quality business need to be cross-matched with a range of services and servicing systems designed to appeal to better educated higher earners or larger established businesses rather than the start-up end of the corporate sector. In essence, corporate image aspirations stem from a series of self-analysis questions:

- What customers have we got?
- What customers do we want?
- What do those chosen customer groups want?
- What needs are not currently being met?
- What needs can be provided profitably?
- What might the chosen customer groups want in future?

This type of fundamental thinking is another illustration of the very core of all marketing decisions and planning processes.

(c) Obsolescence and innovation

All services at some point must be modified or superseded by newer, more relevant or sophisticated services. These changes can be a result of advanced technology, changes in taste, changes in legislation or simply competition arising from a new service which represents better value for money.

Obsolescence can be built in, planned or derived from competitor influences in the marketplace. Mass produced goods are an obvious case for built-in obsolescence. In most cases they are designed and made in such a way as to have a predetermined life span. Ultimately a buyer will change to a new product on finding that the cost of maintaining an old one has become prohibitive. Worldwide acceptability of plastic cards is gradually making travellers' cheques obsolescent and without doubt some of the new high technology computer-based services have an obsolescence factor built into them.

Planned obsolescence is achieved by introducing a new service which supersedes an existing facility. Introducing newer models of motor cars is the obvious example of vehicle manufacturers' planning obsolescence, but the situation is more complex for financial services. For example, banks found budget accounts with highly structured review and sanctioning features time-consuming and costly to maintain. New revolving credit facilities were introduced with features which did not require annual review or restrictions on what bills could be paid. Nevertheless, budget accounts are still used by customers, despite pleas from the banks to change users over to revolving credit schemes. As a direct result of a bank's not wishing to create adverse publicity by forcibly terminating a service, the planned obsolescence influence on service policy is not as clinical as it is in manufacturing. Administrative and organisational systems have to remain in place long after the service stops being available to new customers.

Alternative strategies

These market difficulties and influences apart, what is clear is that there are too many retail services offered by banks, and this creates administrative costs as well as buyer and seller confusion. It is more difficult for a bank than it is for a manufacturer to streamline its range of services, but part of the service policy will be to reduce all forms of servicing costs to a prudent minimum.

Accepting that in some cases terminating a service is desirable, albeit difficult to achieve, then the following broad service strategies are available to the banks to support their 'service policy':

(1) Expand the range of some services for selected market segments.
(2) Reduce the range of some services in selected market segments.
(3) Modify existing services rather than introduce new ones.
(4) Re-position services in chosen market segments to give them a fresh image.
(5) By altering the price, widen or contract markets and types of markets in which the services are sold.
(6) By skilful promotion, differentiate the service from those of competitors so that there is greater appeal in chosen market segments.
(7) Find new untapped markets for existing services.

Later in this chapter the ways in which services can be modified and differentiated will be examined as alternatives to the risks inherent in developing and launching completely new services.

Before leaving the strategic alternatives, there is one which could be considered but in practice hopefully rejected. That is selling only those services a bank already has rather than giving consideration to what the market requires.

Servicing the market or selling existing services?

This question brings into focus the old and the new bank marketing approach. The change of emphasis from offering traditional services to identifying market needs and new service requirements has largely been brought about by competition.

Meeting customers' wants, desires, tastes and attitudes is the basis of the marketing philosophy, provided, of course, that it can be profitably achieved. The alternative is to sell services by persuading customers to buy with scant regard for the users' actual needs. Little time, money or effort would be spent on research to predict market changes now or in the future. Nor would there be any attempt made to create a lead over competitors. The accent would be more on copying competitors should it prove necessary. In this way, the service features become the focus of the sale, not the needs of customers. Ultimately the whole relationship between bank and customer could be sacrificed in the interests of short-term sales results.

Development costs of creating new services can be heavy, and the failure rate high. It is, therefore, essential to gain a considerable depth of understanding of the market and a fundamental identification of needs. Products on the other hand can often be produced more quickly, and are easier and cheaper to promote, because they are tangible, but they often have a much shorter life cycle.

Rubik cubes and hula hoops are examples where pressure sales-manship is necessary as part of a selling process of short product life cycles requiring 'first in and first out' strategies. Servicing a market can be called consultative selling. In the banking industry this approach recognises the special demands imposed by a wide range of services and customers. It offers flexibility, not just in terms of selling to individual customers, but also allows for the industrial and demographic varia-tions seen geographically through a national network of branches.

By placing greater emphasis on customer needs, rather than service benefits, banks are better able to recognise and satisfy those needs and hence sell their services.

The backbone of a clearing bank's service range is money transmis-sion. These transmission services, and there are others, are suitable for a product-orientated sales activity. They have reached the same degree of acceptability as food. People must eat to live, and apart from market price variations and an element of branding, there is little perceived difference – beans are beans and money transmission is money trans-mission. Nevertheless, profit objectives will to some extent influence choice of markets and weight of sales activity.

Both approaches – selling services and servicing a market – can be used, provided the services are as appropriate as possible and potentially profitable either in their own right or as part of a package. It should not be forgotten also that some customers have needs that they are not aware of and that can only be exposed by an aggressive service-selling campaign.

To achieve maximum gain there is also a need for a switch in emphasis from marketing to selling towards the end of the service life cycle, especially when competitive activity makes the going even tougher.

Cross-selling, or return business, is the main factor that encourages consultative selling. The wide range and nature of bank services demands lasting relationships. As people grow older their financial needs change; so profitability from service usage and improving lifestyles creating lodgements and sales opportunities will only continue so long as customers have not been alienated by pressure selling.

The service life cycle

Financial services go through the same life cycle stages as any other product. Analysing and monitoring the life cycle of services can help to identify promotional needs and ultimately opportunities for new services. There are two elements to consider when looking at take-up levels of any given service. The apparent speed of acceptability of the service by the buyers and, within any given market, the likely sales saturation percentage. Buyer behaviour can be illustrated diagrammatically in broad bands (Fig. 4.1).

The life cycle graph (Fig. 4.2) is very similar to the behavioural illustration, for it looks at the same issues but from a slightly different perspective. The simple diagram unfortunately fails to indicate quantities measured along each axis because in practice the time-scale from the birth of a new service to its demise can vary tremendously. Moreover, some services are more easily adapted to changes in requirements than others, and therefore remain in demand for a longer period. Nevertheless this life cycle concept is valuable in assessing market requirements and taking into account competitive elements. If tactical changes to a service or the repositioning of it fail to arrest a

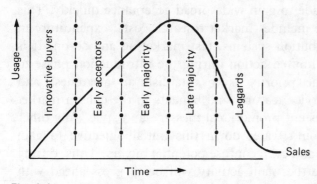

Fig. 4.1

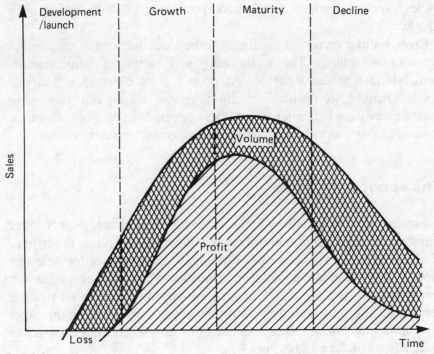

Fig. 4.2

downturn in demand, then other marketing measures should be considered.

Extending the stages of the life cycle

The introduction stage is characterised by slow growth in the sales of the service and generally there is a negative profit. Expenses incurred from the introduction and promotion of the service at this early stage are high, as efforts are made to gain widespread acceptance quickly. This phase in the life cycle includes market research costs, expenditure in establishing the distribution systems, test marketing and so on. It is only possible to take limited action during the introduction phase to increase revenue. The priority is to establish an awareness and appreciation of the service features and benefits in the chosen market segments with a consistent promotional message and style. Any other promotional efforts could water down this initial objective to gain widespread awareness and even confuse potential buyers. Thus, during the introduction stage the main activity will be to press ahead with promoting the service.

During the *growth stage* an increase in sales volumes occurs whilst costs tend to remain stable. Profitability will therefore increase as economies of scale come into play. As the growth stage goes through its cycle it is possible to accelerate take-up levels and improve market acceptance in a number of ways:

(1) Improve service quality/features
(2) Sell to wider market segments
(3) Sell through other distribution channels
(4) Realign advertising from obtaining high levels of awareness to getting service conviction
(5) Reduce price when appropriate to attract the next layer of price conscious buyers

Maturity is reached when over-capacity occurs as the profitability of the growth stage encourages competitors to enter the arena. It is evidenced by dropping sales, increased advertising, increasing costs and falling profits.

There are ways to slow down the rate of decline in revenue and sales in the short term, but eventually service replacement will be necessary. The following strategies may extend the active life of the service especially the timespan of the 'maturity' period:

(1) Modifying the service to appeal to other market segments.
(2) Price cutting to at least retain market but preferably improve market share.
(3) Alter selling strategy by packaging with other compatible services to give broader appeal.

Finally, *the decline stage* will ensue, and is characterised by stable fixed costs but reducing revenue, especially if prices have been cut. When considering what to do about the inevitable, there are two courses of action. Firstly, the bank could terminate or withdraw the service completely and thereby immediately arrest any losses that may be arising. This clinical approach would also release scarce resources to generate increased sales of other services, but withdrawing a financial service from existing users is notoriously difficult to do without upsetting customers. Usually a natural decay is the compromise solution for those who cannot be persuaded to take up the replacement service if there is one on offer. Alternatively, as competition falls away, it might be justifiable to carry on, in markets considered likely to be the most profitable, with the promotion of a modified service adapted to contain only the best features for those audiences which are most highly regarded and least costly or time-consuming from a sales and administration standpoint. Some of the problems of revenue flow are overcome by an organisation that has a range of products or services each at various stages in their life cycle.

Before leaving the service life cycle concept, it is worth highlighting once again the vital role research plays in monitoring each of the stages which, as stated earlier, in real terms are nowhere near as clear-cut. Without the data from research to aid and support management judgement it would be easy to over-react or choose the wrong time to make changes to elements of the marketing mix at some considerable cost to profits and future business growth prospects.

Modifying and differentiating services

As has been indicated, modifying existing services generally occurs at the maturity stage of the life cycle and these modifications are usually in the quality, features and style of the service. Differentiation may also be an end result but this area is a strategy in itself. So far, banks have failed to differentiate themselves from others in the high street. The problem is growing as the previously different roles of building societies, insurance companies and banks become distinctly blurred following relaxation of government controls.

A distinctive range of services is as important as having a distinctive identity in the high street, for it denotes service leadership and encourages buyers to choose. The alternative is a grey featureless and almost indistinguishable image in the marketplace, leaving growth and performance very susceptible to competitors with an innovative style.

Modification is initially sometimes preferable to introducing a new service as there are less financial risks, but the commercial advantages of modifying rather than introducing a new service must be carefully weighed beforehand.

(a) Quality modifications

The objective of quality modifications is to improve reliability, quality and durability of the service. This is done to

(1) Attract a significant proportion of a market segment which offers higher than normal profit opportunities. The American Express Gold Card first launched as a joint service package with Lloyds Bank is a good example of upgrading various services into one quality facility. It was meant to have 'exclusive' appeal at a price.
(2) Ensure higher net profit by charging higher prices.
(3) Produce a service which is consistent with, or will help to reinforce, a desired quality corporate image.

(4) Ward off other competitors who are also entering the same market.

Once quality modifications have been decided, other elements of the marketing mix, particularly advertising and promotion, must blend with the revised service. So too might the choice of target markets.

(b) Feature modifications

Adding on new benefits to an existing service is the most expedient and generally the cheapest way of keeping ahead in a competitive market-place. This may take the form of merely upgrading existing benefits: for example, increasing the value of automatic insurance cover under a loan protection policy or introducing entirely new features.

The main commercial advantages of these modifications are that they are relatively cheap to incorporate and can be adapted or abandoned quickly if that remedial action proves necessary. There are also corporate image benefits if the changes paint a picture of a progressive bank aware of and responding to the customers' requirements. One disadvantage of course is that they can be easily and quickly copied by competitors.

(c) Style modifications

It was said at the very beginning that the majority of customers are particularly wary of sudden changes in an industry which has tradition-ally developed fairly slowly. Nevertheless, the ways in which a bank goes about its business are changing, especially in the corporate sector where the importance of protecting middle- to large-sized accounts necessitates a much closer liaison. New Account Managers are now the vogue who regularly call on customers at their premises. This compares with the old traditional methods of servicing where the corporate customer visited the bank.

The advantages to the bank of style modifications are sometimes difficult to predict. A new servicing system may be welcomed by one customer whereas traditional customers may prefer the old style.

Introducing new services

New services carry the highest business risks even though research is carried out at every stage of the process from development to launch. Guidance on whether or not a new service should be developed is found in the bank's corporate plan. This corporate plan (which is discussed in Chapter 9) is the control document for all major marketing developments. It states the short-, medium- and longer-term aspirations of the bank, and any new services must obviously support those stated corporate goals.

A service may be new to the bank but not considered new by the customer and vice versa. However, if the customer does not perceive it as a new service, then clearly it cannot be regarded as one. Alternatively a service can be regarded as new to everyone. This opportunity to provide a completely new service can arise from changes in the law, technology or society. In practice, opportunities to provide completely new services are few and far between. Mostly, new services for a bank stem from copying a competitor, with or without improvements, or extensively modifying an existing service or services to create a new set or package of interrelated benefits.

(a) Need for new services

There are many commercial factors which may create the need to introduce a new service:

(1) Falling sales and profit. Unless the bank is prepared to adapt to a radically changing environment the end results could be catastrophic.
(2) Competition generally which could reduce market share and undermine future profitability.
(3) Strategic considerations depending upon whether the bank wishes to be aggressive or defensive in the marketplace.
(4) New profitable markets identified by research which calls for a new service.

Other factors will influence a decision on whether or not to introduce a new service. These include the assessment of the effect of a new service on cash flow and other resources. Costs of developing new services are high, and so are the demands on available staff selling time, sometimes to the detriment of other mainstream services. Finally a new service might be so closely related to other services that it adversely affects existing service sales and profit earnings.

The size of the potential market for a new service and the ease with which it can be reached will also impact on the decision. So also will the likely life expectancy of the service. A quick life cycle will lower sales volumes, shorten the profit period and create pressure to keep down development and other costs. Again the name of the game is profit.

Although some services are regarded as loss-leaders, the overwhelming factor in all decisions about services is likely profit levels.

(b)   For and against copying competitors

There are several marketing and commercial advantages in following the lead of a competitor. Therefore there must be good reasons for not doing so, and these will be considered shortly.

The main reasons for copying a competitor's service are:

(1) Saving in heavy development costs and scarce resources compared with developing and launching a completely new service.
(2) Copying is more likely to be commercially viable, especially if the competitor's service is successful.
(3) Spin-off benefits for own promotional efforts if the competitor's advertising has made the service widely known and understood.
(4) Copying the service has the effect of partially neutralising the advantages established by the competitor of being first. This is especially true if, when copying the service, it is also improved.

Nevertheless there are also circumstances where launching an entirely new service would be better than a 'follow my leader' approach. The corporate objectives create priorities and should ensure the overall marketing thrust is not pulled off course by tactical reactions to competitor marketing activity. If these corporate plans are well founded they should ensure that all resources are fully utilised and only when competition seriously encroaches on these corporate goals in key market segments should a response be necessary. The corporate plan may also identify the areas where new services are required to support marketing goals and the development of these services will need to be given priority.

Other reasons for not copying a successful service are related to the practical issues where organisational and marketing strengths and opportunities do not correlate with those of competitors. Customer profiles may differ, so may the degree of a bank's staff expertise and servicing capability. For example, the ability to program the support requirements of a new service by one bank on its computer may not be possible for another.

Limitations of size and the geographical spread of a bank's network of branches may also dissuade it from imitating another's service. This is especially relevant if profitability is dependent upon volume growth in areas where opportunity levels are high but the bank's representation is low. If the new service is just one part of a comprehensive package and the appeal is due to the range, then copying would depend on the ability to provide a similar package of services. In isolation it may have little chance of success.

Research and development

Market research information is vital at all the stages of the development process. These may be listed as follows:

(1) Evaluation of concept and assessing the likelihood of acceptability.
(2) Assessment and testing of reasons for development.
(3) Evaluation of resource requirements to develop and manage the new service.
(4) Cost and profitability forecasts.
(5) Marketability and promotional requirements.
(6) Test marketing before a full launch is undertaken.
(7) Monitoring sales, profitability, customer attitudes and competitor reaction once the service is launched.

Any one of the research requirements could be omitted if there are good grounds for doing so. For example, if the cost of research by test marketing is more than a full launch, then on cost grounds alone the test marketing stage could be waived.

New service development

(a) Creating ideas

The process starts with an idea which could come from internal or external sources. One of the prime internal sources is the bank's own formal research and development function where specialists seek to devise services which meet corporate goals, and changing economic and environmental circumstances. A further internal source is that part of the bank's marketing operation which seeks to translate customer needs and the competitive requirements of the marketplace into service ideas. Finally, the bank may look to its own staff to provide ideas based upon their own expertise or experience. External sources of ideas for new services come from customers, associate companies or subsidiaries and the government, through adaptation of legal considerations or budgetary measures. Personal Equity Plans (PEPs) were introduced as a new service in January 1987 as a direct result of budget influences. Other external sources will also stem from what the competition is doing, and finally from outside academic and technical organisations as they carry out their own research and development programmes.

(b) Screening and viability analysis

Having generated new service ideas, the bank must now screen these to ensure that the good ideas are not dropped and that the poor ones are not progressed. Preliminary judgements must be made in the light of the ideas' apparent conflict or compatibility with overall service objectives, policies and bank resources.

Ideas which survive the screening phase can be developed into service concepts and, once developed, the concepts must then be tested with the appropriate target consumer groups.

Following development of a preliminary service concept, the bank can begin to develop a marketing analysis. This will consist of three distinct parts; first, the likely size, structure and behaviour of the target market, as well as the sales, market share and profit goals, sought for the service in its first few years. Second, the service's intended price, distribution, strategy and marketing budget for the first year. Finally, the long-run sales and profit goals and projected marketing-mix strategy.

Once the service concept and market analysis have been developed, the bank is in a position to make a final decision concerning the need for a new service. This decision will rest on the outcome of a final in-depth business analysis in which the service's future sales, costs and profits estimates will be set against the bank's overall objectives.

(c) Developing the service and presentation

The service development programme will ultimately involve commitment of resources to a full-scale introduction. This is known as the commercialisation stage. However, prior to this, it may be prudent to carry out a limited test marketing exercise. The pilot launch of a service, if time and competitive pressures allow, can provide important information on the service features and also on ways in which it can be ultimately marketed. For example, a pilot test could provide guidance on systems and operational requirements, staff training, the packaging and promotion mix options.

At this stage the answers to four questions have to be considered:

(1) *When* (timing)? The answer rests not only on identifying the optimum marketing and competitive conditions for the launch,

but also how long it will take to establish the back-up resources, staff training, promotion material and any computer support that may be required.

(2) *Where* (geographic strategy)? The bank must decide whether it is to launch the service regionally, nationally or even internationally. Furthermore, if the branch network is segmented into various types – corporate, personal, money transmission, etc. – then a decision has to be made on which branches are excluded. The nature of the new service will determine this outcome.

(3) *To whom* (target markets)? The earlier development research will largely decide the choice of markets and when the markets are chosen the price, promotion and distribution mix can be refined. A test launch later may reveal that the marketing mix may subsequently need fine tuning.

(4) *How* (introductory marketing strategy)? This question involves giving consideration to the allocation of a budget to cover the cost of launch and agreeing the promotional mix including the media advertising programme and timetable.

(d) The launch

During the development and commercialisation stages a number of important decisions or assumptions will have been made, not least the sales or revenue-earning targets for the new service. Part of the launch stage will be to communicate these objectives or targets to all those involved with the launch. It will also be necessary to brief the staff on their expected actions and degrees of responsibility in generating take-up levels. Feedback systems will also be beneficial as part of the launch stage to ascertain the impact of the new service on the chosen market segments and the bank's competitors' reactions.

(e) Monitoring results

Once the service is launched, it will still need to be managed for a period of time, if only to undertake a final review and any corrective action.

When auditing the performance of any service, especially one only recently launched, a number of areas need to be explored:

(1) The extent to which customer needs are being satisfied compared with competitor services.

(2) The extent and speed to which the service can adjust to changes in the marketplace.

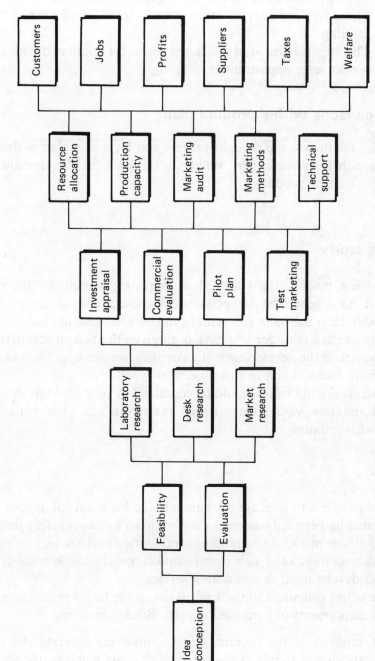

Fig. 4.3 Manufacturer's plan to develop, test and launch a new product — issues to be considered

(3) Profitability, sales and costs levels including the relationship between costs of supply and perceived benefits by the customer.
(4) The position of the service in its expected life cycle.
(5) The effect on sales of other similar services which may need pruning.
(6) The apportionment of effort and resources compared with other service sales opportunities.

Comparisons with a product plan

As Fig. 4.3 shows, the thought process and logic of a plan to develop and launch a service is very similar to the plan for the creation and supply of a new product.

Case study

Your bank has identified a need to increase substantially the retail deposit base generated by personal customers and to do so more profitably than the bank can achieve in the wholesale market.

As marketing manager you have been given the task of identifying a new service or the development of an existing service which will make a significant contribution to this objective.

What marketing issues would be contained in your final report to the board and how would these issues guide you and your bank to a successful solution?

The objective is to increase substantially the bank's retail deposit base generated by personal customers and to do so more profitably than via the wholesale market. A significant contribution to the objective is to be the identification of a new retail deposit generating service or the further development of an existing service.

The issues contained in the final report to the board would form the major components of a marketing plan. Briefly these are:

1 An analysis of the current market situation, covering the characteristics and trends in the personal deposits markets, the sources and types of competition and a review of the bank's own recent performance and present capabilities in the personal sector.

From the analysis, a summary of the bank's strengths and

weaknesses, opportunities and threats can be prepared. This provides the basic raw material for the establishment of marketing goals and the development of a marketing strategy for their achievement.
2   The selection of the target market(s).
3   The selection of service strategies to meet target market needs.
4   The development of associated pricing, promotion and distribution strategies.
5   The establishment of monitoring and evaluation procedures.

The report would seek to address each of these issues in detail as follows:

1 *Current market situation*
  (a) The size of the personal deposits market covering both interest-bearing and non-interest-bearing accounts. Recent historical patterns of growth/decline and discussion of factors underlying changes.
  (b) Market segmentation. An analysis of the market by value of deposits held and the establishment of characteristics of the 20–25 per cent of customers controlling 75–80 per cent of deposits – for example by demographics life cycle group.
  (c) Review of the bank's own personal deposit-generating service range. Analysis of funds deposited, by customer demographics. Summary of pricing, promotion and distribution strategies applicable to retail deposits.
  (d) Competitive structure. The organisations represented in the retail deposits market, the market shares held and any changes in recent years, service ranges and structures, pricing and distribution policies, extent and types of marketing support given. Identification of trends and projected future changes, including new entrants and new services potential.
  (e) Customer behaviour patterns. Examination of current lodgement patterns and considerations influencing them – for example: perceptions of security, ease of access, price sensitivities, taxation issues, imagery of various financial institutions. Evaluation of the needs of different customer groups and the establishment of factors which would induce customers to move deposits from one organisation to another and those which would reinforce existing bank customers' loyalty.
  (f) Future economic, legislative and regulatory scenarios including the impact of retail price inflation, employment and wage/salary prospects upon the level of personal disposable income saved.

From the analysis of the current and projected future market situation, a summary of the strengths, weaknesses, opportunities and threats to the bank in the retail deposits market would be prepared.

This would provide a basis for the setting of financial and marketing objectives and goals which the marketing strategy would be designed to achieve.

2 *Target market*

The target market(s) would be selected by using the market analysis and focusing particularly on the summary of strengths, weaknesses, opportunities and threats.

On a low risk strategy, the market sector(s) offering the greatest deposit potential with the lowest projected organisational cost would be selected. 'Organisational cost' would include not only marketing, promotional and systems development costs but also relative ease of organisational adaptation to achieve the required level of market success.

The target market adopted could either involve pitching at a market sub-sector not presently covered by the bank successfully, or reinforcing or extending marketing activity directed towards existing customer profiles.

Definition of the target market could be in terms of demographics, life cycle stage, media usage, attitudinal groupings, etc.

3 *Service strategy*

The service strategy or strategies adopted would stem from the target market definition. Which benefits would be required and how would they be translated into service features? How do the proposed features and benefits differ from those currently available in the market? Are the differences real or apparent? Is the enhancement of existing bank services proposed or is it the development of new ones or a combination of both?

How do the proposed services fit in with the existing bank service range? Are they realistic and credible? Do they enhance or correct the perceived imagery of the bank amongst the key market sectors? If they represent a significant departure from current service strategy, can all the relevant organisational support be provided to guide the service from introduction or relaunch to maturity?

Equally essential would be to examine the degree of compatibility of the proposed service development with external operating constraints – for example: existing or known future legislative or regulatory constraints, acceptability to consumerist groups.

Finally, the potential competitor reactions to the service strategy. What response would be likely to be made and how could the bank protect or defend its service strategy?

4 *Pricing strategy*

As the only income-generating component of a marketing plan, careful consideration of both an overall pricing policy and its individual constituents is vital.

In a personal sector deposit service, the relationship between the credit interest rates offered and any service charge or interest rate penalty levied is central to pricing. As a guideline, the ceiling for the cost to the bank of the service development is that it should be lower on a net basis than future funds acquired from the wholesale market. How are interest rates to be structured both within the service – for example: progressive tiering of interest rates by minimum deposit thresholds, bonus rates for length of deposit held, absence of withdrawals, etc. – and secondly, relative to general market interest rates? Which combination of interest rates and prices would have the greatest target market appeal?

Are the principles of the strategy capable of supporting the service beyond launch and into maturity with individual components flexible enough to be adapted tactically? Computer models would ideally be used to assess the effect on deposit levels of any change or combination of changes either in terms of pricing attributes or as a result of external changes – for example: a change in personal taxation regulations.

– *Distribution strategy*

How will the target market requirements of the service influence its distribution? How will 'convenience' be translated into hours and days of access as well as geographical proximity to where prospective customers live, work or shop? What are the distribution considerations affecting initial purchase and post-purchase customer advice and information? How well do the bank's existing distribution channels fit these needs and what are the criteria to be adopted for selection amongst existing channels to meet market or service requirements?

Should all existing channels be unsuitable, what are the new types of distribution needed? How many, how would they be acquired and set up? How would new business flowing through blend in with existing business passing through existing distribution channels?

– *Sales and promotional strategies*

A preliminary step to the development of sound sales and promotional strategies would be the forecasting of total deposit volumes over time and their make-up in terms of customer numbers and average deposit levels, given stated assumptions regarding the operating environment – for example: interest rate levels and types and levels of competitor activity.

These forecasts would be the base-line information for cost, profit and budgetary projections and would also provide the company resource implications in terms of systems capability and capacity, staffing levels and types and premises required.

At this stage a commitment to the service development or new service launch should be gained from all the relevant 'supplier' departments in the bank.

Sales and promotional strategies and plans would be developed from predetermined budgetary levels. Marketing and sales objectives would be specified with key attributes of the plans including the identification and targeting of sales and customer servicing personnel, their education, training and motivation and the securing of their commitment to the service development.

Promotional plans would consider issues of media advertising and advertising support material such as leaflets, posters, point of sale merchandising, sales promotion techniques for the launch and post-launch periods and the role played by public relations and publicity activities such as exhibitions.

Presentation or 'packaging' considerations would include the identification of promotional platforms and themes and their creative styling.

The timings and interrelationships of all selected promotional activities would be covered in the plans.

Since new service launches and even existing service development campaigns can involve significant sums of money, a test market or pilot launch stage could be used both to test aspects of marketing or promotional activity and/or systems capabilities. As with a full national launch, objectives and goals should be specified, measured and evaluated with criteria set for modification of marketing components and for commitment to a full-scale launch.

5 *Monitoring and evaluation procedures*

Systems for the monitoring and measurement of marketing activity would be required at the launch stage to provide a reliable information flow upon which decisions to alter, extend or reinforce elements of the marketing plan could be made.

Full-scale reviews and evaluations should be carried out at specified periods to examine performance against the target, to set or revise goals for the forthcoming period and to consider whether a reorientation, down-scaling or up-weighting of activity is needed.

A successful solution to the task of increasing substantially the bank's retail deposit base by personal customers would be one that was carefully planned within the framework outlined and sufficiently flexible to adapt to new information emerging at each stage of the planning and review process.

Summary

Services differ from products in that they have characteristics such as intangibility, a degree of inseparability from the seller, heterogeneity, and fluctuating levels of demand. As such, marketing financial services presents special challenges which may not be inherent in selling products. There are many internal and external influences affecting service policies and strategies but there is also a need to ensure that new services develop logically and the existing service range creates an image of stability.

Meeting customers' needs with new or improved services is important, but so is the need to balance this desire with resource capability and profit goals. All new services should be compatible with the medium- and longer-term corporate goals unless they provide only very short-term but major tactical benefits.

There are many environmental, social, technological and economic influences affecting a bank's decisions on whether to refrain from meeting identified needs, modify existing services or create new ones. Some fundamental thinking is required to choose a bank's best course of action.

Obsolescence can be planned or derived from competitor influences in the marketplace.

A bank's strategies for its range of service include expanding them, reducing the numbers, modifying, updating and repositioning certain services or altering elements of the marketing mix to create different market segment demand, acceptability and availability.

Buyer behaviour, the speed of acceptance of a new service, and the life cycle concept for a service follow similar patterns. However, timing and take-up cannot normally be quantified when looking at these two theoretical concepts.

The growth and maturity and decline stages in the service life cycle can all be massaged to improve overall business performance by innovative and correctly timed use of the marketing mix elements.

New services are the prerequisite for long-term corporate survival but the reasons and objectives for introducing new services should be clearly defined at the outset.

Research plays a crucial part in the development and launch of new services and can be used to minimise risk at all stages of the process from concept evaluation through to monitoring results.

The elements in the development programme for creating a new service from conception to launch should be understood. At the commercialisation stage the answers to questions when? where? to whom? and how? need careful consideration.

Revision questions

1 Before considering the development of a new service what basic questions require resolution? Also explain why some services fail.
2 What do you understand by the term 'service life cycle'? What implications has the concept for bank marketing activity?
3 Outline the stages in a new service development programme and indicate the contribution that market research can make.
4 Under what conditions is it better to prepare and launch a new service rather than to copy a successful service of a competitor?
5 Identify four services marketed by your bank which you consider are in each of the four life cycle stages. Explain how you know they have reached that stage.

Chapter 5
The Marketing Mix – Prices and Discounts

Background to pricing

Pricing is a very important element in the marketing mix for it is the only one which produces revenue. All the other parts of the marketing mix are cost driven. Despite being so critical to the profitability of a bank, aggressive pricing strategies have in the past seldom been adopted. Although in recent years, since the abolition of the interest rate cartel, price competition among the banks has grown. The most memorable example of this growing competition was the advent of 'free banking' for personal current account holders if they remain in funds. Among the 'big four' Midland Bank was the first to break ranks and introduce 'free banking'. Despite strong resistance to following the Midland Bank's lead, the remaining clearers succumbed to competitive pressure and introduced 'free banking' some months later.

More recently the question whether or not to pay interest on current account credit balances has become a serious discussion point. This is another form of pricing, although a general move to pay interest on all current account funds could be very damaging to retail bank earnings. It is interesting to note how the purchase of lodgements by paying competitive rates of interest on the funds attracted is on the one hand a pricing mechanism. But to a bank it is also a cost as the interest paid for lodgements reduces profit. However, if the price paid to account holders for lodgements is lower than the cost of gaining funds in some other way, in the wholesale money markets for example, then there is a cost saving. Moreover, if the interest rates paid increase lodgements and this, in turn, enables lending to be increased, then there will be profit return based on what is paid for the lodgements compared with the higher rates earned from on lending these funds.

When considering the unusual trading nature of a retail bank which buys in funds and relends them it should not be overlooked that costs are both fixed and variable. Where variable costs are involved, their impact is affected by volume. Fixed costs need to be recovered irrespective of sales by means of an appropriate pricing policy. Variable costs that are volume-related need controlling.

Before leaving the semantics of pricing and costing it is worth highlighting the difficulties most banks have in assessing true direct and indirect costs for each individual service or related range of services. If pricing is based on cost recovery, then knowing the cost is normally an essential prerequisite. In the case of the retail banks, great strides are being made to identify and apportion direct costs to individual services but indirect cost allocation is very much more arbitrary. This is not surprising when you have an organisation with 200–300 separate services sold through a network of over 1000 high street branches. Rapid progress is being made to make each separate unit of a bank either a cost or profit centre, and this research, coupled with growing computer technology, is improving the knowledge about pricing generally. This should result in more concise pricing policies and strategies, and ultimately result in more effective use of pricing as a marketing tool.

Relationship of price with marketing mix

The guidelines for pricing policy and the pricing strategies used to attract business can be found in the corporate plan. This plan should identify where the bank is now in the marketplace, where it wants to be within a period of time and, lastly, what should be done to ensure that the planned outcome is successful. No single marketing activity will achieve the desired results which are most likely to stem from the co-ordinated use of all the available marketing skills and functions. Pricing is just one element, but it must be used to support and blend with the ways other elements of the marketing mix are being applied. Just as in the previous chapter we looked at services and service strategies in isolation, so in the next few pages we shall treat 'price' in the same way. However, the strong interrelationship between services, promotion and distribution strategies must not be forgotten or ignored.

Moreover, pricing can tend to be a once or twice a year activity whereas assessing other parts of the marketing mix is a more continuous process. This reluctance to review and change prices on a regular basis is partially due to the fact that setting prices is not a simple exercise. What competitors charge has a profound influence on the marketplace, since consumers regard banks, and bank services, as very much alike. Laws of supply and demand do affect pricing, but these laws, which are considered in more detail later in this chapter, have less effect on financial services than they do on brand foods or mass-produced products, where quality variations, packaging and image of the company have much more influence on consumer demand.

The final decision on what price to levy is influenced by an amalgamation of the following within a total marketing mix designed to stimulate demand:

(1) Government reaction to price levels
(2) The bank's overall corporate objectives
(3) The bank's shorter-term marketing objectives, particularly volume and profit targets
(4) Likely adverse or beneficial customer reaction to price changes. Market research has an important role here.
(5) Likely competitor counter-measures and the general competitive atmosphere in the marketplace.

Elasticity of demand

The way in which a service is priced is a key factor in the attainment of profit and volume objectives. As such, price is a crucial element in the marketing mix and if handled badly can jeopardise sales to an extent where a service, with otherwise acceptable features, could be regarded as a failure. Because price affects both profitability and sales volumes, it cannot be fixed in isolation. Market forces, the cost structure underpinning the creation, maintenance and promotion will all impact on the final price level. Ultimately the task will be to ensure that price is geared to cover expenditure and attract sufficient sales volumes to achieve stated corporate profit and volume objectives.

The theory of 'elasticity of demand' tries to show how the market will react in response to price changes. If a bank is forewarned with this information, pricing strategies can then be chosen for individual services or groups of related services.

Generally speaking, the demand for a service is directly related to its price. If the price goes up, demand should fall and vice versa. The elasticity of demand theory tries to relate the percentage change in price to its effect on the percentage change in the sale of services.

There are three possible outcomes to consider when prices change

(1) Demand can rise or fall by exactly the same percentage as the price rises or falls.
(2) Demand can rise or fall by more than the percentage rise or fall of prices (said to be elastic).
(3) Demand can rise or fall by less than the percentage rise or fall of prices (said to be inelastic).

In other words, when demand is inelastic a price increase can actually increase total revenue even though sales of the service actually decline.

Whereas with a price increase which reduces total revenue through a sharp decline in sales the demand is elastic (Fig. 5.1).

As price affects take-up, the theory of 'elasticity of demand' in relation to finding out the optimum balance is sometimes a matter of trial and error but, for a new service especially, research will be required to gauge buyers' reaction to price levels and price changes.

Some services are more sensitive to price than others and there are a number of factors which affect price sensitivity; they are:

● The existence of similar or substitute services;
● General buyer awareness of prices of alternative services;
● The length of time since a price change was implemented;
● The range of benefits offered by the service;
● How often the service is purchased and the significance of the service to the buyer.

It is a fact that customers tend to use only one bank and, because they share a common belief that all bank services are similar, seldom shop around. Hence demand elasticity is not normally a major factor with existing customers, but inelasticity is becoming less as competitive activity, especially advertising, increases.

When considering elasticity, it is important to distinguish between market elasticity of demand and bank elasticity of demand. If market demand is elastic, a reduction in price will increase sales, as this assumes that many potential buyers are being put off by price. If market demand is inelastic, any price cut will not materially affect sales volumes. Thus market elasticity tells us how total market demand reacts to changes in price. Bank elasticity on the other hand indicates the willingness of customers to shift banks on the basis of price. If one bank cuts prices it may experience an upsurge in demand which could continue until competitors follow suit. In this situation we could experience bank elasticity but market inelasticity, as no new users are attracted, and there is merely a change of customer allegiance.

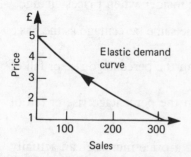 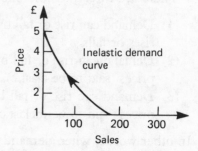

Fig. 5.1　Elastic and inelastic demand curves

In pricing particular services, especially new ones, other strategic factors come into focus. The two most important are 'skimming' – a strategy aimed at attracting only certain segments of a total market which are less price-sensitive – and penetration pricing. The latter is designed to capture a large share of the market as quickly as possible. These pricing strategies are marketing orientated but the cost of developing, launching and monitoring a service cannot be ignored, and ultimately these issues will be considered in the longer-term pricing decisions. Pricing alternatives are considered in greater detail later in this chapter.

Apart from these factors, which influence price and pricing policy, there are others which should not be overlooked. These include:

(1) The overall blend of the chosen pricing policy with the other elements of the marketing mix so that all are complementary;

(2) The degree of automation in the service and the cost over time of providing and maintaining the machinery needed to deliver the service;

(3) The bank's corporate objectives in terms of the image and degree of exclusivity it wants to achieve;

(4) The period in the life cycle that the service has reached especially when it is at the decline stage where price may be less important than maximising sales volumes;

(5) External influences such as government policy and competition levels, which will influence pricing directly or indirectly depending on the strength of these external influences.

Pricing is the only income-generating element in the marketing mix for a retail bank with a large established delivery system. The object is not to be the cheapest in the marketplace but to pitch price at a level which maximises profit/volume objectives.

Researching price change reactions

Market research will improve the quality of management decisions by providing an understanding of all the market forces impacting on pricing and the suitability, in a given environment, of the current pricing policy that has been adopted.

Users of bank services have their own perceptions of what they consider to be value for money. But, generally, when asked to make value judgements on financial services which are free or offer more benefits than others they have little conception of how to actually quantify those benefits. It is much easier to assess and compare financial services that are purely interest-related. Even then, many users are more concerned with how much per month they receive or need to pay rather than the true cost or return compared with what is generally available in the marketplace.

Nevertheless customer financial awareness and sophistication is growing, and reaction to price changes should be researched before and after they are made. This is especially important for new services or for the relaunch of existing services that have been substantially modified and improved. A number of simple research methods can be used to test customer reactions to price levels and price changes.

(a) Attitude surveys

Quantitative research can be used to measure reactions and the relative appeals of alternative pricing. A representative sample of potential or existing users is chosen. Then the sample is asked to complete questionnaires that have been carefully constructed so that degrees of reaction to price structures can be quantified. In this way, an optimum level can be found between price and its effect on customers' general attitudes and their propensity to buy in particular.

(b) Qualitative research

These interviews can be used to try and measure the relationships between price and perceived value. This in-depth research could also highlight the likelihood of price changes resulting in a movement of business to competitors. This qualitative research could also identify customers' preferences when different charging methods are possible. In 1986 some of the banks moved away from item-linked current account quarterly charging to a flat rate monthly system. This is one example of alternative pricing methods which followed extensive research into customers' preferences.

(c) Statistical research

This type of research can take two forms, depending upon the type and quality of the data available to the researcher. Historical analysis can reveal demand fluctuations following price changes and it can also analyse the extent to which changes in demand have been affected by the choice of prices of similar services available in the marketplace. Service take-up information among the major banks is usually available through the survey and statistical reports produced by many of the research organisations specialising in this field – IBRO, MORI and AGB are just three worthy of a mention.

(d) Test research

The features of a new service can be tested prior to a full-scale launch, and again at the post-launch stage. Price will often be a major feature. The impact of each price alternative on demand and what is considered to be the optimum choice to achieve objectives set will need careful analysis.

Price can also be affected by geographical areas and this research in turn will give a lead to the choice of distribution and promotional plans. Pre-launch testing by taking a random sample of the chosen target audiences in those areas considered to offer the best sales opportunities makes its possible to gauge the reaction after launch and assess the sales potential.

Pricing policies

Although pricing policy takes its direction and is derived initially from the corporate plan, there are other factors which have to be taken into account. The two main market influences on the price of a service are levels of demand and the prices of a similar competitor service. These two determining factors will need to be balanced against desired profitability levels.

Price also has a material impact upon other areas which extend beyond sales volumes, demand and profit objectives. The market sectors penetrated, consumer perceptions of the service and competitors' evaluation of its attractiveness are all influenced by the pricing policy selected. When launching a new service, the status, characteristics and attitudinal trends in chosen target market segments will also need to be assessed. Also, if there is a similar service currently offered, consideration should be given to the effect that the price of a new service will have on present sales, likely degree of switching by users of the existing service and organisational and marketing ability to meet expected demands.

Pricing policy alternatives

In practice, price setting can be used strategically or tactically, and there are several major pricing alternatives:

(1) *Skimming price* – a high initial price is set to skim off the cream of demand. This pricing strategy is often used for new services as in the early days competitive issues are less influential. Moreover, an image of quality may undermine price sensitivity and the objective is to sell first to those customers who have the greatest need and will therefore pay a higher price.

(2) *Penetration pricing* – a lower price is set which is designed to win market share initially. This is the opposite to skimming pricing and is generally used if the market is regarded as price sensitive, where there are economies from volume sales and where it is felt the threat of competition necessitates getting a major percentage of the available market share quickly.

(3) *Competitive pricing* – an arbitrary price is set to match competitive pressures, but this price should be at a level which will at least cover costs and allow a margin for profit. Sometimes this pricing policy is described as 'slotting in'. The approach is especially useful when a bank wishes to obtain some early experience of operating either a specific service or in a specific market. Nevertheless, the bank will also need to be reasonably satisfied that the service is launched within a price range acceptable in the market.

(4) *Going rate or market price* – involves fixing prices which match others in the marketplace. With this pricing strategy no consideration is normally given to cost/revenue considerations. It is simply a defensive measure to protect existing business.

(5) *'Loss leader' pricing* – used to attract opportunities to provide other services that are more profitable.

(6) *Segmentation pricing* has similarities to skimming. It involves setting a price structure designed to appeal to specific market sectors. For example, middle income groups, the over-45 age group or those in a particular locality, thus effectively segmenting the market by using this pricing policy.

(7) *Value and relationship pricing* are perhaps the most customer-orientated in that they focus on what is believed to be the price a customer would pay, based upon that customer's perceived value derived from the service. Theoretically, the more benefits that can be attached to a service, the higher its perceived value, and the higher the price that can be charged.

Relationship pricing takes into account a customer's full relationship with the bank rather than one individual service used. Prices would be set on the basis of customers having a certain pattern to the services they use or are likely to use.

(8) *Tactical pricing* is aimed at stimulating demand and is therefore essentially a promotional device. Tactical pricing can be seen in a number of ways, apart from those described above, when these pricing strategies are used for short periods only to affect business volumes. For example, an early announcement of a future price rise might be an appropriate tactic to stimulate sales, as might also a temporary reduction or even 'give away' offers. The banks have used limited-period special reductions in interest rates to gain mortgage business, and these tactical manoeuvres are likely to become much more commonplace.

Nevertheless, with tactical pricing it is an unavoidable fact that at some stage prices must cover costs and include a profit element.

These pricing policies are, generally speaking, market-orientated but there are also cost-orientated pricing methods. Cost plus or mark-up pricing involves the setting of a margin over and above identified costs to cover profit, and it is this feature that determines the price, not the marketplace. The policy is dependent upon the identification and allocation of all relevant costs, and on these grounds alone can lead to a multiplicity of approaches according to the definitions of fixed and variable, direct and indirect costs. A cost-plus policy may or may not result in a price which will generate sales.

A cost reduction pricing policy is one which fixes a price that is estimated to generate certain threshold levels of business which allow the bank to achieve economies of scale and thereby reduce actual costs per service sold.

Before leaving pricing policies and how they can be applied, it should be emphasised that particular pricing policies can be appropriate at different stages of the service life cycle and in accordance with different market conditions. The influence of price in trying to massage the growth, maturity, and decline stages was covered in Chapter 4. Although broadly trying to maintain price stability in banking is also important, as was said at the outset, market conditions do not remain constant. Therefore it is essential that pricing reviews be undertaken regularly, especially in the light of the progression through the service life cycle stages.

Reasons for price changes

(a) Corporate objectives

If the bank has carefully identified its target markets and the services which it wishes to sell to those audiences, then how the market mix, including price, is blended should be fairly clear. The first task, therefore, is to identify markets and market segments, as pricing policy stems from the characteristics of the chosen markets. Corporate pricing policies will be related to achieving objectives that are fundamental to the growth aspirations of the bank. At the lowest end of this spectrum is merely survival, and in times of crisis this objective can be more important than generating profit. Normally maximising profit would be the main corporate influence on pricing policy especially in the medium and longer term. However, there are also shorter-term corporate objectives which may necessitate using price as a tactical weapon. One example is the desire for market leadership in selected markets or for chosen services. Both objectives can be assisted by price manipulation, but other elements of the market mix may also need to be adjusted to support these corporate goals. Price can also be used to change the corporate image. If the bank wants to achieve an air of quality, then pricing to achieve usage exclusivity or simply making some of the services with 'popular' appeal more expensive than the competitors will help to achieve these image changes. Once again, other elements of the marketing mix must be blended with the pricing policy. It would be self-defeating to have scruffy branches and poor standards of service if the pricing policy was geared to achieving a quality image.

(b) Marketing objectives

Many of the reasons for price changes have been identified earlier in this chapter. Nevertheless, it is worth summarising the more commercial reasons as a reminder of the many marketing ramifications that can flow directly from price changes:

(1) To arrest and ultimately improve declining sales;
(2) As a defensive or offensive measure in the face of competition;
(3) To improve profitability if costs have increased or there is heavy demand and little sign of price sensitivity;
(4) The price of one service is having a detrimental effect on the sale of others and there are advantages in creating uniformity;
(5) The present price of a service is proving off-putting to customers or attracting the wrong customer segments;
(6) To undermine adverse publicity about bank pricing policy which could damage future business growth.

There are other less important reasons for changing pricing policy or the price of individual services. The skill of the marketing manager is to know when, and when not to react. This point is clearly shown in the case study which now follows. It also highlights the need to think and research as much as possible before price changes are made which could destabilise the market as a whole or upset customers who are currently using or thinking of using the service.

Case study

With no reduction in service quality, a major competitor has reduced its tariff for a service where your bank is market leader and which earns good profits for you.

    (a) What business issues would you consider before formulating your response?
    (b) What pricing options are open to you?

――――――――

Before formulating specific responses to the competitor's price-cutting activity, some key questions need to be asked. Finding the answers to these questions might be difficult but it must be remembered that a bank should not, and cannot, react to every competitor pressure. The whole purpose of marketing planning is to establish a co-ordinated sense of direction and purpose throughout a given period. If this type of predetermined activity is to be successful, then only major competitive activity, in chosen profitable or particularly rewarding markets, should be allowed to intervene.

In this instance, the competitor has managed to retain quality of service yet reduce the price, thus posing a real threat to future sales of a profitable service. If buyers feel there is little perceived difference between the features and benefits of services offered by different banks, a reduction in price will have repercussions on market share of this business. However, if there are clearly visible real differences between two services, then price is only one element influencing consumers. Therefore, the first reaction will be to compare services and try and determine to what extent price changes are likely to affect subsequent sales.

Reasons why

Reasons why the competitor bank reduced its tariffs need to be quantified. It may be that it is a temporary ploy to buy market share. Or it may be part of a wider strategy to penetrate a market using this particular service, at a cut price, to create opportunities to sell others. There will be commercial reasons why the competitor reduced the price, and when these are known it should be possible to gauge whether the change is likely to be temporary or permanent.

The outcome of any delay by the bank's taking defensive measures to protect market share will also need to be assessed. So too will the effect on profitability by maintaining the present price or reducing it to match that of the competitor. Calculating the profit contribution of individual services is generally very difficult for a bank. It is almost impossible to allocate costs proportionally across the range of over 200 services that a retail bank currently administers. Marginal cost calculations can be very arbitrary, and quantifying the 'spin-off' benefits from providing 'loss leader' services almost impossible. Nevertheless, an attempt will need to be made to assess the overall impact on profit, and business development generally, by doing nothing, matching the competitor's tariffs, or undercutting them.

Finally, the bank will have to consider the likely reactions from any other competitors with a similar service operating in similar market sectors. If these competitors follow suit, and the bank does nothing, then it will be left isolated and seen as a very uncompetitive provider of this service and perhaps others. The overall strategic importance of the service to the bank's business goals will also affect the final choice of response to an aggressive pricing policy by the competition.

Pricing options

Although there are other elements of the marketing mix which can be changed to counter price-cutting by competitors the problem posed only calls for pricing strategies to be considered. These are:

- Maintain current price.
- Maintain price but with non-price counter-attack.
- Reduce price and go for increased sales to compensate.
- Increase price but differentiate service and add features which would give added value.
- Differentiate price according to business or geographic concentration/representation.

Before making any decision on pricing it is important to ascertain any likely reactions from customers, non-customers, competitors and employees. A well-thought-out response will also include contingency plans for dealing with any 'knock on' competitor actions.

Price maintenance

A decision not to react will be based on an assessment of the effect on profit and market share. If the price-cutting is considered to be temporary, retaining the current price for a service might prevent a chain reaction by other competitors. How the service is sold is also an important issue. The bank is market leader and may well have the largest customer base and number of branches. If the service requires a high level of personal selling then, with a traditionally loyal and established customer profile, it may feel that the real risk to its existing business opportunities does not justify even short-term tactical price changes.

Non-price counter-attack

The feelings of current users of the service, who have paid the present price, their attitudes to any reduction and the danger of their demanding retrospective refunds must also be borne in mind. Promotional activity designed to differentiate the service in the minds of the users from the 'cheaper' service of the competitors will help to encourage customer loyalty. This advertising will be designed to reassure users and potential users that the service, at its present price, gives value for money. After all, perceived value is in the eye of the user not the seller. Bankers often make the mistake of undermining their own sales effort by expressing their personal perceptions of the comparative value of 'in-house' services – the fiduciary dilemma!

Price reduction and going for volume

Before deciding to increase sales by reducing the price, it must be evident that current sales opportunities in chosen markets are well below saturation level. Otherwise, sales volume will not grow at an adequate rate to maintain total revenue by increased sales. It may be possible to reduce costs through economies of scale in order to minimise the effect on profit from a price reduction.

Price increase with added value

This alternative choice of action is arguably the bravest but most difficult to take. Improving the features of the service in a way that potential users will appreciate is just one aspect. Trying to add value in a way that cannot be quickly copied by the competition is also vital. In practice, amending the features of a service and convincing the public that the modified service is good value could take a very long time. If costs of providing the service are not related to volume, they will rise proportionally as sales fall directly due to price increases introducing a degree of exclusivity. Thus the estimated reduction in sales may impact on costs, profit and 'spin-off' benefits if the number of new users is reduced.

Varying price by area

It may be possible to avoid price reductions in localities or regions where the competitor is poorly represented, especially when the service features rely heavily on branch support or sales in turn are dependent on personal face-to-face contact. Severe price reductions in areas where the bank is poorly represented may also be practical if a lower resultant profit margin is offset by the absence of costs arising from running branches in those localities. Adopting variations in pricing, according to area and competition, may well cause promotional difficulties, customer confusion and increased movement of accounts between branches. The likely effect of these issues will need careful considera-tion before embarking on price differentiation based on the level of branch network representation compared with the competitors.

Summary

Pricing is a very important element of the marketing mix, especially when used in competitive situations. It should be blended with the other marketing mix variables and can seldom be considered or used in isolation.

Corporate objectives indicate what pricing policies should be adopted to achieve the longer-term objectives, but there are marketing reasons why, in the shorter term, a wide variation of pricing strategies will be used.

The 'elasticity of demand' concept tries to show how the market can react to price changes, and grades the extent of reactions from little effect on sales (inelastic) to a substantial effect on sales (elastic). In practice, elasticity of demand is difficult to quantify, because differing price changes have differing effects on demand, buyer attitudes vary and competitor activity will influence demand, irrespective of effects caused by price changes.

Likely effects and after effects of price changes should be researched using qualitative and quantitative methods. This research will improve the quality of management decisions by providing an understanding of all the market forces and the suitability of the current or proposed pricing policy.

The theory of pricing policies should be understood, as should also how these alternatives can be applied to bank services in a given set of circumstances. The following pricing policies are important:

- Skimming pricing
- Penetration pricing
- Competitive pricing
- Going rate or market pricing
- Loss leader pricing
- Segmentation pricing
- Value and relationship pricing
- Tactical pricing

Revision questions

1 What is meant by 'elasticity of demand'? How does this concept affect pricing policies?
2 Describe the main tactical alternatives which can be used when competitive activity in an important market segment necessitates a response.
3 By selecting a service to illustrate your answer, show the interrelationship between pricing and the other elements of the marketing mix.
4 The price of a service will normally be somewhere between one that is too low to produce a profit and one that is too high to produce any demand. Describe four different pricing strategies that may be appropriate for a banking service.
5 Describe the various approaches and methods that could be used to arrive at a pricing policy for a new bank service.

Chapter 6
The Marketing Mix – Promotion

Generally speaking, promotion in banking occurs at two levels. The first is through central or head office departments or divisions which are responsible for the major advertising budget and how it is spent in pursuit of the corporate and marketing objectives. Publicity and public relations activities are also usually controlled centrally, although modest levels of responsibility and control can sometimes be found at a regional or area level. The second level for promotional activity is in high street branches where managers are responsible for supporting their marketing objectives with direct mailings, branch displays, personal selling and any other forms of promotion which might, in given circumstances, prove cost-effective and judicious.

Because there are these dividing lines in promotional activity within a major retail bank relating to responsibility, capability and requirement, this very important marketing mix element has been split into two chapters. This chapter will cover the major functions normally carried out by specialist teams at head office level; advertising; public relations and publicity. Chapter 7 will take the scenario of the nationwide promotional efforts and examine what additional supporting activity is possible and practical by branch managers. This chapter will also consider the difficult tasks of setting sales objectives and assessing profitability.

Although the vast subject of promotion has been split into two parts for the sake of expediency and clarity, according to where responsibility for the activity falls, there must, nevertheless, be a high degree of co-ordination between head office promotions and what the branches are doing. Good internal communication is fundamental to all marketing efforts and to the successful growth of the bank's business.

Communication requirements

Communicating directly with staff, customers, potential customers and even shareholders is possibly the most single important factor in the marketing of financial services. Even with the most imaginative range of services, sales will be constrained by poor communication whether it be internal or external.

For communication to be effective it must have the following characteristics:

(1) Be interesting enough to command attention;
(2) Convey concise accurate information and create impact;
(3) Stimulate credibility and belief;
(4) Encourage action.

Yet again there are a series of logical questions which, when answered, will aid good communication.

(1) Who is being addressed?
(2) What are the messages?
(3) When should the communication take place?
(4) How should the communication be undertaken?
(5) Where should the communication be undertaken?

The allocation of authority and responsibility for communication varies from bank to bank. This allocation is not in itself important so long as the outcome is effective. All branches of the major banks communicate with customers when undertaking direct mail exercises and arranging in-branch displays. This activity gives the branch manager and his staff opportunities to test, in a practical way, their individual skill in answering the above questions. Each time any form of communication is made it should be checked to see if the 'who' and 'what' are obvious, the nature of the message right for the chosen audience, the timing right and the benefits or requirements clearly stated. Getting the message timing and method right for the recipient is only one aspect of good communication. Other factors also need to be considered, not least the cost and, if funds are limited, the effect of a limited budget on the final choice of communication alternatives.

Moreover, the budget cannot be considered in isolation, as some recipients of the message or information can be easily reached whilst with others it may prove to be much more difficult. The subject of 'reach' and 'frequency' when applied to advertising is considered later in this chapter.

Banks communicate with various audiences in a number of direct and indirect ways. For example, the image that a bank has created for itself is a form of indirect communication, as this image will influence the actions of people in a variety of different ways. Supporting this type of image communication will be the ways in which customers are treated. Customer care is paramount in a retail bank and a reputation for efficiency and courtesy will assist the marketing communication process. Being rude or unhelpful will of course have the opposite effect.

Promotional mix

However, the main ways a bank communicates are through one or a combination of the following six advertising channels:

(1) Press advertising which can be national, regional or local
(2) Professional journals, trade publications and the bank's annual reports
(3) Television
(4) Radio
(5) Exhibitions and outdoor posters
(6) Public relations, publicity and sponsorship.

In the main the responsibility for effective use rests with the bank's marketing and public relations departments. The channels provide the main promotional mix alternatives and should be supported by back-up literature including leaflets and brochures, personal selling, direct mail and local display programmes. These latter promotion methods are mainly branch controlled and will be covered more fully when we discuss the role of 'campaign' marketing in the next chapter.

Advertising

(a) Historical growth in importance

Some fundamental changes in the nature of bank advertising took place during the 1970s. Prior to that period the major advertisers were the large multinational companies whose businesses had been built up on marketing skills. The power of advertising was used to develop markets for everything from detergents to motorcars, pet food to washing machines.

Then came the growth in television advertising expenditure on financial services which has outpaced by a considerable margin growth in expenditure of every other category. In the last fifteen years the banks have considerably improved their advertising skills, and the nature of the advertising has also changed. The early years saw the banks using advertising to help create an image in the collective sense as an industry (many people still remember the bank manager in the cupboard television commercial) and latterly to differentiate themselves from each other. Banks have also progressed from rather bland advertising to a stage where today individual services or packages of services are regularly advertised. This calls for special marketing appreciation in the choice of media, message and focusing, especially when corporate sector services are promoted in this 'mass media' way.

There have been special problems for the banks when trying to use mass media channels, not least the long-standing 'stuffy' image which has created public indifference to banking and financial issues. Moreover, bank services tend not to be exciting, and certainly cannot be described as glossy or gimmicky. It would be tempting to pretend that banks and bank services are something they are not; to 'dress up' the advertising to create 'borrowed' interest. The result would almost certainly be that the public would regard the advertising as even less relevant to them. They would recognise the fantasy gap between what they consider is factual and informative and what advertising by banks was trying to make them believe.

Therefore, the advertising of bank services has developed fairly slowly and has concentrated upon differentiating between the banks, encouraging good reputations for professionalism and understanding customer problems. Having largely achieved these goals, the advertising of actual services is now becoming more prevalent.

(b) Why advertise?

If a bank is already regarded as successful and enjoys a good reputation it could be argued that it need not embark on the expensive business of advertising.

Advertising is mass 'paid-for communication, the ultimate purpose of which is to impart information, develop attitudes and induce action beneficial to the advertiser'. Thus the strategic nature of advertising and its importance in the overall marketing mix is very clear and, like the other elements of the mix, will take a lead from the corporate objectives and, more specifically, from the marketing plan which is compiled in order to achieve these corporate aims.

Mass advertising can fulfil a variety of roles. In the broadest terms it acts as a contributor to sales – though rarely, except in cases of advertising which carries direct response coupons, is it the sole determinant of sales. As a communications tool, communications objectives are appropriate and are usually classified in terms of informing, persuading and reminding an audience.

Informative advertising is often used in the early stages of a service life cycle to advise the market of a new service or new feature or to describe new uses for an existing range of services. It assists in market positioning and can, as has already been stated, be used to build an image.

Persuasive advertising is associated with the establishment of customer preference in a competitive situation. By aiming to change potential customers' perceptions of a service or of the bank generally and encourage switching, persuasive advertising campaigns sometimes include direct comparisons with named competitive services which they seek to undermine.

For well-established and well-known services, advertising can have an important role in reminding customers of particular attributes and in reinforcing loyalty. In such cases, advertising campaigns are conducted in order to maintain or increase market share, against threats of erosion from aggressively promoted alternatives offered by smaller, lesser-known financial institutions.

(c) Blending the marketing and communications mix

In the longer term, a decision whether to advertise or not is an economic decision, based on the anticipated return from the investment. On a shorter-term basis, though, other forms of marketing communication, or indeed other elements of the marketing mix, may be able to perform the roles required of advertising.

For example, to promote a new feature added to an existing service, a bank may use in-branch displays, statement accompanied mailings or other forms of sales promotion activity. Equally, for a personal sector service, a publicity campaign may be conducted, concentrating upon journalists who have a reputation, and family finance writers and broadcasters.

A limited-period price reduction may boost sales in the short term more effectively than an advertising campaign designed to encourage greater take-up or switching of business from other banks. Similarly, changes in the presentation of key locations in the branch network could well contribute to a change in the customer profile, for example, designating some university town branches as 'student banks' to attract the better educated up-market younger customers who should be the professionals or captains of industry in the future.

To enjoy long-term success in a highly competitive environment, the communications policy must be credible, relevant, meaningful and consistent to the recipients. In order to achieve this it may also need to be repetitious and supported by publicity and sales promotions. Using all three is likely to have more dramatic results than just relying on any one of the elements of the communication mix.

Advertising media budgets

The main alternatives for advertising are television, radio, newspapers and magazines, trade and professional journals, and a variety of directories and year-books. Before a bank can select any one media channel or a combination of several, it will need to have a clear appreciation of the characteristics of the audience it is trying to reach. Then, with the needs of the audiences properly matched with the service features and benefits, the bank will take a close look at the viewing and reading habits of the chosen target audiences.

Before looking more closely at the role that television, radio, newspapers and other media channels can play, it is worth while spending a few moments considering the implications of budget constraints and also the relationship between 'reach' (number of target audience likely to see the first and subsequent advertisements) and 'frequency' (the number of times an advertisement is shown).

(a) Budgets

There is no simple formula for deciding how much money should be allocated to a media campaign. However, the overriding task is to achieve the maximum level of profit or volume sales for the smallest cost. This is a tall order and has been compared to crystal ball gazing as the marketing media specialists try to justify their financial requirements by assessing likely results. At worst, establishing a budget for a media campaign is an educated guess linking the proposed 'spend' with projected results. However, there are other factors which come into play and which prohibit the budget's being considered in isolation. The characteristics of the target audience will influence the choice of media and the nature of the message will also determine which media channel to use.

If the target audience is relatively small, television advertising might not be justified. Equally, if the projected profitability of the service is low, then again more expensive media alternatives may not be justifiable. Television is ideal for 'popular' services with a potentially wide acceptance or when there is a strong element of public image building in the message. In both instances, profit is less significant than reaching large numbers.

Choice of media will also be influenced by the nature of the message. If the text of the message is complex or requires constant repetition to persuade the target audience, then television advertising could prove very expensive. In these circumstances, press advertising will be used, with or without an initial television burst, as it allows for a more detailed message.

In practice, there are four methods of budgeting, and they are as follows:

(1) *The maximum required approach*

The media campaign would be budget-driven in the sense that whatever the advertising campaign requirements were, the cost would be fully met.

(2) *Percentage of anticipated sales approach*

This approach is only logical when there is past experience that a given level of advertising will generate a certain level of sales. Where there is a direct relationship between sales and advertising then the higher the 'spend' the more sales will be achieved. Even so, there must be a limit to the 'spend' and at some point in time service usage saturation levels will begin to impact on the equation.

(3) *The competitive matching approach*

There are weaknesses in this approach as it assumes that all banks are the same for the purpose of advertising expenditure and that all the advertising will have similar levels of awareness or impact. Therefore simply matching a rival's advertising budget will not necessarily have a neutralising effect nor does it take into account the influence of the various marketing strategies and way the media mix is used.

(4) *The objective and task method*

This is the most important approach to assessing a budget as it takes pre-defined objectives and systematically assesses the media strategies and alternatives which could achieve the desired results. With this information, choices can be made in the light of knowing the relationships between the objectives, media mix and costs of the various alternatives.

(b) Relationship between 'reach' and 'frequency'

The goal of advertising is to reach the greatest proportion of the target audience for the least cost – part of the total cost being the number of times (frequency) it is necessary to advertise to obtain an acceptable reach or coverage. Reach and frequency are inextricably linked because both aspects influence the number of people seeing the advertisement. Also they are linked because the advertising budget will almost certainly necessitate a compromise between reach that can be achieved and the frequency which can be afforded. No medium is likely to give 100 per cent reach or coverage but a very high reach can be achieved with a cumulative advertising schedule. However, when more than one advertisement is used there will be wastage from repeats, because part of the target audience will have seen the advertisement first or second time round.

For example, newspapers and periodicals included in the National Readership Survey (NRS) or similar data source can be evaluated by various modelling techniques. Included in the 'model' will be average readership for the selected publication and reading frequency behaviour. The average number of readers per publication can be multiplied by circulation to give total readership figures. This, when expressed as a percentage of the universe in question (the total size of the chosen target audience), can be taken as the 'reach' of that publication for a single insertion.

The cumulative readership of several insertions in different issues of the same publication can be calculated from 'reading frequency' data, from which the number of new readers attracted by the second, third and fourth insertions is estimated. The cost of reach will rise with the number of insertions, but the progressive expansion of reach, however, will diminish. Graphically what is happening is shown in Fig. 6.1. Since readership of most established publications is covered by the six-monthly NRS broad audience data, reach (or coverage) can be calculated by using the NRS information. By deducting from the readership of the second, third insertions etc., those who also read the first, it is possible to estimate net readership and therefore the reach of any one publication. On the whole, such calculations, either by hand or by computer model, are considered accurate to within 95 per cent of confidence limits. Clearly it is important, when comparing reach performance to ensure that the same computer model is used, since different methods can produce variations in the results.

Required frequency of the advertisement is assessed by dividing the gross readership with the net, to get the average number of times the advertisement will be seen by the target audience. Then it is a

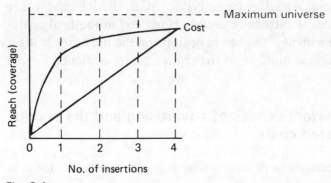

Fig. 6.1

marketing planning function to decide the optimum frequency based upon the reach data available.

The principle is much the same within broadcast media, but given the ever-changing nature of audience behaviour because of programming changes and so on, it is sometimes felt to be beneficial to run a TV schedule against actual Audits of Great Britain (AGB) viewing figures, based on the weekly British Advertising Research Bureau (BARB) panel, in order to measure success in effective spot buying (the time when the commercial is shown).

(c) Optimum balance

Because of the nature of the TV viewing audience it is generally quite difficult to achieve high levels of coverage without correspondingly high frequency figures. Quite simply the audience is made up of a large proportion of viewers who watch regularly and a much smaller number of people who view very seldom. By the time coverage has built to the point where the so-called 'light viewer' will have seen a commercial, the heavy viewer will have seen it several times. This somewhat wasteful phenomenon is something many buyers strive to overcome by seeking to reduce the length of the frequency distribution 'tail' and produce the more efficient 'bell-shaped' curve.

When press is used, it is possible to choose whether to go for high coverage and low frequency or low coverage and higher frequency for the same sum of money. This is partly a question of planning philosophy but may equally reflect the task in hand. For example, if a coupon is to be used allowing only one application for each reader, it is obviously better to limit frequency and aim for the highest reach possible. If, on the other hand, the audience can be tightly defined, for example at the launch of a new service, it may be considered more efficient to confine broad coverage and reach the 'real' target audience as frequently as the budget will allow.

The research data available from NRS, AGB, BARB and other lesser-known sources is extremely useful. However, in the final analysis, managerial judgement is the key to optimising the use of the budget by reaching the highest number of the chosen target audience for the least possible cost.

(d) Measuring effectiveness of advertising and the results from its associated costs

Evaluating the effectiveness of advertising is not an easy task, for it is not always possible to take into account the many other marketing mix factors which may have been used to achieve a successful outcome. For example, a new service may have sold well because it was very competitively priced and not because the advertising was particularly impressive. Moreover, many advertisements do not have a primary sales objective but are purely informatory, related to creating the right image or simply used as a softening-up process for later sales advertising campaigns.

Thus it is clear that service take-up is not a satisfactory measure of advertising effectiveness, as no allowance can be made for the effects of other elements in the total marketing mix.

Advertising impact can be assessed prior to its being used (pre-testing) and then subsequently (post-testing) to see what influence it has had on a target audience.

Pre-testing actively involves showing the advertisement to a representative sample drawn from the chosen target audience in order to elicit a reaction before it is released as part of the promotion.

Another pre-testing method is to ask a panel of experts to assess the advertisement in comparison with other institutions' promotions by asking the question: which one has the most persuasive appeal? Alternatively, a portfolio of advertisements can be judged by a group of consumers to see which ones make the best impact using recall or memory testing techniques where appropriate. Some banks also involve staff in their pre-advertising assessment programme. It appears that staff are more than willing, voluntarily or otherwise, to give their opinions of their bank's latest promotion.

Post-testing is invariably undertaken by recall or recognition testing but attitudinal changes can also be measured. After the advertisement has appeared in the chosen medium, researchers ask those who have seen the advertisement to recall all they can remember.

By allocating scores to the salient message points the advertisement's power to be noticed and remembered can be quantified. Recognition tests rely on an audience being able to say what advertising they have seen before, when shown a range of samples. It can also be used to determine the degree of association between a logo or symbol and the actual name of the institution. For example, is an advertisement depicting a black horse (and with the bank's name removed) correctly associated with Lloyds? This is important if the bank is using a logo or caricature to enforce a particular image to persuade the consumer to take up the services.

Pre- and post-testing advertising material and the choice of media is a vital part of any promotional campaign.

Advertising media – alternative roles

(a) Press advertising and magazines

We are a nation of newspaper and magazine readers and these are produced nationally, regionally, locally and in certain other specialist forms. Thus the choice of newspaper and indeed the choice of area covered by newspapers is very wide indeed. As such they offer the opportunity for an advertiser to reach all types of audiences with similar demographic characteristics. They also offer a wide choice of cost alternatives depending upon size of advertisement, the published position in the newspaper and the type of newspaper it is.

The other main marketing advantage of press advertising is that it is a relatively economic way of getting complex messages across to a large number of people. In the case of magazine advertising, the target audience and the nature of the message can be cross-matched in a very specific manner which it would not be possible to achieve with television advertising.

Finally, press and magazine advertising offer a useful back-up facility to a television commercial. Press advertising with its ability to get specific information over to readers can be an important cost-effective way of riding on the back and reinforcing the higher levels of awareness which are created by television commercials.

(b) Television

Television is ideal for reaching a mass audience but it can also be very discriminatory. Choosing the right time to advertise is the crucial factor, not just at peak viewing times but also when programmes are being shown that attract certain types of people who are also target audiences for the services being advertised. Adopting this selective approach to television advertising when services are being promoted should ensure a high level of cost-effectiveness as greater numbers of viewers are likely to be receptive and persuaded. This is largely due to television's being intrusive by nature, and the mixture of colour and sound gives it greater impact than other media.

Geographical choice is also possible with television, as it is with press advertising. In this way, national and regional activity can be supported separately and there is generally a greater empathy with viewers if advertising has a regional flavour.

Unfortunately, television advertising is costly, which is why it usually needs to be blended into a campaign that also uses less expensive media channels. Moreover, it lacks the refer back facility – a newspaper advertisement can be looked at over and over again and shown to others whereas television advertising cannot.

(c) Radio

The growth in local radio offers a relatively new communication channel for bank advertising. It has the advantages of relatively low cost, flexibility in the way it can be used, and above all a very local market flavour. Expertise in using this new medium is growing and, when regional or local marketing opportunities are identified, has the capacity to provide a cost-effective way of reaching target audiences. Timing of radio advertising is important, for the characteristics of listening audiences can be cross-matched with times of day and types of programme just as they can with television.

(d) Exhibitions and outdoor posters

The usefulness of exhibitions as a communications medium is open to debate and although banks traditionally attend agricultural shows and some major indoor exhibitions, such displays are more regarded now as a defensive exercise. Most banking facilities at exhibitions provide back-up services and are a public relations measure, as the exhibitors are too busy attending to their own clients to be interested in what the supporting banks have to offer. As a result, the number of banks attending exhibitions has declined as costs of attending these functions have mounted, to the detriment of providing the after-sales service which a corporate customer at the exhibition might wish to enjoy.

Billboard posters are another medium which is regarded by some banks as an important element of the communication mix and ignored by others. It is a relatively cheap form of mass advertising, albeit very non-selective, and provides limited scope for creativity.

Contribution from the advertising mix

Although not an end in itself, advertising does make an important contribution to the total sales efforts and to the image of the bank, as it seeks to create the right atmosphere for encouraging future business growth.

More specifically, the advertising industry provides a substantial volume of work for employees and, for the public in general, can help to raise living standards and the quality of life. The continuous research associated with advertising provides material which enables advertisers to quantify the risks and benefits and this is helpful to the welfare of all those engaged in profitably selling goods and services so that commerce and industry may continue to expand.

As we saw when the service life cycle was considered in Chapter 4, advertising can also be used to prolong the life of services. Finally, advertising legislation can also ensure quality standards, as well as improve other benefits through the competitiveness which media communication brings.

The media plan

The importance of planning is continually stressed throughout this book and is no less important when considering media expenditure. Figure 6.2 highlights the considerable number of factors that need to be taken into account when formulating a media plan, and it is interesting to note how this apparent subsection of a marketing plan is also a comprehensive plan in its own right.

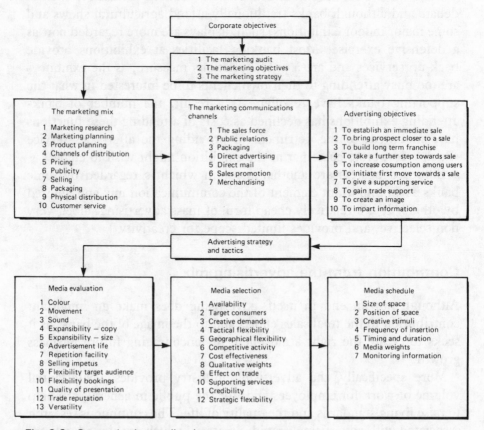

Fig. 6.2 Stages in the media plan

Public relations (PR)

The British Institute of Public Relations defines public relations as 'the deliberate, planned and sustained effort to establish and maintain mutual understanding between an organisation and its public'. This definition highlights the need consciously to make a determined effort over a long period; so clearly PR, like other elements of the communications mix, requires policy guidelines and strategies. It is not simply an exercise in reacting to adverse publicity as and when it occurs, but more a process of prevention and creating the right atmosphere rather than a reactionary cure. Note too that whereas advertising tries directly to manipulate buyers' opinion, public relations concentrates on giving information to ensure that the organisation's motives and actions are properly understood – as such, it is not a selling process.

Good public relations require some basic but important features. Firstly, the PR communication should be authentic to encourage trust, and secondly newsworthy in order to encourage understanding and achieve impact. The way public relations are applied is also important, as ideally they should be channelled to support the corporate business goals and the image of the bank. This channelling can be done in a variety of ways. In practice, PR is mainly undertaken by supporting community projects and worthwhile educational activities, and by assisting other organisations which link directly or indirectly with those customer and non-customer groups that are considered to be most important.

When used to counter adverse publicity any PR response must first be very carefully researched. The true facts need to be known before the extent of the likely damage can be estimated and the alternative courses of mitigating action assessed to find the most favourable or least damaging route. The worst possible outcome should also be considered.

In pursuing this research and mental reasoning, over-reaction will be avoided and some of the more likely questions to be asked by the media will become evident. Considering the sort of answers which could be given will also have a bearing on the final course of action which the public relations man or woman will try to follow. How the medium is handled will also have a bearing on the outcome and will require professional public relations skills. Somebody used to dealing with sensitive public relations issues is more likely to do a better job than an untrained person.

Publicity and sponsorship

Publicity can be viewed as the 'securing of editorial space as divorced from paid space in all media, read, viewed or heard by a bank's customers or potential customers for the specific purpose of assisting in the meeting of sales goals'.

This part of the communication and promotional mix can be generated through press releases, press briefings, radio and television news comment or interviews and sponsorship.

It is perhaps the least utilised element of the communication mix, despite the potential which it offers banks for building awareness and preference. One of the principal qualities of publicity lies in the fact that since, unlike advertising and sales promotion, it cannot be paid for, it can attain a high level of credibility. In many respects it is similar to advertising in the way it can dramatise a service. However, because it is not so overt as advertising, it also has the ability to catch 'off-guard' those customers who might otherwise reject traditional sales and advertising techniques.

Publicity's greatest drawback is the relative lack of control that a bank may have over the effect it can cause. Whilst public relations departments are charged with the specific task of trying to control publicity this does not mean that adverse publicity will not arise and, no matter how unavoidable its cause, it will be just as credible in the eyes of the public. Some efforts will be exerted through public relations releasing press releases to create a good image. These releases will only get 'pad space' if newsworthy, and even then may, because of the nature of the service, result in unfavourable comparisons being made by journalists with competitor services. This pro-active approach is more controllable than the adverse publicity which is not self-started, such as lending a student too much money. This publicity is even harder to neutralise or pre-empt.

Sponsorship is also a part of the total communication and promotional mix, but the extent and ways in which it is used vary considerably among the banks. Some banks sponsor sports, others the arts, but whatever the nature of the sponsorship there must be sound commercial reasons for this type of expenditure. The case for sponsorship is strongest where the expenditure is likely to be seen and appreciated by television viewers.

Overall, the main reasons for sponsorship are to support marketing activity, gain publicity and help to improve the bank's reputation or image in support of the public relations efforts.

Case study

A consumer association has just published a report which has generated hostile, but reasonable, comments about the bank where you are public relations manager.

How would you advise senior management regarding:

(a) what are generally regarded as the basic rights of consumers;

(b) the short- and medium-term action to be taken to extract the bank from its current position?

_____

As the marketing of services has become more sophisticated and more complex over the past twenty years, so the pressures for marketing actions to be accountable to society have increased. One important example of the concern of social responsibility is the rise of the consumer movement to rectify perceived business injustices.

The objectives of consumerism (see Chapter 3) are to enforce the rights to safety, the right to be properly informed or advised, the right to be heard and the right to choose.

The right to safety refers not simply to protection against products that are unsafe to use, or instructions which fail to provide adequate guidance on product usage, but also to the need for competent repair and realistic guarantee services. In banking, prudent controls relating to lending and deposit taking provide frameworks for consumer safety, supplemented by the recommendations of bodies such as the National Consumer Council and trade associations such as the Consumer Credit Trade Association.

The right to be informed aims to protect consumers against inadequate and misleading information and deceptive packaging. The right to information also calls for protection against questionable personal selling tactics and deceptive pricing or credit terms. The 1979 Banking Act and the 1974 Consumer Credit Act contain numerous examples of the content and format of information to be provided for consumers in the area of personal financial services.

The right to choose refers to the need for a genuinely competitive environment in which suppliers can operate and to the provision of appropriate information to allow potential purchasers to make a realistic choice amongst brands, products and package sizes. Collusion amongst companies and price-fixing by cartels are seen as restricting consumer choice. The moves to deregulation of the financial services' operating environments on almost a worldwide basis in the 1980s are fuelled by growing demands for more consumer choice in terms of suppliers, product ranges, designs and prices.

The right to be heard demands that suppliers should be responsive to consumer grievances and requests for information, and that consumers should have a right to influence product design and features in order to augment their 'quality of life'. In the banking industry, consumer pressure for more convenient banking services in terms of hours, days and locations has resulted in the provision of a wider variety of outlets than simply the traditional branch – from automatic teller machines (ATMs) to in-store and workplace representation.

Over and above these specific consumer rights, in the current social environment a major concern is that organisations, whether commercial or non-commercial, are seen to act in a socially responsible manner and to respond positively to the demands placed on them by changing social values.

The role of the public relations manager in ensuring that a bank considers and actively supports consumer interests and rights is clearly a critical one. In the situation outlined, that of 'hostile but reasonable comments' from the consumers' association, the short-term strategy is to contain the negative commentary as far as possible whilst investigating and rectifying the sources of criticism identified in the association's report.

(a) Short-term action – damage limitation exercise

The public relations manager should discuss with the report's authors not only the areas of criticism but the bank's overall approach to the business activities covered by the association's research – for example, consumer credit or deposit services or pricing. Those policies and actions supportive of consumer rights and interests should be highlighted.

The bank should respond with its own press statement, aiming to redress the balance of criticism and stemming any further expansion of negative comment whilst an internal research programme is investigating the sources of criticism, remedying weaknesses in customer relations activities and redressing any inappropriate actions taken. Instead of aiming to deflect public criticism which can clearly be substantiated, the bank should emphasise its willingness and desire to correct any justifiable deficiencies and refer to the setting up of its own research programme to tackle the relevant issues.

(b) Medium-term action – institutional change

The short-term action programme should be underpinned by the setting up of a comprehensive review programme covering all aspects of the bank's customer relations activity. Policies and practices should be examined to ensure that they both conform to and are seen to demonstrate consumerist philosophy. The aim is to encourage the adoption of a more socially responsible outlook throughout the organisation. Campaigns to inform staff of consumers' rights and how to translate them into company action should be undertaken, as well as more detailed training courses for all customer contact staff.

Rather than acting simply as a passive respondent, the public relations manager should encourage a pro-active stance to be taken in key areas of consumer and environmental concern as input to the longer-term image and credibility of the bank.

Summary

Good communication is an essential ingredient of promotion in all its forms. To meet this standard, all communication should be able to attract attention, stimulate interest, convey accurate information and finally encourage action.

Communication can be direct (person to person and through media channels) or indirect: for example, the portraying of an image which the bank has built. Whichever combination of forms of communication are used they must be blended together to gain maximum impact. The best timing for the communication also needs careful consideration.

The main elements of the promotional mix which are usually controlled by specialist head office departments are press, television, journals and trade publications, radio, exhibitions and outdoor posters, public relations, publicity generally and sponsorship.

The mix of communication channels and the timing are mainly influenced in varying ways by the corporate objectives, the nature of the message and the service being promoted, the characteristics of the chosen target audience and the allocated budget.

Fixing a suitable budget for a media campaign is a difficult task as the media mix will be affected by the nature of the message, the complexity of the service features and benefits and the characteristics of the chosen target audience. In practice there are four alternative ways of deriving an amount:

- The maximum required approach;
- Percentage of anticipated sales approach;
- Matching the competition approach;
- Basing it on an evaluation to achieve the objectives and tasks.

Reach (proportion of target audience seeing the advertisement) and frequency (number of times it is necessary to show an advertisement to obtain a desired percentage coverage of the target audience) are important aspects of media selection and budget issues. The information and skill required to strike an optimum balance should be appreciated.

Service sales levels are not an adequate measurement of advertising effectiveness as too many other market mix influences, including price and availability, impact on sales figures. Market research should be undertaken at pre- and post-testing stages, using a combination of opinion research and memory or recall analysis.

Each of the media channels has advantages and disadvantages depending on the nature of the advertising task. These features should be fully understood as a prerequisite to media selection.

The overall objective of public relations is to create and sustain the best possible marketing environment in which the bank operates. As such it tries to influence attitudes and opinions of customers, non-customers, employees, shareholders and local and national government.

Sponsorship is part of the promotional mix and can be used to support marketing goals when focused on key sectors of the market-place. Alternatively it can be *ad hoc*, socially or community-relations based. The aims of sponsorship are to enhance marketing prospects through publicity, improved image and relations generally with the public.

Revision questions

1 What is advertising and what contributions can it make to the bank's marketing efforts?
2 With a service of your own choice indicate how the various media options could be considered and blended for the best effect.
3 Compare and contrast the roles of advertising, publicity and public relations in the communication process of a bank.
4 Some major and successful retailers do not advertise. Should a major and successful bank advertise and, if so, why and to what purpose?
5 What are the benefits of sponsorship? If your bank undertakes sponsorship, explain the extent to which you think the activity supports the marketing efforts. If no sponsorship is undertaken show how using this form of communication might be beneficial.

Chapter 7

The Marketing Mix – Organising and Undertaking Branch Promotions

No book on marketing in retail banking is complete without some coverage of the promotional and sales activities carried out within a network of branches. This activity is sometimes referred to as business development rather than marketing, although many of the same skills and marketing appreciation are required by a branch manager launching a promotional campaign as are required at a regional or national level. However, it is fair to say that some of the major marketing functions such as research and the marketing mix elements of services, price and distribution are at best lower key or, at worst, outside the scope of the branch operation. Perhaps for these reasons business development is a more apt description of branch marketing but, nevertheless, the concept of marketing – getting the right services to the right target audience at the right price and in the right way – is a fundamental to the success of a branch marketing efforts as it is anywhere else in the infrastructure of a major retail organisation such as a bank.

What can be done at a branch level in the pursuit of marketing goals is wide-ranging. This chapter cannot hope to cover all the business development activities that go on, but the main promotional tools available to branches will be covered: displays, direct mail and personal selling.

The way in which a branch can organise a promotional campaign is also included here and so are two other important branch marketing planning tasks, namely creating sales objectives and assessing profitability. Chapter 11 looks at the branch marketing plan in considerable detail and the next few pages should help to prepare the ground by providing some understanding of the very important planning process.

Another no less important task within the overall marketing effort is co-ordinating and integrating all the staff in a branch into a marketing team. Some branches have a marketing clerk in their midst whose job is to organise the day-to-day branch business development activities and in this way ensure that the branch marketing plan is carried through.

The case study at the end of this chapter takes a series of branch marketing plan objectives and shows how an action programme and timetable can be constructed to achieve the stated branch business goals. The actions listed in the programme are not intended to be a 'foolproof' list but just an indication of the sort of things that can be done by a wide cross-section of staff.

Branch displays

Most branches of the major banks occupy prime high street sites; so the opportunity to use them for promotional displays is vast. Nevertheless, the banks have some way to go to catch up with other high street retailers, although it should be stated that some retailer display methods might prove unsuitable for the current image that the public has of banks. However, there is scope for improvement, and many bankers have had first-hand experience of how beneficial to sales an eye-catching and properly timed display can be.

There are two display areas in most branches; the windows and public banking hall. Each branch will be different and have various degrees of potential for in-branch displays. Moreover, each branch will have key spots that are more visible than others. Different parts of the branch are more suitable for some services than others: for example, premier charge card literature should be displayed where people with higher incomes are more likely to see it, such as near the securities counter and in any manager's interview waiting areas. Finally, the overall impact an in-branch display creates can be enhanced if not too many different leaflets and brochures appear together.

The quality and contribution of in-branch displays to the integrated business development activities should be improved if the following guidelines are followed:

(1) One person should be responsible for the overall look of the display areas, for ensuring staff are aware of the services being promoted and for synchronising the displays with the main business development programme laid down by the branch marketing plan or with national advertising or other special campaign activity.

(2) In a familiar working environment it is easy for branch display areas to become untidy and neglected. All staff should habitually straighten leaflets, replenish stocks and generally try to see the exterior and interior of the branch as the customer sees it – with a fresh eye.

(3) Siting of displays is important. Some areas of the branch are seen by more people than others. Spots where people who are likely to remain stationary for a short time and can see displays are prime areas. So too are parts of the branch near to entrance doorways.

(4) Change displays regularly, perhaps once a month, and make sure that supporting material such as posters and brochures ties in with the services leaflets. It is sometimes beneficial to concentrate on a maximum of three or four services at a time and as the two major services are interest bearing lodgements and lending it is arguable that two of the services should always be lodgement and lending related.

(5) Avoid using Sellotape and Blu-tack fixing materials and do not allow a proliferation of notices to build up even though it is accepted that some have to be displayed to meet statutory requirements. Even then, that type of notice should not occupy a prime sales area.

Effective displays can influence and improve branch sales performance, as this type of merchandising increases buyer awareness and reinforces any other advertising and personal selling activity being undertaken. Moreover, when service leaflets and brochures are properly used it can reduce sales interview time, as the features and benefits are carefully listed and should need little or no further explanation.

Direct mail

Bankers only see a very small percentage of their total customers each year. Therefore it is important to find other ways of reaching them with information about services which should interest them. Compiling a list of suitable customers to mail and the level of response rate will depend on the segmentation capabilities of the branch. Identifying the right customers with the right services features and benefits is at the heart of the mailing process. A considerable amount of literature is posted out by a wide spectrum of organisations canvassing for leads. Most of it finishes up in the waste-paper bin, but even so a response rate of two or three per cent is regarded as acceptable, and usually justifies the cost. These are sales opportunities which would not have been generated without direct mailing. Moreover, there is an information and reassurance spin-off that could lead to customers applying for the service at a later date. For example, a letter offering a home improvement loan, or a credit card, implies the bank is favourably disposed to say 'yes'. This reassures customers and the more they know about bank services the less likely they are to buy elsewhere. How many bankers have had to live with the comment when asked to hold in safekeeping a new life policy – 'I didn't know banks sold insurance!'

Mailing to business customers can also be effective on a small and very selective scale but may require a telephoned follow-up or a visit to spur the customer into action. As a softening up tool for a subsequent planned personal call, a direct mail letter can be invaluable. Choosing the right services to promote to business customers is covered more fully in Chapters 16, 17 and 18. To be effective, direct mail needs to go to the right segments and offer services where the benefits can be easily appreciated. It should also be made as personal as possible – 'Dear Sir or Madam' will hardly make the best impact. Wherever possible, ease of acceptance of the service should be such that the customer is not put off by massive form-filling, and there should be a telephone number where customers can seek clarification or make an appointment.

The seasonality of demand for some services should be borne in mind. There are prevalent times when customers go on holiday, change a motor car and indeed buy or sell houses. Those various services which can resolve these sorts of financial issues should be directly mailed at the most appropriate times of the year.

Personal selling

Aesthetically there really is no better way to sell financial services than during a face-to-face interview. Some people have a natural flair for selling whilst others find it very difficult to achieve. Nor should it be forgotten that it may take more than one discussion to clinch a sale; so the importance of follow-up activity is just as great as it is for direct mailing.

The staff personal sales role is vital at a branch level where the bulk of retail personal and small business customers come to transact their financial affairs and consequently meet the staff.

Thus selling is now a responsibility which envelops all the staff to varying degrees. To have any chance of success, some training is required on communication skills including recognising opportunities and overcoming objections. Furthermore, staff cannot sell unless they understand and believe in the services. This understanding of the service should include an ability to see the *customer's* perspective of the features and benefits.

Selling is not easy, it is delicate and hard work, calling for special communication skills including the power of conviction. Advertising, direct mail and a host of other promotional alternatives help to persuade but the personal communication skills actually close the sale.

Cold calling

This is a frequently misunderstood phrase and an activity which bankers have found hard to come to terms with. It is not a sales call, but a personal visit to a potential customer without an appointment. Used judiciously, with or without some background information, and with a clear appreciation of what the caller is seeking to achieve, it can be a useful way to build real contacts. It needs to be stressed that the prime purposes of a 'cold call' should be to arrange another meeting at a later date and meanwhile gather information that will be useful to promote contact. Names of decision-makers, nature of any financial circumstances and needs, type of business and so on. On no account should the first interview be used to sell services, as it may be that subsequent information shows that the bank, on reflection, would prefer not to do business. In any case, correct identification of needs is the first task, for without that any selling discussions may well fall on very stony ground.

Ideally, as much background information as possible should be obtained before any contact is made with a prospective customer, and making an appointment prior to calling cold also saves a wasted journey and makes a better impression.

Telephone selling

Those major UK retail banks with subsidiary banking operations in the USA are probably already engaged in telephone selling which has grown there much quicker than on this side of the Atlantic. Double-glazing suppliers, vacuum manufacturers and a host of other industries are turning to telephone selling to generate leads for the salesman. It can only be a short period before the UK banks also get involved in a similar sales technique – they are already using the telephone to gather market research data.

However, if telephone selling is to prove successful when used by the major banks some fundamental marketing principles need to be applied which are similar for all types of promotion.

(1) The list of telephone prospects must be properly compiled with the service features and benefits closely matched with the prospects characteristics and likely needs.

(2) The person telephoning must have telephone skills as well as banking expertise and service knowledge.

(3) Success will to some extent hinge on the length of experience of selling on the telephone and the ability to concentrate on explaining the benefits to the customer from having the service rather than the features that tend to be for the benefit of the supplier.

Sales promotions and merchandising

It may not be possible for some branches to create their own sales promotion packages which are really short-term incentives to encourage the take-up of a service. Nevertheless, sales promotions are now widely used by the banks and the role of the branch is to exploit the markets where these incentives, special offers or discounts will have appeal.

The most prolific use of sales promotion incentives has probably been in the student market, as each of the major banks tries to outbid the others with low interest rate loan schemes, book tokens, rail cards and the like. American Express, Visa and Access also make 'special offers' to cardholders who introduce their friends. Sales promotions will continue to grow. So too will special cut-price deals, such as a half per cent off mortgage interest rates for new business, at certain times of the year.

Sales promotions and merchandising encompass the way in which these incentives are marketed, usually at the point of sale, and they depend heavily on visual impact, using leaflets and other point of sale literature and visual aids.

There are other promotion methods that can be used to assist the branch business development effort – messages on statements, leaflets posted with cheque cards and cheque books, cashiers handing out leaflets as they serve the customers, and many more.

Any activities that take place must be undertaken as professionally as possible, be integrated to gain maximum impact, be ongoing parts of a planned programme and be followed up and monitored constantly to ensure that time and resources are not being wasted. These requirements call for promotional plans to guide all the staff and the activities through a number of logical thought and action stages.

Promotional campaigns

Promotional campaigns can be nationally instigated or stem from a branch initiative, but in both instances the planning steps will be similar and will require a framework which will help to ensure that the promotion is properly carried through. If done well, the framework will also ensure the best results are obtained from the promotion or, alternatively, provide a means by which to assess whether or not the preparatory work was the cause of a poor outcome.

Figure 7.1 identifies eight basic steps in planning and executing a

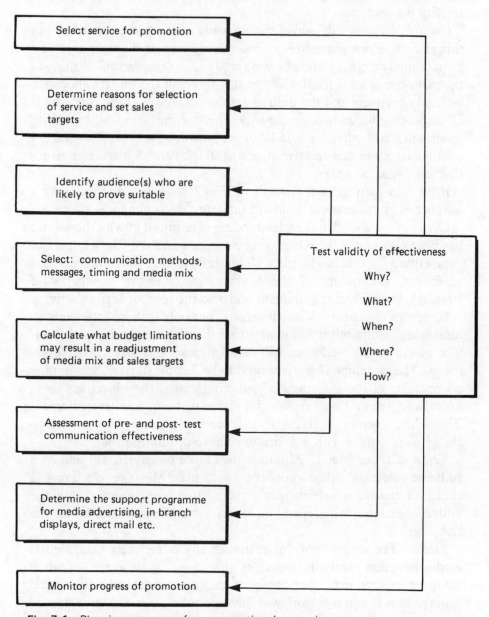

Fig. 7.1   Planning sequence for a promotional campaign

promotional campaign. It also uses probing questions – why, what, when, where and how? – to test the logic and validity of each step.

It should be noted that the steps are interrelated and will impact on one another – they cannot be compiled or considered in isolation. For example, the objectives of the promotion will heavily influence the choice of communication method and the budget requirements. The target audiences chosen to receive the communication will also influence the choice of media mix and the nature of the supporting activity programme.

Careful planning will help eliminate waste of effort and resources, but this alone will not guarantee success. Every step of the operation of a promotional campaign must be subjected to the same careful scrutiny as the planning process itself. Only in this way will the budget allocation be used effectively and the desired results achieved. There is no single all-embracing formula or framework, the circumstance and capability levels will shape what needs to be done. However, what is also vital is a continuous active and reactive stance to all the various marketing issues that can come into play.

If we now turn to each element of Fig. 7.1 we find that there are a number of considerations that will influence decisions to be taken.

Choice of service A full understanding is required of why the service has been chosen for the advertising campaign and the likely impact of competition in the marketplace. This information will influence the objectives, the nature of the advertising (defensive or aggressive strategy), the budget requirement and also the level of branch activity.

Campaign objectives Without targets, not only is there little point in measuring results but it is arguable that the planning and implementation of every other element will lack purpose and direction. Nevertheless, the campaign objectives need to be flexible during the planning process. If, in the information gathering stage, the objectives seem unrealistic, then rational reasons for changing them will have emerged. This whole exercise is trying to balance likely sales, cost, and availability of resources with a desire to achieve optimum profit.

Target audience groups Although the choice of service will influence audience selection, other forces come into play. Message selection and choice of media, which in turn have a strong relationship with the budget allocation, will depend on the target audiences selected for the campaign.

Media The central core of planning any advertising campaign is media selection, and the messages that need to be communicated. Budget allocation may affect choice of medium, volume advertising and timing. This is where a bank will rely upon the skills of a good agency to make sure that the budget is well spent. Generally more than one medium will be used. For instance, the main thrust could be television with awareness levels being maintained with support from newspaper advertising and branch mailings to customers. Choice of timing on television, the stations to be used, and newspaper selection, will all be influenced by the target audience the bank is trying to reach.

If the promotion campaign is branch instigated, the promotion mix will be a selection of branch displays, direct mail, personal selling and any other merchandising benefits that might be available. Even so, the messages, timing, and the way the branch promotional mix is blended, are just as important.

Budget   Often the budget is the first element to crystallise against the objectives initially set by the bank. However, some flexibility is required, and the amount available kept as a broad guideline at least until the pre-test stage. When the amount is fixed, it must also be justifiable.

Pre- and post-testing   This will prove or disprove the harmony and choice of all the other elements in the campaign structure. It is particularly important to test the impact of the advertising media method and timing upon a selection of the chosen target audience. Branch research is also possible.

Support programme and follow-up activity   What needs to be done, when and how, are all important areas to cover in any planned process. The answers to these questions will reveal the degree of special training or other forms of motivation necessary. The objective is to ensure that branch activity can handle business generated and become integrated to obtain maximum impact.

Measurement/monitoring of results   This information will shape any changes considered necessary to the ongoing campaign in order to maximise results and terminate any waste in the use of resources. Again the questions when, what and how can be used to monitor and measure results against objectives.

Role of a branch marketing organiser

It is impossible here to give a graphic account of all the things a marketing organiser can do to support the business development activities of the branch. The extent of the role will be partially dependent upon the experience and capabilities of the person chosen for this work. Nevertheless, there are some key organisational areas which could be delegated to even most junior staff, always accepting that they are prepared to take a lead and receive regular guidance and support from the branch manager. The member of staff nominated will need a degree of creative flair and drive. He or she will also need to have a methodical nature and the ability to explain clearly what needs to be done, how the tasks can be carried out and when the activity should take place. Note that this is an organisational co-ordinating and preparatory function, and a marketing clerk should not be expected to do all the business development work.

More specifically the marketing organiser can:

(1) Identify business development opportunities
(2) Look after the quality and content of in-branch displays and other promotional matters
(3) Organise target audience lists and recommend messages and methods of contact together with the nature and timing of follow-up activities
(4) Monitor the progress of the business development efforts and compare and contrast results with the branch marketing plan.

The most important task the marketing organiser has is to involve all the staff by keeping them up to date with activities and progress. As the organiser's experience grows, this task of involving others can be broadened to include an advisory, even educational, role so that other staff acquire at least an appreciation of the importance of knowing what the requirements are and how marketing activity can be successfully undertaken. Before leaving the marketing organiser's role, and other factors which can influence the results of branch business development activity, the in-house clues to business opportunities which can be spotted by staff need to be considered. Staff in the high street branches have two ways of spotting sales opportunities. Firstly, those with personal or telephone customer contact – managers, securities counter staff, cashiers, and those responsible for issuing statements, cheque books and handling routine clerical queries have face-to-face contact. As they talk to customers with queries, problems and routine financial transactions, sales opportunities can be revealed and developed. Secondly, back-room staff who have little or no customer contact do, nevertheless, see a wealth of information which may in turn prompt further examination for business development prospects. The following list is a small selection of the sort of business opportunities that could be spotted and developed from parts of the various clerical routines that are necessary in a branch operation (Table 7.1).

There are many other financial transactions which when considered could lead to business development opportunities. Additionally, requests from customers to change address records could mean that they require a variety of financial services including revolving credit, and insurance cover. Advice of marriage is another situation where the

Table 7.1   Branch business opportunities

Clerical roles	Nature of marketing opportunity	Suggested service required
Cashier	Customer cashing cheque	Cash dispenser card
	Regular encashment of cheques drawn on another branch or bank	Transfer of account
	Large credit over counter	Investment advice
	Large credits from business customers	Night safe
	Request for regular encashment arrangement	Cash dispenser card/cheque card or credit card
Voucher filing or inspection clerks	Cheques to holiday organisations	Travel facilities and insurance
	Cheques to finance companies and store accounts	Credit card or personal loans
	Large dividend payments	Investment advice and stock and share services generally
	Cheques to insurance companies	Insurance portfolio review and advice
	Cheques to building societies and other savings institutions	Investment accounts
	Large monthly salary credits	Investment facilities and premier charge card
Standing order clerk	New HP standing orders or request for status report from finance house	Personal loan
	New mortgage repayments	Insurance cover, revolving credit or budget account
	Cancellation of HP payment	Regular savings account
	Cancellation of insurance premium on maturity	Investment advice New insurance policy

need for services could be triggered – making a will, insurance, joint account, personal loan and many more. There is one golden rule when communicating with customers, and that is not to offer more than two services, as any more could be too confusing. Life cycle trigger points such as leaving school, getting married, starting a family, buying a house and retiring, and the opportunities these changes in circumstances create for selling financial services are looked at in greater detail in Chapters 13 and 14.

Setting sales targets

Target setting is the almost inevitable outcome of corporate planning, which addresses some fundamental questions:

- What markets is the bank exploiting now and what has been achieved?
- What markets does the bank wish to concentrate on in the future?
- What is the bank's growth and profit aspirations in the future from these markets?

Once these questions have been answered, the next step is to formulate sales targets to meet the corporate objectives.

(a) Targeting alternatives

Targets are often based on the following planning methods:

(1) Extrapolation planning – where the management simply continues its current strategies and uses the actual profit and sales of the current period as the basis for targets for the next budget period.

(2) Goal planning – where profits and sales targets are set at a level which will satisfy the executive and shareholders. Managers are then left to accomplish these targets in any way they can.

(3) Optimisation planning – where each aspect and alternative is systematically examined to see its likely impact on profit and sales growth. The optimum targets are then chosen. Bank planning procedures are still in a relatively early stage of development and there is a lack of precise marketing data, both internally and externally. Therefore, all three planning alternatives are still influencing bank target setting. There is a gradual trend towards optimisation planning as appreciations of marketing forces and information systems improve. Penetration-based targeting is also rapidly finding favour.

(b) Relationship with corporate objectives

The planning process, leading up to the target setting stage, is well known and includes the following:

(1) Review of past performance. Information on sales results and growth will need to be covered as a prelude to new targets.

(2) Assumptions based on the review which will include conclusions on future areas of opportunity for sales and profit growth.

(3) Determining key market segments.

(4) Corporative objectives on which targets for sales and profit growth will be based. (Care should be taken not to confuse objectives with targets. Objectives are short- medium- and long-term. Targets are specific goals measured in money or volume terms and set for a given budget period.)

It can be seen that corporate objectives provide the parameters for sales targets and the review, including the assumptions of potential, assists the selection of priority targets from the range of available alternatives.

(c)   Setting targets

Targets can be specified as either revenue, profit numbers or penetration levels. It is important, when setting targets, that the goals are clearly defined, for any which merely require profit or revenue to be increased without stating a specific amount will hardly prove challenging. Moreover, where progress is not capable of being measured it is less likely that the efforts of staff will be sustained throughout a given marketing campaign or period.

Sales targets or sales objectives are important to the marketing process, for without pre-determined goals, effort, and the use of resources generally, will lack direction and purpose. Neither is it possible to evaluate progress or results without the yardstick provided by specific targets.

When setting targets at both bank and branch levels, there are a number of considerations to bear in mind:

(1) When setting profit targets a balance is required between a realistic profit, continued competitiveness and ongoing customer loyalty. Short-term profitability is of little benefit if it leads to longer-term falling sales or loss of accounts to competitors.

(2) The basis of accurate target setting is a precise analysis of market and market opportunities. This includes an assessment of opportunities based upon the demographic profiles of existing customers as well as potential customers. The difficulties of accurately assessing opportunities, and the impact of penetration levels, are considered in more detail later in this chapter.

(3) Setting targets should be a 'top down/bottom up' process. (In a target setting operation the executive would take the views of branches (bottom up) before setting their targets (top down). In this way, the targets set will be credible in the eyes of all those charged with the task of achieving them.

(4) When setting growth targets (either quantified by revenue or sales volumes) it is important to ensure growth can be handled with existing or readily available resources. These resources include financial capability, branch size or network size, location, staffing levels, skill and so on. Gaining new business at a rate which reduces a bank's ability to cope (either as a whole or at a local branch level) and thereby allows standards of service to fall is likely to prove counter-productive in the longer term.

(5) The cost implication of trying to achieve, or actually achieving the targeted growth in business, should not be ignored. Numbers for numbers sake without the prospect of increased profitability not to mention the use of resources which could be more profitably employed achieving other marketing targets is not the best approach. This point shows that growth and profit targets cannot be set independently. There is only so much time and so much of other resources available, and profit is the main factor when selecting targets and priorities for marketing activity.

(6) Finally the timing of activity to achieve sales targets is an important aspect. Many bank services and revenue cycles have a seasonality trait.

(d) Penetration considerations

The greater the number of customers using a particular service the harder it is to find new potential users. Some of the 'popular' bank services are now reaching user levels as high as 70 per cent. Plastic cards, including cash dispenser and credit cards, are now widely accepted and it is becoming increasingly difficult to increase the percentage of customers using these services. There is an argument that at given levels of penetration the effort and cost of improving the percentage is not worth while, especially if it also reduces the resources that can be used to sell other services more effectively.

Penetration targeting has been introduced only recently and is particularly relevant for the more widely accepted and most used services. This targeting method also takes into account the increase in opportunities to sell services to new customers. If customer numbers grow by ten per cent per year then to achieve a ten per cent penetration for a given service one in ten of the new customers, as well as existing customers, also need to be users at the end of the period. Where growth in account numbers is static, volume targets are as relevant as penetration levels, but volume targets cannot so easily take into account likely fresh business during the marketing period being measured.

Moreover, penetration targets do allow for the effects of saturation, and the more this type of targeting is used the greater will be the understanding of what 'saturation' levels are likely to be for any given service or group of services. Penetration targets also highlight areas of higher opportunity. If one branch has a penetration level of, say, 25 per cent, and the average for a group of branches with a similar customer profile is 40 per cent, it is fairly safe to assume that the branch with a low penetration has considerable scope for sales. This grouping of branches with similar characteristics to ascertain and compare past performance is known as peer grouping. Making comparisons of this sort is not a perfect method of gauging opportunities but at least it ensures that some very blunt questions are asked about target levels and performance to date.

The difficulty in accurately assessing sales opportunities is the main reason why targeting has been such a slow development in banking. There are still major problems in assessing opportunities, but peer grouping and penetration measurements are beginning to highlight areas where a bank and its branches can do better.

(e)   Testing the targets' suitability

Having set the targets, it is prudent to test their relevance with the following questions;

– Are the targets achievable?
– Are they consistent with corporate objectives?
– Do they play on the bank's strengths and avoid the weaknesses?
– How do they compare with what is known about competitor targets?
– Do they fully utilise all the bank's resources?

Finally, the monitoring of progress needs to be considered. If the targets prove to be unattainable or even too easily attainable, there should be sufficient flexibility to bring them into line with the bank's capabilities before too much time and money is wasted.

Assessing profitability

Much can be written on the subject of how banks assess profitability. The sceptics will say that because of the difficulty in precisely allocating a vast number of fixed and variable costs to individual services, groups of services or indeed market segments, any cost/profit analysis is futile.

(a)   Services profitability

This stance rather ducks the issue. Just as banks are getting to grips with the measurement of opportunities in their attempts to set realistic sales targets, so too efforts and progress are being made to measure profitability. The degree of accuracy possible is largely dependent upon the sophistication of the computerised management accounting systems currently operated by a bank. Some branches do have the ability to measure the profitability of various lodgement gathering services by comparing the interest margins over or below the cost of buying alternative funds to sustain the current level of advance from the London Inter-Bank Market (the London Inter-Bank Offer Rate – LIBOR). If a branch lends less than its total lodgements, the profitability calculation is similar, except that there is a surplus of funds left over at the branch to lend to other parts of the bank. Care must be taken to distinguish between the profitability of the branch as opposed to the profitability derived from a given service.

A simple example (Table 7.2) shows how margin calculations can be used to assess profitability. This table also reflects the value of credit balances on current account and highlights the diminishing returns to the bank as funds become less volatile.

Assessing the profitability of groups of services such as those related to travel – travellers cheques, currency and holiday insurance, etc. – is also possible, as the time spent by the staff responsible for administering these services and related overheads can be monitored and priced.

Table 7.2

	Total branch balances	Gross daily interest at	Daily margin with 3 month LIBOR = 11%	Daily margin profit
Current account	£3 m	2% (notional)	9%	£740
7 day deposits	£3 m	7%	4%	£329
1 month notice deposits	£3 m	10%	1%	£82

Note: (a)   The profit in this schedule is expressed as profitability for all the branch accounts grouped by type of service. This can then be broken down into smaller units, for example profit per £100.

(b)   No allowance has been made for branch overhead costs but it is possible to calculate these as a single or overall unit cost per £100 per day, or per annum lent or held in lodgements using branch expenses data.

(c)   Similar profitability calculations can be undertaken for lending services at various rates based on flat or base rate structures.

Revenue earnings can then be compared with the cost of administration to see the profit or loss contribution, ignoring apportionment of other house expenses such as light and heat which would only complicate the calculations.

Overall, the most important profitability factor is to ensure that the calculations, and the components making up the costs, are treated in the same way year after year. Then increases or decreases in profitability, using the same base figures, will be worthwhile pointers on profitability and what marketing action might be necessary to improve any decline in profit trends.

(b)   Market segment profitability

Perhaps the most difficult area to measure for profitability is a market segment such as student customers where the pay-back period can be lengthy, or the small business market where bad debts can be high. These two are important segments, and for this reason have been chosen to illustrate what major factors should be taken into consideration when assessing their profitability.

(i)   Student market

Calculating profitability involves assessing if earnings exceed costs both in the short and longer term. However, one other profitability aspect applies to this market; that is the benefit of business earnings more likely to come from this better-educated segment when it moves into employment in the professions or industry.

Firstly, the profitability or otherwise of accounts of students can be quantified whilst they remain students. Secondly, profitability when they move into employment can be examined to see when, on average, the total cost to the bank is recouped – i.e. breakeven date. Student account costs are relatively easy to ascertain and are mainly incurred as follows:

– Student account recruitment campaigns including cost of incentives such as book tokens.

– Revenue loss through maintaining accounts free of charge or at reduced rates whilst customers remain students. In the most simplistic assessment, marginal cost factors could be ignored, as could the cost of special low interest loan schemes.

– Losses through bad debts.

To offset some of these costs, revenue and benefits are to be derived from the following:

– Use of ancillary services particularly loans and travel facilities.

– Credit balances. Because grants are usually received only once a term, and the balance is drawn down over two to three months, the average student credit balance is higher than those of the accounts of weekly-paid customers.

– Their simple needs, usually money transmission through a cash dispenser, means that they should be relatively straightforward to service. This is more so at branches where the main customer group is students.

– Parental influence is the main reason for students opening an account with a particular bank. Therefore, there are opportunities to enhance the relationship with parents who are customers and often also better-educated high earners.

To summarise, costs can be assessed, but the benefits are less easy to quantify. Losses sustained on student accounts need to be recouped after they start employment and, in the short term, bank servicing costs should be kept to a minimum. For example, any troublesome student accounts should be closed.

Graduated student account costings can be obtained by continually maintaining data on a sample of student accounts over a period of several years. Costs and revenue, adjusted for inflation, can be calculated and the average period to breakeven obtained. It can never be an exact computation but it is a guide on which to base marketing strategies.

Costs
– It takes seven to nine years on average for revenue from student accounts to pay back costs incurred whilst they are at seats of learning or articled.

– As many as 15 per cent of all students transfer to another bank when they graduate, and the previous years' costs cannot then be recovered.

Benefits
– Ex-students usually acquire higher monthly salaried employment and thus keep higher than average credit balances.
– Many enter the professions and commerce where they can be 'good connections' for new business acquisition.
– This group has a greater need than the average customer for ancillary

services, so providing the bank with opportunities to obtain additional sources of revenue.

Clearly a bank has to nurture and fund student accounts for many years before a profit can be made. At the time of graduation these accounts can be lost to a competitor who will have avoided the early costs and is likely to show a profit very quickly.

Consequently there are two alternative marketing strategies open to a bank:

– Continue to gather student accounts as the basis for longer-term profitability and be prepared to accept all the risks involved or

– Attract accounts of the better-paid from the competition through service tailoring and pricing policies. The problem is that any heavy activity of this sort is unlikely to stay unmatched, with the danger of further erosion all round of bank margins.

Retention of the student's account when he or she graduates and needs to transfer to another location is a key issue. The relationship created during the student years, and the continuation of this relationship when the account is transferred to another branch, will be fundamental.

Attempts to determine the profitability or otherwise of the student market especially in the longer term, can never be an exact science.

Nevertheless, it is possible to obtain a general picture for the segment, and by scrutinising individual students' accounts it may be possible to be even more precise.

Internal sources
Maintaining a computer-based sample is the most accurate method. The information will need to be updated annually, either by returns from the branches where the accounts are kept or by linking the sample program to the main bank accounting computer. Without computer assistance, the analysis operation becomes clerical, so increasing work-loads and probably reducing the size of the sample and thus the accuracy.

It may be possible to segment the student market even further by profitability, or account usage or analyse students at different types of educational establishments.

External sources
The Association for Business Clearing Services (ABCs) undertakes extensive research on behalf of all the banks. This is both quantitative and qualitative and includes market share analysis.

As student accounts are profitable in the long run (provided they are retained after graduation) market share performance is relevant to any views on total profitability of this segment.

Moreover, without market share data it might be impossible to determine the success of incentives and of campaign activity designed to attract student business. It might also be impossible to assess the cost of incentives and other promotions for each account gathered.

(ii) Small business market

There are several definitions of a small business, mostly based upon number of employees or turnover. The Committee of Inquiry on Small Firms in 1971 (Bolton Committee) and the Committee to Review the Function of Financial Institutions in 1979 (Wilson Committee) based their definitions on employees and turnover but differed on the maximum level of both criteria according to the type of industry. In general terms, any firm employing less than 200 people and/or having an annual turnover of less than £200 000 falls within the category of a small business. The definition of a small business is particularly important when collecting data.

Between 90 and 95 per cent of all firms in Britain are regarded as small, according to the Bolton and Wilson definitions. Therefore, they are an important market segment for banks. Its profitability as a sector is crucial to the ongoing expansion of many financial institutions who cater for their needs.

Market characteristics
An interesting fact which emerged from the Wilson Committee's report was that half the 'smaller companies' and a quarter of the 'medium-small' companies had no bank overdrafts or loans on their balance sheets in 1975. However, economic recessions and even 'boom' periods could have altered this picture quickly and drastically.

For the purpose of the question it is the small businesses which borrow that create the most difficulty when assessing profitability. Those with credit balances are obviously profitable and this profitability is easy to measure.

The growing pains of a small business, which wishes to expand, have resulted in considerable government pressure upon the banks to provide easily available and practical financial support. As a result, many term-lending schemes and other structured financial packages have emerged. Many of these schemes take a balanced view between long-term repayment and reduced cashflow which can be recycled. With fixed rates of interest, the banks are also forced to take a view on interest rates over a long period. This is especially important to the profitability achieved from the small business sector, as banks, in the main, 'balance their books' daily and make little attempt to match long-term fixed-interest lending portfolios with long-term sources of funds, also at a fixed rate.

Expansion loans, venture loans, start-up loans and many other term schemes also usually have features which reflect, not so much on the level of profitability to the bank, but when the profit becomes available. Novel features such as no repayment of capital in the first few years, or no interest (subsequently interest is linked to sales levels to recoup) reduce income and therefore profitability in the early stages.

Moreover, the longer lending terms now available call for a higher degree of interpretation of business prospects than before. With this type of support it is also more difficult to withdraw help in the earlier stages if the business takes a turn for the worse. Consequently the risk of bad debts increases.

Clearly the small business segment is potentially very profitable for a bank, although quantifying the precise level of profitability could prove very difficult. The name of the game for this very large market sector is to pick more winners than losers. For every firm which survives in the first year at least another one will die.

Assessing profitability

Just as the Wilson and Bolton Committees found it necessary to consider the characteristics of the industry when defining a small business, so profitability levels will differ according to industry types. Profit margins of a grocer's shop are likely to be lower than a business selling motor cars. Professional and consultancy practices, such as estate agents also create a higher level of profit for assets employed than an engineering firm.

So any cost/revenue analysis of the whole sector can only be undertaken in very general terms, although it is accepted that banks would prefer to attract the business of firms which have the highest profitability potential.

Costs to banks are mainly twofold; the losses through bad debts and secondly the higher level of management time necessary to administer small business accounts, especially in the first year and when they wish to expand. This level of contact is also influenced by the profitability potential of the type of business.

However, the revenue potential from being able to charge higher interest rates than those for a 'blue chip' company offsets some of the costs. Credit balances, as mentioned above, must also not be overlooked when considering profitability of the whole segment.

There are other important benefits which, although less quantifiable, nevertheless add to the profitability of the segment. Apart from the future prospects from a segment where the majority of constituents are growth-orientated, other factors are:

- future loyalty stemming from support through the difficult years;
- good personal account business can ensue from grateful proprietors who have achieved financial success;
- the small business sector is not multi-banked and thus competitive pressures are not so great.

So, on balance, the small business segment is profitable. Also the future profitability growth potential is unequalled when success flows from professional banking expertise. Lending support in the early years is critical, with often no track record to aid the lending judgement.

There are other influences that can adversely affect lending risks and, particularly in today's climate, nothing can be totally certain in the small business segment. Recession, industrial action, unexpected competition, a change in the market, even technology and legal changes can all cause a profitable small business rapidly to become unprofitable. Such business risks can be mitigated, to some extent, through diversification, for the bank in the small business sector can spread its risks by not going solely for one type of industry that may be more attractive because of its potential profitability.

Collecting data

A bank will wish to have information on three matters:

(1) Profitability from the segment as a whole and how this can be increased;
(2) Profitability from individual subsections of the segment and how this can be increased;
(3) Causes of success/failure so that profit potential can be maximised and undue risks avoided.

There is a wealth of information about the nature of small firms and their needs, but little which particularly assists a bank in assessing profitability. Consequently, it is necessary to undertake specific research programmes in order to obtain information of this nature.

Data required is both qualitative and quantitative. It can be collected by a combination of internal and external research involving desk analysis and interview techniques with samples of small businesses. One key to profitability for the bank is the classic marketing route of establishing needs and then providing services, that are profitable, to meet these needs. Sales and revenue levels of specific services can then be assessed.

Sources of information will depend on the actual aspect of the profitability area that is being researched. Business balance sheets, government data, Bank of England classification by type of business data, and many other external sources can all provide useful information. However, when assessing profitability to the bank of the whole sector, or any given subsection, an analysis of internal bank information from actual experience of conducting accounts, including revenue generated and advances experience, is likely to be the most useful. Once again a computer model may be the best way to produce quality information.

Case study

This case study takes a series of branch objectives and demonstrates what action could be taken to achieve the stated goals. Only two of the stages normally found in a marketing plan are shown. Chapters 9 to 11 look at the total planning process in much greater depth. However, this case study does emphasise the variety of activity that is possible at a branch level, and that can be used to control the branch's own destiny and support the corporate objectives that have influenced the choice of marketing goals it has formulated.

Lilliput branch, in support of its bank's corporate objectives for 1989, has set the following business targets:

(1) To improve total net business profit by £25 500 (+ 30 per cent) to raise its interest margin from 7.5 to 7.6 per cent and produce a net profit of £3750 per head of staff;
(2) To improve standards of service;
(3) To expand business development activity by better use of staff;
(4) To increase the average advances for the coming year by £700 000;
(5) To increase total lodgements by £500 000;
(6) To increase income from services which are non-interest-related by 7 per cent;
(7) To increase fee income by 10 per cent.

The schedules on pages 144–148 detail some of the action that can be taken and indicates the time-scales. When some activity takes place will be influenced by the bank's national advertising programmes.

Branch: Lilliput

Supporting prime objectives
(1) To improve total net business profit by £25 500 (+30%) and achieve ROC (B) 35%
Absorption ratio 40%   Interest margin 7.6%   Net profit per head £3750

Programme objective	Action	Time-scale		Monitoring report
		Start	Finish	Quarter 1|2|3|4|
To improve non-interest income	Review all non-personal tariffs under manager's discretionary lending limit where accounts are overdrawn	January	June	
	Review all non-personal credit accounts under manager's discretionary lending limit	July	December	
	Enforce minimum 1% A/Fees for all new loans and overdrafts	Continuous		
	Consider 'renewal' of facility A/Fees' where applicable—minimum ¼%	Continuous		
To reduce bad debts	Closer control of all existing manager's discretionary lending power and greater selectivity with new business	Continuous		
To widen interest margins	New business loans and other non-personal loans to be minimum 3½% over the bank's base rate of interest except for 'blue chips'	Continuous		
	Funding non-personal current account hardcore whenever possible at higher interest rates	Continuous		
To reduce costs	Improving office efficiency and reduce relief staff costs and overtime by: — Progressive clerical training programme to improve flexibility. — Close end of day supervision to reduce overtime.	Continuous		Continuous

Supporting prime objectives
(2) To improve standards of service

Programme objective	Action	Time-scale		Monitoring report
		Start	Finish	Quarter 1/2/3/4
Improve premises appearance and visual impact of public space	● Appoint in-branch display clerk with daily responsibility for literature displays and public space appearance	Continuous		
	● Deputy Manager to be responsible for monitoring all other premises features which impact on image	Continuous		
Increase staff knowledge and enhance 'customer care' attitudes	● Regular review of service standards by complaints committee and at bi-monthly staff meetings	Continuous		
	● Special training sessions using video films and applicable interactive video programmes	Continuous		
	● Compile survey questionnaire to go out with cheque books and/or statements to assess performance (Discuss with Market Research Manager, H.O.)	September	November	
	● 'Opening account' seminars	January	May	
	● 'New service' seminars			
	● 'Service knowledge' 10-minute talks by selected staff			
Position branch as a serious professional adviser	● Evening seminars to invited audience of small/medium business customers/non-customers covering financial cash control/management using H.O. support resources	April	April	
	● Maintain regular personal contacts with accountants, solicitors and brokers in area	Continuous		

Supporting prime objectives
(3) Expand staff business development activity (4) Increase the average advances for year by £700 000

Programme objective	Action	Time-scale Start	Time-scale Finish	Monitoring report Quarter 1/2/3/4
Expand business development activity through better use of motivated knowledgeable staff	● Nominate business development teams for – Access – Insurance – Lodgement services – When necessary to support other national activity.		To dovetail with national campaigns	
	● Increase mailing activity	Continuous		
	● Dovetail in-branch display programme with business development team activity	Continuous		
	● Nominated member of staff to co-ordinate, control and monitor trust division service sales including arranging 'clinics'	Continuous		
	● Erect a staff business development notice board	January	—	
	● Support regional training programmes by sending maximum number of staff to courses and seminars	Continuous		
	● Aggressive home loan marketing with in-branch displays	February	May	
Increase average advances by £700 000	● Continue to seek new accounts from established businesses using local professional firms for introductions, Gold Card connections and where principal controlling officers have private accounts	Continuous		

Supporting prime objectives
(5) Increase total lodgements by £500 000

Programme objective	Action	Time-scale		Monitoring report
		Start	Finish	Quarter 1/2/3/4
Increase total lodgements by £500 000	● Very selective adoption of marginal cost quotes for competitors' business customers with an established history of credit balances	Continuous		
	● Selective mailing of interest-bearing lodgement accounts to all premier card customers and principal officers of firms where we have private accounts	February	February	
	● In-branch display programmes for interest-bearing lodgement accounts	October	October	
		See separate schedule		
	● Selective mailing using computer output to identify good credit customers	February	February	
		October	October	

Supporting prime objectives

(6) Increase non-interest-related income by 7%   (7) Increase fee income by 10%

Programme objective	Action	Time-scale		Monitoring report
		Start	Finish	Quarter 1|2|3|4
Insurance (£11 000 total – 10% increase)	• Priority activity to be given to pension plans and low cost endowment home loan insurance. Action to include selective mailings, displays and regional insurance adviser clinics.	Continuous		
	• Special-branch displays.	See separate schedule		
Overseas services (£7200 total 2.5% increase)	• Special mailing to larger customers who are potential importers/exporters. Arrange visits by Overseas Manager.	Continuous / February	July	
Arrangement fees (£9500 total 11.8% increase)	• Charge ¼% on renewals and consider rates charged on all temporary facilities.	Continuous		
Access cards (150 new cards)	• Permanent in-branch display rack.	Continuous		
	• Mailshot in conjunction with national campaign.	February	February	
	• Market to all new accounts at the six month review.	Continuous		
	• Leaflets to be included with travel facilities and cheque card renewals.	Continuous		

Summary

Branch displays are an important branch promotional activity. To be effective, one person should be responsible for ensuring that they are presentable, properly sited and changed regularly. Direct mail is a cost-effective means of generating sales opportunities to a wider group of customers than those interviewed in the branch during the course of a year. Good results rely on correctly identifying and cross-matching customer groups with the benefits of the service(s) being promoted. Considering seasonal factors and making the letter as individual and personal as possible will help improve response levels. Follow-up activity is also important.

There are other forms of promoting services including personal selling, cold calling and telephone selling. All have a part to play and can be successful, provided the appropriate skills are properly applied.

The sequence of steps in planning and executing a promotional campaign should be fully understood. So too should the reasons why, and the methods that can be used to test the validity of each interlinking stage with questions beginning with the words why, what, when, where, how.

There are some key organisational responsibilities which, if carried out professionally by a person chosen to do the work, will improve the quality of business development activity. These responsibilities include identifying and selecting target audiences, ensuring the business development activity is co-ordinated, and monitoring progress.

Most of the branch staff have the chance to spot business development opportunities as they carry out their clerical functions. These opportunities should be identified for each clerical role and a system introduced for action to be undertaken by the person who has the skill and authority to make these decisions. Specific sales targets are fundamental to the marketing process. How these targets can be set will vary widely from bank to bank. The basic alternatives and the reasons why a particular target setting system is used by your bank and branch should be understood.

Expertise is growing and management accounting systems improving, so that profitability of a service, groups of services or segmented customer profile can be assessed more accurately. Consider, from your own knowledge and experience, how accurate profit assessments are becoming and how the process could be further improved.

Revision questions

1 Select a lodgement-gathering service of your own choice and

construct the framework of a branch promotion. Show how each element of the framework impacts on the others.

2 What tasks would a marketing organiser perform in your branch? Give reasons for your answer.

3 What are the key issues in organising and implementing a direct mail campaign?

4 How are targets set in your branch? Describe the ways in which profitability and penetration levels impact on the system used, choice of service and target levels.

5 Describe how and to what extent your bank or branch assesses the profit contribution from lodgement and lending services. How do these assessments of profitability influence the marketing objectives?

Chapter 8
The Marketing Mix – Distribution

The way in which the major banks distribute services is, without doubt, one of the most discussed aspects of marketing. New technology is bringing with it new ways to distribute services and opening up new markets, not just for the high street banks but also for building societies and a range of much smaller and less well represented financial institutions.

During the next few years all the banks will slim down their network, partially to contain costs, but also in recognition that market requirements are also changing as a result of the increasing automation of money transmission services. A large branch network has been called a hindrance, suggesting that its importance will diminish as automation proceeds. This judgement makes the mistake of over-simplifying the cost/benefit issues arising from a branch network which has been the platform on which a substantial profitability record has been consistently built over many years.

It is true that some reshaping of the branch network is now necessary, but the business potential derived from personal contact with customers should not be ignored when deciding what the optimum size of a branch network should be.

Moreover, the type of distribution channel is also changing as the major banks buy estate agency firms, open up branches in stores, create fully automated banking offices and are currently introducing corporate offices designed to service the medium to large corporate customer.

So it is clear that a lot is happening now, and changes will continue for the next few years. The task of this chapter is to highlight the role of distribution in the total marketing mix and look at the marketing factors which will create changes. Finally, it is possible to forecast how these influences will impact on future bank distribution systems, and some of the influence of technology can be foreseen.

Principles of distribution channels

Distribution is a complex subject spanning the process of getting the goods or services from the supplier to the customer. It includes the selection of the most expedient channel or channels and the servicing of these channels.

The choice of a distribution system is an important one, for if it has to be changed at a later date, making these alterations could prove expensive and time-consuming. In general terms, an organisation has two broad distribution alternatives: taking its goods or services directly to the consumer without using outside intermediaries, or using wholesalers or agents (middlemen) to support the distribution process. Many factors will influence the choice of distribution system, not least the characteristics of the product or service and the chosen target audience. It is worth stating that the distribution system chosen will affect many of the other marketing mix elements. Before looking in more detail at the four alternative channels of distribution, it must be stressed that the choice of channel will need to take account of tomorrow's requirements if the marketplace is changing.

(a) Benefits of having intermediaries

A manufacturer or service provider selling direct to the consumer can be advantageous. This is especially the case where goods decay quickly or have a seasonal demand where an expensive or complex distribution channel might not be cost-effective for a short period.

By using intermediaries there should be economies of scale and cost savings from having the right facilities required to store goods and get them to the marketplace. This specialisation of roles can be as important for the manufacturer as it is for the middlemen (wholesalers, agents and retailers). It allows manufacturers to focus on production and allows others to introduce retail selling expertise.

Moreover, there may be a lack of financial resources to allow direct marketing to the consumer especially where the market is geographically widespread.

(b) Alternative distribution systems

There are four general systems of distribution:

(1) *Direct distribution* whereby the goods or services are supplied direct to the consumer, and there are no intermediary links to consider. Avon cosmetics are an obvious example of direct distribution of a product, as that company uses its own sales

people to market direct to the housewife. Other forms of direct selling include the use of mail-order direct response advertising, and telephone selling where the consumer in one way or another ultimately obtains the goods or services directly from the manufacturer or provider.

(2) *Vertical distribution* is used to describe a distribution channel which uses intermediaries that are owned or unified into the same organisation as the manufacturer or service provider. The channel may include wholesalers and retailers, but the important characteristic is that successive stages of production and distribution are carried out within the same organisation. Many multiple stores use the vertical distribution system and in the financial services industry, home banking and automatic teller machines are two examples of services supplied direct to the customer through wholly-owned delivery channels.

(3) *Horizontal distribution* involves two or more companies joining together to exploit the market. They may work together or create a separate organisation which may even appear to operate in competition.

   This system is often found where a market for a product or service is expanding rapidly. To take advantage of the opportunities presented, it is necessary to buy in products or a service to satisfy demand which cannot be met from existing production capacity.

   In financial services terms, the plastic credit card industry is a good example of horizontal marketing. Many of the store cards use either Access or Visa technology and facilities under their own branding in the form of a franchising arrangement.

(4) *Multichannel distribution* usually describes the use of more than one channel of distribution for supplying a product. It may, for example, be cost-effective to reach different markets for the product or service by using different marketing systems which often could be in competition with one another.

   An insurance company may sell direct or through intermediaries, such as banks or brokers. American Express sell their charge cards through agents such as banks, direct through response advertising and through their travel offices. When using several channels it is important to 'harmonise' the more important elements of the marketing mix such as price, product features and benefits, and general advertising style. In this way, maximum marketing impact will be gained rather than maximum consumer confusion.

Considerations when distributing services

Marketing decisions relating to the distribution of services are inextricably linked with how the other elements of the marketing mix are applied. Moreover, in an organisation such as a major retail bank, distribution of services can be within geographical areas as well as nationally or internationally spread. However, the overriding influences on how services have been distributed to date are the unique characteristics of the traditional range of bank services.

Effect of financial services characteristics

Whilst there are many parallels in the marketing of physical products and the marketing of services, services have particular characteristics that are not shared by physical products and that have influenced the distribution systems used by the banks. These characteristics, which were fully considered in Chapter 4, include intangibility, inseparability, heterogeneity and fluctuating demand. Applied to the banking industry, together with another factor – that of an ongoing customer relationship – these characteristics have been instrumental in the way branch networks have developed. Moreover, the branch network will continue to be a major distribution system in the future, but the formal structure, style and atmosphere will undoubtedly change.

As services are intangible, sales and promotional efforts need to concentrate on the benefits of their usage to consumers. Traditionally, the explanation of the sometimes complex benefits of banking services required selling by knowledgeable and experienced staff directly under the control of the bank. The need for a direct channel of distribution led to the development of the branch concept. This is of course in marked contrast to the lengthy chain of distribution used by some producers of consumer goods as seen earlier in this chapter.

The application of the product standardisation concept of banking services, progress in promotional techniques, and the diffusion of interest in banking across broad sectors of the consumer market, have enabled marketeers to focus on the tangible features of established banking services such as cheque-book and statement design. The imagery portrayed by these tangible aspects assists consumers' perception of particular services and contributes to sales efforts. Undoubtedly for some audiences and for some more complex banking services, intangibility will remain an issue to be tackled by personal advice and explanation, and will thus continue to influence the type and format of distribution systems.

In many service industries the actual service is inseparable from its supplier – for example, financial advice – so that personal sale is the only feasible method of distribution. Traditionally, account opening procedures and the sanctioning of credit required personal contact between bank staff and prospective customers. As methods of prospective customer identification have improved, the separation of service from supplier has become a viable proposition – for example, the use of direct mail to recruit customers and the use of ATMs to service customers' day-to-day account needs.

Whilst much has been achieved in the establishment of uniform features for banking services, some key aspects of services are heterogeneous – for example, length of queuing time in branches, branch design and layout. Apart from customers' perceived differences in the quality of service from outlet to outlet, the provision of precisely the same objective service standards across a number of outlets at the same time is difficult. Attention is therefore concentrated by banks on sales and product knowledge training and customer servicing to mitigate the effects of heterogeneity, and to provide quality control standards.

Service industries are often subject to major fluctuations in demand by season, day of the week or hours of the day – for example, empty banking halls staffed with cashiers and personal bankers. The problems of servicing cost-effectively the peaks and troughs of demand within acceptable customer response times have been major issues in banks' distribution network planning and design, leading to developments such as reopening on Saturday mornings, 24-hour ATM facilities and the early experiments in home banking with use of computer terminals. The importance of servicing customer demand, as and when needed, is highlighted by the fact that decisions to buy financial services are made relatively infrequently, and missed sales opportunities may not recur for a period of years or even at all.

A special characteristic of banking services is that they form the basis of an ongoing relationship between supplier and customer – markedly different from buying most consumer goods. The quality of a bank–customer relationship is often highly regarded by both personal and corporate customers, involving issues of trust and the provision of reliable financial counselling and advice. Traditionally, the customer's educational and advisory roles have been undertaken by branch staff for personal and corporate customers.

However, better knowledge of customer needs and a more sophisticated marketing orientation have led to the updating and streamlining of distribution systems in banks. With clearly defined products and well-maintained customer information systems, prospective customers for many personal sector services can be contacted and recruited by mail whilst information and advice can often be provided by telephone.

Increasing automation of basic services and a more financially know-ledgeable audience amongst personal customers offers fewer opportunities for face-to-face contact between bank and customer. Some banks have countered this with the introduction of 'personal bankers', members of staff designated as the customer contact points responsible for maintaining and developing the bank's relationship with identified personal customers.

A parallel concept is that of corporate account or corporate business executives. Since the financial service needs of businesses are generally more complex than those of individuals and can require individual tailoring and presentation, this approach to corporate customer servicing has required different distribution networks. A typical configuration involves the day-to-day money transmission and financial service needs of corporate customers handled at local branch level. This is supported by corporate account executives located at area or regional centres with direct access to a number of specialist financial advisers. Increasingly, corporate account executives visit their customers rather than vice versa, as was traditional.

The old approach of distributing almost the whole range of banking services through all the branches has been superseded by the adoption of market segmentation techniques. A primary objective for banks, in distribution planning, is to select channels to optimise their profit position in the long term. There is now less concern to modify markets and services to fit into the traditional distribution system and more willingness to consider the implications of the particular characteristics of banking services for the evolution and development of cost-efficient distribution systems. Later in this chapter the part played by improving technology in shaping future services and the choice of delivery is considered.

Distribution strategies

The main influences on the determination of strategies for distributing services are the characteristics of the marketplace, including target audiences and competition. What the customer wants is, as we saw with other elements of the marketing mix, paramount, but often these requirements are shaped in the short term by the activity of competitors as well as the other evolutions of the marketplace, including changing banking habits and new technology.

Yet again there has to be a balance between matching competitor activity, meeting customer requirements, and the overall cost of trying to do both. At the same time, some customer segments will have different requirements to others and some will be more important to the bank's long-term profitability goals than others. So we see a movement away from the 'catch all' branch distribution network with its attendant costs to more tailored distribution systems which meet the particular needs of key customer groups or segments.

Any distribution strategy should derive from the bank's long-term planning process. It takes a considerable time, and a large sum of money, to change traditional bank distribution systems. Before taking any precipitate action the reasons for the change and benefits to be derived must be clearly visible to customers, staff and the public at large. The corporate plan will address three very basic questions:

(1) How can we get services or groups of services to the marketplace cost effectively?
(2) When do customers want these services available?
(3) Where are the markets we want to reach, and what are the characteristics of the services and planned new services for those markets?

These three questions also highlight the close relationship of distribution to other elements of the marketing mix. For example, if a service has complex features, then a more personal selling approach is necessary, both to sell and also to service it once customers become users. Technology might not help in this situation in the same way that money transmission or simple lending facilities can be automated so that they can be sold and serviced with minimal staff involvement. Pricing policies will also impact on distribution strategies in terms of the need to automate the distribution of those services which generate little or no profit. Moreover, where pricing is complex or multivariable and has a negotiating element, automation is not the answer – technology has yet to develop a machine that can make subjective decisions on pricing. There are a multitude of other interrelating factors between distribution and the other marketing mix elements which could create difficulties when trying to establish broad distribution strategies. It would be easy to opt for simple routes when establishing the best ways in which to tackle the problems, associated with getting services to the market, in the most cost-effective as opposed to the cheapest manner. The strategies for distribution could be mainly technology driven, market driven, or, bank expediency driven. Probably the right approach is a strategy based upon an amalgamation of all three forces.

(a) Getting the services to the market

Before making changes to distribution systems, research will be required to ascertain the extent that chosen markets are being satisfied by existing methods and whether or not customer satisfaction and after-sales service could be improved with resultant profit benefits to the bank. Customer satisfaction and profit are, as we know, at the very heart of marketing. A retail bank ignores these facets at its peril. Equally important is the personal relationship between banker and customer, and automated delivery systems can undermine this important requirement so vital to any financial institution seeking return business as customers go through the life cycle. Any feelings of remoteness will leave bank customers vulnerable to a host of other financial service providers who are prepared to create close contact often outside normal banking hours. These issues are explained in the second case study at the end of this chapter — it compares and contrasts the current branch role with a financial supermarket approach.

This problem of getting the services to the chosen markets is ongoing and in recent years has created a groundswell which will probably change the traditional branch network system in so many different ways that within the next decade the current high street branches with their 'cloistered' image will have largely disappeared.

(b) Providing services when customers want them

Later in this chapter the effects of technology on extending the 9.30 to 3.30, five days per week hours of business banks have clung to, despite fierce competition from the building societies, will be considered in some depth. At this stage, whilst looking at the main influences on distribution strategies, it is only necessary to stress the importance of availability, no matter what delivery systems are used. However, some services do have seasonal demands and others have features which lend themselves to delivery systems that are not tied to branch opening hours or indeed the branch network itself.

Where there are peaks and troughs in demand, the distribution and delivery systems must be capable of adjusting to these fluctuations. So too must the financial infrastructure, as a bank must balance its books. If lending is substantially higher at certain times of the year because of a farming or industrial cash flow cycle, then matching funds must be gathered in one way or another to meet these peaks. At a local level, customer demands on branches at Christmas time, for example, require a distribution or delivery capability that can also match these abnormal demand levels.

These are market demands on delivery times and capabilities but of course there are also bank demands to consider. During the 1950s, branches closed their doors on Saturdays and it is only in the last few years that a very restricted Saturday opening service has been re-introduced, probably at some considerable cost rather than profit to the major retail banks. Staff willingness to work on a Saturday was a fundamental requirement, so too was technology improvement if a restricted service was to be effective in meeting some customer requirements. It seems likely that full six-day banking will return in one form or another. This will either be through selected larger branches or by using subsidiary organisations such as estate agents where these are wholly owned. 'Money shops' where 'popular' services can be acquired quickly and easily from specially trained sales staff away from the security conscious, processing clerical environment of the high street branch bank are another attraction. Once again, the close relationship between the service characteristics, the public requirements, and the bank's ability to provide selected services outside 'normal' bank trading hours, must be stressed. In the corporate market, which is now being serviced by account executives regularly visiting the larger customers (turnover of £1 million plus), constraints imposed on delivery by bank opening hours are no longer so significant.

(c) Service characteristics and market locations

The branch networks of the major retail banks have developed partially by the desire to serve the larger conurbations and specialist industrial sites where the prospects of volume business was greatest and partially as a result of mergers and trade-offs agreed between the banks at the start of the Second World War. So not all networks are uniformly spread throughout England and Wales. In some areas, for example, Lloyds Bank is poorly represented – the North East of England and some parts of the Midlands other than Birmingham are prime examples. By comparison, in the South West and South East, Lloyds is particularly strongly represented. A similar lack of uniform spread can be identified in the other clearing banks' networks and thus when developing services the characteristics of the markets which can be reached, whether geographically or demographically segmented, must be considered.

   In the next section of this chapter those factors, including technology, that influence decisions to expand representation by creating a new branch or reducing the size and style of existing branches is covered fully. However, it must be said that branch network decisions are more often cost containment driven than service characteristic or market location driven. This is not so of course for automated delivery systems which are regarded as cost-saving systems and as a means of expanding availability in a way which would not be profitable or practical by expanding the number of branches.

Marketing issues affecting retail network size

It is already clear that the traditional branch network is contracting as well as changing its role and style. Some major branches are introducing specialist offices to service the accounts of corporate customers, others are introducing a satelliting operation which pools expertise in a centrally located branch which is readily available to customers of a number of branches nearby. This system reduces salary costs and theoretically provides a higher standard of financial advice than would otherwise be available.

Whatever delivery systems are used, they all have to consider some fundamental marketing issues especially for the 90 per cent of customers who make up the personal market. The issues are these:

(1) What market share and volume of personal sector business does the bank wish to develop in the future? This broad but fundamental question can impact directly on the use of bank branches within the distribution strategy. Branches are neither cheap nor mobile, so where a bank has decided significantly to increase its market share and volume, market targets must either be catered for profitably within the existing network, if necessary by modifying existing branch formats, or else the bank must consider the viability of either creating extra sales outlets or adopting completely new channels of delivery.

(2) Following on from the above point: which segment or segments of the personal sector is the bank aiming at? What are the characteristics of these customers and importantly what is and what will be their requirements and perceptions of the channel through which bank services are provided? For example, the young may be responsive to alternative and radical forms of delivering services, and to the new technology which this frequently entails, but what of the older customer who has grown up with the traditional branch outlet and the high degree of personal contact that it provides?

(3) It will be necessary to consider fully the role of convenience and availability in terms of days of the week and hours of the day for the personal sector in general, and selected target segments in particular. Branches can be made more 'flexible' through extended opening hours, Saturday opening or through the installation of automated

teller machines, but at a cost which must be justified either in terms of increased profitable business or at least as a response to customer demand or competitive pressure.

(4) Location is another important issue. A network of existing branches can provide the important personal interface between the bank and its customers, but few banks are fortunate enough to possess an ideal network. Social and economic changes mean that once profitable locations can decline just as new opportunities for business development may occur elsewhere. Nevertheless, the costs involved in new representation are such that even the strongest customer demand, or competitive pressure, may have to be resisted and the bank forced to consider utilising alternative means of delivering its services.

(5) It is important to establish the delivery systems currently used by the bank and by its direct competitors. For most banks, the main distribution channel for services is unquestionably still the branch, but to what degree and with what success has the bank or its competitors already changed the format of these outlets? It may be that the network has begun to be segmented with the creation of personal branches and specially trained staff or that branches have become more clearly divided into personal and non-personal service areas. Perhaps even temporary or 'short-life' branches are being used to supplement or replace parts of the existing network. Again, to what extent, and with what success, has the bank or its competitors moved away from the branch as a delivery system and adopted alternatives such as centralised mailing sales techniques, coupon response in papers and magazines, centrally administered products, card based products or even home banking?

(6) New competitors moving into the markets for financial services must also be considered. The building societies, insurance companies and even the high street multiples are now increasingly engaged in providing services which were once the sole province of the banks. What is their current and likely future strategy with regard to the provision of these 'banking' services and how will this affect the long-term viability of the banks' branch networks?

(7) The role of existing and future technology will be of central importance in determining the use of current and new delivery systems. It is sometimes difficult to determine whether service development is technology driven or customer/bank led, but the rate of progress is such that there is constant pressure to try new delivery methods. There is little doubt that the current branch networks could not have survived without the labour- and paper-saving

technology installed to date, but as technology has moved into the forefront of the sales and delivery function, it must be no less rigorously judged than the bank branch, in terms of its cost, efficiency and degree of customer acceptance.

(8) Consideration must be given to the potential increase in volume, productivity and profitability, through using alternative delivery systems. An existing bank branch may be modified, or a new branch custom-built to deliver services more efficiently than before, but how will this compare with the cost and return on non-branch delivery systems? The traditional branch unit will undoubtedly deliver a range of personal sector services profitably and in greater numbers than through any other distribution channel but how limited is this product range? Is it growing or diminishing, and what implications does this have for the bank's overall marketing strategy?

(9) The bank must also consider what role existing and potential pricing strategies will play in any move towards alternative delivery systems. The successful adoption of say, cost-plus pricing for services, will help to absorb the overheads of maintaining a branch network. However, a reliance on loss-leader or penetration pricing for example, to gain market share, may not be compatible, even in the short term, with the maintenance of the branch and associated costs, at existing levels.

(10) There must be evaluation of the role of personal selling in current and future sales as opposed to automated and direct response delivery systems. Because of the intangible and inseparable characteristics of many bank services, personal selling is often the only means for selling and delivering them. As such the physical branch structure may provide the ideal focus for productive and profitable contact between staff and customers.

(11) It is of prime importance that the bank considers the likely impact on staff, of adopting or retaining a particular delivery system or systems. Relocation may be required where a network is thinned, and compensation agreed if the staff function is reduced beyond that which retirement and natural wastage will allow. Changes in selling techniques may require incentives to staff and will certainly entail effective retraining. Performance related pay is now being introduced.

The above points highlight the main marketing issues, but by no means do they constitute an exhaustive list. Other factors such as the effect on internal controls, the maintenance of corporate identity, and the importance of the 'after-sales' function of a branch, would also be

relevant to a broad evaluation of the branch and its likely contin-
uance in the face of alternative delivery systems.

The case for specialised offices

Local characteristics will generally determine whether there are commercial advantages in concentrating all promotional activity on certain
market sectors and then providing almost exclusively for the needs of
these chosen sectors.

Specialisation is not a new phenomenon. Coutts and Co is a specialist
bank and segment by wealth; Child & Co is another. Lloyds has its Cox
and Kings branch which caters mainly for armed forces personnel and
there are many student orientated branches. Most recently Midland has
opened its first branch catering for women only. Thus some degree of
specialisation already exists and there is ample evidence of the commercial advantages.

However, specialised offices are an important development in the
structure of branch networks, namely satellite grouping and the
formation of branches specialising in corporate business. Satellite
grouping involves moving some clerical routines and even some types of
business to a conveniently situated 'mother' branch. It can also involve
centralising and thus concentrating managers and staff with specialist
skills. In this case, customer problems, which are out of the ordinary,
necessitate either the customer going to the main branch, or the banker
from the main branch travelling to see the customer.

The reasons for wanting to realign the services provided at a given
branch to match more closely the dominant requirements of the
customer profile can result from trading pressures, not least rising bank
costs and the need to match aggressive competition. On the one hand,
corporate customers are demanding, and, as a result of increasing
competition among the banks, getting a more sophisticated service
based upon a bank's greater understanding of complex business issues.
Nevertheless, in the personal market, a speedy and relatively cheap
money transmission service is the primary requirement. Therefore,
corporate and personal market requirements differ. Cash dispensers
and other forms of computerised technology are providing the need for
money transmission and helping to cope with escalating transaction
volumes as the number of personal customers grows.

This is the broad economic scenario, but in the case of the major
clearing banks, with a well-spread network of offices, there will always
be those in the more remote areas which will endeavour to meet both
corporate and personal customer requirements. Specialist branches can

only function effectively if there is sufficient profitable business of one type locally to justify the costs of an office and keep the prudent minimum number of staff fully employed.

Where the market characteristics reflect a need for a specialist branch, there are benefits for both the bank and the customer.

But before a specialist branch is established, the profit, or profit potential, must justify the decision not to supply a more broadly-based banking service. Equally the question should be asked: when does specialisation cease to be a good thing?

(a) Bank benefits from specialisation

There are five main types of benefit that a bank may derive from specialisation.

(1) Relatively senior staff can be grouped in one branch where the demand for a higher level of knowledge and expertise will ensure it is fully utilised.

(2) Concentration of expertise in one place has a number of spin-off benefits. Training is more effective and easier to implement, specialist learning is accelerated.

(3) Pricing of service strategies can be more easily controlled to counter competitive activity. This comes from a closer understanding of the type of business served and what the market will bear.

(4) The branch image will be improved within a specialist market as standards of service and expertise are more tailored to customer needs.

(5) Cost savings generally should be possible in a specialist branch through the optimum use of the resources available.

(b) Benefits to customers from specialisation

There are few benefits for those that are not the type of customers which the specialist branch has been structured to service. Indeed, their business could be actively or passively discouraged. For the selected market there are real benefits, namely:

(1) Lower pricing from cost savings generally.

(2) Higher standards of service brought about by greater understanding and more expertise.

So what about the demerits?

(1) Some business, because it is not catered for by the specialist branch, will be lost.

(2) Some staff career opportunities may be lost to the bank or restricted because individuals have specialised.

(3) Changing market characteristics may not be recognised. This could lead to increasing costs and the loss of future business opportunities and even stagnation of business growth if changes become drastic – for example, if part or all of the business in the locality goes into decline.

(4) Adverse economic, or environmental trends may seriously affect the type of market being served. In turn, this will affect the profitability of the specialist branch through a drop in demand for services.

From this comparison of the pros and cons of a specialist branch, it can be seen that the bank must maintain some flexibility of stance. Market opportunities can change rapidly in a locality and there will always be pressures from industry for a local branch to also service its employees. Some lower quality personal accounts may be unprofitable today, but tomorrow the situation may have changed. Branches serving a wide range of customers have this flexibility to adapt quickly to local changing profit opportunities.

Moreover, personal customers are a sizeable source of new corporate business – one which might be lost to the specialist corporate branch which has discouraged personal customers.

Impact of technology on distribution and allied marketing mix elements

Technology is having a growing influence on marketing, especially delivery systems, by not only changing banker/customer relationships (sometimes detrimentally) but also by opening up new opportunities among non-customer segments which may previously have been considered unprofitable.

When banks offer new technology-based financial services and payments systems to customers it is sometimes assumed that this is in response to consumer demand. However, with some new technology-based services the consumer benefits are arguable. Part of the stimulation for new technology may not, therefore, be the marketing desire to satisfy customer needs but may be brought about by the fear that another bank will steal a competitive advantage. Alternatively it might simply be just weakness to sales pressure from technology suppliers.

Care must also be taken not to confuse the technology necessary in banking to keep the operational wheels turning, with the technology primarily designed to impact on marketing activity.

(a) Areas influenced

Technology affects the following areas of marketing:

(1) *The marketing mix*, particularly distribution and communication channels, prices, and the types of services available. Improvement in technology enables the service range to be extended and improves the availability of services through new distribution methods. Availability can also be extended simply through price reductions from economies of scale or from reducing costs as a result of technological improvements in providing the service.

(2) *The market segments*. New opportunities can arise either as services become more easily available or the appeal of new services creates new demands.

(3) *The basic banking functions; customer information and retrieval systems*. Additional profit is generated by reduction in costs, or unprofitable services becoming profitable through the streamlining of manual processes. Moreover, more efficient customer information systems improve the quality and the results of bank marketing.

(4) *Consumer behaviour* and levels of financial sophistication.

To summarise, it can be seen that the areas of influence split broadly into two groups. Firstly, where technology primarily changes banking processes in an effort to improve profitability/efficiency and secondly where technology is more specifically aimed at customers and designed to encourage business growth.

(b) Changes to the marketing mix

Without doubt, technology's main task has been to help overcome the constraints on marketing imposed by limited hours of opening. Money transmission services have been the first challenge and the expanding number of cash dispensers, through the wall and in 'remote' locations, have gone some way to blunting consumer demand for longer banking hours. Well over 80 per cent of customers use cash dispensers which extend the availability of banking service and reduce the number of cheques issued. This is an example of technology providing an operational and marketing benefit.

Developments in dispensers will continue, as the facilities offered are extended beyond cash withdrawals. Various instructions can be given relating to most aspects of account administration. It should also be possible, in the not too distant future, to process loan applications which are 'credit scored' by a machine and the decision transmitted automatically back to the applicant.

Perhaps the greatest technological progress has been made in communication, both for staff marketing training, using audio visual systems, and also for customer communication. Messages on statements are the forerunner of improvements in customers' information. New concepts, popularly known as 'home banking' using Prestel and other national communication networks are now available. Cable television, with its ability to reach regional audiences with messages which have local appeal, is yet another development that will soon have an impact on bank marketing.

With the new ways of reaching customers, additional services are being developed especially in the corporate sector. Selling time on a bank computer, and creating a linked accounts facility for the multi-banked through an inter-bank computer, to aid funds transfer, are two new developments. In fact company terminals can be linked directly to the bank's computer to facilitate minute by minute financial data transfer.

In the personal market, point-of-sale terminals (EFTPOS) will give the shopper a convenient and safe payment mechanism and the retail outlets a quicker access to 'cleared funds'.

Many technological possibilities have advantages and disadvantages. For the banks' point-of-sale terminals may stimulate more people to want bank accounts and reduce paper handling problems. Customers however, lose the benefit of credit for the time it takes now to clear a cheque and also the ability to stop the cheque at any time before it reaches their bank account. Consumer benefits from this type of technology are arguable except that it reduces the risk of carrying cash. The ability of a company customer to switch funds more quickly will reduce the benefit of static credit balances to the bank. Here again improvements in technology and the impact of technologically based competition are hardly making bank marketing easier if the objective is to gather and hold lodgements. Rates of interest for lending and lodgements will also become 'finer' as technology aids fund switching. Again, hardly a plus point for the bank, but the need to compete will create the need to find other ways of creating the profit previously attributed to customer inertia or a slow bookkeeping process.

Price sensitivity will increase in both the personal and corporate markets, threatening the banks' so-called endowment (current account credit balances on which no interest is paid). This in turn will affect the choice of services a bank will be willing to offer and, with increased volume growth necessary to compensate for smaller profit margins, may even mean readjustment of general attitudes to some services and the selling methods employed.

(c) New markets and effect on customer relationships

Improved communication due to technology has helped to improve consumer financial sophistication, and has resulted in new and more complex services.

At the same time technology has caused a reduction in customer contact.

As 'self-service' banking, through the use of terminals and cash dispensers spreads, so the bank's face-to-face contact with customers drops, and personal selling opportunities diminish. Consequently, two fears emerge; the use of new technology will not be as successful at marketing as the customer interview. Moreover, it is feared, the relationship with some customers, especially with older, wealthier customers, will decay and lead to a loss of this profitable business to specialist institutions.

It is an established fact that older, wealthier customers do not accept technology readily, and as they keep substantial lodgements their wishes cannot be ignored.

At the other end of the social scale, new technology capability may differ. For instance, the ability to program the support requirements of a new service by one bank on its computer may not be possible for another.

Current distribution developments

Given the present pace of change it is impossible to keep any textbook up to date. Nevertheless the general direction of changes in distribution or delivery systems will still be similar, even if the degree of sophistication of these changes has improved.

The retail banks have two major but distinctly separate markets – personal customers and business customers. Traditionally delivery systems have been the same to both markets despite the fact that their characteristics, and thus their needs, can be very different, especially when comparisons are made with the larger business customers. As a direct result of recognising these differing requirements, and growing competition for the profitable corporate sector banking business, new distribution systems are being introduced to supplement or enhance the traditional role of the branch.

(a) Delivery developments in personal market

Once a bank has established what market segments it regards as important to profitable volume growth, and has then identified the specific characteristics and requirements of these market segments, it is possible to tailor channels of distribution which most suit these needs and are cost effective.

It is a safe assumption that all the major retail banks are looking for quality business and that quality segments can be identified in any given age band of people. In Chapter 3, the various ways to segment markets were covered fairly fully. The next few paragraphs will build on this basic understanding and illustrate how consumer attitudes and behaviour are influencing delivery systems for certain types of services.

There are two broad types of market within the personal sector. One is the volume market which consists of customers who are happy to accept technology, especially if it extends time of availability of bank services and at the same time speeds up service. At the other end of the total personal market spectrum are those which do not accept automation either because of age or they have a requirement for more specialised services which require 'one-to-one' or 'face-to-face' delivery. It is not coincidental that the younger age groups are those more likely to be happy with volume-related automation and the older often more wealthy age group seek a more personal type of distribution of services.

Accepting that in Fig. 8.1 there are some very arbitrary cut-off assumptions in terms of age-related service requirements, the figure, nevertheless, clearly shows how new distribution systems for certain 'popular' services including financial advice started to develop during the late 1980s.

Not surprisingly, those services now available have been influenced by the characteristics of customers in the various age bands and the types of delivery systems now available. Figure 8.2 shows these servicing systems as they appeal in very broad terms to the segmented customer profile age bands.

(b) Delivery developments in the corporate market

Current delivery system developments are based mainly on the size of

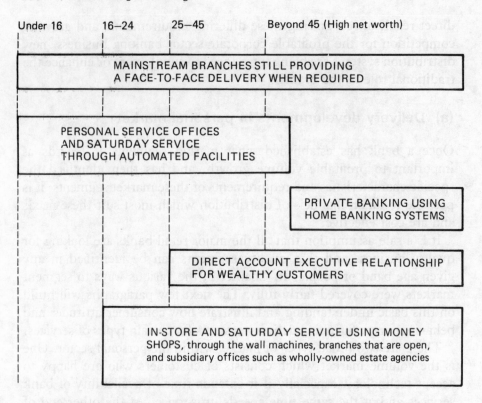

Under 16   16—24   25—45   Beyond 45 (High net worth)

MAINSTREAM BRANCHES STILL PROVIDING
A FACE-TO-FACE DELIVERY WHEN REQUIRED

PERSONAL SERVICE OFFICES
AND SATURDAY SERVICE
THROUGH AUTOMATED FACILITIES

PRIVATE BANKING USING
HOME BANKING SYSTEMS

DIRECT ACCOUNT EXECUTIVE RELATIONSHIP
FOR WEALTHY CUSTOMERS

IN-STORE AND SATURDAY SERVICE USING MONEY
SHOPS, through the wall machines, branches that are open,
and subsidiary offices such as wholly-owned estate agencies

Note: The exact cut-offs are unimportant as they are very arbitrary.
What is important is the way that distribution systems are
dividing out among the overall banking population.

Fig. 8.1 Main distribution channels and methods

companies measured by turnover but in some specialist segments, such
as agriculture, there are trained staff who can function as mobile
account executives or advisers if called upon to do so by the branch
manager.

Servicing the complex corporate market is proving time-consuming
and costly for the banks, but the competitive threat from overseas
banks for the banking business of the larger corporate clients is such
that cost of delivery and servicing is not the major factor; preservation
and improvement of market share is. Overseas banks, especially from
the USA and Japan, are buying market share by offering very fine prices
and a highly attentive service. They are happy to leave the costly money
transmission services with the UK retail banks and concentrate on
lodgement and lending facilities that are both competitive and
innovatory.

The vast majority of businesses are small. The breakdown of the
corporate market by annual turnover which is VAT registered is

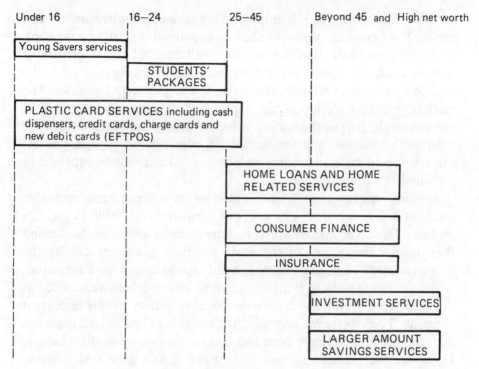

Note: The exact cut-offs are unimportant as they are very arbitrary.
What is important is the way that distribution systems are
dividing out among the overall banking population.

Fig. 8.2 Popular service requirement, influencing development of distribution channels

roughly as follows:

Less than £100 000	£100 000–£½ m	£½ m–£5 m	£5 m–£10 m	£10 m plus
68.6%	23%	7.3%	0.5%	0.6%

Professional firms and farmers have always enjoyed a special rapport with the traditional branch network and the managers who run these branches. Nevertheless, centrally based support teams have been formed by the banks to help deliver the more complex administration support schemes, often computer-linked lending facilities and advisory services.

The smaller businesses, with turnovers up to say £½ million, are time-consuming and make a lower profit contribution to bank earnings than the larger business. The majority of business customers fall into this category and in relation to the effort and time spent by banks in administering these accounts they are very much less profitable than the larger customers which are substantially fewer in number. Nevertheless, these small turnover accounts are important, as they are the seed corn from which larger more profitable businesses will emerge.

'*The Times* top 1000' companies are usually multi-banked and serviced by personal account executives appointed specially by the bank to co-ordinate all the banking services both national and international that are available. They deliver these as a comprehensive package to the finance directors or corporate treasurers in a sophisticated manner. The modern phrase is 'relationship banking' and demands a very close rapport on the part of the banker as well as a deep understanding of the customer's business, and the markets in which he or she operates. At this level, banking is extending well beyond what could be expected or provided at a branch level.

Arguably, the most important segment of the corporate market is that group of businesses with a turnover of between say £1 million and £25 million. These companies are very important to the retail banks and their branch networks. In the past they have been serviced by the branch manager, but as competition and sophistication have increased, so the ability of the branch manager to give a comprehensive service has declined. New ways have had to be found to deliver to this important segment. These systems, including the benefits of specialised branches and satellite groups, have been touched on previously in this chapter. However, the main focus now is to provide this group of business customers with 'account executives' who have similar skills and responsibilities as their colleagues who look after the mega-businesses including *The Times* top 1000.

Table 8.1

Bank	Delivery/servicing system	Target segment size by turnover
Barclays	100 Specialist corporate branches or offices	£25 million–£100 million
Lloyds	55 Commercial offices not incorporated in branches	£½ million–£35 million
Midland	30 Specialist offices	£5 million–£100 million or where borrowing £1 million plus
National Westminster	100 Corporate banking centres (some branch-based others new locations)	£1 million plus
TSB	300 Corporate branches	Primarily all corporate accounts

Currently, the major clearing banks are either providing, or propose providing, the servicing/delivery systems to the 'middle market size' businesses, as indicated in Table 8.1.

Specialisation of delivery systems enables a much higher degree of expertise in the co-ordination of various service departments and subsidiaries to take place and closer, more frequent contact, to be maintained. Costs are high in providing these new delivery systems but it is doubtless hoped that increased profitable business will offset some or all of this front-loaded expenditure. What is clear is that the new delivery systems are being market and competition driven.

Case study I

Your bank has decided to expand its branch network. What strategic factors need to be taken into account when deciding where to locate a new branch?

The corporate decision to expand the branch network has been taken, but in this process the objectives of doing so will have been determined. These corporate objectives would be based upon:

(1) The results of research leading up to the decision, including research into the profitability, competitive factors, and the likely effect on the existing resources of the bank following network expansion.

(2) Defined business development objectives including the priorities for service sales and the type of customers the bank wishes to attract.

Thus it can be seen there are two aspects to consider:

(1) The reasons for network expansion

(2) The identification of where new branches should be located to satisfy these reasons.

Both these stages in the decision-making process are closely connected, as the corporate reasons for expansion influence the selection of suitable areas for new branches.

Before looking for answers to those questions that relate mainly to the choice of a location for a new branch there are some strategic considerations for a bank with a retail network of branches.

In its efforts to serve its customers, the uniformity of distribution of branches needs to be taken into account. There may be areas where poor representation is undermining the credible image of a viable national network. However, an examination of the historical reasons for this lack of national spread will reveal the problems of the bank in expanding into those areas, as will an analysis of the competitors' representation. As a result, it may be considered more expedient, or cost-effective, to concentrate network spread in areas where existing representation is relatively stronger. This could be better than breaking new ground in localities where acceptability of the bank by personal and corporate customers would be much harder and more expensive to achieve.

So what are the other criteria that need to be considered once the corporate decisions have been made and the main guidelines of the bank's expansion policy are known?

Here, marketing aspirations are taken into account and relate to providing for the needs of viable numbers of customers as profitably as possible. Information is therefore required on potential customers' needs in any given locality and figures of potential customer density. If both need and numbers appear to be potentially profitable and viable, the siting of the branch will depend upon finding a suitable spot most convenient to the largest numbers of these potential customers the bank wishes to attract.

The geo-demographic data obtainable from Finpin/Mosaic as outlined in Chapter 3, together with the mapping techniques will help to establish public expenditure zones, financial characteristics of the populations in given areas, existing market share and thus the likely market potential of any given area. This information will also be invaluable when constructing a business plan.

The decision on locality will take into account the analysis of the environmental and social elements which may affect the longer-term growth prospects of a new branch. It is an expensive operation to set up a new office, and the bank will need to be reasonably satisfied that the present profit potential of the locality is likely to continue and that future customer density and traffic flows will not, after a period, become adverse.

Because of the cost of new branches, and therefore the need for profitable growth, the proximity of existing branches and the offices of competitor banks need to be taken into account. If the new branch is close to an existing branch there is a danger of splitting the existing customer base between them, merely because the new branch is that much nearer to some existing customers. This increases the overhead costs which may not be offset by new business to the bank. Equally, it is important to consider the location of competitor banks in relation to their prime customers. Where the siting of a new branch can offer other banks' customers greater convenience this will be a major factor in persuading them to change banks.

Before leaving the question of attacking business already banked, and the potential new business coming into the marketplace, the value and location of existing influential connections should not be overlooked. High on the list will be associations with accountants, solicitors and large employers of labour. In order to establish a new branch quickly the support of 'business providers' such as these will prove invaluable.

The research into the quality of business in the vicinity identified for a new branch and existing connections may also have a bearing on the nature of service the branch should give. A strong personal bias would suggest the need for automatic cash dispensers, whilst corporate potential will require higher levels of technical staffing and ready availability of corporate services provided by the bank's specialist departments. Ease of communication, the distances from these specialist support teams, the ease of car parking and the availability of suitable staff will all influence the final choice of site.

It is doubtful if it will be possible to find a branch location which matches all these requirements perfectly. At the end of the day each aspect will need to be weighed in importance and the final decision on a site will hopefully be the best possible compromise in support of the original corporate objectives.

Case study II

'Segment the market or operate as a financial supermarket': both these approaches are common currency these days when discussing the future of financial services. Compare and contrast the relative merits of these two avenues for a major retail bank with a nationwide network of branches.

Banks have been accused of becoming more like financial supermarkets, which implies a 'catch-all' servicing style. It could also be implied that a supermarket approach reduces the individual care each customer can expect and that it erodes the bank's marketing philosophy of ascertaining a customer's needs and correctly cross-matching these requirements with specific service benefits.

On the other hand, the segmentation approach intimates a higher level of cross-matching or tailoring within the total marketing effort, but, for a bank, this more discerning process has disadvantages that are sometimes overlooked. In a fast changing competitive world, there are opportunities to explore the supermarket style of distribution alongside a segmented market approach as two parts of a bank's overall marketing strategy.

Financial supermarkets

There are many arguments in favour of a bank's using this approach. They are:

- Customers will be attracted by the simplicity of getting all of their financial requirements from one bank. This is largely possible now for, with a few notable exceptions, most key market segments needs can be catered for. Nevertheless there remain some gaps still to be filled – banks do not sell holidays, or offer accounting services except in some exceptional circumstances, and they have only recently begun to introduce 60/90-day term investment facilities similar to those investment accounts and bonds offered by building societies.

- If all the financial services are under one roof, any packaging of facilities to cover a variety of needs is made easier. This would prove attractive to many customers and enhance cross-selling activity to maximise business development opportunities.

- There are organisational benefits to be derived by the banks. Sales efforts can be concentrated and a network of servicing outlets streamlined. It may also be possible to focus more effort on sales training as well as make other marketing cost savings through economies of scale and standardisation.

There are some disadvantages for banks who create financial supermarkets. Sales results might suffer if customers are unwilling to put all their eggs in one basket and, despite the inconvenience, continue to shop around. Moreover, some customers may feel vulnerable when providing one bank with full details of their financial life.

Organisational problems are also evident, not least those created by having a large number of services, some very complex, sold by one sales force. It would be very expensive to have a large number of experts at every outlet to service the needs of a minority of customers.

Finally, although it may be easier more accurately to monitor the sales levels of individual services, this would be at the expense of allocating promotional costs evenly across the board as the supermarket approach presumes each service would be marketed in a similar way with little regard to varying degrees of demand or levels of profitability.

Segmentation

As with financial supermarkets there are disadvantages in a segmented distribution approach. If a segment is difficult to identify or reach there will be a tendency to ignore that element of the customer profile when planning marketing activity. Some of these people would, however, be picked up by the supermarket approach.

Moreover, segments and segment characteristics overlap, so that there could be a multiplicity of effort and a diversity of resources. The 'catch-all' supermarket will generally avoid these problems. Finally there is also a danger that profitable segments will quickly become over-supplied with services. Whilst sales efforts can be concentrated, service efforts will still need to be widespread, since segments are not likely to be located in a small coherent area. As such, the servicing capability of a branch network would still be required even if much of the selling activity was handled centrally or through specially selected locations.

Summary

Bank distribution systems are changing rapidly to meet changing customer requirements and also as a result of competition and new technology opening up markets which were previously considered unprofitable.

Automated delivery systems reduce customer contact. Finding ways to retain and maintain a personal relationship with customers will be a major challenge in the future.

There are various distribution systems, and as marketing activity by the bank increases and expands into new areas, these systems, whether direct, vertical, horizontal or multichannel, become more significant to the banks as alternatives to the direct (branch-orientated) system used in the past.

The changing characteristics of financial services are enabling new delivery systems to be introduced in different segments of the personal and corporate markets. Even so, before introducing these delivery systems, they must conform with the longer-term corporate objectives and not merely be a reaction to competitive activity in the marketplace.

When choosing distribution channels, consideration needs to be given to whether they are likely to be cost-effective, whether they deliver services to the right audiences when customers want them and, finally, whether they are suitable for delivering those services required by the chosen segments.

There are many marketing issues affecting the current network size of a retail bank including

- The bank's future market share and profit aspirations;

- Where the prospective target markets are situated;

- The future requirements of chosen market segments and how various delivery systems can be used to provide services;

- The role of convenience and availability and the cost and profit implications associated with these two factors;

- The location in relation to the competition and other branches;

- The likelihood of further new delivery systems which may provide a more cost-effective distribution system than opening a branch;

- The part which can be played by using other marketing mix elements – price and promotion – as an alternative business acquisition method to creating a new branch;

- The availability of staff to man the new branch.

Specialised offices are being introduced as a way to improve standards of service and exploit business development opportunities among key customer groups. There are many benefits to the bank and its customers from introducing specialised branches. The main benefits to the bank are concentration of expertise, cost savings and enhancement of business development results. The benefits to the customer include higher standards of service including advice and support and possibly lower prices.

Technology is influencing the way the marketing mix can be used, the choice of market segments, the operation of the bank and not least consumer behaviour. The effect of technology on these marketing and operational areas should be understood and future developments watched very closely.

Revision questions

1 Bank branches have been the traditional delivery system for bank services. What are the marketing issues which need to be considered in order to establish whether they will remain so?

2 The introduction of technology is enabling the bank to use more than

just a direct distribution system. Describe the main distribution alternatives and illustrate how each might be used by a bank as a delivery system.

3 Using a personal market service and corporate market service of your own choice as examples, show how the characteristics of the service and the target markets influence the way(s) they are distributed.

4 Discuss the proposition that, from a marketing point of view, it is better to have bank branches dealing with whatever customers they can get, than have specialist branches dealing with only a limited range of customer.

Part 2
The Management of Marketing

Chapter 9
Organising the Marketing Planning Process

This chapter covers the very important area of planning at corporate and marketing department levels. As a prerequisite to passing on marketing guidelines and objectives to a network of branches, both plans must be compatible and achievable. Branch planning, its role and structure, follow in Chapter 11.

There are many variations of corporate and marketing plans and the examples used in this chapter may differ from the structure of the plans in any one particular bank. What is important is that there is a logical progression from an historical and current analysis of business, through to the setting of objectives and formulation of action programmes to fulfil the planned objectives.

Planning should not be a rigid structure without sufficient flexibility to meet sudden unexpected market changes. Nor is it a process which, by itself, will guarantee success. However, a skilfully prepared marketing plan will keep the organisation's marketing efforts on course. Successful results are more likely to be attained if all available resources are made to work in unison and in a cost effective and efficient manner.

Importance of planning

You plan to market then you market to plan. These few words encapsulate the fundamental reasons behind the marketing planning process. Marketing is the way in which a bank achieves prosperity; it requires the identification of market needs and their subsequent conversion into positive demand. Obviously, there is a time lag between identifying market requirements and satisfying them. This period is also the marketing planning period, and involves accurately determining customer needs, setting objectives and deciding what action is required to achieve stated aims. Once again, note that the starting point of marketing planning is the identification of customers' needs – as has been said before, marketing starts in the marketplace.

Marketing plans governing the sale of financial services can be defined as an administrative and management system to control future volume growth, profits, costs and market share in accordance with pre-ordained and quantifiable objectives. Without a clearly laid down system, a bank's marketing effort will lack direction, co-ordination, purpose and the ability to measure the success or failure of its efforts. A plan should be the driving force for all activities aimed at increasing revenue and volume growth. It takes a considerable time to collect all the information required to construct a marketing plan, so it should be taken seriously. However, the marketing results will be influenced by the quality of the plan. It should also be noted that this quality stems from actual management judgement in assessing the opportunities, formulating fresh objectives and constructing the programme of activity which will fulfil those objectives – the information gathering process is not an end in itself. Undoubtedly, the first marketing plan will have deficiencies both in the type and amount of data collected but also in judging what marketing opportunities exist. Selecting priorities and setting objectives also requires a depth of experience and understanding. Marketing skill and astute judgement will improve through the experience gained from refining the marketing planning process over several planning periods. After all, marketing is a practical and constantly evolving management science. This again highlights the important fact that marketing plans play a supporting role in improving effective marketing and management, and are not a substitute for it.

The marketing plan format can be tailored to any shape which best fits the background problems, conditions and circumstances that the planning process is addressing. However, marketing plans and indeed any sort of structured plans all make similar major contributions to the systematic growth of business.

More particularly the main benefits of planning are as follows:

(1) Plans provide a control system which enables marketing activity to be co-ordinated, focused and measured. Without the detailed objectives stated in the plan it would be impossible to monitor progress.

(2) The requirement to gather information on which a marketing plan can be based is also a time to reflect on past results. In this way, management is compelled to assess past performance, and the quality of previous plans, with a view to improving performance and quality in the future. If some of the assumptions and

objectives in the past are shown to have been unrealistic this will encourage the planner to be more careful when thinking ahead.

(3) When there are clearly defined objectives that are accepted as realistic at all levels, planning will stimulate the organisation to make the maximum effort. Good communication is of course a prerequisite.

Corporate plans

Corporate plans are not the same as marketing plans but they will include the bank's broad marketing aspirations.

Corporate and marketing plans are drawn up within two distinct cycles of time. The first cycle is the preparatory period and entails the collection of input from all sections of the bank. This input will be influenced by the analysis of previous results and will thereby indicate priorities for the next plan.

One department which will make a major contribution to the preparation of a corporate plan will be the bank's marketing department. Having gathered whatever data is available, a corporate plan is formulated which will give a lead to the individual plans of departments and divisions of the bank – this is the second cycle and is covered later in this chapter.

The corporate plan will stipulate short-, medium- and long-term objectives. These periods are, normally, short term up to one year, medium term say two to five years and long term over five years. Figure 9.1 will help to put this structure in perspective.

Because of the contribution from every corner of the bank, this process is sometimes known as 'bottom up/top down' planning. However, information also moves sideways between departments so that the objectives of each can be blended with the others – they are, therefore, examined for compatibility. It is the function of the corporate planning process to identify and resolve areas of likely conflict of interest between the various departments of the bank.

There are other advantages in having a systematic approach to planning at corporate level:

(1) Management is forced to think about problems and try to anticipate future events.

(2) Constraints are clearly identified and specific consideration can be given to overcoming them.

(3) Many opportunities for business growth are revealed and the bank's

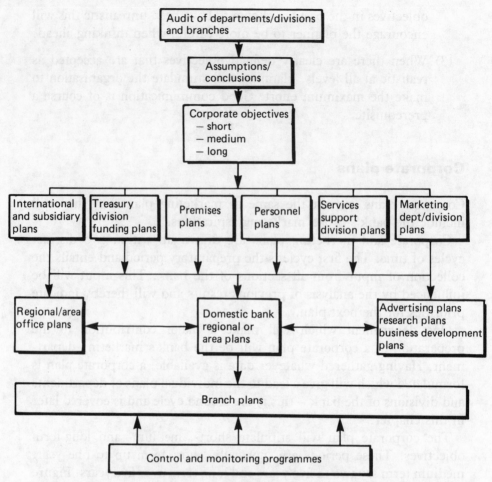

Fig. 9.1 Corporate plan structure. The general managers of the bank will need to ensure there is no conflict in the various plans. For example, corporate staffing levels are the responsibilities of Personnel Division but marketing requirements will influence employee levels and even the qualities of some of those recruited

resources can be quantified to see which of, and how best, these growth opportunities should be exploited.

(4) Efforts at all levels are directed and co-ordinated.

(5) Planning objectives allows performance standards to be measured and responsibility for results to be pinpointed.

Interpreting corporate objectives

As the corporate plan is the driving force, corporate objectives must be set very carefully. Unrealistic aims, or those which are not challenging

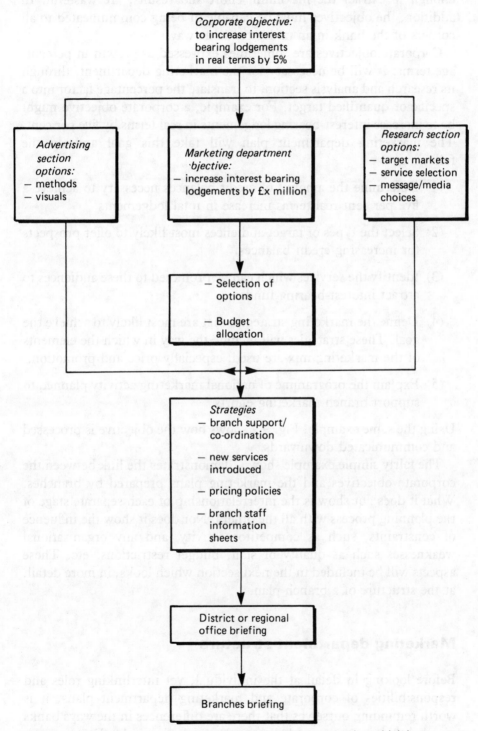

Fig. 9.2 Structure of a section of the marketing department plan which interprets and communicates the objective

enough to extract the maximum effort and results, are wasteful. In addition, the objectives must be capable of being communicated to all corners of the bank in an understandable way.

Corporate objectives are sometimes expressed as growth in percentage terms. It will be necessary for the marketing department, through its research and analysis section, to translate the percentage factor into a specific or quantified target. For example, a corporate objective might be to increase interest-bearing lodgements in real terms by five per cent. The marketing department plan will take this goal and do the following:

(1) Determine the amount of credit balances necessary to achieve a five per cent real terms increase in total lodgements.

(2) Select the types of target audiences most likely to offer prospects for increasing credit balances.

(3) Identify the services which can be promoted to these audiences to attract interest-bearing funds.

(4) Define the marketing strategies that are most likely to achieve the goal. These strategies will include the way in which the elements of the marketing mix are used, especially price and promotion.

(5) Explain the programme of national marketing activity planned to support branch marketing efforts.

Using the same example, Fig. 9.2 shows how the objective is processed and communicated downwards.

The fairly simple example shown, demonstrates the link between the corporate objectives and the marketing plans prepared by branches. What it does not show is the interrelationship of each separate stage of the planning process with all the others. Nor does it show the influence of constraints, such as competitor activity, and any organisational weaknesses such as quality of staff, budget restrictions, etc. These aspects will be included in the next section which looks, in more detail, at the structure of a branch plan.

Marketing department structure

Before looking in detail at the individual, yet interlinking roles and responsibilities of corporate and marketing department plans, it is worth reminding ourselves that there are differences in the ways banks marshal their resources and allocate the marketing tasks. For example, Lloyds Bank does not currently have a marketing department, and prefers to split the main marketing functions among other divisions. It has a Communications Division responsible for internal and external communication including advertising, publicity, and public relations. Service development and service enhancement comes under the domain of a Retail Banking Division and a planning section is responsible for co-ordinating the activities and deciding the future direction and shape of Lloyds Bank.

Nevertheless, within Lloyds, all the marketing functions can be fully undertaken, albeit they are not bound together within what would perhaps be described as a conventional marketing department. It is not possible to cater in this book for the differing ways marketing roles and responsibilities are allocated within the major banks. Readers should digest the resource requirements of marketing outlined here, and study their own organisation in order to understand the rationale behind the arrangements across the divisions and departments of their banks.

Overall, the organisation of the departments collectively responsible for marketing must allow for flexibility and adaptability in a rapidly changing world. This requires an outward attitude by people in marketing coupled with a high level of motivation. Figure 9.3 shows the main sections and a number of subsections to be found in a typical bank marketing department. The titles also indicate the way in which

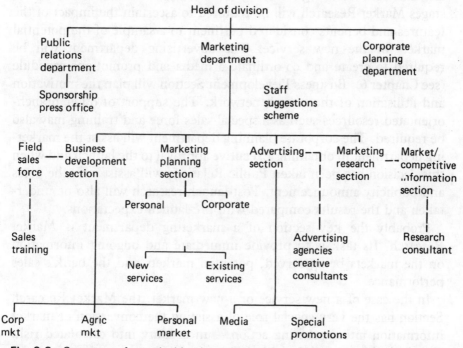

Fig. 9.3 Structure of a typical bank marketing department

responsibilities can be shared. This illustration also highlights the vertical reporting lines.

In the following areas much closer liaison, which extends beyond horizontal reporting, will be necessary between many of the sections:

(1) New service development and service improvement
(2) Improving sales performance
(3) Corporate planning short-, medium- and long-term.

These three main areas of activity and responsibility cover a wide spectrum, but the development and launch of a new service probably provides the best illustration of a marketing organisation at work.

All marketing departments are expected to work to financial budgets. To obtain the best results from the most effective use of these funds will require a close association between the management of corporate planning, public relations and marketing department.

New service development – illustration (see also Chapter 4)

This process begins with an idea and Market Research will be required to identify market potential and the nature of any of the competitive alternatives. Marketing Planning will develop the idea and at various stages Market Research will be required to ascertain the impact of the features and benefits considered pertinent to a sample of the potential market for the new service. The advertising department will be required to create and co-ordinate a media and promotions schedule (see Chapter 6). Business Development Section will plan the motivation and utilisation of the branch network. The support of other branch-orientated resources such as a special sales force and training may also be required. The corporate planning department will assist the marketing department in obtaining Executive approval to the launch and when this decision has been taken Public Relations will assist with the press and publicity announcement. Post-launch research will also be undertaken and the results compared with pre-launch expectations.

Probably the key section of a marketing department is Market Research. Its task is to provide immediate and ongoing information on the markets being served, potential markets and the bank's sales performance.

In the case of a new service or a new market, the Market Research Section has the very special role of assisting the conversion of market information into marketing action – uncertainty into calculated risk. This is the heart of all decisions where correct interpretation of data by

Market Research helps to minimise the risk of the executive's making the worst decision.

Planning role of marketing department

Before we examine in some depth a marketing plan which could be suitable for a high street branch of one of the major retail banks, it is worth examining the role and content of a plan which might be used in the bank's marketing department. Although the aims of a branch marketing plan and a marketing department plan are similar, the tasks each performs are different. A marketing department plan has a much wider role; it provides the links between the corporate plan requirements and branch marketing plans but also is a plan in its own right. Marketing departments have responsibility for many developing business areas including new services, network shapes, national advertising, research programmes responding to major competitive pressures, marketing education and so on. These plans also include medium- and longer-term marketing objectives taking a lead from the longer-term corporate aspirations so these can be ultimately fulfilled by advance preparation for future marketing activity.

Branch plans may address some of these issues, but they seldom extend beyond one year and generally do not include some of the marketing mix issues such as pricing, distribution and advertising. Nevertheless, the branch marketing plan has an important part to play – it is the cutting edge of the bank's total marketing efforts in the chosen marketplaces and, as such, needs to dovetail with the marketing department plan. It must also gel with any other marketing plans in the organisation which might impact on branch efforts. Synergy through harnessing all the various marketing forces into one co-ordinated activity can best be achieved by having a central marketing plan (Fig. 9.4).

Very few bankers will gain firsthand experience from working in a marketing department. Nevertheless, it is worth while spending a little time identifying broad areas of responsibility which need to be considered in a marketing department plan.

The following is only a sample selection of those business facets which impact at head office rather than regional or branch level and therefore need to be considered as part of a plan compiled by a marketing department:

(1) Review of corporate objectives and quantification into revenue and volume growth targets.

(2) Review of all bank chosen markets and potential markets.

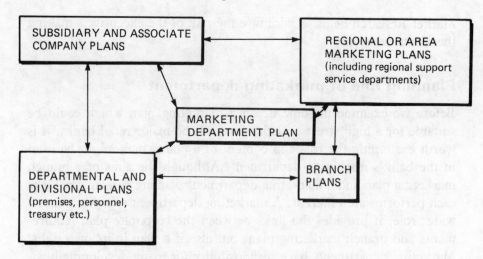

Note: The channels used for communicating between the four segments and the areas of responsibility shown above will be dictated by corporate policy and may well vary between the banks.

Fig. 9.4 Central marketing plan

(3) Review of past performance and trends.

(4) Strengths, weaknesses, opportunities and threats analysis and summary on which marketing management assumptions and recommendations can be based.

(5) Objectives, strategies and activity programmes by segmented markets. The market segments could merely be broken into corporate and personal or refined further into much smaller sub-groups each with its own tailored marketing plan.

(6) Advertising and promotional programmes and publicity material requirements. These will include details covering budgets and monitoring effectiveness.

(7) Service development and enhancement programmes including service rationalisation costs and profitability projections by service or groups of services. This section would also include pricing policy and the alternatives, together with other user benefits/ competitor features comparisons.

(8) Branch network and other distribution systems development programmes.

(9) Marketing personnel utilisation and allocation. This will include educational requirements and improving the co-ordination and support systems throughout the organisation.

There are many other aspects that a marketing department plan will need to consider specifically and which may well fall outside the scope of a plan constructed and implemented at branch level. However, this list demonstrates again the importance of constructing a plan based upon the chosen goals and circumstances. There is no ideal framework for a plan that will cater for all circumstances or situations. But a brief outline of a marketing department plan could well be as in Fig. 9.5.

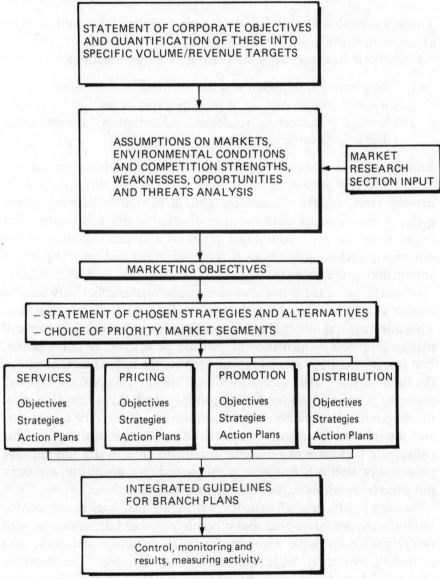

Note: No budget is included in the above. If the budget is pre-determined it will affect the choice of action at the time the marketing objectives are set.

Fig. 9.5 Marketing department plan structure

If the cost of implementing the plan is established after the activity programmes have been agreed, then a budget statement will appear towards the end of the planning process.

Relationship between corporate and marketing planning functions

This is a difficult area and the relationship will vary from bank to bank as has been highlighted at the beginning of this chapter.

Every bank has three basic marketing planning functions:

(1) The planned production and administration of services;
(2) Financial control over its marketing expenditure;
(3) Developing marketing strategies and activities to meet stated growth or revenue objectives.

Bearing in mind that each of these functions can be departmentalised, there could be a conflict between them, especially in three major areas namely: time, capital and labour. Thus it is vital to have an overall policy – the corporate policy – to resolve any conflict of interest that might arise between marketing aspirations and other sections of the organisation whose job it is to control personnel and other aspects of administering the network.

In recent years there has also been a personal conflict between the banker as an administrator, as he was, and his new role as a salesman. This dilemma was also highlighted in Chapter 1. Therefore, an overall planning process, which includes setting objectives, is fundamental. Not just for harmony but also to ensure that the individual elements of the bank all pull in the same direction. One key part of the total bank planning process is the marketing plan(s) which takes direction from the corporate plan and also has the authority to call on the operational and administrative sections to achieve the corporate business goals. The paramount objectives of a bank are usually to grow in size and improve profitability – all other objectives are generally subordinate, although not everybody would agree with this statement.

As has already been shown, the marketing plan makes one contribution to the corporate plan. But other divisions and departments, with responsibility for large resources such as premises and staff, also contribute by stating their requirements and objectives. The corporate plan should ensure harmony by taking account of all these issues and seeking objectives that are acceptable to all sections of the bank.

This is not an easy task for corporate planners who additionally plan over a longer time-scale and include in their corporate plans considerations on major issues such as network spread, choice of markets, at home and abroad, and the growth of other subsidiary companies.

Financial planning is also contained in the corporate plan. This is when strategic growth and profit ratio goals are set. In turn, the marketing department plan takes these financial objectives into account when choosing the marketing growth areas and determining which services should be promoted in priority to others.

The need for close liaison between marketing and corporate planning is self-evident. It would be impossible to set corporate growth objectives without sufficient data on which to base these judgements. Much of this data is obtained from the previous marketing plans. Therefore a number of similarities will emerge between the corporate and marketing plans if the desired level of fraternisation has been achieved. Equally, setting corporate objectives which are totally unattainable by marketing plans is a waste of time.

Resources available to achieve the marketing plan objectives might also be detailed in the corporate plan, and this too will give a lead to organisational and administrative sections of the bank. It was once said, rather unfairly, that most head office departments and divisions of a bank were only interested in keeping the 'ship' well painted and ready to sail. When the marketing department moved the vessel and put a strain on the machinery, the administrative sections were upset. In today's environment it is necessary for all sections of the bank to support those who actually compete in the marketplace irrespective of wear and tear considerations.

The need for flexibility

Marketing in the banking industry is evolving rapidly, and although a plan provides the basic programme for action over a given period other competitive activity may intervene and force a counter-measure at short notice. Changes to a marketing programme should not be taken lightly; the essence of structuring the plan in the first place is to provide a period of concerted effort with co-ordination at all levels, so attaining sustained progress in a chosen direction by the whole organisation.

Apart from the need to retain flexibility of action within a planning period, the way in which plans are compiled also needs to be tailored and to have contingency elements if, ultimately, progress does not work out according to plan. This emphasises again that there is no set format for a plan which will meet all possible issues and circumstances. Not all the elements of a conventional plan might be needed, especially if a set of steps is required to overcome a problem at short notice.

For example, if a bank identified that it was losing market share and profit in a priority market segment, a plan to counter this should not include 'back to the drawing-board research' which would take many months. These circumstances require a prompt remedial solution. Some strategic thinking is required about the market and how performance has faltered compared with that of competition. Therefore, in these circumstances, fresh objectives included in a plan of action would require a high level of management skill based on information which could be gleaned quickly, so that any change to the marketing mix had a reasoned basis and was not just a shot in the dark.

Thus it is clear that plans are a tool of marketing and can assume many shapes, depending upon the job they are required to do.

Whether an existing plan is being amended, or another plan compiled to meet unexpected but important competitor activity, a fresh assessment of the situation is necessary. Revised objectives may also be required and this shows that plans can be updated where conditions merit despite the cost and disruption this may cause.

Case study

You are the chief executive of a bank which operates in a number of financial markets. Performance could definitely be improved: profit opportunities are missed: scarce resources are occasionally misapplied: and the communication process needs to be reconsidered.

You wish to issue fresh guidelines to those responsible for researching and preparing the marketing plan. Describe four key issues on which a marketing plan should concentrate. What guidance will you give on each issue?

It is clear that profitability, or lack of it, is the prime issue, and it should be stated at the outset that marketing planning, including the setting of business and marketing objectives, is usually profit driven.

We are not told how the chief executive knows performance is below par and that profit opportunities are being missed. Some research may have been carried out or perhaps marketing targets, which are considered reasonable, are not being attained. Alternatively, it might simply be that the bank is comparing its profit performance and growth with its competitors' achievements. Whatever information is already available will be valuable when trying to assess the magnitude of the problem and identify a course of action to improve matters.

Urgency required

Before guidance can be given to those responsible for preparing a marketing plan designed to improve sales and profitability, some research will be necessary. However, the urgency of the situation must not be overlooked, and this in turn will influence the areas of research, depth of information and methods used to obtain the information. Nevertheless, the research programme, despite the urgency, will need to look closely at all the elements of the marketing mix; especially how well the bank promotes its services. Establishing if customers understand the benefits of the services is clearly paramount. The question implies that market saturation has not been reached and thus there is ample scope to improve sales of current services in existing markets.

Areas of research

Prior to establishing planning priorities and courses of action, a plan will need to concentrate on analysing the present situation. Concentrating on the following would be beneficial:

- Customer requirements and those segments of the market which are more profitable than others.

- Underlying reasons for poor performance; is it communication difficulties internally, externally, training problems, morale?

- Marketing mix. Impact and effect of pricing, relevance of service features and benefits, advertising and promotional deficiencies and the way in which the services are distributed.

- Nature and effect of competitor marketing activity on performance.

- A Strengths, Weaknesses, Opportunities and Threats (SWOT) summary to highlight what changes are needed to improve service, sales and profitability.

Armed with this information, including the identification of customers' needs, profitable segments, and target markets, attention can now focus on the elements of the marketing mix. Marketing staff responsible for service features, pricing, advertising, promotion, and branch business development activity generally, will need to formulate new objectives based upon the changes considered necessary in the situation analysis review and assumptions already made. The amount of guidance needed will depend upon many factors, not least their existing expertise.

Guidelines must also ensure co-ordination of all the various contributions to the new plan.

The market mix

Thus the chief executive will be looking for a marketing plan which establishes service sales priorities, considers enhancements to meet customer requirements and assesses costs and profitability arising from these improvements. As the bank will set revised sales/profit targets, these projections should match the executive's aspirations. As a separate exercise, or as part of enhancing the service, pricing and pricing policy will need to be reconsidered. Customer and competitor reaction to price changes will need to be gauged. Where a service is price sensitive in a chosen target market segment, the effect on sales

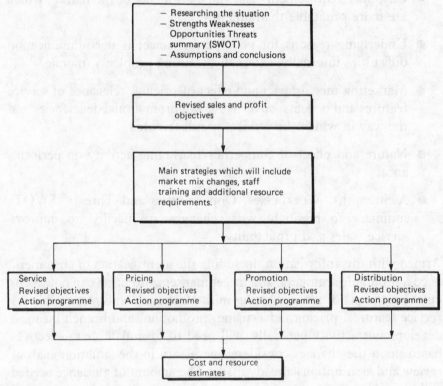

Fig. 9.6

volume, and any 'spin-off' business opportunities, should be assessed. It is worth stating again that the corporate profit objective should not be overlooked when making pricing decisions.

Another way to improve profitability is to cut costs, and here the major consideration for a retail bank is the overheads incurred from having a branch network. Reaching customers with services is expensive, and part of the guidance given to those responsible for devising and implementing a new marketing plan will be to look at the service range and consider other ways of distributing them. New electronic systems are constantly evolving, of which home banking, EFTPOS, and debit cards are just three that will help to change the face of a branch network and the attendant incurred costs over the next few years.

Finally those responsible for the advertising and sales promotion plan will need to be given guidance. Advertising is a vast subject, but even with the best range of services in the marketplace customers will need to be persuaded to use them, especially if take-up is required in large numbers. Getting the promotional package and timing right so that results justify the promotional cost will be vital to the task of achieving the corporate sales/profit objectives. The problem stressed there were deficiencies in the communication process so that those responsible for internal and external communication would be told to look very closely at all the elements of the promotional mix and their total impact on staff and customers.

A broad outline of a plan could well be as in Fig. 9.6. Prior to implementation of the new plan, and in order to gain acceptance, satisfactory answers should be forthcoming to these questions.

- Will the plan work?
- Is it challenging?
- Is it flexible enough to meet further changing market conditions?
- How easy will it be to monitor progress?

Summary

You plan to market and then you market to plan. In this way effort, through the plan, has direction and co-ordination, and there is the ability to measure and control progress.

Marketing plans should be capable of adapting to changing market conditions. This does not mean that, for example, it is necessary to react to every competitive innovation, as this would only disrupt the main thrust of your marketing plan. Some flexibility is required, so that tactical action can be taken if activity and results are threatened by a competitor. Flexibility is also required when drawing up a plan so that the elements focus correctly on the important areas and take into account how quickly results are required from a planned programme of activity.

A corporate plan is the main driving force for marketing plans and activity at all other operational and administrative levels within the bank. The corporate plan and its objectives should be based on input collated from all areas in the organisation. The key to corporate and marketing planning is communication using top down/bottom up methods.

The advantages of systematic planning include the need to think about problems, identify resources and constraints, quantify opportunities and assess what efforts can be made by whom, where and when to achieve stated objectives. It also enables performance standards to be measured, and pinpoints responsibility for results. Corporate objectives must be carefully formulated, be realistic yet challenging, and also capable of being communicated in an understandable manner to those responsible for achieving the corporate goals.

The organisation, role and responsibilities of marketing functions and marketing departments vary from bank to bank. However, the underlying marketing resources, nature of work and requirements remain, no matter how these elements are arranged within the bank's basic infrastructure.

A marketing department plan is a key link between the corporate objectives and marketing activity at all other levels. It is also responsible for ensuring that the marketing activities of subsidiaries, area offices and other departments are in unison. The marketing department is also responsible for achieving the maximum support and impact in the marketplace, by co-ordinating and correctly timing these various plans and activity programmes.

There are some major differences in the role and responsibilities between a corporate plan and a marketing department plan. These differences should be fully appreciated.

The logic of the sequence of corporate and marketing plans together with the content of the various stages must be understood. It is worth while comparing the outlines of the plans in this chapter with an outline of a corporate or departmental plan in your bank to see how they differ. If there are major variations in the structures, try and understand why. When studying these plans concentrate on the interrelationship of the elements by using hypothetical objectives and tracing how these objectives would ripple through the various stages.

Revision questions

1 What problems may arise if a bank does not have a written marketing plan?
2 Describe the functions and responsibilities of a corporate plan and a marketing department plan. Show how the two plans interrelate.
3 Describe the way in which your bank organises its marketing planning at various levels. Show how a corporate objective of your choice is communicated to all areas of the bank.
4 Describe how a marketing department is organised and highlight the vertical and horizontal communication that is vital to this department's success.
5 Structure the planning steps you would expect to see at corporate and marketing department level when considering whether or not to expand the existing network of branches.

Chapter 10
Improving the Marketing Planning Process

Implementing the planning system, by itself, will not guarantee success. Other factors will play a major part in the results achieved. Moreover, it should be appreciated that marketing planning is a process of gradual refinement. The first plan will inevitably lack some information and therefore quality. A planner's skill in interpreting the data, and setting objectives based on information gathered, will improve as experience grows over time.

Setting objectives is just one factor which will need skill and understanding. Harnessing the right resources and motivating all those who are required to achieve stated goals is another crucial requirement for the successful outcome from the marketing planning process. Man management is an attribute that not all managers possess. Many readers must have suffered the frustrations and setbacks of poor management and have seen how this undermines the achievements that otherwise could be derived from a well-structured marketing plan.

This chapter looks at a number of especially important areas which can impact on the final outcome from creating and operating a marketing plan. These areas include the following:

(1) The special role and benefits of the analysis and assumptions section of a plan;

(2) The importance of objectives, strategies and tactics including the relevance of management by objectives;

(3) Considerations relating to the setting of challenging yet realistic sales targets.

(4) Ways in which branch staff can help to create the best possible environment in which to develop the business.

The situation analysis

All elements of a marketing plan are, in given circumstances both relevant and important parts of the whole process. However, if the base data gathered during the early stages of the planning process is poor, it follows that the overall quality of the plan will suffer. So starting off on the right path is the key to the outcome and, as such, the situation analysis, and its strengths, weaknesses, opportunities and threats summary, have a special significance. The situation analysis involves systematically gathering relevant usable information which, when summarised, is the raw material used by managers when setting, objectives.

This crucial step is also important because it helps management understand the environment in which the business is operating, focuses the mind on what needs to be done, and helps to eradicate or confirm subjective thinking. The situation analysis includes a review of past performance and tries to establish the quality and accuracy of previous objectives by relating historic targets to results. The task of setting objectives is not an exact science and the situation analysis should help to improve management's judgement in an effort to establish goals which are challenging yet attainable.

It should not be overlooked that the situation analysis is ongoing and trend data is fundamental. This highlights the point that it is not an exercise carried out just once a year for the purpose of writing a marketing plan. Collecting data and reviewing performance is a continuous process. In this way the information will be readily available so that action can be taken at any time to exploit a market, attack a competitor or defend a position against unexpected predators.

Most textbooks state that the situation analysis is in four parts:

– An analysis of the economic and social environment
– An analysis of the competitive scene
– A self-analysis
– A summary of all this information collated under the headings, Strengths, Weaknesses, Opportunities and Threats (SWOT).

The ability to gather information, and the type of information required, varies at different levels in a bank. A marketing department has extensive research resources, whereas the manager of a branch has less research capability and, in any case, will primarily require local rather than national data. The following is a 'shopping list' of the type of information that might be gathered at most hierarchical levels in a bank. The list is not exhaustive but demonstrates what might be considered useful. However, information which is seen as useful to a marketing department might not be so relevant to a branch manager. A choice has to be made, and the time available for gathering information will also dictate the final selection of areas of research.

Economic and Social Analysis
(To plan successfully a retail bank and its branches must know what is happening in the marketplace.)

Information could include:

● Population characteristics (numbers, demographic profiles or socio-economic bands)

● Employment and prospects

● Industry growth, types of industry and changes in profile

● Retail growth prospects

● Inflation trends and impact on real income, purchasing power and consumer spending, industrial costs

● Consumerism and likely trends

● Educational standards and trends

This information is most easily gathered by the research section of a marketing department on a countrywide basis. Nevertheless, branch managers can collate similar information relevant to their location.

Competitor Analysis
(First identify who the competitors are, and it may be necessary to restrict comparison to broad market or service areas to avoid being 'swamped' by a mass of information.)

Information could be marshalled and gathered as follows:

● Profit performance statistics and operating ratio comparisons such as earnings per share, post tax return on average total assets, post tax return on average equity. Profit per head of staff.

● Market performance comparisons including lending and lodgement growth and ancillary service sales. Cash dispenser networks and share of plastic user markets. Computer-based service sales results.

● Market share trends including account gains/losses, consumer lending and term lending share, account relationships in personal, professional, commercial, industrial and agricultural market shares.

● Marketing philosophy and strategy comparisons including the way in which the marketing mix is used. Major changes in strategy which could include new services, outlets, location variations and ways in which the domestic network and staff are utilised.

Much of this information can be monitored locally by branch managers and should provide a clear picture of competitive threats so that counter-measures can be planned.

Self-analysis

The information we can gather about ourselves is wide-ranging. Some of the key areas of analysis include:

- Image/reputation among personal and corporate market sectors and includes customer and non-customer views

- Effectiveness of staff training

- Level of staff morale

- Communication effectiveness

- Marketing skills and performance

- Ability of organisation at all levels to innovate, cope with change including technical, legal, social, environmental, financial and consumer demands

- Computer accounting sophistication and flexibility to accept new services and provide marketing and financial information in the most desirable form.

Any bank which fails closely to monitor and review these aspects of its operation is hardly likely to remain a competitive force in the financial services industry for very long.

The SWOT summary

The final step is the Strengths, Weaknesses, Opportunities and Threats (SWOT) summary which gathers the information together and marshals it in a digestible form. Some aspects could be regarded as strengths and weaknesses and some market conditions pose threats as well as offer market opportunities. For example, an increase in consumer financial awareness could be a threat to lodgements (the so-called current account endowment) as surplus funds are more actively managed by customers to earn higher rates of interest, but this also provides greater opportunities to sell profitable ancillary services to a more enlightened customer base.

Again, the SWOT summary needs to be tailored to the issues posed, and there is no set content or structure. But whatever it contains the information must accurately reflect the data, including trends, gathered in the situation analysis. The 1986 Institute of Bankers Cambridge Seminar on Bank Strategies for the 1990s contains a case study entitled 'Century Bank Plc' which includes an in-depth SWOT summary. This case study, is reproduced at the end of this chapter. It should be carefully read for it is a good example of a comprehensive SWOT summary based on a detailed situation analysis.

This case study is a highly detailed SWOT analysis and covers strategic issues. A marketing department SWOT summary will be somewhat different in content and emphasis. It could well include assumptions and facts relating to the following:

Environmental aspects
Economic factors
Technical changes
Social and cultural trends
Political and legal changes

External marketing influences
Consumer attitudes
Competitor activity and strategies
Professional and other valuable account connections
Account relationships (profiles of both personal and corporate)
Representation and spread including special advantages/disadvantages
    re other competitors
Service range and special features/benefits
Gaps in service range matched to consumer demand potential

Internal factors including
Marketing skills and planning capabilities
Marketing information and control systems
Organisational support capabilities
Use of market mix
Quality of staff
Service penetration
Account relationships, number, type, demographic profile, etc.

At a branch level, the first SWOT summary may be even more basic in its coverage, but the important point is that the analysis and the summary is done and becomes a discipline which can be improved over time.

The following are a sample of headings under which any branch manager could collect relevant information and make comparisons in a SWOT format with his major competitors who also operate in his catchment area:

(1) Favourability of branch and sub-branch locations in his catchment area;

(2) Appearance and suitability of branch premises including special factors such as car parking;

(3) Special services including cash dispensers and other automated facilities, and corporate or account manager support systems;

(4) Standards of branch service including strengths/expertise of management team;

(5) Business connections especially those with accountants, solicitors, insurance brokers, estate agents, schools and larger employers of labour;

(6) Shared business and assessment of primary banker/secondary banker situations;

(7) Staff numbers, staff involvement in community;

(8) Marketing activity/impact especially where promotional effort has a strong area or local bias;

(9) Any other aspects which might impact on future marketing plans and activity.

Even from this broad list of areas which could be covered it is clear that some perceived weaknesses may be impossible to resolve in the short term whereas others can, with little expense or effort, be quickly overcome. The relative ease with which weaknesses can be eradicated may also be a factor when marshalling the information into a SWOT summary.

When considering the requirements of a situation analysis, it may help to get the right stance and understanding of the practical issues if the following questions are posed:

(1) What are the main issues requiring solutions?

(2) What information is required in order to consider these issues?

(3) What relevant information can be gathered?

(4) How quickly is a solution required to the problems posed, and does this impact on research areas and methods?

(5) What will it cost to gather all the information and is the potential expenditure acceptable in relation to the perceived value of the information?

Objectives, strategies and tactics

These three words are the core of a marketing plan and must gel
together in an interactive way so that each supports the other. Having
undertaken a situation analysis, and summarised the information
gathered, assumptions can then be drawn. These assumptions on the
problems and opportunities facing the planner provide the basis on
which objectives will be established.

As such, objectives are, in turn, a guide for planning suitable
strategies and tactics, but they also form the basis of the budgeting
issues and the evaluation of performance, and they assist in the process
of determining corrective action when goals are exceeded or not
achieved. From this it can be seen that setting the best objectives is
crucial. If poor objectives are set, based on the lack of quality
information or influenced by a low standard of marketing management,
then the whole planning process is likely to fail.

There is no set of guidelines which will ensure that the objectives
chosen are the most appropriate in all conditions. Nevertheless some
factors should be kept in mind when developing goals:

- They should be developed in such a way that they can accomplish
  the corporate and marketing objectives.

- Everybody and every section of the organisation should have goals
  that are realistic within the context of the various roles and duties
  performed.

- There must be flexibility so that if objectives are unrealistic the
  requirements of the plan can be revised.

- Finally all objectives should be challenging and stretch the whole
  organisation collectively and individual sections and departments in
  it to a level of excellence.

Once the goals or objectives have been set, the marketing strategy can
be developed. This marketing strategy encompasses the marketing mix
elements; how they will be blended and used to achieve the stated
objectives. Undoubtedly there will be many marketing mix combina-
tions or alternatives and it is unlikely any organisation will wish for, or
can afford, the time and expense of trying them all. So, once again, the
planner is faced with the problems of making a choice and then putting
the chosen strategies into some sort of priority order. Managerial
judgement will play a vital role in this selection process.

Finally, having defined its targets (objectives) and selected the various
routes it will take (strategies), tactics will need to be selected. This

requires defining what actions need to be taken, by whom, and at what cost, so that the targets are reached. It may well be necessary to draw up contingency plans in case the first action programmes adopted fail to produce the results required within the given time-span.

The quality of the objectives, strategies and tactics will largely determine the success of the marketing planning process. They form the structural skeleton and for maximum effect must complement each other so that effort and direction are properly co-ordinated.

Sales targets

Sales targets are widely used. They are the almost inevitable outcome of any corporate plan which addresses the question 'what future growth and profit goals in selected markets do we want to achieve? Until recently, banks have tended to set future targets solely on historic results. Now more sophisticated targeting is being undertaken as marketing data becomes computerised. Penetration targets are clearly a fairer system than numbers targets but it is first necessary for information on service usage and customer profile to come together. Traditionally, bank computers have been designed to cope with administrative and clerical records, so new marketing orientated computer programs have had to be developed. Peer grouping a selection of similar sized branches which have a predominance of certain types of business or other characteristics is also widely used. It enables performances to be compared, and this in turn will show some branches within a given peer group to have more marketing opportunity or have been less successful than others.

In theory, targets are generally based on the following planning methods (see Chapter 7):

- Extrapolation planning – where the management simply continues its current strategies and uses the actual profit and sales of the current period as the basis for targets for the next budget period.

- Goal planning – where profit and sales targets are set at a level that will satisfy the executive and shareholders. Managers are then left to accomplish these targets any way they can.

- Optimisation planning – where each aspect and alternative is systematically examined to see its likely impact on profit and sales growth. The optimum targets are then chosen.

Bank planning procedures are still in a relatively early stage of development and there is a lack of precise marketing data, both internally and externally. Therefore, all three planning alternatives are still influencing bank target setting. There is a gradual trend towards optimisation planning as an appreciation of marketing forces and information systems improves.

The planning process leading up to the target setting stage is well covered in previous chapters, but to recap includes the following:

- Review of past performance. Information on sales results and growth will need to be covered as a prelude to new targets.
- Assumptions based on the review which will include conclusions on future areas of opportunity for sales and profit growth.
- Determining key market segments.
- Corporate objectives on which targets for sales and profit growth will be based. (Care should be taken not to confuse objectives with targets. Objectives are short-, medium- and long-term. Targets are specific goals measured in money or volume terms and set for a given budget period.)

It can be seen that corporate objectives provide the parameters for sales targets and the review, including the assumptions of potential, assists the selection of priority targets from the range of available alternatives.

Target criteria

Targets can be specified in terms of either revenue, profit or numbers. A target which merely requires profit or revenue to be increased, but no specific amount is mentioned, hardly portrays a challenging or realistic goal. Moreover, where progress is not capable of being measured, sustaining maximum effort over a given period from the available resources is unlikely.

Additionally, there are a number of other considerations when setting targets at both bank and branch levels:

(1) When setting profit targets a balance is required between a realistic profit, continued competitiveness and ongoing customer loyalty. Short-term profitability is of little benefit if it results in longer-term falling sales or loss of accounts to competitors.

(2) The basis of accurate target setting is a precise analysis of market and market opportunities. This includes an assessment of the demographic profiles of existing customers as well as potential customers.

(3) Setting targets should be a 'top down/bottom up' process. In this

way, the targets set will be credible in the eyes of all staff who are charged with the task of achieving them.

(4) When setting growth targets (either quantified by revenue or sales volumes) it is important to ensure that growth can be handled with existing or available resources. These resources include financial capability, branch network size and location, staffing levels, capabilities and so on. Gaining new customers at a rate which reduces the existing staff capacity to maintain a high level of service to existing account holders is likely to prove counter-productive.

(5) The cost implications of growth targets should not be ignored. Numbers or revenue growth without the prospect of profitability is also counter-productive. This point shows that growth and profit targets cannot be set independently.

(6) Consideration of the alternatives available in the timing of activity is an important aspect. Many bank services and revenue cycles have a seasonality aspect.

Having devised the targets it is prudent to test their relevance with the following questions:

– Are the targets achievable?
– Are the targets consistent with corporate objectives?
– Do they play on the bank's strengths and minimise its weaknesses?
– How do they compare with what is known about competitor targets?
– Do they fully utilise all the bank's resources?

Finally, the monitoring of progress needs to be considered. If the targets prove unattainable or even too easily attainable, then sufficient flexibility should exist to bring them into line with the bank's capabilities before too much time and money is wasted.

Creating the best environment

Customers are the life blood of any bank which offers a range of services to the public. Therefore, 'customer care' is paramount, the ways in which service to the public can be improved are numerous and banks go to considerable expense researching their servicing image and reputation. The public relations department of a bank usually has the main task of ensuring that the mainstream marketing efforts are fully supported through winning the esteem of customers and the public at large.

Without a good reputation for understanding customer problems and requirements a bank will lose existing customers and fail to attract at least its market share of new business. Typical research into the image and reputation of a bank, compared with its major competitors, will involve exploring the responses and perceptions among key customer and non-customer groups to some of these topics:

(1) The bank's ability to make quick decisions;

(2) Ability of the bank to administrate efficiently;

(3) The degree to which the bank is seen to be helpful and friendly;

(4) The professional level of skill and objectiveness exhibited by the bank when giving financial advice;

(5) Appreciation of customer problems shown by the bank and the public's perception on the degree of support they get when times are hard;

(6) Availability of services, approachability and general convenience factors both in terms of opening hours and branch location.

This is not an exhaustive list of questions which would be posed by a bank trying to measure its own esteem and that of its competitors in the marketplace. However, it demonstrates that more is required of a bank than having the right range of products at the right prices, readily available. Banks are still perceived by the public to be much alike and offering a similar range of services. Thus relying on product and price alone will not with this 'all alike' situation generate a higher than normal market share of business. There are, therefore, a number of areas which can be massaged to support the marketing thrust of a bank:

- Service quality
- Promotion of corporate values and separate identity
- Press and media relations
- Public relations and sponsorship
- Customer information and service availability
- Customer convenience
- Staff knowledge and skill

(a)   Service quality

This is the main platform on which a retail bank builds its business. Politeness, efficiency, general attitudes and even the way staff are dressed all play a part in convincing the public that the bank appreciates and can provide the standards its customers want. For most customers, the bank is their local branch and the staff they meet there. Good PR and advertising will not overcome poor service at this level.

All banks receive complaints, and these should be monitored to see which aspects of the service are breaking down. How these complaints are dealt with is also an important facet of 'customer care'. Some banks have gone further in striving for the ultimate in service quality. Specially trained personal bankers in the banking hall, giving customer contact that is not inhibited by bandit screens are now commonplace. Customer newsletters is another feature. As competition in the high street increases, the present burdensome clerical function will need to be replaced to allow more staff time to develop the quality of service and expand the selling role.

(b) Promotion of corporate image

There are four broad groups of people which a bank will wish to convince that it has a distinctive identity and socially responsible corporate goals. These are the shareholders, the government, employees and the public.

Major clearing banks have approached the problem of getting across corporate values and identity in a number of different ways. Some use the logo to good effect – Lloyds Bank's black horse conjures up a picture of a long history of reliability based upon service – the horse is a well-loved servant of man. Midland has animated the griffin and created the slogan of 'the listening bank', the TSB like to say 'yes' and so on.

To the banks, creating the right image, which supports their business growth goals, is now seen as important for them as it is for the major high street stores. Consider for example the different identities portrayed by Woolworth and Marks & Spencer. Existing customers and shareholders will be reassured by effective image and value promotion and, hopefully, targeted non-customers will be attracted to use the bank.

(c) Press and media relations

Media include TV, radio, newspapers and magazines. All are vital communication arteries for a bank. Good media relations are important, so that adverse events, for example a bank defalcation (a member of staff using his/her position in the bank to do something dishonest), are publicised accurately, and worthwhile happenings are given maximum publicity.

The public relations department has the responsibility for ensuring good media relations and for releasing information which would be interesting to the public and promotionally beneficial to the bank. Press conferences and news releases are the main ways of providing the media with this flow of information, especially of new service launches. The extent of the publicity received to support the marketing effort will depend upon the relationship that exists with those who provide the media coverage.

(d) Public relations and sponsorship

Public relations activity and sponsorship are important elements of the communication mix and when used effectively will give valuable support to the bank's mainstream marketing activity. The overall aim of public relations (PR) is to establish and maintain mutual understanding between the bank and the public at large. Good PR material requires features which include newsworthiness, honesty and authenticity. Without these ingredients, little or no impact will be achieved on public attitudes towards the bank and the likelihood that the public will use the services on offer. Sponsorship is also a form of publicity and provides a background promotional activity which can also help to characterise the bank. If a stated corporate aim of the bank is to improve the quality of its customer profile, then sponsorship should be directed to those areas where its selected quality target audiences are likely to see it. It can also be used to enforce the corporate image and logo branding advertising – Lloyds Bank for example sponsors some junior horse-riding competitions, which fit in nicely with its 'black horse' and is compatible with its aim of attracting quality new accounts from the higher educated and wealthier background school-leaver fraternity.

Another example of sponsorship being used to support key corporate aspirations is the Barclays link with the Football League, an association which started in 1987. Barclays Bank wanted to raise its profile in a cost-effective way. Ultimately it will be looking for an increased share in some market segments, especially in the smaller business market.

Barclays' rationale was that the ongoing repetitive nature of the football programme and results would keep the bank in the public eye. It is the national game and has a large following, interest and appeal. The bank had some concern about the 'hooligan' problems but felt that crowd control was improving to a point where families were being enticed back – another broad but important customer group. As part of the sponsorship package, local branches of Barclays Bank are given ten complimentary tickets to all League and League Cup matches. These are used for entertainment purposes, especially business customers. In summary, the sponsorship deal was expensive, but Barclays receive constant coverage in the media at possibly less cost than the alternative of direct advertising.

Local branch managers have an inexpensive vehicle for entertaining customers and non-customers at football matches, and ultimately Barclays will expect new business account acquisitions and an improved share of the personal market.

(e) Customer information and service availability

The main debate currently is on 'hours of opening'. The activity of pressure groups and competition has brought about the return of a Saturday service and some evening opening of branches. Undoubtedly building societies have made inroads into the business traditionally regarded as the banks' because they are open six days a week. It now seems inevitable that banks will follow suit, but in the interim they are using externally located machines to give a 'limited service' extension to their current opening hours. Nevertheless, machines cannot deal with all customer requirements and the business customer has been excluded from using the Saturday service.

In addition to an extension of opening hours, there is also the need to support the marketing efforts of a bank by providing customer information in a readily digestible form. This does not simply relate to leaflets on services but includes a whole spectrum of data including account information. New delivery and information systems are appearing. These include 'home banking' and Prestel using TV terminal links with a bank's own computers, allowing corporate treasurers to collate information and move money from place to place without moving out from their own offices. We may also mention lobby banks, accessible by using a magnetic card in the door and offering a selection of facilities through machines and, most recently, service centres. These are high street locations manned by staff trained to sell the 'popular' services including loans, savings schemes, insurance and money transmission facilities. Making the services and information on services readily available is an essential task in support of the marketing effort.

(f) Customer convenience

Convenience of location is an important factor in gathering new business, and providing existing customers with a viable network of branches and cash dispenser facilities is important for a retail bank.

However, traditional branches are costly to run. The major banks are having to rationalise their branch networks in the face of changing customer requirements and the need to cut costs as margins are eroded through fierce competition for lodgements and lending. Nevertheless, providing customers with service convenience is an important prop for the marketing effort, since 'distribution' is an essential element of the marketing mix.

(g)   Staff knowledge of services

Staff are a very expensive resource. As the emphasis continues to move from a purely clerical function to more of a selling role, their knowledge of services and selling ability takes on greater significance. Motivation, training and creating the right environment in which staff can identify and exploit business opportunities are arguably the greatest challenges facing the major banks. It is a cultural revolution and one which will take time to achieve at all levels.

Having a competitively priced range of services, with attractive customer benefits, is only part of the marketing thrust. Ensuring the staff are capable of selling them is also a crucial factor. In summary, it must be said that all these aspects listed above, have been considered in isolation. In practice, many are linked together and it is combined activity through co-ordinated planning on a number of fronts which will ensure maximum success in supporting the marketing efforts.

Case study

The following case study appeared in the Chartered Institute of Bankers' Cambridge Seminar publication *Bank Strategies for the 1990s*. It highlights the real issues facing a retail bank in the current trading climate and shows how these problems will influence the planning process. The logical development of the plan, the assumptions and decisions taken are also interesting. This study encapsulates and shows the interrelationships of many of the marketing issues considered in the previous chapters.

Century Bank PLC – strategic review

1   Introduction

The strategic review was carried out against the background of the radical changes that are taking place and are expected to occur during the next ten years in the financial markets in the UK. Whilst an overview of likely developments during this period was considered, the time horizon of the strategy which has been formulated has been confined to a period of between three and five years. It was concluded that a shorter period would produce too frequent changes of direction and that, in the case of periods exceeding five years, external factors such as developments in technology and changes in legislation and regulation, as well as economic uncertainty, would make it difficult to produce accurate forecasts.

2 Aims and objectives

(a) To remain an independent clearing bank with the sale and delivery of banking and related financial services remaining as 'core products'.
(b) To expand the range of products and services offered in order to compete effectively in the financial services industry sector.
(c) To be innovative, progressive and responsive to the needs of customers and to ensure that services are provided in the most efficient, productive and cost effective manner.
(d) To continue to achieve a satisfactory rate of return on share-holders' funds to ensure adequate dividends and retentions for future growth.
(e) To develop all aspects of the bank's business in light of varying market opportunities whilst ensuring that there is no undue reliance on a particular sector.
(f) To provide for the career development of all members of staff.

3 Legislative, regulatory and economic background

The changes in the structure of the financial services industry over the next ten years will be derived from a number of factors. The abolition of minimum commissions for Stock Exchange dealings on 27 October 1986, the 'Big Bang', will result in major re-alignments of different and previously competing financial institutions such as clearing banks and stockbrokers to provide the securities dealing and delivery services required by customers. The provisions of the Financial Services Bill, when enacted in 1987, will also contribute further to the blurring of the traditional boundaries between different types of financial institutions. The deregulation entailed in these developments, however, will be balanced by increasing regulatory control and supervision of the participants by the authorities. In clearing banking it is expected that more stringent requirements will be imposed in respect of capital adequacy and prudential control of advances and that proposed revisions to the Banking Act 1979 will produce stricter criteria to be satisfied before banking licences are granted.

The likely changes in the nature and status of building societies will require to be taken into account.

The general economic environment is influenced by the policies of the government which is in the first year of its second term of office, having been returned with a large overall majority. The government is in favour of 'free-enterprise' and encourages competition in all sectors of the economy including the financial services sector. Incentives are available to industry to increase exports. The success of the government's anti-inflation policy is now becoming evident with inflation currently running at the rate of 4 per cent per annum. Gross Domestic Product is increasing in real terms by 2 per cent per annum and, despite the recent fall in world oil prices, this rate of growth is expected to be maintained until the end of the decade. Unemployment remains disappointingly high at an average of 12 per cent and certain more depressed regions of the country are experiencing much higher levels of between 20 per cent to 25 per cent. Consumer expenditure is expected to continue to grow at the current rate of 3 per cent for the next three years but thereafter there will be a reduction in growth of around 1.5 per cent. Interest rates will continue to fall and will be below 9 per cent by the end of 1986 with prospects of further falls in succeeding years. Exchange rates remain volatile although it is believed that recent fiscal measures agreed by the major industrialised countries will produce a degree of stability which has been absent for many years.

4 Future trends in the UK financial services sector

The continuation of deregulation and increased competition at home and abroad will determine the shape of the financial services sector in the UK for the next ten years. With the breakdown in the traditional barriers, the clearing banks will face increased competition from building societies, retail stores (particularly in the field of credit cards and point of sale finance), American and Japanese banks, who intend to be major participants in the securities and capital markets, and from government agencies who will be competing for deposits. In addition, insurance companies will seek to attack the traditional savings market through the development of unit-linked life assurance policies whilst specialised instalment credit and hire purchase companies will attempt to satisfy the demand for consumer lending by the offer of specially tailored products.

The principal external factors with which the clearing banks will need to contend will be legislative and regulatory changes, developments in technology and their application by competitors and the development and use of shared communications networks

Internally, clearing banks will require to consider the best use of traditional branch outlets which are in danger of becoming uncompetitive, whilst contending with outdated and costly organisation structures.

In addition, in order to remain competitive, the clearing banks will need to have regard for and respond to changes in customer requirements and to ensure that they can maintain an effective international market presence.

Banks can expect to find that, as a result of the increased competition, there will be a shortage of deposits from traditional sources and a need to develop new lending products; and failure to meet the challenges in these areas will have serious detrimental effects on both profitability and growth. Furthermore, it is expected that growth in net interest income will come under pressure as a result of the competitive factors mentioned above and, consequently, it will be necessary for banks to increase commission and fee income to maintain earnings growth. It is expected that interest margins on all types of business, but especially corporate lending, will continue to narrow and that the actual volumes will either decrease or remain static. The likely development of a UK sterling commercial paper market will cause a major shift in the traditional methods of meeting working capital requirements of industrial companies which have hitherto been reliant on the clearing banking system for short and medium-term finance.

To combat the greatly increased competition, it is likely that the clearing banks will respond by diversifying still further the range of services they offer. Possible ways of achieving this would be to expand into:

- insurance broking
- insurance underwriting
- securities trading
- commodity and financial futures dealing
- estate agency
- travel services
- the provision of information services
- point-of-sale financing

In summary, therefore, to survive and prosper in the next decade, the clearing banks will require to protect their existing services and develop new products to meet the needs of the marketplace.

5 Century Bank PLC – strengths and weaknesses

(a) *Strengths*

(1) A strong balance sheet on which to base expansion and a sound profit record.

(2) A domestic branch network in England and Wales with the majority of outlets well sited in economically active areas but still moderate representation in depressed areas.

(3) A proven international expertise covering trade investments, trade finance and currency operations.

(4) Subsidiary and associate companies providing a range of ancillary financial services to the retail and corporate sectors.

(5) A comprehensive product range equivalent to those of peer banks in both price and range.

(6) A personal account base with 50 per cent of customers in the ABCI socio-economic group with 50 per cent of customers aged 45 or over.

(7) A business account base where traditional and mature businesses predominate.

(8) Strong customer loyalty.

(9) A staff well-versed in traditional banking skills.

(b) *Weaknesses*

(1) An out-dated image created by poor branch premises where little refurbishment has taken place over the last twenty years.

(2) A computer system which is ten years old and requires to be replaced.

(3) Limited ability to issue an own bank credit card; the bank's existing credit card is issued by a company owned jointly by a number of banks.

(4) A static market share with a 10 per cent turnover of accounts.

(5) A weak market image with little recall of the bank or its products.

(6) A product range which is now at a 'mature' stage within the product life cycles.

(7) An ageing board of directors and a management structure which has not been changed for fifteen years.

(8) A retirement bulge covering the next three years during which 10 per cent of the bank's senior management will retire.

(9) A lack of broad-based management skills and of specialised expertise in respect of 'non-core' activities.

6   Century Bank PLC – opportunities and threats

(a) *Opportunities*

   (1) Government policies that encourage competition and enterprise.
   (2) A domestic economy in which output is increasing.
   (3) Stable exchange rates.
   (4) A domestic market, both personal and business, which is capable
       of expansion as competitive influences come to be felt.
   (5) Increasing numbers of new and high technology industries in
       major areas of economic activity with good export potential.
   (6) Deregulation and the consequent blurring of traditional barriers
       between different types of financial institution.

(b) *Threats*

   (1) Traditional markets and customers are under threat.
   (2) Building societies and other institutions are seeking to provide
       personal financial facilities, particularly those which are 'plastic
       card based'.
   (3) American and Japanese banks are seeking actively to increase
       their market share of medium-sized corporate business.
   (4) Large financial conglomerates are actively entering the securities
       and capital markets.
   (5) Market research indicates that one competitor bank has a suc-
       cessful advertising campaign which is succeeding in taking that
       bank 'up market', thus placing the bank's personal account base
       at risk.
   (6) Margins obtainable on non-UK branch business are becoming
       finer, and regulatory authorities in major financial centres are
       tightening control and imposing increasingly stringent capital
       adequacy rules in the light of some bank failures.
   (7) A global economic crisis which could cause major problems for
       re-scheduling loans by banks to LDCs.
   (8) Potential loss of experienced middle-management staff to those
       institutions which have entered into competition in the bank's
       traditional markets.
   (9) Vulnerability to take-over.

7   Conclusions and recommendations

An examination of the strengths and weaknesses of the bank, coupled
with analysis of the opportunities open to it and the threats facing it has
resulted in the conclusion that positive action will be called for if the
bank is even to maintain its position as the fifth largest clearing bank in

the UK. Moreover, if it is intended to continue to achieve growth, major initiatives will be called for in the following areas:

(a) Products and services

With a mature product range it will be necessary to develop new products to achieve the corporate objectives. In addition existing products should be re-evaluated to ensure that the resultant product mix satisfies customers' requirements.

It is accordingly recommended that the bank should:

(1) seek to develop, as a major part of its mainstream business, lending to medium-sized corporate customers, whilst continuing to service large and small corporate customers;

(2) protect its personal customer base and capitalise on it by developing a full range of banking and ancillary services suited to the high value personal customer, as well as by restructuring the existing products;

(3) ensure that all facets of large volume consumer credit businesses are catered for, including the development of an in-house credit card which would not be subject to restraints on development because of the needs of co-shareholders;

(4) seek to enter or increase its presence in those areas of the financial services market which will become open to development as a result of deregulation;

(5) undertake the necessary research and development to ensure that its products and services will be based on up-to-date technology;

(6) consider the acquisition or formation of additional subsidiary companies to provide additional services.

(b) Merchant banking

It is believed that the development of an 'in-house' merchant banking facility will prove to be insufficient to enable the bank to provide the range of activities required to service other areas of its operations. It is therefore recommended that consideration be given to the acquisition of an existing merchant bank.

(c) Domestic banking – the branch network

Given the principal recommendations arising from this review it is clear that the greater part of the bank's income and, consequently, its costs in the foreseeable future will continue to be derived from the Domestic Banking Division. It is recommended that a full review of all existing branches should be carried out to ascertain their profitability. At the same time, consideration should be given to the most appropriate use for the property contained in the branch network.

It is further recommended that the nature and extent of the branch network of the future should be structured towards the principal target markets of the bank.

(d) International activities

For the bank to maintain its market position, it will require to ensure that the range and scope of its international activities recognises the areas of likely economic growth such as the Pacific Basin. It should therefore be a priority to increase the bank's direct representation in the appropriate areas.

(e) Treasury activities

A further area in which the bank will require to develop its expertise is in treasury operations, both sterling and currency.

(f) Data processing services

The bank has failed to keep abreast of developments in computer technology and the existing mainframe computer is out of date and requires to be replaced. The main priority should be the installation of a new mainframe computer so that all operations will be on-line and with sufficient spare capacity to allow for growth over the next five years. The provision of information terminals at branches is seen as a prime requirement as well as the installation of modern ATMs with the capacity to engage in reciprocal arrangements with other banks and financial institutions.

(g) Organisation structure

The existing organisation structure is not suited to the requirements of the bank in the years ahead, particularly as it develops into a financial services group. It is accordingly recommended that the organisation structure should be revised with this in mind, to achieve the optimum allocation of resources.

(h) Staff

The bank possesses strength in depth in the traditional banking skills but it is recognised that the existing training programme is too narrowly based to provide staff with the necessary skills to sell the complete range of the bank's services in the future. It is also recommended that recruitment policy be reviewed and that specific attention is given to the recruitment of staff with specialist skills.

(i) Market image

The recommendations in the preceding paragraphs will, if accepted and implemented, provide the framework for the future success of the bank and the attainment of its corporative objectives. It is considered essential, however, that action be taken to improve awareness of the bank and its image for both customers and potential customers.

Summary

This chapter only touches the tip of an iceberg. There must be many factors which will influence the outcome of a plan apart from the plan itself. The important message is that even a well-structured plan will achieve little without the support and motivation of all those required to implement it.

The core of the plan is the logical sequence of analysis, assumptions, objectives, strategies and action plans. The quality or relevance and logic of these sequences and the degree of compatibility of each in the given circumstances are paramount to any plan's achieving its stated goals.

An analysis of the situation, and the assumptions drawn from a SWOT summary of this information, provides the raw material on which objectives are based. Clearly, if this section of the plan is poorly compiled, the ability of the planning process to achieve stated aims is undermined. So too is the full utilisation of organisational resources.

There are many marketing areas under which information can be collected. Too much information could be as unhelpful as too little. Information collated must be relevant, in a format which is capable of interpretation and capable of being gathered in any given time and cost constraints. By asking the questions posed on page 207 the best combination of information should be forthcoming.

Objectives must be realistic yet challenging. There must also be sufficient flexibility in the planning process to allow amendments to objectives during the planning period if important market conditions, results or organisational circumstances dictate.

Sales targets are set for limited periods usually a maximum of twelve months. Objectives can be goals over much longer periods. The criteria for setting targets are listed on page 210, but before they are passed forward for implementation their suitability should be tested for achievability, consistency and compatibility with the bank's strengths and resources.

Part of marketing is creating the best possible business environment into which planned marketing can flourish. Creating public esteem and distinctive identity, good relations with the media, customer convenience and service quality, and the right branch atmosphere in terms of staff attitudes and skills are all essential factors.

Revision questions

1 What areas do you consider should appear in a situation analysis which covers your present working environment? Make a list of headings, and under each define how you would gather the information.

2 You have set an objective to increase insurance commission earnings by £50 000 (20 per cent increase) in this planning year. Within the structure of a branch plan, outline the strategies and action plans you would implement. Consider market segment and service priorities as well as the cost of implementing the plan.

3 What considerations should be borne in mind when setting sales targets?

4 Can the environment in which your marketing activities are being undertaken be improved? Show what weaknesses exist and suggest how these can be overcome.

Chapter 11
The Branch Marketing Plan

The branch plan logic

A branch plan is the structure which controls and co-ordinates the activities of branch staff who in turn provide the cutting edge of a bank's business development activity.

Once again, it is worth remembering that the marketing planning of a branch should be designed to maximise profit performance by getting the right services at the right times to the most receptive markets with those features and benefits, including the price, which prove attractive to the selected target audiences. If the branch plan is to do this effectively, it must, like the corporate plan, have a series of stages which together form the planning process. This process should seek to maximise profit performance and also fully utilise the scarce resources in the branch – labour, premises, and of course time. As a backcloth to the business development activities, there are a number of important factors which must be 'managed' in support of the branch marketing effort. These include the availability of services and the hours branches are open to the public. Quality of service and the image or reputation of the branch manager(s) and staff for receptiveness to and appreciation of customer requirements is also a crucial part of this background on which business development is based. These supporting features were considered more fully in the last chapter.

Forming a market plan requires the branch manager and his/her marketing team to ask six related questions:

(1) Where is the branch business now and what sort of business is it? This is the review and analysis stage.

(2) Based upon the information gathered by this review and analysis of the information some assumptions and conclusions are possible. How and in what direction the branch business is developing, and, given a changing environment, how the marketing activities and chosen markets should be revised are the main conclusions which will need to be drawn.

(3) Where should the branch be developing its business in the future, given the opportunities and constraints revealed by the review, and the assumptions and conclusions? Trying to answer this question leads directly to the formation of objectives.

(4) What is required in order that the branch manager utilises his/her resources fully to achieve the marketing objectives? This assessment will indicate what strategies are required to ensure business development activity can be successfully carried through.

(5) What action is necessary by the branch staff to achieve the stated objectives? This activity programme should include the allocation of responsibilities for the chosen business development activity and when it is scheduled to take place.

(6) What methods should be adopted to monitor progress and report results? This is the control stage in the marketing plan process.

Plan content and structure

As already pointed out, there will be variations in the style of branch plans from one bank to another. But, apart from the degree of complexity, the objectives set and the order in which the basic planning steps are scheduled, the thinking or logic behind the planning process will not differ widely. Figure 11.1 shows a possible structure for a branch marketing plan. Each stage will be analysed in detail.

(a) Review of local market and past performance. This historical and current analysis of the economic, cultural and social environment in which the branch is operating is a vital part of any marketing plan covering a given planning period. Information sought will vary from branch to branch but attempts should be made to assess the market share of new customers gathered by size and profile.

A review of the current forces influencing the state of the marketplace especially in economic terms, and the likely future trends, will assist the management decisions relating to formulation of fresh marketing objectives. Of less relevance, but nevertheless important, is an assessment of the national political and economic scene and the impact this may have on the locality. A branch in Consett, Durham, for example, is unlikely to remain unaffected by a government 'shake-out' of the steel industry.

(b) Summary of branch trading features. In marketing jargon, this is often referred to as a SWOT summary (Strengths, Weaknesses,

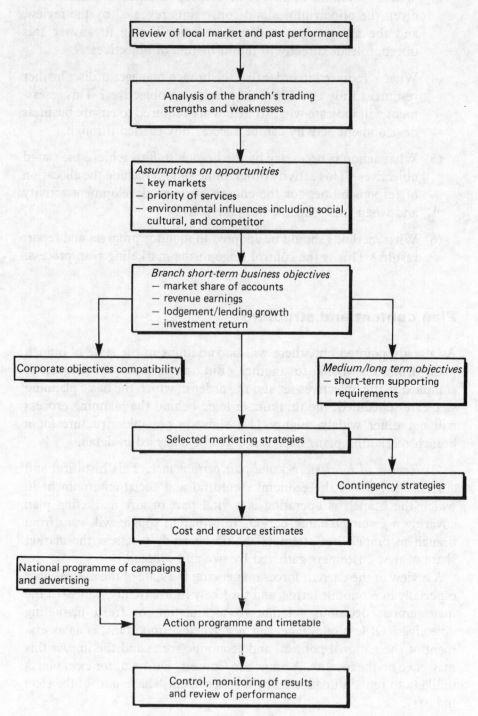

Fig. 11.1 Structure of a branch marketing plan

Opportunities and Threats). This analysis will reveal market potential and the limitations or constraints to be borne in mind when setting objectives.

The SWOT may include even the broadest issues – whether the branch has a customer car park, an external cash dispenser, a desirable share of account relationships with key professionals, the quality of management and staff compared with counterparts in other local banks and so on.

The list could be almost endless, but at the end of the day it will need to be split into two types – those strengths that can be used effectively to attain the marketing objectives and those weaknesses that can be overcome quickly, as opposed to those that cannot be resolved so easily, if at all.

(c) Assumptions on opportunities. This section brings together the information gathered in the first two elements of the marketing planning process. It will take the review, and the SWOT analysis, and start to highlight priorities in key market sectors and the degree of opportunity that exists in them for business development.

Because the review and analysis section which culminate in the SWOT summary is so important to the total planning process, it will be considered in greater practical depth in Chapter 12.

(d) Business development objectives. Two words, 'objectives' and 'strategies', are often misused because their concise meanings are not appreciated.

An objective is something that has to be achieved within a given time-scale, and is capable of being accurately quantified. For example, an objective might be to sell x number of a particular service or increase profit or revenue by $£y$. As a broad rule of thumb, all branch objectives should be stated in numbers or money terms. Moreover, targets or goals are generally short-term objectives bearing in mind that an objective could be a medium- or longer-term aspiration.

If this is not possible, then almost certainly the requirement will be a strategy – something that has to be done so that the marketing objective can be achieved. Examples of a strategy might be to increase levels of appreciation of a particular service among the staff or public, improve a communication method so that more relevant motivational information can be distributed more quickly, or simply to improve the quality of data being collected for key target markets. In a sense, they are objectives, but the lack of ability to quantify them precisely, and their 'support' features makes them strategies in the context of marketing planning.

As Fig. 11.2 shows, branch objectives are shorter-term (usually

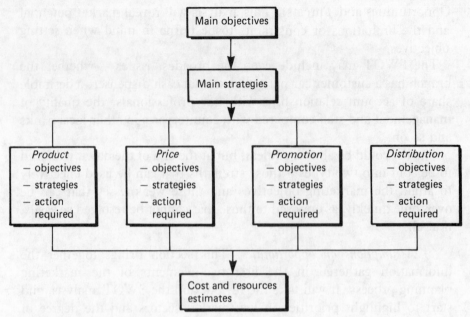

Fig. 11.2 Subsection of a branch marketing plan

maximum twelve months) and need to be split into those goals for the coming planning period and objectives which stretch beyond the immediate horizon. Both the immediate and longer-term objectives should be compatible with the bank's major aspirations as detailed in the corporate plan.

Bearing in mind the need for conciseness in objectives, the main marketing areas on which a branch will set goals will be:

(1) Numbers of new accounts;
(2) Sales targets for key services; measured either in number or penetration terms.
(3) Revenue earning targets;
(4) Target increases in amounts to be lent or lodgements to be gathered;
(5) Return on assets ratio increases.

Longer-term objectives should not be overlooked when setting short-term targets. For example, if the five-year objective is to achieve £x million lent on a fixed rate loan scheme, the goal for the current marketing plan period must reflect this longer-term requirement or say why it does not figure in the plan. However, in practice, the majority of branch plans will probably focus solely on yearly objectives and will not include longer-term goals.

(e) Marketing strategies. The difference between an objective and a

strategy, together with the relationship of one to the other, has already been highlighted.

In the context of marketing, the main strategic issues often revolve around the elements of the marketing mix – product, price, promotion, distribution and so on. These elements are the variables which, when effectively managed, will bring success in achieving marketing objectives. Without wishing to add unnecessary confusion, it must be stated that in each of the marketing mix elements there could be another set of objectives and strategies, but these are subordinate to the main marketing goals. The subsection of a comprehensive plan, which includes the marketing mix variables, is shown diagrammatically in Fig. 11.2.

At a branch level, there may be severe limitations on the nature and extent to which the marketing mix elements can be changed from those which are imposed by the bank. Nor should the need for a measure of flexibility be overlooked; the shaping of contingency strategies in case those first selected do not achieve the desired results are a vital part of the total planning process.

(f) Cost and resource estimates. Marketing is about profitable volume growth – the cost implications of planned marketing activity cannot be ignored. It would also be contrary to the philosophy of bank marketing, as it is known today, to allow branch staff and other expensive resources to escalate faster than profit is generated. Banking is not a philanthropic enterprise, although it is acknowledged that loss-making branches and services do exist when and where there are valid commercial justifications for that situation to occur in the shorter term.

Careful comparison of the likely effect of planned marketing objectives with the existing or obtainable resources is the main platform on which the whole planning process, encompassing the controlled expansion of business, is based.

Marginal cost factors can make it difficult accurately to quantify the costs of planned marketing activity. Nevertheless, some attempt at assessment of costs, no matter how difficult, is vital to ensure the best possible use of the bank's network.

(g) Action programmes and timetable. Who does what, when, where and how? This simple sentence sums up the requirements of an action programme. This section of the plan, like so many others, will help the co-ordination of effort within a branch and ensure that individuals responsible can plan in advance. In this way, they will be properly prepared for the task they have to perform when the time is judged to be right.

Action programmes allocate responsibility and accountability. However, if they have not been agreed beforehand by those who are deputed to carry out the tasks, then the advantages of having accountability will be seriously undermined.

(h) Control, monitoring and results review. Creating a marketing plan is an important starting point but, more important still, is making sure that the predetermined activity achieves the desired results. If, in the course of monitoring and reviewing the results of activity, it is clear that the marketing objectives are not being achieved by the activity programmes, something must be done quickly.

It may be that the objectives are unrealistic, or the wrong type of action is being taken to achieve the goals. Again the important test words – what, when, where, why and how? – can be used to research the validity of the plan in the light of the information obtained from trying to carry it through.

However, the quality of the plan and the pre-set objectives should be tested even before action programmes take place as part of the process of gaining acceptance by all staff charged with the task of implementation. To gain this acceptance, satisfactory answers should be forthcoming to the following questions:

(1) Will the plan work?
(2) Is it challenging yet realistic?
(3) Is it flexible enough to meet any potential changing marketing situations?
(4) How easy is it to evaluate progress?

Case study

As branch manager you have identified the need to increase substantially the retail deposits generated from personal customers.

The manager will need to prepare a plan which can achieve a targeted increase in retail deposits from personal customers. Significant factors include the identification of the retail deposit generating services and the target audiences which provide the best sales opportunities to achieve the objective.

Broadly the branch manager will need his plan to include the following elements:

(a) An analysis of the current market situation, covering the characteristics of his personal market, the impact of competition, a review of his branch performance and an assessment of his capabilities.

This analysis concludes with a summary of his branch strengths, weaknesses, opportunities and threats in the retail deposit sector can be compiled.

(b) Setting objectives which are realistically based using the information gleaned by the analysis.

(c) The selection of priority target audiences and strategies required to ensure the action programmes are likely to be effective.

(d) The development of the most appropriate marketing mix package for the chosen markets.

(e) The establishment of monitoring and evaluation procedures.

In more detail the plan would include the following information.

(a) Current market analysis and setting objectives

(1) The size of the personal deposits market covering both interest bearing and non-interest bearing accounts. Recent historical patterns of growth/decline and discussion of factors underlying changes.

(2) Market segmentation. An analysis of the market by value of deposits held and the establishment of characteristics of the 20–25 per cent of customers controlling 75–80 per cent of deposits – for example by demographics, life cycle group.

(3) Analysis of the branch personal deposits and the value of funds deposited, by customer demographics. Summary of promotion and distribution methods.

(4) Competitive structure. The local organisation represented in the retail deposits market, and any changes in recent years, product ranges and structures, pricing and distribution policies, extent and types of marketing support given. Identification of trends and projected future changes.

(5) Evaluation of the needs of different customer groups and the establishment of factors which would induce customers to move deposits from one organisation to another and those which would reinforce existing bank customers' loyalty.

(6) Future local economic, legislative and regulatory scenarios including the impact of retail price inflation, employment and

wage/salary prospects upon the level of personal disposable income saved.

From the analysis of the current and projected future market situation, a summary of the strengths, weaknesses, opportunities and threats to the branch in the retail deposits market would be prepared.

This would provide a basis for the setting of financial and marketing objectives and goals which the marketing strategy would be designed to achieve.

(b) Target market selection

The target market(s) would be selected using the market analysis and focusing particularly on the summary of strengths, weaknesses, opportunities and threats.

On a low risk strategy the market sector(s) offering the greatest deposit potential with the lowest projected organisational cost would be selected. 'Organisational cost' would include not only marketing and promotional costs but also the time required for this campaign which cannot then be used for other marketing activity.

The target market adopted could either involve pitching at a market sub-sector not presently covered by the bank successfully or reinforcing or extending marketing activity directed towards existing customer profiles. Definition of the target market could be in terms of demographics, life cycle stage, media usage, attitudinal groupings etc.

(c) Service strategy – market mix

(1) The service strategies adopted would stem from the target market definition. Which benefits would be required and how would they be translated into service features? How do the proposed features and benefits differ from those currently available locally? Are the differences considered important or merely cosmetic?

Finally, the potential competitor reactions to the strategies. What response would be likely to be made and how could the branch protect or defend its activity against counter-measures?

(2) *Distribution strategy – market mix*
How will the target market requirements of the product influence its distribution? How will 'convenience' be translated into hours and days of access as well as geographical proximity to where prospective customers live, work or shop? What are the distribution considerations affecting initial purchase and post-purchase customer advice and information?

(3) *Sales and promotional strategies – market mix*

A preliminary step to the development of sound sales and promotional strategies would be the forecasting of total deposit volumes over time and their make-up in terms of customer numbers and average deposit levels, given stated assumptions regarding the operating environment – for example, interest rate levels and types and levels of competitor activity. These forecasts would be the base-line information for cost, profit and budgetary projections and would also provide the resource implications in terms of staffing capability and premises.

Sales and promotional strategies and plans would be developed from predetermined budgetary levels. Marketing and sales objectives would be specified with key attributes of the plans including the identification and targeting of sales and customer servicing personnel, their education, training and motivation and the securing of their commitment. Promotional plans would consider issues relating to advertising support material such as leaflets, posters, sales promotion techniques for the launch and post-launch periods. Presentation or 'packaging' considerations would include the identification of promotional platforms and themes and their creative styling.

The timings and interrelationships of all selected promotional activities would be covered in the plans.

(d)   Monitoring and evaluation procedures

Systems for the monitoring and measurement of marketing activity would be required at the launch stage to provide a reliable information flow upon which decisions to alter, extend or reinforce elements of the marketing plan could be made.

Full-scale reviews and evaluations should be carried out at specified periods to examine performance against target, to set or revise goals for the forthcoming period and to consider whether a reorientation, down-scaling or up-weighting of activity is needed.

A successful solution to the task of increasing substantially the branch retail deposit base by personal customers would be one which was carefully planned within the framework outlined and sufficiently flexible to adapt to new information emerging at each stage of the planning and review process.

Note: This case study indicates what should be done at branch level. All too often pressures of other workloads erode the quality of the marketing effort.

Summary

Once again you plan to market and then you market to plan. In this way organisational effort, through the plan, has direction, co-ordination, sense of purpose and can be controlled. Bank plans, like any other plans must be capable of adapting to changing market conditions but overall they take their lead from the corporate objectives.

The logical structure of a marketing plan must be clearly understood. It is worth while comparing the information in this chapter with an example of a marketing plan used in your bank or financial institution to see if and how they differ. When studying your branch plan, try to concentrate on the interrelationship of the elements by using hypothetical objectives and tracing the interactive effects through the various stages.

When writing a marketing plan the branch manager will need to answer six questions (see page 226).

The last few chapters have looked at the planning responsibilities and procedures at various levels within the bank, but more or less in isolation. Before leaving the subject of planning it needs to be stressed that there is a hierarchy in the planning process within any large financial institution. If the lead comes from the corporate plan then all other plans will focus on this lead. As such, they will all have a large degree of common relevance, purpose and direction.

Moreover, similar market information to help the formulation of objectives at various levels will seep down the hierarchical planning structure. It is also true that a somewhat smaller volume of market information will return upwards from the branches through regional offices and ultimately back to the corporate planners. Therefore, branch managers, when compiling a marketing plan for their branch will have some market information and guidance on which to base their own plan. The volume of data flowing down the planning pyramid will vary in strength and detail, depending on the degree of central leadership the executive wishes to exert. Very few managers will be required to compile a plan from scratch. If this were so there would be little synergy and general co-ordination of effort as each hierarchical level within a bank would decide for itself what was important. Then the marketing strength evolving from being a large corporate with a nationwide network would be largely left unharnessed.

Finally, it must also be recognised that branches are not exactly free agents in matters of policy such as opening hours, pricing of mainstream services, national advertising and so on.

Revision questions

1 Show how the constraints of time-scale might impact on each of the elements of a branch plan.
2 What are the main considerations which will influence the quality of the planning process?
3 Compare and contrast your own branch marketing plan with the outline structure on page 228. Highlight and explain what you think are the reasons for any differences.
4 Why is the marketing planning process so important in the process of achieving profitable growth in any organisation?
5 Explain the differences between objectives, strategies, goals and targets. Give examples.

Chapter 12
Market Forces Including Competition

This is a vast subject, probably too vast to cover adequately in a single chapter of any textbook. Moreover market forces are of course constantly changing. Words written today are unlikely to be completely up to date tomorrow. Nevertheless no book covering the marketing of financial services would be regarded as comprehensive without at least attempting to paint in the broad competitive scenario, in order to provide a basic understanding of what has happened and what could happen in the future.

Answering the questions: what market forces should be taken into account and who are the main competitors? will first depend on what markets you are in and the area of responsibility you cover. For example, the Chief General Manager of a major clearing bank will be interested in these issues at several different levels. Globally, if his bank is operating in world markets with associate companies operating in other countries; and at home, as his retail network and servicing departments and subsidiaries battle for profits and growth against fierce competition on a broad front. The Area or Regional Manager will have more parochial concerns, and the market forces and areas of competition which he/she will need to address will be narrower than the bank's Chief Executive. Nevertheless, the task in understanding what issues may affect the growth of business in his/her own area and what the competition is doing is no less important. Moreover, the underlying marketing aspects are similar to the bank's global problems. Often they are interconnected, as the worldwide fortunes of a UK bank will undoubtedly impact on the operational and profit requirements in other markets. Probably the best example of this interrelationship of world markets with all other markets is the South and Central American debts crisis.

In the early 1970s the OPEC countries were producing massive amounts of money which sought safe and profitable havens. The UK banks looked safe for OPEC money because they could not risk the consequences of not honouring their deposit obligations. This influx of funds triggered off the search for borrowers. Inevitably this money found its way to the developing countries, oilfields around the world and farming. The folly of this lending first came to light in 1982 with the first Mexican debt crisis and then subsequently with the collapse of the Continental Illinois Bank. Since then, the UK banks, with varying degrees of exposure in Brazil, Mexico and other smaller South American countries, have sought ways of diluting these questionable debts in their books.

They turned to trying to increase income outside the worldwide deposit and loan business by expanding services or developing new ones – mortgages, premier charge cards, insurance, estate agencies, stock-broking and many others. It might be that as the debt burden of individuals in the UK rises to an apparent saturation level public or government views on prudence will cause intervention and the brakes to be applied to consumer borrowing. At that stage the strategy for developing the so-called safe home market will need to be reconsidered. The burden of debt per capita in the UK is below that of the USA and some European countries, so that it may be some time before increasing debt defalcations and other pointers begin to support the views of some pressure groups that credit curbs should be imposed. Meanwhile the problems of 'easy credit' are beginning to emerge and the banks are now discussing the need for a Central Credit Register.

At a branch manager level these worldwide issues are interesting but of less importance to localised marketing activity. The branch manager will know the main competitors in his/her neighbourhood and will have an appreciation of those nationally-based institutions who also actively canvass on his patch. Here again, the problems of market forces and competition could differ widely from branch to branch. A manager of a large city branch will have more competition than a manager operating in a quiet market town where his/her bank might be the only one in the high street. Furthermore, the north/south economic divide will also impact on the nature and degree of market forces. The problems of running a bank in the Surrey stockbroker belt are quite different from those of a banker in any other town largely dependent upon one industry or employer.

The marketing environment

The need to understand the marketing environment as it affects particular levels and types of operation has already been highlighted. There is no substitute for maintaining an up-to-date and detailed analysis of competition and other market forces as they emerge. Each new competitive development affecting the market's environment should be studied so that the reasons for it are understood and the likely effects on the bank's own marketing activity appreciated. In this way, reaction to the changes can be considered quickly to mitigate damage to profit or volume growth in chosen markets or, indeed, latch on to a new marketing initiative which has emerged.

Banking is a diverse service industry; market forces will vary between market segments and thus influence opportunities in various ways. There can be no argument that the last decade has added to the complexity of banking in all its forms and this has, in turn, increased the momentum of change. The economy has suffered violent fluctuations; the number of bank account holders has increased; and automated technology has greatly improved servicing capabilities and opened up new markets. However, technology has also enabled competitor institutions, without a network of branches, to operate in markets traditionally regarded as belonging to the banks. These are a few of the market forces and all have played a part in changing the nature of bank marketing activity.

Even though the marketing environment in which banks operate has become more complex, a simplified approach can be adopted to meet new marketing issues and increased competitive challenges. However, such an approach does stress the importance of making the right commercial decisions, and this in turn means knowing the facts and understanding what these might mean.

(a) Internal forces

Before looking in greater depth at the marketing environment as it affects the branch network, it is worth spending a few moments looking at a marketing system which encompasses the environmental forces of change. Diagrammatically it can be illustrated in Fig. 12.1.

This illustration clearly shows that within the marketing system there are limitations. For example the bank's resources are not unlimited, and neither is the level of demand in chosen market segments. Therefore, irrespective of other market forces, assessing the capabilities of the bank and matching these with likely demand levels is the first priority. However, it is the likely demand levels which will be influenced by the environmental and competitive forces, so these issues cannot simply be ignored.

(b) External forces affecting the bank and branch

Economic, political and legislative forces will all affect the marketing

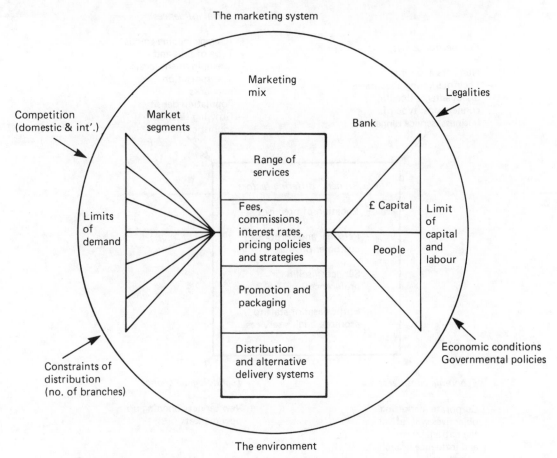

Fig. 12.1   The marketing system and factors affecting it

effort, but the extent of the impact of these influences will vary from bank to bank and also from branch to branch. The types of customers and the nature of the industry served in any given locality will dictate the degree to which the network as a whole, or an individual branch, needs to react to the situations these forces create.

Underlying these more immediate forces are also a series of broad socio-economic and environmental trends. These include the redistribution of wealth among social classes as evidenced, for example, by the growing number of people becoming homeowners. These social trends have helped to contribute to an increased financial sophistication among the public, and this has increased demand for new financial services.

Figure 12.2 shows the typical range of forces which confront the bank nationally and the branch manager locally when reaching marketing decisions through the planning process. These forces are as real at

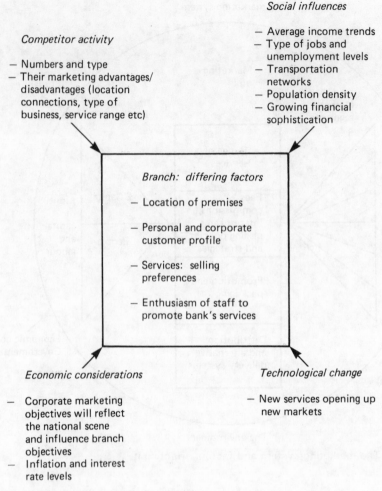

Social influences

— Average income trends
— Type of jobs and
  unemployment levels
— Transportation
  networks
— Population density
— Growing financial
  sophistication

Competitor activity

— Numbers and type
— Their marketing advantages/
  disadvantages (location
  connections, type of
  business, service range etc)

Branch: differing factors

— Location of premises

— Personal and corporate
  customer profile

— Services: selling
  preferences

— Enthusiasm of staff to
  promote bank's services

Economic considerations

— Corporate marketing
  objectives will reflect
  the national scene
  and influence branch
  objectives
— Inflation and interest
  rate levels

Technological change

— New services opening up
  new markets

Fig. 12.2   Making marketing decisions

branch level as they are for those who have responsibility for planning the marketing thrust for the whole bank. Thus the major challenge for the bank at all levels is to gain the necessary level of understanding and skill to meet those forces of change in a way which enables their marketing targets to be achieved. However, a bank cannot react to all the forces as they occur, as its main marketing thrust would become diffused and fragmented, so undermining the likelihood of success from a planned and co-ordinated approach. The corporate plan objectives and the corporate strategy should remain the central core guiding all marketing activity. Any counter-measures taken to meet adverse market forces or capitalise on new opportunities, must therefore also be relevant to the longer-term corporate aspirations.

Importance of the corporate strategy

In 1986 the Fifth International Retail Banking Conference was held in London and its central theme was 'The retail banking revolution – triumph or catastrophe?' The Deputy Chief Executive of Lloyds Bank, Mr Fred Crawley, was one of the speakers and outlined his bank's retail strategy for the future. It would not be surprising if many of the strategic objectives of Lloyds Bank were similar to those of the other UK clearing banks, as they have broadly speaking similar problems and opportunities.

The following are extracts from Mr Crawley's speech and show how deregulation, market forces such as growing financial sophistication and competition, pressure on profits from increasing servicing costs and the impact of technology are all affecting the ways in which a bank will do business in the future.

(1) Consideration of where a bank is going can usefully start with the background to today's retail strategies. The massive growth in competition reflects the attractiveness of UK markets. Traditional rivals are being joined by deregulated building societies, and mainstream retailers like Benetton are also crowding in. Some high street retailers like Marks & Spencer have launched their own financial services – loans and credit cards. Through their quest to gain a share of the lucrative consumer lending services market, they are also eroding the banks' domination of money transmission and creating potentially viable alternatives to the branch network.

(2) Customers are also becoming more demanding and the relationship between the banks and customers is changing. Power has shifted into the hands of customers as they demand higher quality service, giving added value to justify premium prices. Moreover, we can no longer take loyalty for granted.

(3) Strategies, against this changing background, must recognise that the banks no longer have some markets to themselves and that their market is not necessarily where it used to be – markets are now where the customers are, not where the banks are situated.

(4) Customers now shop around, and to meet this trend banks need to create new images through massive expenditure on refurbishment of branches and technology. This in turn means that greater profits have to be earned to pay for these changes.

(5) It also means that a bank will need to be more selective, focus more strongly on chosen markets, concentrate specialist resources to meet specialist threats and create a distinctive personality. To differentiate from other banks in the eyes of the consumer is a very important objective in order to influence consumer choice in favour of the bank which does this successfully.

(6) The branch network remains an important distribution system and will continue to offer tremendous potential for those customers requiring personal contact. However, technology provides the opportunity to reduce network costs whilst yet retaining them as sales outlets.

(7) Introducing new services and new delivery systems will continue to be important, so too will the 'brand' image or identity, with a degree of distinctiveness that these new services will reinforce. Providing value for money remains a key strategy. Quality of service is paramount in any retail operation as part of the added value which justifies a premium price. Staff training and motivation are vital factors in ensuring quality standards.

(8) Technology can be used to improve customer convenience and extend banking service hours of availability. However, the use of technology should not be driven by internal demand or competitor activity. Customer demand should be the driving force, and wide consumer acceptance of technology will depend on customers being carefully introduced to it by well-trained staff.

(9) Lodgements remain the life blood of the industry but current levels of profitability from lodgements are not going to last as customers demand a better deal on savings. The banks are gradually moving towards payment of interest on all current accounts. However, improved service features will attract money from profitable non- or low interest-bearing services such as current accounts and seven-day deposits. The banks are naturally reluctant to pay more for the funds already held if it can be avoided. Understandably they tend to delay introducing more attractive 'value-added' services to defer customer opportunities of 'trading up' their funds. Ultimately adverse movements in market share of personal business must reach a point where an institution is forced to follow a competitive lead.

(10) These pressures on earnings will require clear strategies. There is a need for tighter cost control. Paper, huge networks and a comprehensive service range are expensive. In future the banks

must try to service customers in less expensive, non-traditional ways based on innovation and technology. Ways of reorganising need to be found which will reduce costs yet serve the customer better.

This extract is a sharply focused insight into the problems facing one of the major UK banks and how it proposes to face the pressures with which other retailers are already familiar. Deregulation and new competition signalled the end of a protected environment. It also opened up new challenges for the banks which need to be addressed in a way that ensures that good profits continue to be earned to finance future business and to strengthen capital.

The effect of Big Bang

On 27 October 1986 the Stock Exchange was 'deregulated' and this event was christened the 'Big Bang'. The Act which helped to shape these changes was the Financial Services Act and this far-reaching legislation was designed to introduce measures to protect the general investing public.

The main reasons for deregulating the Stock Exchange were

(1) Following the worldwide trend towards greater competition in securities markets;
(2) The growth of unregulated securities trading in London outside the Stock Exchange, for example in Eurobonds;
(3) The shortage of capital in London firms, compared with the UK's international competitors;
(4) Pressure from the big investing institutions to cut the Stock Exchange commissions that they pay;
(5) The steady decline in profitability amongst the jobbers, endangering the market in smaller stocks.

Government pressure brought all these matters to a head and it was because everything was changed at once that the event was called the Big Bang. The main change was the opening up of the Stock Exchange to outsiders, so creating more competition but also more capital to expand the UK market, so that it could compete with other global financial markets.

(a) Impact on the banks

Most of the major British banks have formed new groups by taking over jobbers and brokers and combining them within their own merchant banks. The big four will use their branch networks to promote high-volume dealing in stocks and shares by customers, and included in this are the Personal Equity Plans with tax exemption on capital gains and dividends. Foreign banks are also able to join the UK Stock Exchange and this will greatly widen the scope of their operations to include trading and broking activities.

(b) The new system and its supervision

The UK has chosen to supervise functions, for example, investment management (see Table 12.1), rather than types of institution, unlike the USA, where the various bank supervisors watch over all types of bank business. A bank which provides different kinds of financial service may thus have to be regulated by several supervisory authorities. There are the twin dangers that some functions – especially financial innovations – will slip through the net and not be supervised

Table 12.1   The Stock Exchange – the players and their roles

Big Bang market participants

Title	Functions
Market-makers	Holding, making markets in, buying and selling securities for clients.
Primary dealers	Market-makers in gilt-edged.
Inter-dealer brokers	Acting as intermediaries between, taking deposits from, and lending securities to market makers.
Broker-dealers	Dealing, buying and selling securities for clients.
Brokers	Buying and selling securities for clients.
International dealers	Broker-dealers in international securities.

New Stock Exchange dealing systems

Title	Functions
Stock Exchange Automated Quotation (SEAQ)	3500 leading shares.
SEAQ Automated Execution Facility (SAEF)	Small bargains (From 1987).
Block Order eXposure (BLOX)	Large bargains.
Stock Exchange Floor	Second line shares.
TAURUS	Automated settlement (from 1989).
Central Gilts Office (CGO)	Gilt-edged.

Table 12.2 The supervisors and their areas of responsibility

The new structure of supervision

Supervisory agency	*Functions to be supervised*
Bank of England	Banking
	Wholesale financial markets
	Gilt-edged
	Foreign exchange
Building Societies Commission	Building society mortgages and other assets, and deposits
Securities and Investments Board (SIB)	Protection of retail investors
Self-Regulating Organisations (SRO)	UK and international securities
International Stock Exchange	Investment management
Investment Management Regulatory Organisation (IMRO)	
Life Assurance and Unit Trust Regulatory Organisation (LAUTRO)	Life assurance and unit trusts
Financial Intermediaries Managers and Brokers Regulatory Association (FIMBRA)	Securities dealing, insurance and unit trust broking and selling
Association of Futures Brokers and Dealers (AFBD)	Futures trading

by anyone, and that some institutions will be supervised twice over in some of their activities which fulfil more than one function.

The Bank of England will continue to supervise the traditional lending and deposit-taking activities of banks, and will have special responsibility for wholesale financial markets, notably the gilt-edged market, but also the markets in foreign exchange, futures and commercial paper. It will share with the Stock Exchange the supervision of the equity market as well as the gilt-edged market. But it is difficult to draw the line between the wholesale markets, for which the Bank of England is responsible, and the retail markets, where the Department of Trade and Industry is trying to protect the small investor, by means of the structure set up by the Financial Services Act.

There have been great debates, in and out of the House of Commons, about the investment protection powers to be given to the Securities and Investments Board (SIB). This body is responsible to the Department of Trade and Industry (DTI), which has a good deal of discretion as to how much power to allow it. It has been established that the Self-Regulatory Organisations (SROs) will be immune from prosecution. It is not clear how effectively the DTI will be able to intervene in the affairs of the SROs, which come under it.

(c)　The new competitive environment

There are three dimensions in which the competition between London and other financial centres may be measured. First, the internal dimension. Second, the European dimension. Third, the global dimension.

Internally, the Big Bang is a further stage in the trend away from specialisation and towards conglomeration in the UK financial services sector. For fifteen years or more the British banks have been transforming themselves into conglomerates, but their leap into the securities business, thanks to the reform of the Stock Exchange, is an important further advance, even though it opens up new kinds of risk.

With traditional high margins being competed downwards, it is impossible to see how the UK financial market can provide a sufficient income to yield a profit to all the British and foreign competitors who are crowding into the City, and spilling out into other parts of London. It is perceived that some competitors will retire hurt from the fray, or disappear altogether. It remains to be seen whether the British banks, or their foreign competitors, will be the main beneficiaries of the Big Bang. The task of the UK authorities may be to facilitate the exit of some of the competitors, without contagion spreading to the others, or affecting the health of the market.

In the European dimension, London has for years been acknowledged as the leading financial centre, not so much because of the size of its market in the UK securities, as because of its markets in leading international shares, foreign exchange, Eurocurrency banking, and Eurobond issuing. Its relative freedom from regulation, especially for foreign banks, has been a major attraction, and since 1979 it has benefited from the complete absence of exchange control. The UK will hope to benefit from the EC Commission's plan to unify the European internal market by 1992. This should mean greater freedom of trade in financial services, as well as in other sectors. Once banking regulations can be harmonised, the way will be open for British banks truly to develop into Eurobanks.

The City's pre-eminence in Europe is likely to continue, given the slow pace of liberalisation in other EC member countries. This will enhance the advantage which London enjoys in the third dimension of global competition against New York, Tokyo and other centres. London has the comparative advantage of being in the time zone that bridges the gap between New York and Tokyo. Its disadvantage is that its own domestic securities market is smaller than those of the USA and Japan, both larger and faster-growing economies. The City therefore has to continue to make its living by acting as a centre for mobile international markets, which it can do only by offering a freer regulatory environment. The banks and other financial institutions of each country are naturally concerned that their own national authorities will subject them to stricter regulation than their competitors from other countries. The British banks are afraid that American and Japanese banks operating in London will be allowed to operate on less demanding capital ratios and less stringent disclosure requirements; hence their demand that competition should be on a level playing field. There is thus pressure on bank supervisors to indulge in a competition in laxity, so as to ensure that their own national banks are not at a disadvantage in competition. On the other hand, investment protection agencies are more concerned to see that investors enjoy the benefit of well-regulated and highly liquid markets. These developments will take time to evolve and it may be that in a few years' time the capital markets in London and the players will be more restricted than was envisaged in the early days of Big Bang.

Banks versus building societies

(a) Historical developments

In their quest for lodgements, a major task for the banks is to combat the vigorous competition from the building societies. The special tax advantages that used to be enjoyed by building societies courtesy of the Inland Revenue was a major factor, for it allowed, in normal economic conditions, as much as an additional one per cent to be paid to depositors over that which the banks could pay.

But the tax advantage was only one reason for the loss of market share of deposits to building societies; a more personal service and more convenient opening hours are two further reasons. The success of building societies has engendered a change in the competitive environment and the banks have been forced as a consequence to introduce new interest-bearing services and offer mortgages to arrest the loss of retail deposits. Figure 12.3 illustrates the extent to which banks have lost market share of savings to the building societies over the last decade.

The clearing banks' entrée into the market for house mortgages – the once sacred preserve of building societies – has sparked off counter-moves, with the larger societies introducing chequing accounts and other money transfer facilities. It is not the job of this book to list all the services available through building societies, and anyway such a list would soon become out of date.

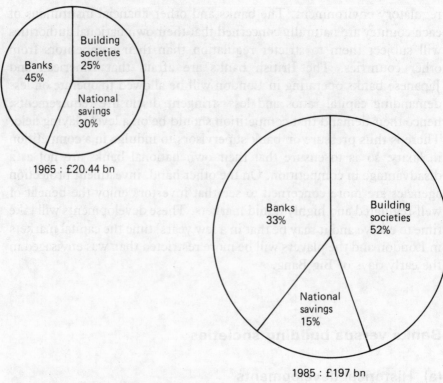

Fig. 12.3 Personal sector liquid assets

But to reinforce the competitive environment and the nature of the threat to the banks in the marketplace it is worth highlighting some of the recent innovative service developments of building societies. As already mentioned in this chapter, there are now building societies operating jointly with a clearing bank's credit card company; a building society operating cheque clearing facilities through a major bank; and another linked with a bank to provide cheque book facilities and no bank charges. Perhaps the most dramatic developments of all are represented by one society's arrangement to provide facilities through some 20 000 post offices, and by many societies' sharing automatic cash dispensers with banks, including those of the Scottish banks, to give a nationwide network facility under the name of LINK. Undoubtedly societies will continue to introduce cash dispensers.

Building societies, with nearly 40 million investors and £7 billion of assets, are a competitive force to be reckoned with by the banks. Collectively they have gathered a substantial share of retail lodgements – the life blood of any financial institution. By the end of 1985 the share of personal lodgement balances was: building societies £103 billion, banks £64 billion and National Savings £30 billion. These figures when compared with total lodgements of £127 billion, at the end of 1982 show just how fast this lucrative savings market is growing.

Meanwhile the banks' attack on the house loans market has also stung the building societies out of any complacency they may have had. Higher interest rates for the larger mortgage or endowment linked scheme have disappeared with increasing competition fuelled by special discounts and other merchandising by the banks to acquire what they would regard as their market share. By December 1985 the market share picture was as shown in Fig 12.4. The latest development in this growing competition between the banks and building societies was the Building Societies Act 1986 which became law on 1 January 1987.

(b) Effects of the Building Societies Act 1986

Under this Act, building societies may provide the following services either themselves or through subsidiaries:

(1)   Money transmission services including the giving of guarantees

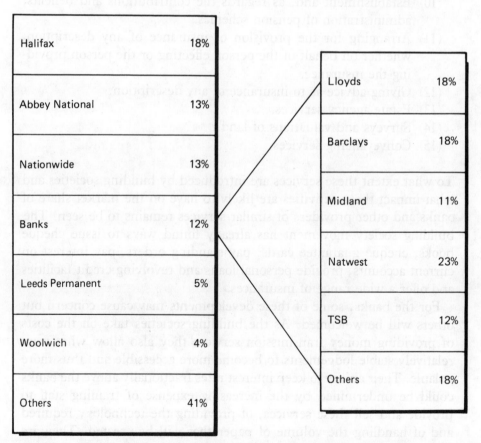

Fig. 12.4   Market share of mortgages as at December 1985

in relation to, or the permitting of occasional overdrawing on, accounts with the society.

(2) Foreign exchange services.

(3) Making or receiving of payments as agents.

(4) Management, as agents, of investments consisting of rights arising out of advances secured on land.

(5) Management, as agents, of land.

(6) Arranging for the provision of services relating to the acquisition or disposal of investments, whether on behalf of the investor or the person providing the service.

(7) Establishment and management of Personal Equity Plans.

(8) Arranging for the provision of credit, whether on behalf of the borrower or the person providing credit, and providing services in connection with current loan agreements to the party providing credit.

(9) Establishment and management of unit trust schemes for the provision of pensions.

(10) Establishment and, as regards the contributions and benefits, administration of pension schemes.

(11) Arranging for the provision of insurance of any description, whether on behalf of the person effecting or the person providing the insurance.

(12) Giving advice as to insurance of any description.

(13) Estate agency services.

(14) Surveys and valuations of land.

(15) Conveyancing services.

To what extent these services are introduced by building societies and what impact these activities are likely to have on the market share of banks and other providers of similar services remains to be seen. The building society movement has already found ways to issue cheque books, cheque guarantee cards, pay standing orders, pay interest on current accounts, provide personal loans and revolving credit facilities and offer a wide range of insurances.

For the banks, some of these developments may cause concern but others will be welcomed. As the building societies take on the costs of providing money transmission services they also allow what were relatively stable lodgements to become more accessible and thus more volatile. Their ability to keep interest rates fractionally above the banks could be undermined by the increasing expense of training staff to provide and sell these services, of providing the technology required and of handling the volume of paper that will be created. They are resting their hopes on generating sufficient profit from consumer lending and other ancillary services to offset these added costs incurred as they encroach further into what has been regarded as traditional bank markets. Moreover, the ability of building societies to pay these higher rates was a function of their being able to 'fix' the rates charged for mortgages when they had a virtual monopoly. The entry of the banks and other niche operators has upset this by creating competitive pricing and bringing building society interest rates into line with those of other institutions now providing mortgages.

It is not inconceivable that some of the smaller building societies, several of which operate from only one branch and rely upon advertising higher than normal rates to attract lodgements, will remain highly competitive by specialising solely in the mortgage and savings markets. These societies, specialising in and offering a relatively small range of services will go for high-volume low-margin business yet remain profitable by keeping administration costs down. It will be several years before the new boundaries of competition become completely clear.

Importance of lending

Against the background of competition, deregulation and new marketing ploys, bank lending will remain the cornerstone of the banks' earnings and indeed of their survival.

Personal consumer finance services abound as the banks and the other financial institutions try to fill the gaps in their own service range and cater for every likely customer requirement. Consequently the competition for consumer finance has become very aggressive, as a variety of lenders, including the building societies, offer ready credit and use a variety of promotional ploys in an effort to increase market share.

Credit-scoring systems, as they became available, have helped the banks, building societies and other finance companies to measure risk and set standards or disciplines which enable them to manage it. Credit-scoring has also replaced the need to have trained staff capable of assessing risk and making a judgement. Thus the consumer credit market has become wide open to anybody capable of providing the credit and administering the repayment systems.

Lending to business customers remains under the influence and control of the major banks but here too the position is changing. Larger corporate customers have a wider range of borrowing options than before as shown in Fig. 12.5. New players will continue to enter this very lucrative marketplace and the road ahead for the banks does not look smooth. They will need to expand and improve their loan schemes

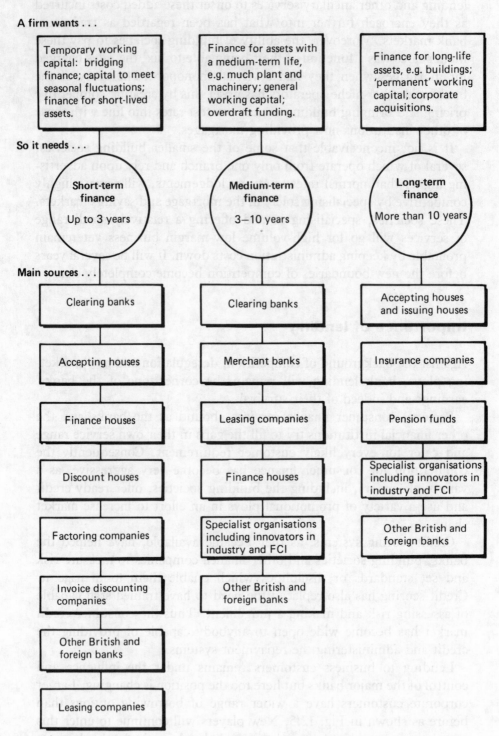

A firm wants . . .

| Temporary working capital: bridging finance; capital to meet seasonal fluctuations; finance for short-lived assets. | Finance for assets with a medium-term life, e.g. much plant and machinery; general working capital; overdraft funding. | Finance for long-life assets, e.g. buildings; 'permanent' working capital; corporate acquisitions. |

So it needs . . .

| Short-term finance
Up to 3 years | Medium-term finance
3–10 years | Long-term finance
More than 10 years |

Main sources . . .

Clearing banks	Clearing banks	Accepting houses and issuing houses
Accepting houses	Merchant banks	Insurance companies
Finance houses	Leasing companies	Pension funds
Discount houses	Finance houses	Specialist organisations including innovators in industry and FCI
Factoring companies	Specialist organisations including innovators in industry and FCI	Other British and foreign banks
Invoice discounting companies	Other British and foreign banks	
Other British and foreign banks		
Leasing companies		

Fig. 12.5   Main providers of corporate finance available in the UK

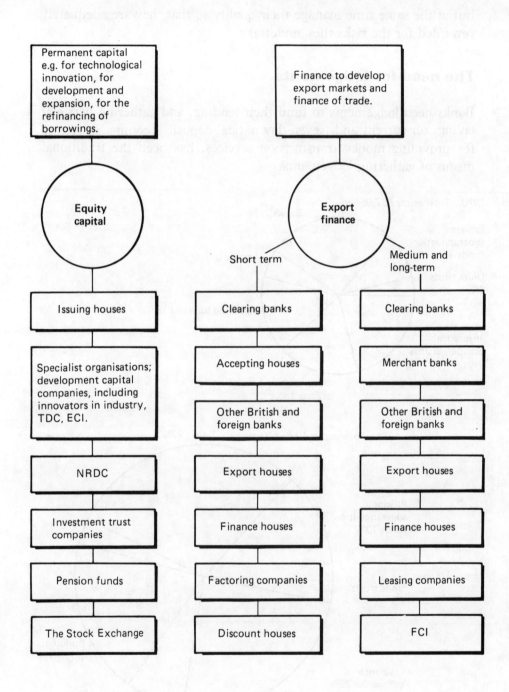

but at the same time manage their quality so that they are adequately rewarded for the risks they undertake.

The need for lodgements

Banks need lodgements to fund their lending, and gathering personal savings on current and 'seven-day notice' deposit accounts, in return for providing money transmission services, has been the traditional means of gathering lodgements.

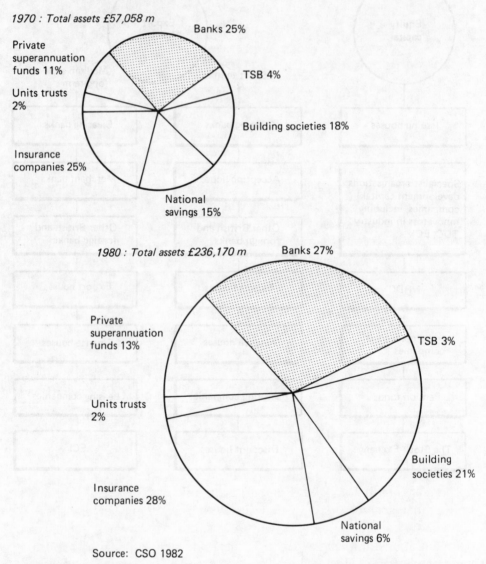

Source: CSO 1982

Fig. 12.6 Total personal lodgements – institutions: total assets withdrawable on demand after notice.

However, since the late 1970s retail lodgements have largely failed to keep pace with the growth in lending. By 1981–2, when the banks lent £14½ billion to the personal sector against only £8½ billion raised in personal deposits, wholesale borrowing (money raised in the money markets) to redress this imbalance began to grow rapidly. There is also an increasing mismatch between the pace of growth of seven-day deposits and an increasing portfolio of longer-term lending.

Marketing cannot escape the consequences of these funding problems, which create a requirement for more selective and responsible marketing activity. Generating lodgements and profits, through service sales revenue and improved margins, to pay for escalating costs, is now a way of life.

Type of lodgements

Balances on current and deposit accounts are retail deposits, and are mainly generated through the branch network. Deposits can be further split into sight deposits, which are those on current account and are withdrawable on demand, and time deposits. The latter can be either for a fixed period or require a period of notice to be given before withdrawal can be made.

Wholesale deposits are funds which originate within the money market or through branch customers placing deposits with the bank at rates of interest linked to the money market. As already noted, the main sources of competition for smaller personal savings are the major clearing banks, the TSB, building societies and the National Savings movement.

Total personal savings and the movement in market share over the last decade is shown in Fig. 12.6.

Competitors in the high street

1971 saw the end of lending restrictions on banks and the unofficial cartel covering interest rates. Until then the competition between the banks was relatively low-key. During the 1970s competition increased among the banks, some of which 'came of age' in the search for market share – notably the TSB, Co-operative Bank and National Girobank. Building societies, licensed deposit-taking institutions, money shops, retail stores offering credit facilities, insurance companies, unit trust organisations and, most recently, the trade union link with the Co-operative Bank to form Unity Trust, all compete in the high street with the major clearing banks.

In all there are some 50 000 retail outlets offering financial services of one description or another. Many of these organisations are competing for personal savings, investment and financial services – particularly lending. Some of these services are profitable in themselves whilst others – money transfer services, for instance – can be loss leaders, suffered in order to gather lodgements.

By looking at the principal functions of a clearing bank, it is possible to identify who are its main competitors. In the more 'popular' areas of financial services, institutions that are in competition with the high street banks are broadly as follows:

Banking function	*Competition*
Money transmission	Post Office
	Secondary banks and smaller licensed deposit-takers
	Credit and charge card companies
	Some building societies
Deposit gathering	Building societies
	Post Office
	National Savings movement
	Local authorities
	Stock Exchange and unit trusts
	Finance houses
	Insurance companies, including friendly societies
	Overseas banks
Lending	Finance houses
	Merchant banks
	Overseas banks
	Local authorities
	Building societies
	Insurance companies
	Some specialist organisations including Finance for Industry and Agricultural Mortgage Corporation
Safe custody	Solicitors
	Overseas banks
	Merchant banks and many licensed deposit-takers or 'secondary' banks
Trustee services	Solicitors
	Public trustee
Overseas and travel services	Overseas banks
	Credit card companies

> Charge card companies
> Travel agencies, particularly those
>   associated with banks, such as Thomas
>   Cook
> Building societies providing personal
>   travel services

This list is not exhaustive, but it does show the extent of competition for business which, in the past, was traditionally regarded almost as the exclusive province of the high street banks.

This growing expansion of the types of services being provided is a direct result of competition, as financial providers try to improve their range of services.

Their objective is to provide the public with 'one-stop shopping' convenience and fill gaps in their range of revenue-earning services, thereby maximising the sales potential of a large and mainly loyal customer base.

A second competitive development is the number of trading links being established between different financial institutions. Sometimes the links are between organisations which had previously been in direct competition with one another, but which now find that there are marketing benefits in packaging their services together. Examples include the American Express Gold Card link with Lloyds Bank, which provides a comprehensive service that includes overdraft and money transmission benefits. Plastic cards are a very convenient method of paying for travel and entertainment throughout the world.

Building societies have linked with credit card companies to provide their depositors with greater flexibility in paying for goods and services. Cheque books issued by building societies are common. They issue travellers cheques and link with banks to provide all the benefits of a bank account and the interest rates of a building society investment (for example, Bank of Scotland and Alliance Building Society).

Some broad conclusions

The rapid pace of change in retail banking is beginning to have an effect on the institutions themselves. A paradoxical feature of the breakdown in distinctions between different types of institutions is that there is a noticeable increase in the individuality of particular institutions. Some of the leading banks and building societies are pursuing strikingly individual lines of development in order to stand out from the crowd, rather than waiting until all are prepared to move together. The future of retail banking may therefore be more difficult to chart than the past, if each institution is pursuing its own line of development. No longer will it be possible to talk about the clearing banks all doing one thing and the building societies all doing something else. No longer will it be possible to talk disparagingly about 'shades of grey'. Naturally, with no patent or copyright protection on banking services it will be difficult for any one institution to monopolise a successful idea for very long, but the first in the field can often build up an unassailable lead.

If there is one key principle of long-range planning in retail banking perhaps it is that each bank's management should be developing a clear and coherent plan of the individual image that it wants to present to the public over the next two decades and the stream of products that it will have to introduce to support that image.

For the major clearing banks, the way to meet competition, especially in the retail markets, is becoming fairly clear. Improving target audience selection and then strongly focusing the marketing effort on those selected groups is becoming much more important. To do this effectively, service features must be precisely tailored to meet chosen market needs and the other marketing mix elements; especially price and delivery must also be more appealing. Getting closer to these target audiences with services which offer convenience, flexibility and value is vital. So too is the way these benefits are communicated and delivered. Not just the advertising but also the quality of service, the speed of delivery, the innovativeness and the ability to anticipate change.

Case study

'Good marketing is managing change.' Discuss the factors that lead to change in financial services markets, and give examples.

The two major influences which can lead to changes in demand for financial services are competition and environmental factors. Before going into greater detail, it is worth stressing that market forces are invariably interlinked, and when assessing their effects cannot usually be looked at in isolation. For example, social environmental forces will impact on the pace of technological change. The pace of change from both of these forces may also be influenced by economic factors or political or legal intervention.

However, for the sake of clarity, each market force will be looked at independently, and examples will be given to highlight the effect of such forces in practice.

Competition

This is arguably the most influential market force and one which creates the quickest change in the marketplace. A recent example of competition bringing about a major change in customer attitudes and demand was the Midland's introducing free banking for current accounts maintained in credit. With some reluctance it was not long before the other major clearing banks were forced to follow suit. Thus a major resistance to opening a bank account was removed, especially for employers striving to reduce payment of wages in cash. The demise of the Truck Acts removed another obstacle to the spread of current accounts and so increased the numbers of the bank customers to whom other financial services could be sold.

Competition comes from a number of sources. It is a growing force, especially as technology, and co-operative links, begin to allow those institutions, without a large branch network, to reach and service large sections of the public. EFTPOS (Electronic Funds Transfer at Point of Sale) facilities will extend non-cash payments throughout the UK. Any financial institution issuing a plastic card could give immediate access to customer funds through EFTPOS so bypassing the need for a very costly branch network. Here we see the forces of competition and technology coming together in a way that could revolutionise the currently largely cash-dominated payments systems.

Apart from the prospect of a continual stream of new competitors entering the marketplace for the first time, impacting on price and demand levels, a bank faces competition from other sources. The other high street banks are a primary force to be countered and so are the building societies, insurance companies and even organisations such as the AA and multiple chain stores.

Each institution or organisation will, by its marketing efforts, stimulate existing areas of demand and occasionally open up new markets. This is a healthy challenge which has to be met. The immediate outcome has resulted in a growing financial sophistication among the public at large, and created a more discerning demand. The new rule, known as 'polarisation', devised by the Securities and Investments Board – the financial services regulator – will however alter the competitor picture. Banks will have to elect whether their branches sell their own house investment services such as unit trusts and insurance or become totally independent unbiased advisers and only sell other organisations' financial services.

Undoubtedly 'polarisation' will lead to some banks developing and expanding their own in-house services where these have an investment content, in order to fill gaps created by the loss of ability to sell those services not already available in-house.

Social and economic factors

Market demand is influenced by cultural and social changes, not least those related to birth rates, educational standards and the ways attitudes change according to the information distributed or the effects of pressure groups.

Closely linked to these social trends are the economic issues that affect demand. The main economic factors likely to have a major influence in the marketplace are inflation, the level of unemployment and incomes.

When the economy is buoyant, and job prospects are good, demand for consumer loans will naturally rise. On past trends, levels of savings tend to increase when the economy appears to be going into recession. Rising house prices, which occur when mortgage money is readily available, also stimulate sales of financial services. Obviously mortgage lending increases, but so does the sale of other services. These include life insurance, and consumer lending generally, as when houses are switched or remortgaged money is unlocked to pay for a wide range of consumer durables and leisure activity.

Technology

Computers in communication and delivery systems continue to create a major impact on financial services markets. Technology is reshaping delivery and marketing communication methods in such a way that new services and new markets are developing rapidly.

We now take ATMs for granted, 'home banking' for the personal and corporate markets is now available, worldwide automated payments systems function efficiently and on the immediate horizon is EFTPOS, already mentioned, which is now at an advanced pilot stage. Credit cards and debit cards are undermining the volumes of payments by cash and cheques, offering customers speed, convenience and safety.

It has been said that the banks are technology driven and not driving technology. An amalgamation of the need to reduce paper, open up availability of financial services beyond restricted banking hours, and meet customer demand for cheap money transmission facilities, are the main thrust of a technological revolution. Perhaps now it is difficult to decide which came first, customer demand or the bank's need to improve efficiency and cut cost. Nevertheless, technology has made changes to market demand and will undoubtedly continue to do so.

Political and legal forces

Regulation, deregulation, privatisation. These words have become commonplace in a banker's world. The Financial Services Act 1986, the Building Societies Act 1986, the Consumer Credit Act 1974, and many other parliamentary Acts, have reshaped the roles of competition in what were traditional financial services markets. On 27 October 1986 we saw 'Big Bang', the deregulation of the stock market, and this legislation continues to have a far-reaching effect on capital markets in Great Britain. New 'players' have emerged and new markets. Competition has brought down investment charges and broadened the appeal of the stock market. Increased interest in shares has also been aided and abetted by the sale of state owned utilities and industries.

New financial schemes and changes in tax regulations occur in most budgets, and the latest in a long line was the introduction of Personal Equity Plans. These fiscal measures stimulate market demand and encourage further competition which in itself also creates demand. Now the banks are faced with polarisation, mentioned earlier, and this will undoubtedly create further market demand changes. Some banks will counter polarisation by developing a wide range of 'in-house' services, especially highly remunerative insurance products. Others may decide to become independent brokers; so the nature of the competition will change and with it market attitudes and demand.

Ever since the bank cartel was removed by the 1971 Act governing Competition and Credit Control, legal changes have continued to exert a major influence on the marketplace and those that service it.

Summary

The impact of competition will depend upon where you are and what your responsibilities are within the bank's structure. Branch managers will have issues which will be narrower than the broader competitive aspects which the Chief Executive will have to address. Nevertheless, the basic importance of knowing who the competitors are and how their impact can be neutralised is similar for all those with marketing responsibilities. Currently all the major clearing banks are trying to increase their revenue from activities that are not directly related to lending money. This has intensified competition to sell ancillary services such as insurance, not just to increase revenue generally but also to enhance customer loyalty and maximise sales opportunities that derive from a retail network.

There is a need for a corporate strategy to keep the bank moving towards stated objectives and to help the decisions which arise on whether or not to take reactive measures if and when competitors' actions could impact on market share in key service areas or markets.

Major changes recently, such as deregulation and growing financial sophistication, have placed pressure on profits. Competition is sharper, there are more players, and servicing and technology costs are increasing. Markets and market needs are changing, and the role of the branch network is also changing. All these factors demand a brave strategy for the future, designed to give customers a better service at an acceptable or competitive price.

The Big Bang and the Building Societies Act 1986 have resulted in a further reduction in the historical demarcation lines between what was regarded as traditional retail bank markets, building society markets and insurance and securities markets. Now there are many more participants offering a wide range of similar services and facilities.

Lending and lodgements remain the life blood of the retail banks, but both are under greater competitive threat from a wide variety of financial institutions, some of whom sell by offering very specialised skills and others by using the price mechanism.

The way forward for the major clearing banks in this very competitive environment is to get closer to chosen target markets with greater appreciation of their needs, stronger marketing using a skilfully blended marketing mix, and the creation of services and distribution systems which offer convenience, flexibility and added value.

Revision questions

1 How has legislation broadened the scope of building societies and how do you think this will affect the retail banks' operations?
2 What competitors do you have in your locality? Describe their marketing strengths and weaknesses and demonstrate how the strengths could be overcome.
3 What are your bank's main corporate strategies to deal with the rapid changes in the marketplace?
4 Identify the main suppliers of medium-term finance to the corporate sector. How can the retail banks overcome the competitor's advantage derived from specialisation?
5 What part can technology play in the bank's efforts to meet competition?

Part 3
Selling Financial Services

Chapter 13

Personal Market – Some Important Customer Groups

Shakespeare's seven ages of man in '*As You Like It*' had a mewling infant, a whining schoolboy, a sighing lover, a quarrelsome soldier, a wise justice, a bespectacled 'sixth age' and finally a time-worn ancient. Although Shakespeare's segmentation was not based upon the requirements of financial marketing, nevertheless he had identified that life does go through stages or cycles and what is suitable for one age may be entirely inappropriate for another.

It is impossible to define precisely where each stage in the life cycle starts and finishes, the only finite dates remain the two which mark our birth and death. However, within a life span of three score years and ten it is possible to identify broad age bands where, in general terms, the needs of people are very similar. By segmenting the personal market into groups it is also possible to select the most likely profitable areas within these groups for selling selected financial services.

In this chapter, grouping by age, by income, by marital status and by home ownership is considered in conjunction with their likely financial requirements. Then each group is looked at in greater depth as a prerequisite to cross-matching financial services which would appear to meet broadly similar needs in each age and income group.

(a) Grouping by age

In the last few years, the banking habit has not only become more widespread among adults, it has also spread down the age scale. During the 1970s, as competition for school-leaver accounts became intense, the major banks introduced 'lollipop' or 'young savers' accounts. In many cases expensive 'give-aways' were introduced to encourage young schoolchildren to open an account, the main aim of this marketing activity being to pre-empt the school-leaver stage where competition among the banks was proving tough and costly. Unfortunately the marketing efforts to gain account relationships with children prior to their leaving school was not entirely successful. The outcome was an expensive account gathering exercise. The value of minimal credit balances was more than offset by the administrative and marketing costs. Moreover, many opened accounts with every bank offering an attractive 'free' incentive; so we now have a vast number of multi-banked children. This, in turn, has undermined the traditional customer loyalty factor – this young age group has become very used to multi-banking.

So the age spread of bank customers is now very wide, and includes children, teenagers, school-leavers, students, young marrieds, those with families, the middle-aged and the retired. For campaign marketing activity, these broad categories are most easily identified within arbitrary age bands. These age bands are merely guidelines and it should not be forgotten that customers are also individuals and may not comply in every respect with their peer group. So although mass marketing activity designed to cater for grouping by age is no substitute for marketing face to face with the individual, it nevertheless provides the easiest starting point for segmenting the personal market into customer groups.

The following age splits are widely used by the banks when grouping customers

(1) Under the age of 16 when there is a heavy reliance on parents;

(2) Age 16–21 when people are leaving school, starting work or going on to higher education;

(3) Age 21–25 when the majority of people in this age group save to get married, actually marry and perhaps buy a house;

(4) Age 25–45 which is the period when many financial services are in most demand as people raise a family;

(5) Over 45 but before retirement. By now children are leaving home, and people are beginning to plan for retirement. It is also a time for more social or holiday expenditure and for amassing liquid and capital assets;

(6) The retired whose financial service needs can be complex or simple, depending upon their wealth and state of health.

(b) Grouping by income

In Chapter 3 the socio-economic classifications of A, B, C1, C2, D and E were highlighted and these, in the main, coincide with income, education and potential income levels. High net worth people are valuable customers of the bank not only because they maintain good credit balances on current and investment accounts but also because they offer the greatest potential for cross-selling ancillary services such as wills, insurance, tax and financial planning facilities, investment portfolio management and so on.

However, so called blue- and white-collar workers also need financial services, and in some cases offer greater potential to banks as they may be less likely to shop around and are prepared to pay higher rates of interest on borrowing. Within this grouping by income there is a further subdivision: that between the weekly paid and those on monthly salaries.

Arguably the most important service is the current account and the credit balances maintained on which, at the present time, no interest is paid by the bank. These so-called 'endowment' funds make a major contribution to bank profits, and it is a well-known fact that monthly-paid current account holders keep higher average balances than those customers who are weekly paid.

Figure 13.1 illustrates the considerable difference between average balances held by monthly-paid customers compared with those receiving a weekly income.

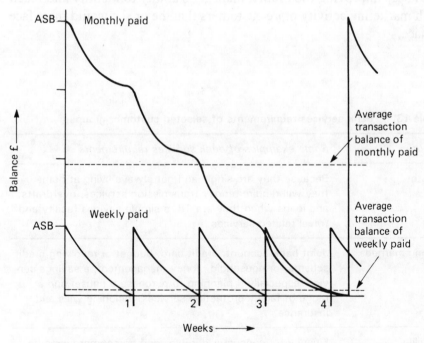

ASB = average starting balance

Fig. 13.1 Schematic of the transaction balance in accounts receiving monthly or weekly wage/salary payments. Some 50 per cent of workers are not paid monthly and approximately 400 000 per annum are switching from cash to a banking account.

(c) Grouping by marital and home ownership status

The consumption pattern of single people is quite different from that of married couples. Similarly the financial needs of those with young children and those buying their own home are different from others with no family or who are not houseowners.

By using these broad distinctions it is again possible to identify financial needs that are similar for all customers who are single, married, or married with a family. Table 13.1 highlights some of the banking service requirements of these groups.

Deciding the most practical method of segmenting the personal customer profile in order to conduct mass-marketing activity, or in choosing which segment or group to exploit in this way, will depend upon the ability of the bank's computer and other information systems to produce customer lists marshalled from the chosen groups.

Many bank information systems were not designed to aid mass marketing and, as a result, identifying customer groups quickly and accurately has in the past been almost impossible. New marketing-orientated computer programs are being introduced, and this is gradually improving the branch manager's ability to identify and reach with marketing activity more customers than he or she would meet face to face.

Table 13.1 Bank services requirements of selected customer groups

Group	Some examples of bank services requirements
Youth	Because they are single and not always living at home they will require money transmission services, overdrafts, and loans when they are 18, a simple savings facility and travel-related services
Young marrieds	Joint bank account, credit card, budget or revolving credit scheme for household money management, a savings service (especially if planning to purchase a house) and a range of family protection services, including wills and insurance.
Families	Finance for consumer durables and home improvements. Savings schemes for parents and children. Advice on finance for education, insurance and financial management generally, wills, insurance and perhaps taxation advice are now important necessities for family protection.

Table 13.2   Matrix of customer variables

Group	Age	Lifestyle	Finance requirements
Schoolchildren	Up to 16	Mainly parental guidance. Limited financial resources	• Simple savings account with occasional access to it
Youth	16–21	Leaving school Further education First job Low earnings	• Money transmission services • Travel facilities • Overdrafts or loans • Simple savings account
Young married	21–25	Going steady or getting married Saving for a home Joint incomes	• Joint account • Budget facilities • Savings accounts • Consumer loans • Insurance, wills and travel services
Householder Married with family	25–45	Income growth but loss of wife's earnings when children born. Buying home and trading up and home/consumer durables	• Joint account • Mortgages and home improvement loans • Longer-term savings for education funding • Insurance, wills, consumer loans • Savings accounts for children
Older persons	Over 45 but before retirement	Higher paid with or without inherited wealth Higher spendable income Need for financial advice and planning	• Savings and investments • Occasional borrowing • Replacement mortgage or home improvement loans • Financial advisory services
Retired	Over 60/65	Accumulated capital Lump sums available Protection for widowed	• Management of capital/income • Trust services and financial advice

Cross-matching services

Before looking more closely at some of the main features of the larger
customer groups in an effort to gain a greater appreciation of their
financial requirements, it is worth spending a few moments matching
the main segmentation variables covered so far in this chapter. These
are age, income and lifestyle features which can all be brought
together in a matrix that also highlights likely needs for bank services
(Table 13.2).

In conclusion, segmentation is necessary in order to channel expensive resources and marketing activity into areas which are judged to be
potentially the most profitable. Moreover, it is vital for the banks to
reduce reliance on interest-related earnings by selling more ancillary
services that are fee or commission-related. There are many ways in
which customers and non-customers can be marshalled into groups for
marketing activity, but whichever way is chosen the underlying reasons
for doing it will be similar. The two main reasons for grouping
customers and non-customers are firstly, as a way to gain a sound
understanding of the needs of selected groups who have been identified
as potentially profitable. Secondly, to enable promotional messages to
be correctly positioned so that they highlight the right service features
to the group being targeted. Without careful grouping or segmentation,
the campaign-style marketing of financial services is unlikely to be
cost-effective.

The young savers' market (up to 16)

The 'lollipop' or junior savings services with gimmicks or give-aways
are now an accepted part of marketing life on both sides of the counter.
The end objective is to gain accounts that are likely to yield profit in
the years to come. Between the ages of 11 and 16 the only guide to
achieving this objective is to concentrate on attracting the accounts of
children at the better quality schools or those who have reached sixth
form study. One other way to control likely quality of account, and thus
improve potential profitability in the years to come, is by concentrating
on those schools in better class areas – another use of geographic
segmentation.

Market potential for new accounts among schoolchildren is considerable since about 550 000 children are born each year in England and
Wales. Four out of five children whose parents have a bank account
have some form of savings, and approximately 35 per cent of customers
have children under the age of 16.

Not surprisingly, parents or grandparents have a strong influence on the choice of a home for childrens' savings, and the balance between child orientation and 'adultness' reflects the bank's appreciation of these family influences. Market research among 11–16-year-olds shows that children are aware of the need to save and in many instances have a fair knowledge of what savings schemes are available. This research also shows that children are keen to start a savings account with a bank as a forerunner to gaining current account facilities.

Until Composite Rate Tax (CRT) was imposed upon the banks, they could pay interest gross on savings accounts and, provided the tax-free income allowance for a single person was not exceeded, no tax was payable on the bank interest earned by these young savers. Nowadays, with very few exceptions, only the National Savings movement can pay gross interest on savings to personal customers and this has given them a very advantageous marketing edge. Currently gross interest paid on a National Savings investment account is 4/5 per cent above the CRT yields on bank and building society schemes for the smaller saver.

The young saver will remain an important market segment especially in order to attract new account customers. Ways need to be found to streamline the administrative processes to keep costs as low as possible. Another vital task is to prevent 'decay' as the novelty of the 'give-away' wears off and gradually accounts go dormant or are closed. Keeping in touch with young saver customers remains important not just to prevent account decay but also to encourage further deposits and thus make the total balances grow. Yet again there is a direct link between cost of communication and perceived benefits derived from it. Several ploys have been tried by the banks including sending birthday cards and newsletters. Switching young savers into current accounts or other forms of savings schemes is also actively pursued by the banks as they try to obtain the primary account relationship at a time when the young saver will have to make a decision on where to bank.

The youth market (age 16–21)

Competition among banks for the unbanked is most visible in this market segment mainly because it allows a degree of selectivity but also because there is little remaining scope to acquire new accounts from the adult population as the vast majority have an account. In certain socio-economic groups and age-brackets – the wealthier middle-aged and older groups – this penetration has virtually reached saturation point. In the early 1970s about 60 per cent of the adult population had a banking account, but the growth of account holding to present levels has not been uniform as Table 13.3 shows.

The youth market in this age group can be split into a further three broad bands

(1) Sixth-form students
(2) College and university students
(3) Those seeking employment

Of these three groups the college or university students have attracted the most marketing activity from the major banks. Incentives to open a bank account have included cash, book tokens, railcards at a discounted price, guaranteed overdrafts, commission-free travel facilities and specialised loan schemes to fund the costs of education. Some banks have paid considerable sums to student unions and other bodies for lists of names and addresses of new students and embarked upon direct mail campaigns to improve market share of new accounts from those going on to higher education. As has already been said, the motive behind such aggressive competition is easy to see – better-educated people are more likely to provide the greatest profit potential to a bank in the ensuing years.

Table 13.3 Current, deposit or savings account held by adults in Great Britain by socio-economic group and age

	1974 %	1977 %	1981 %
All adults	61.9	69.2	73.9
By socio-economic group:			
AB	81.9	86.1	88.7
C1	74.6	81.3	83.8
C2	59.8	68.3	73.8
D	49.0	54.9	63.0
E	41.8	46.8	49.6
By age:			
15–19		40.0	44.7
20–24	56.6	75.7	75.2
25–34	69.1	78.0	83.1
35–44	65.6	76.4	81.3
45–54	64.6	73.8	79.9
55–64	62.5	69.1	76.4
65 +	54.3	63.5	68.9

Source: Target Group Index, British Market Research Bureau (1982)

(a) Student market

Among the age band 16–21 approximately 55 per cent are working and 12 per cent are unemployed. The remaining 33 per cent are still at school, university or polytechnic, in sixth-form or vocational training employed within the various government training schemes.

The size of the potentially unbanked market has gradually reduced over the years and it now numbers approximately 550 000. Another feature of this group is the changing attitudes and the fact that they have more money to spend. Moreover, they are not daunted by a bank because they have more self-confidence. They are also more discerning and sophisticated, which means that marketing campaigns to attract their business must be professional and correctly matched to their requirements.

Despite the shrinking of numbers, accounts opened by students still provide approximately 20 per cent of all new current accounts; so for this reason alone they are an important group. What is more, their value, even whilst at college or university, is considerable, for students keep higher credit balances than other customers of similar age. Higher balances are only part of the potential, since students and especially ex-students tend to use more banking services, and this in turn provides profit opportunities.

Opportunities to attract student accounts exist for only a few months each year, mainly during July to October.

Probably the best time to launch promotions is after the examinations in May and before arriving on campus. Even so, some 25 per cent leave opening an account until they arrive at college or university, probably because they wish to wait and see which bank is the most conveniently situated.

Student needs for financial services are relatively uncomplicated. A current account with cheque book, cheque and cash dispenser cards and perhaps a small overdraft facility is probably sufficient in the early stages of their student life. Travel facilities might be required, a budget or revolving credit account to even out the bumps in the financial issues of living in rented accommodation may also be necessary. Other than these needs, and perhaps a credit card, there is little else they require apart from financial guidance on how to make limited ends meet. Financing the cost of higher education which usually falls upon the parents is covered later in this chapter.

(b) Market for the unbanked workforce

This market is made up of those who have been unemployed since leaving school and have now found a job, and those who leave school with a job to go into. Any marketing activity to gain business will depend largely on whether they are weekly or monthly paid (see page 269) and how easy it is to recruit accounts in sufficient numbers, so reducing initial administration costs involved in opening new accounts.

For many years there has been considerable consumer resistance among older workers to open bank accounts. Apart from the nineteenth-century Truck Acts which guaranteed the rights of workers to be paid in cash (since repealed on 1 January 1987), generally weekly workers have resisted opening a bank account because:

(1) they fear their cash may be inaccessible;
(2) they fear overspending because of the ease and convenience of a cheque book and credit cards;
(3) they fear loss of privacy (often this is linked to the husband not wanting the wife to know what he earns);
(4) they feel intimidated by bank premises/the image of banks.

These issues need to be overcome by carefully positioning bank marketing, but the requirement to reap profit should also be borne in mind. This need for profit has encouraged the major banks to segment the unbanked so that the potentially more rewarding areas receive the greatest weight of marketing. As a result, the choice of selection of unbanked groups by the banks and how they gather this business varies widely. Some concentrate on the better educated, whilst others adopt a policy of quantity rather than quality. One economic factor which will affect a bank's views on attracting the unbanked in large numbers will be the ability of the existing branch network resources to cope with the increased business yet maintain a high quality of service. Automatic cash dispenser machines in factories and shops are helping to meet some of the pressures caused by more and more people having banking accounts.

(c) Advantages of accounts with mandated wages and salaries

If in conjunction with employers, accounts can be opened for employees, with wages or salaries mandated direct to the bank. In this way, the overall administration costs of running the account can be considerably reduced.

On this basis, most banks would agree that weekly-paid customers can be profitable, as they offer potential for savings facilities and generally provide a particularly good source for consumer credit and consumer durable loans. Moreover, in some industries, income levels are relatively high and this in turn opens up potential to sell a much wider range of services than just loans and savings schemes.

With mandated arrangements there are also benefits to the employers and employees. The ways in which these benefits are portrayed is important.

Benefits to employer

(1) cost savings
  - no security service needed;
  - no staff needed to guard the wage packets and distribute them;
  - interest saving with same day debiting.

(2) Cash flow improvement
  - wage cheques debited later (same day debiting);
  - possibility of introducing four weekly payments or one monthly payment;

(3) No security risk;

(4) No disruption of workforce to collect wage packets;

(5) If wage records are computerised, using BACKS exchange of tapes system there is a substantial reduction in paperwork.

Benefits to employees

(1) Wages paid in a more secure format

(2) Enables easier budgeting of own cash resources

(3) An immediate introduction to all the personal services of the bank;

(4) Improved 'status'.

Proposals for implementation

(1) To the employer
  - evaluate cost savings based upon information provided by the company;
  - highlight the benefits;
  - offer concessionary terms for operating employees' accounts for an initial period;
  - offer a financial advisory service to the workforce and simplify the arrangements for account opening by having bank staff attending at the factory;
  - encourage the company to offer incentive to the workforce to accept changeover, especially to a less frequent wages period (e.g. sharing of first year's cost savings).

(2) to the employees
  - meet the unions' representatives to explain the services;
  - meet the workforce to explain bank accounts including cashing cheques, clearing cheques, standing orders, bank statements, credit cards, cheque guarantee cards;
  - indicate concessionary terms for operating accounts;

- explain the bank's savings and mortgage services;
- agree to the issue of credit/cheque guarantee cards soon after the accounts are opened.

In conclusion, the trend towards non-cash payment of wages will undoubtedly continue, largely as a result of pressure from employers. The banks can actively seek this business and streamline their administration and servicing systems so that even weekly-paid customers' accounts are profitable. Alternatively the banks can take a passive stance, but even so some accounts will be attracted through convenience of location or for other reasons. Undoubtedly, where the market is approached *en masse* through employers, costs are reduced and there are substantial benefits to all parties. It may also be possible to use this opportunity to encourage employees to switch to fortnightly or even monthly pay.

Married and homemaker markets (age 25–45)

Arguably this group of customers offers more opportunities to sell financial services than any other. Certainly its needs for mortgages, home improvement loans and consumer durable credit, is very evident. However, this group also needs family protection in the form of will appointments, insurance to protect income and death risks, and longer-term savings schemes generally to fund future expenditure on such items as school fees. It would be impossible to cover in detail all the circumstances which could give rise to this group's requirements for financial services, for within this spread of approximately twenty years many life cycle changes will occur. Table 13.4 shows a shopping list of services which are appropriate at certain stages within the life cycle of this group. But because of the importance of insurance and mortgages to customers, and a bank's profit performance, the markets for these services are singled out and looked at in greater detail in this chapter.

Home loan market

The different types of mortgage schemes available to home buyers are highlighted in Chapter 14, so this section will deal only with the characteristics of this market. In recent years competition has grown as first the high street banks and now specialist mortgage companies have entered this arena. The net result of this competition has been the abolition of differential interest rate tiers based upon the type of mortgage and amount borrowed, finer interest rates generally and, more recently, very favourable fixed-rate offers for up to three years.

Table 13.4 Services for married and homemaker segments

Family circumstances	Likely requirements	Service suitable
Getting married	Joint access to funds	● Joint account
	Furniture and other household goods	● Consumer loans/credit
		● Credit or charge card
	Household money management	● Budget or revolving credit account
	Saving for various items including house deposit	● Savings/investment services
	Family protection	● Insurance and wills
	Leisure pursuits	● Travel facilities
Buying first home	Finance for property	● Mortgages
	Improvements to home	● Home improvement loans
	Furniture and household items	● Consumer loans/credit
	Family protection	● Insurance and wills
	Household money management	● Budget or revolving credit account
	Credit to cover emergency or unexpected bills	● Credit or charge card
Starting a family	Finance for car/consumer durables	● Consumer loans/credit
		● Credit or charge card
	Education provision	● Insurance services
	Family protection	● Will revision, insurance and estate planning
	Childrens savings	● Junior savers' accounts
Moving house/ Extending house	Bridging facilities	● Bridging loan
	Finance for home improvement	● Home improvement loan
	Review of mortgage	● Mortgage/insurance advice
	Review of insurance cover including household	● Insurance and insurance review facilities
	Finance for consumer durables	● Consumer loans/credit
	Investment of surplus proceeds	● Investment services and advice

The latter benefit has been brought about by those institutions which from time to time endeavour to 'buy' market share.

Home ownership has grown considerably in the last decade and this growth has created a substantial market for mortgage funds. Moreover, the average life span of a mortgage is about six to seven years, so there is a large recurring or repeat business. The banks also see this as a low risk service which creates spin-off benefits, since invariably buying a house also creates other requirements for financial services as the chart on page 279 clearly shows. Even the period whilst saving for a deposit on a house has attracted considerable competition, as the banks offer savings schemes linked to a provision which guarantees a mortgage. In this way lodgements are attracted, and when a mortgage is required the bank which offered the links through a savings scheme is in first place to quote for the business. This facility could be important to customers if mortgage funds are in short supply. Both the size of market, and its value to those financial institutions who service it, will continue to grow. In the current political climate, this country is committed to extending home ownership to as many people as possible. Furthermore, the role played by the banks and building societies will remain very important, not just in terms of providing finance, but also in making sure that customer requirements are correctly matched with the most appropriate financial packages. The purchase of a house is probably the most important and costly single financial act in a customer's life. Thus, the need for the best possible advice remains paramount and this re-emphasises the fiduciary responsibilities of a bank manager. However, polarisation has to some extent neutralised fiduciary feelings, as the customer will know if the bank manager is acting in the capacity of a company representative.

Family and school fees market

Bringing up children is expensive, and the cost of a child from birth to adulthood has been estimated at nearly £100 000 or around £100 per week. That sounds a lot, but includes the apportionment of a number of expenses such as housing, heating and holidays which are incurred by the whole family. For many families the weekly cost will be substantially lower than £100 per week but nevertheless the liability remains, and if the parents died somebody else would have to bear the costs. The expense of raising children and the cost of private education are two main drains on family income. They also create the main needs for financial services from this market.

Insurance is the main way many families protect themselves against loss of income, sudden death and the cost of private education. This market's requirements are protection of income, provision in the event of death and ultimately income to fund mortgages, school fees and finally retirement. Table 13.5 outlines these needs and identifies the type of insurance that can be used to cover them. The list is by no means complete but it does give a guide to the main risk areas, which in turn open up sales opportunities in this profitable and financially active market.

Table 13.5 More common insurance contracts

Target customers	Investment		Income		Capital cover
Personal	*From income*	*From capital*	*Protection*	*Provision*	
	Fixed/flexible endowments	*Guaranteed/investment bonds/annuities*	*Permanent health*	*Family income benefits*	*Whole life/term assurance*
Young married working couples	Tax efficient savings from surplus income		Income replacement on disablement		To clear death expenses, debts
Homebuyers	Funding mortgage		Continue mortgage repayments on disablement	To meet running costs of home on death	To clear mortgage/loans
Family	Future expenses/growing reserve of money	School fees	As above	Tax free income for dependants on death	Family emergency fund
Middle age plus (comfortably off)	Capital for investment to supplement pension	Tax efficient capital growth			Inheritance tax planning, death expenses, etc.

Older more affluent market (over-45s)

Understanding the characteristics of this very important market segment is a prerequisite to providing services which meet its financial
needs. By comparison with the under-45 market this is a stable group of
people who keep good credit balances in their bank accounts. They are
also a busy segment and often have little time to look after their own
financial affairs. So they need from their bank a high standard of
personal service, help and advice on making the best use of capital and
surplus income, and finally guidance on how best to plan for ultimate
retirement.

This group, despite enjoying a higher than average income and a
tendency to have capital is not necessarily financially sophisticated.
Senior managers in industry and commerce, and those self-employed,
are usually well educated but often do not take much interest in
financial matters except those which impact on their job or their family
lifestyle. This lack of appreciation of financial facilities is aggravated
by the wide variety and complexity of financial services aimed at this
market. Therefore, they rely heavily on their financial advisers and are
sympathetic to bank managers who demonstrate that they are familiar
with their circumstances and can provide the right services.

The principal needs of this group are borrowing facilities at competitive rates, including home loans, a full range of savings, investment,
estate planning and pension-related services and perhaps school fees
schemes in the early years. Above all, they need personal attention so
that the advice and services are tailored to the individual's specific
needs. Which savings and investment services are most suitable may be
influenced by the customer's income tax liability, and new services will
continue to appear aimed more directly at the higher taxpayer. A recent
example is the Personal Equity Plan which followed the Chancellor of
the Exchequer's budget changes in 1986.

Protection against risk such as loss of income, job, etc. are usually
insurable, and Table 13.6 illustrates areas which can be covered in this
way for the self-employed people in this group. Many of those who are
employed will be more than adequately covered under a variety of
employer pension and protection arrangements.

Table 13.6 Insurance contracts commonly used by business customers

Types of self-employed	Endowments	Pensions	Permanent health for individual or group	Death in service benefits	Whole life/ term	Business covers
Sole traders	Augment retirement provision	Retirement income provision for: (a) self	Income replacement on disablement for: (a) self	(Normally part of pension plan)	Loan repayment on death	Material damage
Partnerships and directors of limited companies	Funding of limited loans	(b) employees (c) partners (d) directors	(b) employees (c) partners (d) directors	Financial provision for dependants of: (a) self (b) employees (c) partners (d) directors	Partnership Share purchase schemes; Key man cover, Repayment of loan accounts	Protection of profits following losses from insured risks; Liabilities to employees /public; Theft, travel, legal expenses, etc.

Note: Many of these risks apply to all self-employed people not just those who are over 45

Approaching retirement

Hopefully some careful and long-range planning has already been done to ensure that retirement is secure and untroubled by money worries. The earlier planning for retirement is started the more successful it is likely to be. However, many will leave these issues to the last minute or get caught out by an unexpected early retirement imposed upon them by unforeseen circumstances. This could be redundancy or simply a general reduction in the retirement age from, say, 65 down to age 60.

The main issues which need to be addressed as part of this planning process are

(1) Savings and how to build up capital;
(2) Investment and how to make existing capital grow;
(3) Pensions and other ways to mitigate income tax and provide for future income;
(4) Getting personal affairs in order by making wills and limiting the effects of inheritance tax.

All these issues can be cross-matched with financial services which include insurance, unit trusts, investment bonds, share purchase, investment management services, Personal Equity Plans, taxation facilities, will appointments and many more. Cross-matching needs with the right features and benefits of services will require a detailed understanding of each customer's financial and family circumstances.

Ultimately, when nearer to retirement, a further set of issues should be considered, some of which are covered in more detail by the Case Study at the end of this chapter. These include: when to actually retire, whether or not to repay a mortgage, how to use commutation funds or other lump sums, whether to continue with some form of part-time employment. Any advice from a bank manager would need to cover most of these issues and be framed in the light of the customer's family circumstances, health and tax position. For these reasons there can be no set or preconceived advice as the circumstances will be different in each case. This list is by no means complete nor do the needs of groups in practice separate as clinically as shown. For example, the requirements of professionals and small businessmen may fall within the range of services suitable for both corporate and personal markets. They may even have needs which fall between both these service segments. Nevertheless the list does give a guide to the main risk areas relating to personal customers and this appreciation in turn will open up sales opportunities in these profitable and financially active markets.

Other important market segments

The personal market can be divided in many different ways, but this chapter has concentrated on using age, income and family circumstances as the main criteria for grouping customers. Although this is probably the easiest way to identify similar groups and cross-match their requirements with financial service features and benefits it does not cover three other groups which are also important from a profit potential point of view:

(1) The women's market
(2) The travel market
(3) The expatriate market

The women's market

There are approximately 20 million women in England and Wales of whom some 11 million work. In fact, the number of working women has steadily increased in recent years, whereas the total number of men in employment has remained fairly constant. As such, women have become important contributors to the family budget, and also in their own right offer considerable opportunities as users of financial services. More women are gaining better-paid jobs, joining the ranks of professionals and running their own businesses. Therefore, their financial needs are similar to those of working men and include financial advice and services across a broad spectrum of lending, savings, investment and ancillary services.

Clearly the wealthier women, and those in better-paid or potential career jobs, offer the major opportunities and thus are the key groups within the total women's market. As such, they have their own salaries to manage, may have surplus income to invest and need to amass capital through investment in insurance, unit trusts and stocks and shares. These women also need consumer loans, budget or revolving credit facilities as well as the range of money transmission/money access services. As they get older, and perhaps depending upon their marital status, women may also require tax, financial planning and pension schemes as well as estate planning services. This is a market where the characteristics continue to change. These changes are influenced by social requirements and attitudes as well as legislation designed to create equal opportunities.

The travel market

Over 20 million people travel from the UK each year either on holidays abroad or on business. Annual sales of travel services including currency, travellers cheques, insurance, accommodation and travel tickets are substantial and this market is highly profitable.

A wide range of travel services exists already and it may not be too long before the banks enter the package tour market directly or establish a chain of travel offices. Meanwhile providers of travel facilities compete very strongly to try and increase market share, especially relating to the following popular travel services:

(1) Travel insurance in all its forms;
(2) Travellers cheques as a safe way to carry funds;
(3) Charge cards and credit cards to ease shopping and provide emergency back up;
(4) Holiday loans and savings schemes prior to a holiday;
(5) Eurocheques and currency facilities

Most of these services are sold on the basis of convenience of availability, security, loss replacement and world-wide acceptance.

Expatriate market

Although this group is small it is a remunerative market for the banks and other financial intermediaries. There are approximately 200 000 British expatriates in the Middle East alone on comparatively high tax-free salaries. For those who are the longer-term expatriates, capital sums will be available for investment and the clearing banks are keen to provide investment advice and offshore investment facilities especially in low-tax areas, such as the Channel Islands where they are represented.

Expatriates need rather specialised financial advice and the major banks will have this expertise within their organisation. The branch manager's role is to ensure that his expatriate customers gain access to this specialist help, and the main areas to consider are:

(1) *Tax position*
   When a customer decides to take up employment overseas the tax position may become extremely complex. There is certainly a need for professional advice before leaving the UK. There are many ways of reducing tax liabilities in the year of departure and good advice can produce favourable results for the customer and the bank.
(2) *Offshore bank accounts*
   There are often advantages in switching savings accounts offshore, and it is preferable to introduce the services of Channel Island subsidiaries.
(3) *Insurance*
   Many areas of insurance need careful consideration before depar-

ture, particularly if property is retained in the UK. It is far easier to arrange the necessary cover while the individual is in the UK.

(4) *Wills*

A will is always important, but the more so with the added risks of working overseas.

(5) *Investments*

Investment planning will be required once the expatriate is in receipt of a regular tax-free income. This might start with a cash reserve offshore to cover contingencies and/or the needs of the short-term expatriate. Usually the regional trust branch will advise about other forms of investments. No two individuals have exactly the same requirements; they will have different future intentions, tax positions, financial goals and so on.

Finally, the majority of expatriates, having completed their term abroad, will return to the UK and continue as wealthier customers. Thus the long-term fee earning and lodgement benefits can continue for many years, provided the right support and guidance is given initially to cement the relationship.

Case study

John Smith has maintained a personal account with his bank for many years. In the past, personal loans have been agreed to assist with the purchase of cars, but the last loan was repaid six years ago when Mr Smith was provided with a car by his company.

Mr Smith calls to see the bank manager by appointment. He explains that he was 58 years old last week. He has worked for his present company for 16 years and currently earns a salary of £12 000 per annum. His company has just offered him early retirement, with effect from the end of the year, and he is disposed to accept it.

He details his financial position as follows:

(1) On retirement a lump sum of £12 000 will be made to him;
(2) He will receive a pension of £6000 per annum;
(3) He owns his home, estimated value £40 000, outstanding endowment mortgage £10 000; supporting life policy, taken out 16 years ago, matures on his sixtieth birthday;
(4) He has about £5000 invested in a building society account as well as £2000 on his accounts at your branch;
(5) He has been offered the post of secretary at his golf club, commencing on 1 April. He would be paid an honorarium of £1750 per annum;
(6) He is married – his wife works part-time as a book-keeper and earns £30 per week – and has two daughters, one of whom is

married and the other, now aged 19, starts a university course next week.

He asks for guidance on investment or other disposition of the £12 000 he would receive if he accepts the retirement offer.

———————

This is a strategic time to review his financial affairs generally and the bank should not miss this opportunity.

There would seem to be a number of areas to consider:

(a) Should he retire?
(b) Should he repay his mortgage?
(c) Investment advice
(d) Car – will he have to buy a new car?
(e) Daughter – funding her university course
(f) Pension arrangements regarding his new job and his wife's work.

Retirement

A calculation of the net income is needed to establish the likely reduction in income.

Current Income

	£	£	£
Salary		12 000	
Tax	2 500		
N.I.	1 000	3 000	8 500
Building society (say 8%)			400
Wife – no tax/N.I. payable			1 500
total net income			£10 400

Proposed

	£	£
Honorarium		1 750
Pension		6 000
Investments – £15 000 at 10%		1 500
		9 250
Tax	say 1 700	
N.I.	—	1 700
		7 550
Wife		1 500
		£9 050

Although the gross income is substantially lower, the net income shows a differential of only £1 350. Allowing for reduced expenses and possibly an increase in his daughter's grant, the differential could be reduced further. In other words, financially a decision to retire should not involve a substantial reduction in income, whilst he would have a useful amount of capital to fall back on if needed.

Repay his mortgage

The net interest payments are about £900 p.a. plus the premium on the life policy which is still tax allowable. Since the net interest rate is probably very competitive and Mr Smith ought to be able to meet these outgoings, it would not be worth his while repaying the mortgage but better to wait until the policy matures. At that stage there may be additional sums available from the policy assuming that it is 'with profits' – further advice on investment may be needed at that time.

Investment

Depending on the purchase of a car and allowing for the funds in the building society and deposit account, there would be in the order of £20 000 to invest. An introduction to the bank's specialist personal adviser would be appropriate. A spread of investment, based on capital growth, extra income or a mix of both, would be sensible. Investments would range from National Savings Certificates, gilt-edged, unit trusts, building society special deposits and banks' high-rate deposits which now offer competitive rates. The specialist personal adviser would prepare a detailed report on which Mr Smith could base his decisions.

Car

His company car will have to be returned on his retirement – what are his proposals for purchasing a replacement vehicle?

Daughter

With his changed circumstances, his daughter's grant could well be increased. Discussions should be held with the local authority to clarify the position urgently.

Pension

If he accepts retirement, both he and his wife will be employed part-time in non-pensionable jobs. There may be a worthwhile investment in 'self-employed' pension schemes in which the contributions are tax allowable. If necessary, the contribution could be made out of capital with the view that the return should be improved later with an increased pension. Reference should be made to the bank's insurance services.

Other areas

Other matters which could be considered include reviewing of wills; insurance cover, particularly as he may already be covered by his company and this cover will cease on retirement; private medical treatment, which again may have been paid for by the company.

Summary

There are many different ways to group elements of the personal market. How this is achieved in practice is largely dependent upon the bank's computer-based ability to provide the type of information that will aid marketing effort. Currently the main methods used by the major banks to group customers are by using the demographics of age, income, marital status and home ownership.

When grouping by age the personal market tends to subdivide as broadly follows:

Under	16
Age	16–21
Age	21–25
Age	25–45
Over	45s
Retired	

These subdivisions correlate roughly with major life cycle characteristics and changes.

Monthly-paid customers keep average balances some ten times higher than those who are weekly paid.

The characteristics that govern the take-up of financial services in the following groups should be fully appreciated

- Youth market including the student segment
- The unbanked

- Married and homemaker market
- School fees market
- Older more affluent market
- Those approaching retirement
- Travellers and expatriate markets

Revision questions

1 Explain how your bank segments the personal market. Outline the reasons for these segmentation methods and identify any weaknesses you feel can be overcome with improved computer systems.
2 You are asked to prepare a marketing campaign to sell credit cards. Select your target audiences, explain why they have been chosen and how you would reach them.
3 John Brown calls to say he has started business on his own as an engineer and is employing two people. What advice can you give him?
4 In what ways can school fees be funded?
5 What are the marketing reasons for trying to obtain employee accounts?

Chapter 14

Personal Market – Lodgement and Lending Services

Estimates of the number of financial services offered by banks and, more recently by building societies, to their personal customers vary widely. It is true to say that there is a considerable number, and more new services continue to emerge at regular intervals. Also another recent trend is the growing co-operation between what were considered to be competitor institutions to provide unique packages of services with a wide range of financial benefits. One example of this co-operation is the American Express Gold Card where a 'charge card company' is joined with a number of individual banks in order to expand the benefits of their card by including some traditional bank services, especially an unsecured overdraft. Building societies and some of the Scottish banks are forging similar partnership links.

This chapter concentrates on the main lending and savings services available to personal customers. Many services now have to be actively promoted, as their complexities grow through competition, and as some are less indigenous to banking than the current account. Recently-launched services are now structured to generate more profit than before by catering for specific and clearly identified needs of some personal customer market segments, reminding us yet again that meeting needs profitably is paramount. It is only when benefits of a service are correctly matched with customer needs, in a way that is clearly appreciated by the sellers and buyers, that customer satisfaction is achieved and 'return business' fostered.

(a) Why do people buy?

The 'Maslow' theory of motivation tries to highlight the needs of individuals and place them in some order of priority or importance. By starting from the most basic needs, and working towards man's materialistic requirements, priorities can be broadly divided as follows:

(1) physical needs or the requirements for food, clothing and warmth;
(2) safety needs,
(3) social needs or the desire to be accepted or loved (a sense of belonging);
(4) status needs;
(5) self-actualisation requirements or the needs of self-achievement.

Recognising which basic need is actually most prevalent in the chosen target audience is vital. For example, trying to sell executor and trustee services to weekly-paid workers under the threat of redundancy would probably prove a waste of marketing effort. The immediate requirements of these people are job security and a simple way of paying bills and budgeting now and in the future.

Therefore, although a customer may have needs, the number and kind largely depend upon a person's standard of living or lifestyle. Some needs will not bother customers unduly; they may not be aware of others, but with some there will be a sufficient level of want which, when converted to desire, will encourage them to buy. Moreover, the strength of the buying motive varies widely from person to person. Some factors which influence this are people's heredity, environment, education, experience and income. The strength of these motives also constantly changes, depending upon time and immediate circumstances. Even the mood of the person will influence the reason for buying or not buying.

Although understanding the psychology of a person's behaviour is important in the recognition of a customer's requirement, the art of selling depends upon:

(1) establishing precisely the needs of a customer;
(2) cross-matching service features to meet these needs;
(3) convincing customers that their requirements will be fulfilled by the benefits of the service on offer.

When this chain of action is effectively achieved then, and only then, will marketing objectives be achieved.

(b) The need for local research

At a branch level, there are limitations on the nature and complexity of the research that can be carried out. This important tool of marketing is usually a function which is carried out by a marketing specialist research department. Nevertheless, customer attitudes, environmental influences, and social and economic factors do have local variations, and these differences will have some bearing on what marketing opportunities cost from branch to branch.

Local knowledge, and an appreciation of the various forces that shape the local marketplace, are valuable assets for any branch manager. The knowledge will affect his/her judgement and influence the choice of what is included in the branch marketing plan. (The main external forces affecting the marketing decisions were covered in Chapter 12 which also examined the current climate in which banks are operating.)

Despite the limited time available, a branch manager should try to undertake some basic research among customers and non-customers. To promote services effectively, he/she must know who uses them in the locality, how they use them, what benefits are particularly appreciated and what customer and potential customer financial needs remain unfulfilled.

Equally important, a banker needs to determine his/her own branch's marketing strengths and weaknesses compared to the trading aspirations and the competition for business that must be faced in that area. Again, this is part of the marketing planning process already covered in a previous chapter, but it is mentioned now because this sort of research is closely linked to the task of target customer selection and meeting these chosen customer requirements through the development of a branch marketing plan.

Probably the most revealing branch research will be that which compares sales results against pre-set targets based upon a reasoned assessment of the market potential. Regular monitoring, capable of allowing for seasonal variations in demand, is vital to branch marketing. As the results become known questions should be posed. Are the results under or over the target and, if so, why? What can be done about it?

Local research into trends in demand and changes in the market potential, through shifts in consumer preferences, are likely to be too difficult for a branch manager to assess accurately. In some instances it will be necessary to rely on intuition. However, no matter how difficult it may seem, a conscious attempt to anticipate any trends or changes which will influence the marketing effort is as important locally as it is for a bank and the industry as a whole.

For the branch banker, the lack of 'in-house' computerised customer profile data, and the limited selectiveness and relevance to branch banking of socio-economic trend information for day-to-day marketing decisions, is a handicap. Nevertheless, the division of customers into groups, with similar needs and profit potential, must be undertaken if scarce and expensive branch resources are to be channelled into areas where they will do the most good.

Personal customers account for approximately 80 per cent of the clearing banks' accounts and it is impractical to rely on face-to-face marketing activity with such large numbers. On average, 75 per cent of customers have an interview with their branch manager less than once a year.

If is therefore necessary to use ways other than face-to-face contact to communicate details of bank services, and this in turn requires customers to be segmented into groups which have similar needs. In this way various forms of campaign activity can be correctly aimed at those groups selected as priority targets. The alternative is to promote to large numbers of customers at random, in the hope that some will recognise the usefulness of the service on offer. Segmentation is often described as having 'rifle accuracy', compared with the random approach which is more akin to using a scattergun. The first step in a branch analysis of personal customers, by using information which is readily available, is usually to group by age and then, within selected age bands, by wealth or income levels.

It is not necessary to look further than the life-cycle concept to understand why this approach to customer grouping is a valid starting point. Most people will recognise that from birth to death an individual goes through a series of stages. For bankers an appreciation of these stages, and, indeed, the recognition of opportunities created by the movement of people from one life-cycle stage to another, is a basic essential to the successful marketing of bank services.

Segmenting personal customers

The total personal market can be segmented into groups according to age and lifestyle as a preliminary to selecting the most likely profitable areas for selling selected financial services.

The following divisions of the life cycle are commonly used as the basis for matching the likely needs of broad categories of customers with the features of bank services when planning promotional campaigns:

Group	Approximate age band	Lifestyle characteristics
Youth market	16–22	Includes students of further education, those entering employment for the first time, and older people in the group saving to get married.

Young marriages	20–35	Includes those who are buying their first home and starting a family. In the earlier years there is higher disposable income if both are earning. Main commitments are house purchase and obtaining labour-saving consumer durables.
Families	25–45	Settled occupation or career but with limited freedom of financial action. Priority commitments include home improvements, family financial protection and educating the children.
Older persons	40–55	Increasing disposable income as family commitments reduce. Security of occupation and beginning to plan for retirement.
About to retire or have retired	55 +	Accumulated capital giving financial security.

The age bands are broad and there are obviously overlaps – not all individuals conform to the norm. They may have typically similar requirements which change as they grow older, but the fact that customers are individuals should never be forgotten.

Income levels also affect customer requirements. However, the influence of income in many cases is only relative to the level of demand and not to the basic need. For instance, a low-paid worker must feed, clothe and house his/her family just as a high earner must. Moreover, both may well need transportation, although the difference is measured by the amount each can afford, or considers should be spent on a vehicle, not by the basic needs which are similar. Both also have the need to budget their expenditure.

(a) Further refinement of the basic customer group

There are a number of ways in which a selected age group of customers can be further refined in order to isolate the best possible target audience with a particular set of financial needs. Using information which is readily available in the branch, the following data is useful for improving the assessment of likely need and, therefore, the demand for the service within a given target group:

(1) *Income level*. The higher the income the greater the chance of selling a properly targeted service.

(2) *Marital status*. The requirements of single people are generally different from those of married couples. This split is especially relevant if the older group needs to be further defined between those still at work and those retired.

(3) *Type of occupation*. Those with careers and job security tend to have a higher demand for bank lending and savings services. They are, therefore, on average better sales prospects for a wider range of revenue generating bank facilities, simply because of their stable and often increasing disposable income which, in turn, moulds their lifestyle and requirements.

On a more individual basis, changes from one stage of the life cycle to another offer opportunities for selling bank services. These changes are sometimes called trigger points. The more obvious examples which are implied by the lists above are:

leaving school;
getting married;
buying first house;
starting a family;
promotion;
moving house;
acquisition of a capital sum;
retirement;
death of spouse.

On each occasion, financial needs, which are clearly identifiable, will exist and these will be considered later in this chapter. At this stage, these changes should be remembered as providing a way of recognising and matching services with segmented customer needs.

Lodgement gathering services

Without attracting lodgements a bank cannot lend. Therefore, the success of a retail bank in gathering essential lodgements is one of the main cornerstones of its other primary activity – lending money. Despite the effects of inflation, most people save by using the banks, building societies and other institutions.

Competition for personal market savings is fierce, and it would be impossible to cover comprehensively all the savings and investment services available. The objective in this section is to highlight the distinctive differences between various groups of savings schemes and consider how they broadly fulfil user needs.

In recent years the banks have lost considerable ground to other financial institutions intent on gathering lodgements. In 1970, banks and building societies each had a 35 per cent share of the total consumer savings market, and the National Savings movement had 30 per cent. By 1982, the banks had increased their market share to 34 per cent but the building societies increased theirs to 46 per cent. The National Savings movement dropped to 20 per cent during the same period, but appears now to be regaining lost ground.

It is undeniable that the fiscal advantages once enjoyed by the building societies over the banks had been partially responsible for the decline in the banks' market share, but the stale image of the traditional bank saving services, coupled with shortcomings in the way banks go about gathering lodgements (including the restricted opening hours), are major factors.

(a) Interest versus term

Banks are now rapidly filling the marketing gaps in their range of savings schemes by introducing services that are designed to attract particular types of savings.

If short-term political or economic influences are ignored, which can distort the laws of supply and demand, there is a very close relationship between the amount of interest paid on savings and the notice required before funds can be withdrawn. The shorter the notice required, the lower the interest given, because all financial institutions prefer stable lodgements and are prepared to pay more to attract the less volatile deposits.

There can also be a link between the interest paid and the size of the deposit. It is cheaper administratively for any financial institution to gather a small number of large sums than a much greater number of smaller deposits. This administrative saving can be passed on to the customer in the form of higher interest rates to the larger investor.

Savings tied up for longer terms are also more attractive to banks as they strive to satisfy demand and fulfil their growth objectives in mortgage advances and term lending to expanding businesses. The sterling interbank market is unsuitable for the acquisition of longer-term funds and, therefore, there is a need to create new forms of matching deposits to fund the growing volume of longer-term lending schemes.

More new savings services will undoubtedly emerge, as will a continuous appraisal of markets which, hitherto, were regarded as low potential or unprofitable. Young savers, and the weekly paid, are two examples of new markets now being closely examined for potential by the banks. Banks are also following building societies by introducing 60-day and 90-day notice of withdrawal savings accounts with higher rates of interest than currently offered for 30-day or 7-day notice services.

(b) Range of lodgement gathering services

It is worth while looking now at the types of services provided by the banks to gather retail lodgements and to identify the basic benefits these services offer to customers. (See Table 14.1.) This list of lodgement-gathering services does not show all the differences between the wide range of competitive services. But it does illustrate the comprehensiveness of the bank services available, each of which is tailored to provide particular benefits to attract a certain type of lodgement.

(c) Categories of savings

Bank savings schemes are intended to attract lodgements of four main kinds:

(1) Short-term deposits where immediate access outweighs the benefit based upon the level of interest paid.

(2) Short-term regular savings plans (up to two years).

(3) Funds not earmarked or likely to be required in the shorter term so interest rates and safety are important aspects.

(4) Larger investments which may or may not be earmarked for use but can be deposited for longer fixed periods.

Deposit or savings accounts for short-term savings. This is the most traditional of all the types of savings accounts offered by the banks and provides a number of benefits to users:

Any sum of money can be deposited as there are no minimum/maximum criteria. Deposits are simple to make and withdrawals are allowable on demand. However, it is possible that there is a loss of seven days' interest on amounts withdrawn if no notice is given.

Additionally, bearing in mind that withdrawal can be immediate, a 'fair' rate of interest is paid. There is also the benefit of passbooks or statements showing a 'running' balance and therefore making funds control an easy matter.

Table 14.1

Type of service and features	Benefits
Current account: Money transmission facility with regular statements.	Keeps money safe. Ease of withdrawal and simple account control.
Deposit and savings accounts: Normally 7 days notice required but immediate withdrawal is possible. No commitment to regular savings or any limitations on amount that can be withdrawn.	Simple savings facility. Interest paid plus safety, accessibility and convenience.
Regular savings schemes: Minimum/maximum monthly contributions. Some in the past when mortgage funds have been scarce were linked to mortgage provision or at least special consideration for home loan. (Compete with building society subscription accounts.)	Higher rate of interest than 7 days notice accounts. Interest paid at regular intervals to encourage saving.
Premium interest accounts: Higher interest paid for larger deposits provided a high minimum balance is maintained. Some have cheque books but restrictions on number of cheques and amount of each withdrawal stop the facility from becoming another interest-bearing current account. Some premium interest accounts require notice to be given before withdrawal (generically known as money fund accounts).	Higher rate of interest than other types of bank accounts on which interest is paid but some flexibility in how funds are withdrawn.
Fixed rate of interest facilities: Investment of fixed amount for fixed period of time ranging from 1 to 10 months. Interest is linked to money market rates and, therefore, quotations for lodgements will vary daily. Term chosen and amount invested will also affect rate of interest.	Guaranteed interest rate for duration of investment. Higher rates which reflect the fixed nature of the deposit.
Special longer-term deposit schemes: Commitment to invest a sum for a longer period, up to seven years. Especially suitable for customers looking for income either monthly or half-yearly. The longer the term chosen the higher the rate.	High rate of interest paid either monthly, quarterly or half-yearly. Interest payments can be used as income.
Money market facilities: For larger sums when daily money market rates apply. No early withdrawal. Funds are usually placed within the banking group including the hire purchase subsidiary company. Tiered rate structure based on term, and amount.	Most competitive rate of interest. Ideal investment for funds which are available for only a short period of days or months.

This account will satisfy the needs of all sections of the community, young and old, who have surplus funds they wish to keep readily available. Building societies' plastic card-based accounts giving instant access with no penalty are also a haven for short-term savings.

Regular savings schemes. Special savings schemes were introduced by the banks in the early 1980s to fill a gap in their range of services for the savings market. Savings schemes are aimed primarily at younger people, especially those who are planning to get married or are actually married homeowners wishing to improve its comfort and conveniences or, if not homeowners, wish to save for a deposit on a property. Thus, if the customer saves for a car, house deposit or even a holiday this type of service is very suitable.

The main features of regular savings schemes include stipulating a minimum/maximum monthly subscription which must be maintained for a set term – usually a minimum of twelve months. For early withdrawal, a penalty could be payable. Interest paid is higher than seven-day deposit/savings accounts and extra attractions can include special consideration for a loan or mortgage, sometimes at preferential interest rates. These schemes are, therefore, flexible, provide quick access to savings and a reasonable rate of interest on accumulated funds.

Higher interest accounts. The drive for lodgements, coupled with the need to meet the investment requirements of groups such as the older wealthier customers, prompted the introduction of higher-interest accounts.

A premium rate of interest is offered for larger deposits without the need to tie up these funds for a period of years. As such, these accounts are an ideal resting place for funds over the shorter periods and will attract 'windfalls' such as redundancy/pension payments, legacy receipts and life policy maturity proceeds. Corporate customers also use these accounts, so that the potential market for this type of lodgement is substantial.

Main features of most higher-interest accounts include a minimum deposit of £2000 and a minimum investment period of 30 days with a similar period required as notice of withdrawal. Interest is higher than seven-day deposit/savings accounts, and can be paid monthly, quarterly or half-yearly. The method of deposit is easy and once the minimum balance requirement is satisfied further sums can be added, no matter how small, at any time.

Fixed amount and rate deposits. This type of investment is usually channelled from branches to the money market division of the bank.

As the descriptive title implies, customers agree to deposit a sum of money for a fixed period of time – usually for terms from 14 days to 18 months. The interest earned is fixed for the whole term. As the minimum acceptable investment is usually £2500, higher rates of interest apply which reflect the nature of the deposit. Interest is paid gross at the end of the term on deposits of £50 000 or more for periods of 28 days or longer. Other deposits are subject to composite tax rate.

Variable rate longer-term deposit schemes. If longer terms than 18 months are required, deposit schemes are offered by the banks for larger lodgements up to a period of seven years. For this type of investment, interest is usually paid half-yearly or compounded and the rate of interest is usually linked to the bank base rates. It would clearly be very difficult to project interest rate movements over a period of seven years and thereby offer fixed rates to customers.

Competition for this type of larger investment, which remains static for a lengthy period, is keen. The matrix in Table 14.2 shows the main areas open to investors who wish to tuck money away for a year or longer.

Money funds. Money funds, an interest-bearing account coupled with a cheque book facility, were first introduced in 1983. They evidence the growing fusion of what were once distinct areas of operation of two different institutions, as the building societies and banks encroach upon each others' traditional roles.

Table 14.2 Variable rate deposit alternatives

Financial institution	Example of term	Minimum/maximum	Other comments
Bank	3 months–7 years	£2500–£100 000	Fixed interest rates can be obtained up to two years. Otherwise yield is linked to bank base rates.
Building society	1–5 years	£500–£20 000	There is a wide range of term shares available.
Finance houses	1–5 years	£1000+	Rate of interest is linked to size of deposit and term.
Local authorities (negotiable bonds)	3–5 years	£1000	Quotations are given on individual transactions.
Gilt-edged securities	1–3 years treasury variable rate stock	None	Yield is related to the rate paid on treasury bills.

To date, not all the banks have entered this market as there is a substantial risk of customers' trading up – switching non-interest earning balances from current account or lower interest-bearing schemes – to a money fund. A result of trading-up is that the banks simply pay substantially more for the same funds. Competition from merchant banks, savings institutions (such as Save and Prosper) and finance houses (such as Western Trust and Tyndall) have opened up this latest highly sought after market. Only the traditional clearing banks, with the heavy costs of a network of branches and substantial lodgements in the form of current account balances, stand to lose. Primarily for self-preservation, first the Bank of Scotland and then the Midland followed suit by introducing interest-bearing cheque accounts.

Generally the main features of money funds can include a minimum balance level of £1000 or more and interest paid at a rate which reflects this minimum balance requirement. Sometimes, only large withdrawals are permitted – usually £250 or more – and in some instances seven days' notice or a longer period is required. Charges can be levied if withdrawals rise above a predetermined number. Money funds are still in the development stage and further features will evolve for some time to come. Tiered interest rates linked to the size of the lodgement are already available and there will be other developments. The bank schemes will add on many of their traditional money transmission services in order to differentiate and give their money fund a competitive edge.

Summary

No attempt has been made to explain in detail the wide range of savings services available to the public. Nevertheless, it is hoped that this information has concentrated the mind on the broad areas of need and the types of services available to meet customers' requirements. Accurate cross-matching of service features with customer requirements remains an essential aspect of successful marketing. There is also overlapping of features and benefits throughout the range of savings services. Nevertheless, they can be marshalled broadly in an order which demonstrates how the total range of customers' savings needs can be provided. Table 14.3 gives a list of cross-matches. What this table does not show is the conflict of interest between consumers' requirements for immediate access and high interest rates with the banks' desires to seek long-term stable investment accounts at the lowest possible interest cost. How both bank and consumer requirements are

Table 14.3 Savings/investment services

Service	Examples of amount range	Usual term	Main features and benefits
Savings services for the young *Target market*: 11–16	£0–unlimited. Some stipulations on a minimum sum to open account	No minimum/maximum	Higher rate of interest than 7-day deposit. Wide variety of 'give aways' – money boxes, pen sets, folders, calculators, etc.
7-day deposit/savings accounts *Target market*: Those who have surplus funds not required for immediate use	£0–unlimited	7 days' notice on withdrawals or loss of 7 days' interest on amount withdrawn	Convenient and simple to deposit and withdraw funds. No minimum/maximum criterion. Easy to keep track of funds
Regular savings schemes *Target market*: Those saving to get married or getting a home together. Saving to purchase consumer durables or provide house purchase deposit	£10–no maximum or £100 depending upon the bank	Minimum 12 months. Early withdrawal under penalty	Higher rate of interest than 7-day deposit. Some schemes offer preferential consideration if saver requires a loan
Higher interest accounts *Target market*: Older, wealthier and those who have received windfalls such as a legacy or life policy maturity	£2000–no maximum	30 days minimum and 1 month's notice of withdrawal	Higher rate of interest than 7-day deposit

	Target market	Minimum	Term	Rates of interest
Fixed rate deposits	Investors with substantial sums not required for immediate use	£2500–no maximum	14 days–18 months	Rates of interest based on money market rates. Interest paid gross at end of term on deposits of £50 000 or more where term is 28 days or longer. Interest rate fixed for whole period of investment. Interest rate applied linked to size of investment
Variable rate deposits	investors looking for a larger term investment which is safe and will provide return on a regular cycle	£2500–no maximum	Up to 7 years	Rates of interest fluctuate and are linked to money market rates or directly to bank base rates. Interest is usually paid half-yearly. Interest rate applied linked to size of investments
Money funds	wealthier people looking for convenience of immediate access to funds	£1000–no maximum	Immediate withdrawal but some institutions stipulate 7 days' notice and limit the minimum amount of withdrawals	Good rate of interest on a current account type facility with quick access to funds by using a cheque book

mutually satisfied is the job of marketing. Resolving the banks' funding and profitability issues is a major and ongoing marketing task.

Consumer lending services and mortgages

For many years, the banks have provided a range of loan and overdraft services which satisfy most customers' borrowing requirements. Nevertheless, structured schemes, tailored to specific financial circumstances, have been introduced from time to time and these new services have helped stimulate additional business growth for the banks. Services such as charge cards, credit cards, budget accounts and revolving credit plans, not previously available, have made customers more aware of the financial flexibility that these types of services can provide. Personal loans, budget and revolving credit accounts, property improvement loans, bank mortgages, credit cards and charge cards are now considered in detail.

Competition for this profitable business is fierce and is increasing as the building societies and other institutions enter the consumer finance market supported by credit-scoring systems. The main providers of money for 'white' and 'brown' goods (consumer items such as fridges, washing machines, furniture and furnishings) are still the banks and hire purchase companies. At the end of 1986 market shares were as shown in Table 14.4.

Personal loans

This service is mainly used for the purchase of consumer durables and is normally only granted by banks to existing customers. The advantages of a personal loan to a customer include speed with which it can be arranged, a fixed repayment which makes for easier budgeting and no

Table 14.4

	Bank loan	HP (Finance house)	Other
New car	44%	45%	11%
Used car	69%	21%	10%
Central heating	55%	36%	9%
Kitchens/bathrooms	54%	40%	6%
Furniture/carpets	27%	68%	5%
Electrical goods		90%	10%
Gas appliances		84%	16%

penalty for early repayment. For some loans interest may be allowable against tax.

Where availability of life cover is built into the service this can be an added selling feature. Some loan schemes also offer the chance to take out sickness or redundancy protection for a single payment. For the customer with limited financial resources and a need to protect his family circumstances as best he can, this type of insurance arrangement provides a real benefit, initially in the form of peace of mind.

The market for consumer lending is vast – 23 per cent of all retail sales are taken on credit – and with computerised credit scoring and other means of automatic decision-making systems, bank lending services will become more readily available to a wider audience, especially to non-customers.

No precise data is available, but in 1981/82 the estimated amount spent on cars and vehicles was £6.4 billion, while that spent on pursuit of leisure was £11.6 billion and on home comforts (white goods and furnishings) £8 billion. Hence the market then was large and will have grown substantially since that time. It offers considerable profit potential for those institutions, including the banks, offering consumer finance.

Budget and revolving credit accounts

Budget accounts have largely been superseded by the more flexible revolving credit account. Nevertheless, it is worth spending a few minutes considering the function of the budget account and highlighting how it differs from a revolving credit facility.

A budget plan is designed to provide finance to meet pre-identified commitments other than those that are paid monthly. Rates, electricity, gas and clothing are some of the types of bill that can be estimated. The annual costs can then be provided for by dividing the projected annual cost by twelve and contributing the resultant figure as a monthly sum into a separate account from which only nominated commitments are paid.

A revolving credit account is not so rigid; future commitments do not have to be identified and assessed. The only major stipulation is that the level of borrowing on the account should not exceed a chosen multiple of this fixed monthly contribution to the account. Thus, the benefits to users of a revolving credit can be easily appreciated. No special arrangements to purchase items, even major ones, have to be made, provided the credit limit based on the monthly contributions is not exceeded.

With a revolving credit account, customers are not required to undertake any regular interviews with the bank to review the facility. The fixed monthly transfer to the revolving credit aids financial budgeting and, in the majority of the schemes on offer by the banks, modest interest is paid on any credit balances.

If there is evidence that a customer needs the discipline of careful monitoring and strict financial control then the budget account is more likely to meet these particular requirements.

Credit cards, for example Access and Barclaycard, are also revolving credit schemes which have become an integral and widely accepted part of the financial flexibility now available to personal customers.

Property improvement loans

There are a growing number of 'special' loan schemes to meet particular items of expenditure. Car and holiday loans are two obvious examples.

These loans, apart from the name which makes the facility more visible to the customer, are invariably cosmetic adjustments of the basic personal loan. Some may have features which tie in with the purpose of the loan. A holiday loan, for instance, may only be for a twelve-month term and may offer a lower interest rate on borrowing, if there is a stipulation to save for six months prior to the holiday and the commencement of borrowing for the remaining six months.

Property improvement loans are rather different, because of the variations of some features depending upon the term of the loan. For example, interest on a property improvement loan may be at a fixed rate for up to five years. Loans for periods of over five years could have interest linked to bank base rates. Security may or may not be required, again this facet may also be linked to the amount of the loan, or the term, or simply influence the rate of interest levied. Unsecured loans would naturally be more expensive. Property improvement loans often have optional benefits such as unemployment, sickness and accident insurance. This family and personal protection can be taken up by customers if their circumstances make them consider it desirable. Other selling points include no penalty for early repayment and a quick decision on whether or not financial support is forthcoming.

The market for property improvement loans is also large. In 1983, £5 billion was spent on home extensions, repairs and renovations. Many customers seeking loans also own their own houses, which reduces the lending risk appreciably.

Mortgages

Mortgages are a comparatively recent addition to the range of lending services offered to personal customers. Previously, banks had stuck rigidly to shorter-term advances but competition, and availability of funds, coupled with a growing expertise in handling commercial term advances has encouraged banks to enter the home buyer market.

For those who may not have purchased a property, it will be worth considering the basic differences between a repayment mortgage and an endowment linked mortgage.

With a *repayment mortgage*, monthly repayments include an interest and capital contribution. In the early stages, the overwhelming part of the monthly repayment is swallowed up by interest but in later years, the pendulum swings the other way as the debt is reduced. To protect the family, a special insurance policy can be effected to repay the outstanding mortgage if the mortgagor dies. This annual insurance premium should be included when considering the annual cost of the mortgage repayments.

Endowment mortgages function differently. The amount of the mortgage advance is not reduced annually, only the interest levied on the borrowing is paid – usually monthly. An insurance policy (or several policies) is written to yield on maturity sufficient to repay the mortgage advance. It also provides death cover during the life of the mortgage so protecting the financial interests of any family. The insurance premiums have to be paid regularly as well as the mortgage interest. There are many variations of endowment mortgages using both non-profit and with-profit policies. But to fully understand this complex subject it is necessary to research other more detailed information sources. As a general rule, endowment mortgages require a larger monthly outlay than an ordinary repayment mortgage (see Table 14.5). Consequently, for house buyers on a tight financial budget, or those who are only temporarily resident in the UK, a repayment scheme is probably best for them.

Pension mortgages

Those customers who are self-employed or in non-pensionable employment and whose earnings are assessable to UK tax are eligible for pension policies. These policies are drawn under the terms of Section 226A of the Income and Corporation Tax Act 1970 and the Inland Revenue allows these policies to earn their income without tax deduction. Moreover, the policy holder can qualify for tax relief on the premiums at the highest rate of tax being paid. Thus there are

Table 14.5   Mortgage repayment comparisons

For male aged 30 borrowing £30 000 over 25 years	25-year term repayment mortgage	Low cost endowment mortgage
Interest rate	13%	13%
Net monthly mortgage payment	£266.88	£227.50
Monthly premium to insurance company	£4.60 (Mortgage protection)	£37.90 (Endowment)
Average or net monthly cost	£271.48 (average cost)	£265.40 (net cost)
Reversionary bonus	Nil	£4 948
Possible terminal bonus	Nil	£16 099
Total cost	£81 444	£79 620
Less estimated surplus	Nil	£21 047
Total Net cost	£81 444	£55 873

considerable advantages for the higher rate taxpayer especially as the annual growth of the policy and the ultimate cash commutable value (CCV) when paid on retirement is tax-free.

Policy holders can also agree with a mortgage provider to use the CCV of the policy to repay the mortgage. The CCV is in turn linked to the annual pension policy premium paid, so the older the mortgagor the higher the cost of funding his mortgage in this way. The pension policy itself is non-assignable, so a bank or building society would probably want whole life insurance cover to clear the mortgage if death occurred before retirement as well as a legal charge over the deeds of the property.

The combination of annual outgoings for the premiums on the pension policy and whole life insurance with the interest on the mortgage may be considerably higher than the low-cost or repayment mortgages. However, after tax relief, tax exemptions and mortgage interest relief at source (MIRAS) allowance, the net cost after the CCV has paid off the mortgage could be lower than a conventional mortgage. This is particularly so for higher-rate taxpayers, and in addition the pension policy will also provide a retirement pension for life.

Credit cards and charge cards

No chapter on consumer lending services would be complete without including credit and charge card facilities. The difference between the two is simply that the monthly outstanding expenditure on a charge card must be paid in full immediately the statement is received, whereas a credit card company only expects a fixed minimum percentage of the amount owing to be paid monthly. Available statistics for December 1986 give a good indication (Table 14.6) of the widespread use of the main credit and charge cards. It is generally accepted that a charge or credit card is an ideal payment method for customers who travel widely at home and abroad. However, there are other benefits for users of these 'plastics'. These are:

(a) The cards constitute a simple and easy method of payment.
(b) Credit cards have the convenience of extended credit when required without formality.
(c) There is safety in not carrying cash and protection if card is lost or stolen.
(d) There is flexibility of use and the monthly statement which itemises expenditure assists financial control.
(e) Many expenditure items can be settled with just one payment. Fewer cheques issued could mean lower bank charges.
(f) Cash advances are available immediately.
(g) A secondary card can be issued to a nominated person so extending the financial convenience enjoyed by the holder.
(h) They are increasingly usable for 'telephone' shopping.

The credit card companies also offer as a separate service a special loan scheme which provides all the benefits of ordinary personal loan finance.

Table 14.6

	Credit Cards		
	Access (MasterCard)	Barclaycard (Visa)	Trustcard (Visa)
UK holders	6.5 million +	7 million +	2 million approx.
Retail outlets	200 000	200 000	200 000
Payment requirement	Minimum £5 or 5% of total	Minimum £5 or 5% of total	Minimum £5 or 5% of total
Payment due	Within 25 days of statement receipt	Within 25 days of statement receipt	Within 25 days of statement receipt

	Charge cards	
	American Express Green card	Diners Club
UK Holders	850 000 approx.	400 000 approx.
Retail outlets	70 000 approx.	60 000 approx.
Payment requirements	In full immediately statement is received	In full immediately statement is received

Case study

Frank Jones, whose wife banks with you, has made an appointment to see you. During the discussion you learn that he is a director of a large company which banks with a competitor. His net monthly salary is £1500 and he has a mortgage of £8000 and £2500 savings in a building society.

Mr Jones explains that he has decided to purchase a house in an adjoining town in preparation for retirement in five years time. His offer of £75 000 for the property has been accepted. His present house is on the market and he has received an offer of £65 000. This property was purchased ten years ago. Mr and Mrs Jones wish to issue a cheque for £7500 and complete the purchase six weeks from now.

How would you react to Mr Jones and, in helping him, what security requirements might you feel necessary?

The customers initially require a bridging loan but the main opportunity is the chance to make a mortgage advance and pick up some useful insurance business, especially if the customers wish to have part of the mortgage endowment-linked.

Clearly, Mr Jones earns a salary in excess of £25 000 per annum and, although only five years from retirement, his pension income should be sufficient to cover payments on any mortgage he decides to carry into retirement. The financial position looks like this:

Sales of present house	£65 000	Purchase of new house	£75 000
Mortgage	£8 000	Surplus from present house	£53 000
	£57 000	Shortfall-mortgage requirement	£22 000
Legal fees, etc. estimated	£4 000		
Surplus	£53 000		

If the bank would not normally allow a mortgage term which continues after retirement, the considerable scope for insurance business and estate planning generally, not forgetting the connection with a potential corporate account, may well encourage them to make an exception in Mr Jones' case.

Summary

As the range and complexity of consumer lending services expands

Table 14.7 Consumer finance services

Range of services	Example of amount range	Main features and benefits
Personal loans for the larger single purchase	£0–£5000	Fixed or flat interest rate. Fixed monthly repayment programme. Easy to arrange. Security not normally required.
Budget accounts for the household bills that cannot be paid monthly	£0–2500	Fixed monthly repayment programme. Easy to arrange. Security not normally required. Ensures funds are available to pay commitments earmarked in the budget plan. Immediate payment can result in a discount.
Revolving credit facilities for regular borrowing and budgeting with a savings option	£500–£500	Freedom and flexibility to purchase goods as and when desired. Can be useful alternative to a budget account. No annual renewal formalities. Interest paid on credit balances. Allow a larger repayment than perhaps allowable on a personal loan.
Home improvement loans	£100–£2500	Enables repairs and improvements which maintain or increase the value of the property. Allows extension of the property without the need and expense of moving house. Fixed monthly repayments. Longer term than personal loans usually up to 10 years.
Credit cards for payment of domestic and leisure purchases and for cash advances	Subject to credit rating – normally between £300–£2000	Convenient and safe mechanism which can be free if monthly expenditure is cleared within the stipulated period. Can be used for purchases over £50 and widespread acceptability at home and abroad. Ideal to cover unexpected bills. Convenient payment method for mail order or telephoned purchases.

there is more difficulty for the sellers and purchasers to distinguish which facility is best to meet their particular circumstances.

Some bank services actually appear to be in direct competition with one another; Access or Barclaycard services do look very similar to the banks' revolving credit accounts. In fact, a closer analysis soon shows that these two separate services are more complementary than competitive, and if one is being offered to a customer it generally means that both would be welcome.

The banks have tried to provide a comprehensive range of financial services to meet consumer needs in a way that is likely to produce the most profit. Do not forget profit can come from interest earnings or by reducing administrative costs. Hence smaller loans will cost more and be structured to require less time to sell. A revolving credit service will also be more cost-effective for the provider than a budget facility which requires regular monitoring.

Accepting that in a range of services (Table 14.7) there is bound to be some overlapping features and benefits to customers, it is, nevertheless, possible to construct a matrix which differentiates the services. Hopefully this will aid the process of understanding and matching customer needs with service benefits.

This chapter has tended to focus on the features and benefits of bank services and it could be construed that what a bank wishes to provide takes precedence over what customers actually want. In fact the features and benefits of services will have largely evolved from consumer research findings into what customers want. Fixed monthly repayment facilities or a revolving credits flexibility so that the user can buy and determine repayments without reference to the bank are customer requirements, not evidence of a bank's wishing to fill gaps in its service range. They may not be features which a bank would provide if they could be avoided. There are also undoubtedly other services or features which the customer would like but currently the banks do not feel obliged to provide. Yet again we see the dichotomy between banks' and customers' requirements which can only be resolved by skilful marketing. Nevertheless, in broad terms, customers' requirements are generally paramount in the marketing philosophy and there must be good commercial reasons for ignoring this basic principle.

Revision questions

1 Outline the various ways your branch can segment its personal customer profile.
2 Explain the basis of the customer life cycle concept and show how

its use can enhance or support the planning of a promotional campaign.

3 List six 'trigger points'. Then identify three bank services which could be appropriate for each trigger point situation and demonstrate the relationship in each example of the service features with customer needs.

4 What are the main issues which affect the rates of interest paid by banks for lodgements? What gaps exist in your bank's lodgement gathering service range compared with competitor services?

5 What are the main benefits to users of a credit card?

Chapter 15
Trust Department Services

Trust departments of the major banks usually provide the following separate but often interrelated services: executor, administrator and trustee services, taxation advice, investment management, estate planning, insurance and investment services.

Historically, these are some of the longest established bank services and, over the years, business in all these areas has grown substantially. This growth has not been trouble-free for, apart from insurance, some of the other trust department services have not been particularly profitable. Despite the banks' undoubted specialist expertise in this field, branches have tended to regard selling some of them as no more than an ancillary activity. The public too have remained far from convinced of the wisdom of using the services of trust departments of the major banks rather than competitor facilities provided by other professional organisations. Solicitors have not been slow in condemning published charging scales for executorships and further claim that banks cannot give impartial advice. Some are also upset that the banks can advertise their services without restriction whilst, until recently, solicitors could not compete in this way. Another problem is a perceived remoteness of trust department specialists who may have to give advice and support to many branches in a widespread region.

So this is the current climate in which the banks are operating and seeking new business opportunities. In this chapter it is not intended to give space to the complex legal and technical requirements of trust services. Our objective is to provide sufficient information to be able to appreciate customer requirements and know how, generally speaking, the various trust services can meet these needs.

Personal Equity Plans, introduced in the 1986 Budget are also included in this chapter. Not all banks administer PEPs through their trust departments but nevertheless the nature of the service fits into this chapter as they are designed to be tax efficient investments. As such, they form an integral part of an investment adviser's armoury.

Administration of estates

Why make a will? The answer to this question is fundamental for any banker trying to convince his customer to make one. To understand the advantages of making a will, the rules of intestacy must be appreciated.

Briefly the main problems that arise from dying intestate can be summarised as follows:

Intestate dies leaving	*Distribution*
(1) One of the married partners and there are no issue, parents, brothers, sisters of the whole blood	Other party takes the whole of the estate.
(2) Husband or wife dies and there are issue	Survivor takes personal estate, £75 000 free of duty and costs, and a life interest in half the balance of the estate which is held in trust for the issue.
(3) Husband or wife dies and no issue but there is a parent or brother or sister	Survivor takes personal effects, £125 000 free of duty and one half of the residue. The other half of the residue is taken by parents absolutely or, if no parents survive, it will be held in trust for brothers and sisters.
(4) The intestate dies having no husband, wife or relatives	Whole estate passes to the crown as ownerless property.

There are other aspects not covered above, but it is plain that a customer is unlikely to be very happy when he/she realises the intestacy rules. Making a will is the only way to protect and care for dependants in the way one would wish. Moreover, the legal procedures that the law insists upon, for estates for which there is no will can involve costs and delays. These can, in turn, cause unnecessary distress to the deceased's family.

Nature of executor and trustee services

Banks will act as executors and as trustees and the appointment is made either in a will, or by a codicil to an existing will. If there is no will, an executor or trustee has not been named in a will or the named executor/trustee is dead, unwilling or unable to undertake the duties then banks will also take up their role and act as an administrator and/or trustee.

The roles of executor or administrator are virtually identical; it is only the way in which their powers are vested which is different. Under the will or letters of administration the duties will include:

- the funeral arrangements;
- collection, realisation and distribution of assets;
- payment of all debts/expenses;
- agreeing estate valuation with Collector of Taxes and payment of taxation;
- accounting to the beneficiaries for the way in which the deceased's affairs are settled.

If under the terms of the will or letters of administration, the executors'/administrators' duties are to continue for any length of time their function becomes that of a trustee. Banks are willing, in appropriate cases to act as trustees and there are several advantages to be gained by appointing a bank rather than individuals:

(1) The bank's trustee department is an organisation with extensive business and financial expertise.
(2) The bank never dies – it provides perpetual existence no matter how long trustee duties last.
(3) Secrecy and impartiality when dealing with family cases are important. Both these essential elements are provided by banks.
(4) Many routine administration matters involve using banking services – these are quickly and easily provided when a bank is acting as executor/trustee.
(5) Fees are competitive and not payable until the bank commences its duties.

Banks are prepared to act solely or jointly as an executor or trustee. They will also arrange for wills to be drawn up and give advice on draft wills drawn up by others.

Before leaving the subject of trusteeship is should not be forgotten that trusts are often established by a settlement *inter vivos*. This is a trust created during the lifetime of the settlor, either as a fixed trust or discretionary trust and such settlements provide a further opportunity to sell the bank's trustee service.

We started by highlighting some of the difficulties which must be overcome by banks when selling executor and trustee services. On a more positive note, an executor and trustee appointment undoubtedly helps to cement the banker/customer relationship more closely. Perhaps this is the biggest single argument for branch bankers to promote a service which will not show an immediate financial return for their efforts.

Promotional opportunities At some time or other making a will becomes particularly important for an adult. Although the subject is sometimes branded as morbid and brushed aside, the need is real and the following occasions provide opportunities for bankers to press home the merits of making a will:

Event	*Special remarks*
Marriage	A will is essential. If there is a previous will it will be revoked and a new will needs to be drawn up
As children are born	Will needs revision
Customer buying a home	Will is important especially in view of intestacy rules
Foreign travel or overseas working	
Going self-employed	
Divorce or separation	
Receipt of large sums including redundancy, legacy, maturity of life policy	
Death of existing executor	

Estate planning

Closely allied to making a will is estate planning. This involves rearranging a person's assets in order to reduce the liability to taxation, especially inheritance tax. To a large extent, estate planning relies upon life assurance, and in most cases specialist advice is essential. To ensure that the value of the estate is maintained, the possible effects of inheritance tax have to be allowed for. Inheritance tax is a tax on capital – your home, car, furniture, jewellery – virtually everything owned.

Essentially this tax is designed mainly to attain maximum coverage of assets, but certain exemptions and reliefs are allowed. However, for inheritance tax savings to be achieved, early action is essential, which is where the estate planning services offered by banks can be most useful.

The estate planning service, usually includes advice on the following:

(a) The most efficient use of available inheritance tax exemptions and allowances;
(b) The most effective way of drawing a will and arranging settlements;
(c) Provision of life insurance to meet inheritance tax on death and enable lifetime gifts of a business to be made.

Other peripheral services to estate planning include advice on tax-efficient investment schemes, especially those linked to life assurance, savings plans and schemes related to provision of school fees.

Inheritance tax rates

Table 15.1 shows current inheritance tax rates but it is intended in future years to index the banks and link increases to the retail price index. Although this chart may soon become out of date, it emphasises the need for effective estate planning where assets amount to over £110 000. This is not a large sum when you include the value of a house.

Expert advice is essential and the branch role is simply to understand the problems created by inheritance tax and be able to identify customer situations which demand counselling. Moreover, the branch banker can stress four advantages for the customer if he/she elects to ask the bank to assist in estate planning:

(1) Advice from a bank will be unbiased.
(2) Recommendations will be made only after a close examination of the particular needs of a customer by an expert department.
(3) The service is wide ranging and not entirely insurance orientated as is that of some of the bank's competitors.

Table 15.1: Inheritance tax rates

Cumulative total gifts or estate	Lifetime scale rate of tax
£	%
Nil–110 000	Nil
Above 110 000	40

(Correct as at 15 March 1988)

(4) Initially the service is free of charge, but if a detailed scheme is prepared a reasonable charge may be requested.

Moreover, if the banker has a sound grasp of the customer's affairs he will be able to produce 'tailored' solutions which help to preserve the assets for dependants and thereby relieve worry and stress.

Opportunities to promote estate planning

The circumstances for promoting will appointments also provide opportunities to offer an estate planning service, especially to the older and wealthier customer. For the younger married age groups, advice on how to protect the family in the event of adversity is a form of estate planning. However, these people are unlikely to want a detailed plan drawn up if their only major asset is the family home.

Event	Main customer requirement
Marriage	Life insurance for protection and saving
Addition to family	School fees planning and additional family protection with life insurance
Starting a business	Estate planning to fund inheritance tax using life and pensions insurance
Receipt of large sums of money through inheritance, maturity of life policy, redundancy etc.	Cover against inheritance tax and investment advice generally
Making a will	Estate planning advice is appropriate in most cases
Death of husband/wife	Estate planning and reviewing will.

Taxation service

Banks will undertake tax work of all descriptions from the straightforward to the very complex cases. Nowadays this work includes handling any form of taxation claims on personal income, trust income and capital gains. The service also covers the preparation of income and capital statements for purposes other than taxation, such as rent and rates rebates claims and educational grant applications. Accounts for self-employed customers are also drawn up by some of the banks' taxation departments for submission to the appropriate Inspector of Taxes.

The principal advantages of a taxation service to the customer include:

(1) Saving in time and effort in looking after their own tax affairs.
(2) The knowledge that matters are being handled by experts and that the correct amount of tax will be paid.
(3) An automatic link with other bank services which may be appropriate to mitigate tax. A good knowledge of customers' financial circumstances enabling 'tax-saving' solutions to be suggested to customers.
(4) Advice on specific tax issues even though the customer is not using the full taxation service.

Customers with taxation problems need specialist advice. The branch role is to know the 'break points' of income tax and capital gains tax. This will enable customers, who need advice, to be identified and the benefits of using the bank's specialists can be promoted.

Table 15.2

Income tax bands	Correct at 4 April 1988	Correct at (Pencil in current rates)
Income £1–19 300	Tax rate 25%	
Over £19 300	Tax rate 40%	
Tax allowances		
Married man	£4095	
Single person or working wife	£2605	
Age allowance (65–80)		
Single person	£3180	
Married couple	£5030	
Income limit	£10600	
Age allowance (over 80)		
Single person	£3310	
Married person	£5205	
Income limit	£10600	
Capital gains tax		
Individuals		
First £5000 p.a.	Exempt	
over £5000	At top rate of tax payable	
Most settlements		
First £2500 p.a.	Exempt	
over £2500 p.a.	At top rate of tax payable	

Without a basic knowledge of the tax structure a branch banker is unlikely to be able to gain sufficient interest from a potential user to make the customer buy the tax service. The matrix in Table 15.2 covers the main points on which customer questions are likely to arise.

There is considerable market potential for the taxation service, especially among higher income earners and the self-employed. There are over 21 million taxpayers in the UK, and it is estimated that the clearing banks only administer the tax affairs of 200 000 customers.

It is no secret, however, that the banks are not geared up to coping with a substantial growth of tax cases. Therefore, a highly selective sales drive is more appropriate, seeking out the prospects offering the best profit potential. As has been highlighted, numerous opportunities arise to introduce the taxation service – marriage, divorce, changes in employment, retirement, working abroad, receipt of large sums, etc. However it may well be bank policy to restrain sales activity that merely increases the number of customers using its taxation service.

Where taxation cases are handled by the banks, the customer relationship is strengthened and the intimate knowledge of customers' financial affairs can, in turn, highlight other business development opportunities.

Other trust department services

Investment management

This service should not be confused with investment advice which is obtained from stockbrokers or specialist investment departments and then passed on to customers. Investment management, or portfolio management as it is sometimes called, entails day-to-day supervision and control of investments. The service is primarily intended for customers with large sums to invest – at least £20 000 or more. In some cases, smaller capital sums may be managed initially where a customer is in the process of building up an investment portfolio.

Property and land investments are not generally considered suitable for the investment management service, which almost exclusively deals with stocks and shares, government and local authority investments, building society and bank deposits and money market funds.

Because of the very nature of this service, it is mainly designed for the long-term investor and is not suitable for customers wishing to speculate. The administration of this service is very flexible, with the customer having, if he/she wishes, a substantial say on investment policy. Customers can either allow the bank to act at its discretion or elect to be consulted before investment changes are made.

As with the other trust department services, the branch role is primarily to have a broad understanding of how the service works, to know for whom it may be suitable and to be able to state the principal advantages to the customer before calling on specialist help to complete the sale.

How the service works has been explained already, and for whom it is suitable is self-evident. The principal advantages to the user are:

(1) Professional management of investments by experts on a day-to-day basis;
(2) An investment policy determined by the user's own personal circumstances and wishes;
(3) Prompt action on good opportunities to invest, with the risk of making poor investments being minimised;
(4) No danger of overlooking rights or bonus issues and all purchases/sales are dealt with quickly without inconvenience to the customer.

Priority target groups for this service include the older, wealthier customers, especially the busy executive who does not have the time, or the retired person who does not want the worry. Those customers working abroad also offer a likely source of investment management business.

Unit trust service and share exchange schemes

Development and growth in the number of unit trust schemes have gathered pace in recent years, fuelled by higher disposable incomes and the propensity to save for a rainy day. For the smaller investor/saver, unit trusts are an ideal investment. The multiplicity of unit trust schemes allows considerable choice, depending on whether income or capital appreciation, or a mixture of both, is the investor's primary objective. Bank unit trusts offer a number of advantages to the would-be investor/saver, and include the following:

(a) They are designed to achieve a wide spread of investment which ordinarily the investor could not obtain. In this way risks are reduced.
(b) Initial outlay can be as low as £250 with the opportunity to add to holdings by investment amounts as small as £25.

(c) The professional portfolio management within the bank relieves customers of investment problems.

(d) Compared with the direct purchase of shares in a company the cost of buying unit trusts is lower.

(e) Units can be valued easily and sold quickly at an ascertainable price.

Branch staff should know what unit trusts are sold by their organisation and appreciate the investment policy of the different types of unit trust on offer.

The share exchange scheme is intended for those who already hold shares and want to exchange their portfolio for an equivalent value in bank unit trusts. For customers agreeing to this exchange, the advantages are simply that the investment risk is spread wider and they no longer have the headaches of managing a portfolio.

As a general rule, the scheme is most attractive where the shares being exchanged are suitable for inclusion in the bank's share holdings. Those shares that are outside the investment criteria, or are surplus to the bank's requirements, will be sold in the market.

Personal Equity Plans (PEP)

This investment scheme was the surprise in the 1986 Budget. For the first time it allowed private investors to invest in a tax-free environment without tying themselves down to a personal pension plan or limiting themselves to £100 per year and the ten-year minimum period of the savings plans offered by the friendly society/insurance-linked schemes.

Shares in a Personal Equity Plan (PEP) will be free of capital gains tax liability and provided that dividend income is reinvested, that too will be exempt from income tax. However, PEPs go further than pension plans or other insurance schemes which are tax exempt, in that the investor can choose how and where the money is invested. However, only the ordinary shares of fully quoted UK companies and those in the Unlisted Securities market are allowed as PEP investments together with unit trusts. The key features of a PEP investment are:

(1) Maximum annual PEP investment whether by regular savings or lump sum is £3000

(2) Up to 25% (maximum £540) of the PEP can be invested in unit trusts

(3) The PEP must be held for a full calendar year after the year in which it was taken out if it is to qualify for the tax exemptions and income tax relief

(4) One plan per year can be taken out by individual UK residents over the age of 18.

Promotional opportunities

For a higher-rate taxpayer, a PEP will be a very good way to mitigate tax, but for ordinary rate taxpayers the initial charge and management charges may offset part of the tax savings in the first year. Apart from the higher-rate taxpayer group which offers the best promotional opportunities, other customers who wish to save a regular sum each month or have small lump sums to invest are suitable targets for PEPs. With recent state sell-offs – British Telecom, British Gas, British Airways and others – roughly 20 per cent of the population now own shares. Share ownership should continue to grow, and for those who want to avoid the paperwork, a PEP is a good alternative to unit trusts.

Insurance

Insurance services are some of the banks' fastest growing services, and how insurance can be used as a savings, investment and protection service is mentioned frequently in the last few chapters of this book. Therefore in this section it is not proposed to cover how and in what circumstances insurance can be used but merely to concentrate on the advantages of using the insurance services provided by the banks as an alternative to using insurance companies direct or another broker. Ascertaining what insurance cover is required and finding the best policy terms are the two most difficult tasks facing a customer. The insurance industry is fast moving and the different types of cover now available are quite bewildering to the average man in the street. Moreover, it is now possible to tailor insurance cover to match individual needs in a way that was not possible only a few years ago. The impact of taxation also has to be borne in mind, as some policies are more tax-efficient than others when used or applied correctly to mitigate tax liabilities. The personal pension policy is just one example where substantial tax sums can be avoided by those eligible to have policies drawn up under Section 226A of the Corporation and Tax Act 1970.

This complexity when delving into life insurance is the main reason for a customer's turning for help and guidance to an insurance broker. A bank's insurance broking subsidiary, when used through the local branch manager, can provide an expert service, for a bank can also cover those situations where there may be more appropriate ways of resolving a customer's problems or circumstances than by using insurance.

Indeed the most important single aspect is having a good understanding of a customer's financial and personal circumstances and being able to offer a wider range of services than just insurance. For example, the savings and investment needs of an individual are strongly influenced by that person's personal circumstances – married, single, widowed or divorced – and partly by the person's philosophy, income and tax position. An insurance bond may be suitable for one person, a unit trust for a second and National Savings Certificates for a third – or perhaps even a cocktail of all three.

Bank insurance staff also provide impartial advice, what is best for the customer rather than how much commission can be earned, is invariably uppermost in their minds. An insurance agent is not so impartial, his role is to sell his insurance company's policies. This impartiality is also claimed by all brokers, but the bank's insurance staff in the branch are more likely to have an in-depth knowledge of the customer's personal and financial affairs.

New bank schemes and services are also emerging, the latest being a free insurance review facility. Banks will record all the customer's details including insurance contracts on a computer and provide annual updates of this information. The benefit to users of this free service is a comprehensive record of their insurance, and to the bank an ability to spot gaps in the cover and provide a customer base which feels committed by convenience as much as anything else to using the bank's insurance facilities.

Polarisation

This chapter would not be complete without a few words on the introduction of investor protection rules resulting from the Financial Services Act 1986. In 1988 all banks and building societies were forced to decide whether to sell only their 'in-house' investment services (mainly life insurance and unit trusts) or alternatively offer an independent service advising on the whole range of services available on the open market.

Insurance brokers were also obliged to decide whether to become 'tied agents' or go 'independent' by registering as members of FIMBRA (Financial Intermediaries, Managers and Brokers Association). This is one of the five self-regulatory watchdog organisations, given formal recognition by the Act, and able to authorise members to do business.

In early 1988, the major 'tied agents' included Barclays, Lloyds, Midland, Royal Bank of Scotland, TSB and the Abbey National Building Society. 'Independent Advisers' include the National West-minster Bank and most of the other major building societies including Alliance-Leicester, Halifax, Nationwide Anglia, Woolwich and Leeds.

Thus the ability to sell 'house services' alongside others in the marketplace on a brokerage/commission basis has been severely curtailed. The two options have now been polarised into one – hence the expression 'polarisation'.

Clarity of the status of the financial service provider is fundamental to investor protection, and polarisation will ensure that the buyer knows if he/she is dealing with a 'tied agent' or an 'independent' adviser. It will not be possible to be both through the same type of outlet. Never-theless, it will still be possible for 'tied agents' to introduce customers to other subsidiary companies within the group who have, by virtue of their level of expertise or for other reasons, satisfied FIMBRA require-ments and remain 'independent' advisers.

Polarisation has closed some doors of business opportunity but opened others. Banks electing to be 'tied agents' have widened the range of the 'in-house' life insurances and investment services and this process will continue. Success will depend on convincing customers that these new services are likely to prove competitive over time and value for money. How banks use their branch network delivery systems to promote 'in-house' life contracts, unit trusts and investment bond contracts will also be a crucial factor. General insurance is not affected by polarisation and will continue to be sold as at present by the various financial institutions in the high street.

It must have been a difficult choice for banks and building societies to make, and time will tell whether they have been able to take full advantage of the changes brought about by polarisation.

Case study I

A Mr Smith, who is not a customer, calls with a letter from a long-standing customer.

'Dear Sir,
I am writing to introduce Mr Smith whom I have known for fifteen years. He tells me that unexpectedly he has inherited a lot of money and needs guidance. I have recommended you.'

During the interview Mr Smith tells you he is married with one grown-up daughter and son. He owns a modest house with no mortgage but has no desire to move. He wants to use the money to care for his family and produces a cheque for £120 000. Describe the various services which the bank could provide to meet Mr Smith's needs and briefly state the benefits of each.

At the heart of this situation lay a request from an unsophisticated person who, with appreciable funds at his disposal, was seeking sound guidance and the comfort that his affairs would be managed on his behalf. It is clear that he would not be capable of monitoring or supervising his own investments and dealing with the associated taxation and inheritance tax matters, and it is appropriate to suggest that an introduction to the bank's trust company would have been right and proper. The trust company would be able to offer investment management for a modest portfolio of stocks and shares, the taxation division could assist with his income tax affairs and the trust company could also advise generally concerning the making of a will, with the possibility of the bank being appointed executor and trustee of his estate.

So far as the specific benefits are concerned, each service could show specific benefits, which could be illustrated as follows.

(a) Investment management

(1) The appointment of the bank would relieve the customer of dealing with the many dividends, bonus issues, rights issues and reports that he would undoubtedly receive.

(2) The customer would be able to appoint the bank in such a way that it could make changes in the investments, using the discretionary powers vested in it, and thus relieving the customer of the anxiety and decision-making in switching investment in the light of any appreciable movement on the Stock Exchange.

(3) The customer would have the comfort of knowing that his portfolio would be reviewed at regular intervals by specially-trained bank personnel.

(4) The customer would always have access to funds by instructing the bank to sell shares should cash be needed at any time in the future.

(b) Taxation service

(1) The bank would be able to deal with his income tax return which would be slightly complex as a result of the income derived from the investment of his inheritance.

(2) As part of the taxation service, the bank would be able to deal with the capital gains tax liabilities as and when they became due.

(3) The customer would receive expert advice in using all of his allowances, not only personal but those set out in various finance acts.

(c) Trustee and executorship

(1) The bank would be able to advise on the drawing up of his will to ensure that his wishes are met.
(2) The appointment of the trust company would relieve a relative or friend of carrying out the terms of the will and the winding-up of the estate, which in view of the recent inheritance, could entail a considerable amount of work.
(3) Advice would also be offered on the latest provisions of inheritance tax to ensure that all the allowances are used in full.
(4) The continuous existence of the trust company would ensure that the estate was administered without any undue delay, whereas the prior death of friends or relatives, who might otherwise have been appointed executors and trustees, would give rise to complications on the death of the testator.

Case study II

You have received a letter from Mr White, managing director and majority shareholder (he owns 90 per cent of the issued share capital) of White's Engineering Limited, one of your old-established customers. In his letter, he mentions that he will be calling to discuss temporary overdraft facilities to meet corporation tax that is now due. From the balance sheet figures you have on file, you expect no difficulty in acceding to the request, although an exact amount of the overdraft required is not stated in the letter.

You know from Mr White's file that he is 58 years old, a widower with two sons, both of whom are involved in the business which has operated from its original factory for many years. Your branch holds the unencumbered deeds of his house, which you value at approximately £45 000, together with various uncharged Stock Exchange security certificates with a valuation of approximately £15 000. No other documents or securities are held, either for Mr White or for the company.

You are required from the general information already in your possession to identify the areas in which Mr White might have problems and indicate those bank departments and services which could assist in solving or mitigating those problems, to the mutual benefit of the bank and the customer.

The most important considerations are as follows:

(a) The most obvious problem facing Mr White is the potential inheritance tax liability, bearing in mind that he is a widower and any estate must, under present legislation, be subject to taxation. Not only does Mr White own easily identifiable assets in the form of the house and the investments, but he also owns 90 per cent of the company shares and the value of these will further enhance the estate. The shares in themselves will probably be worth more than they appear at first glance, bearing in mind the hidden reserve described as the 'land/building' asset in the balance sheet.

(b) Mr White should be made aware of the problems he faces, particularly the area of difficulty of passing his interests in the company to his sons on the assumption that he wishes to do so. This would be a fair assumption, bearing in mind that his sons are already involved with the company.

(c) He should be advised that the bank's trust company will be able to offer expert advice on methods of assessing the potential inheritance tax and making provisions through life assurance schemes, or as an alternative, using the lifetime gift facilities (whereby inheritance tax is assessed at a reduced rate). He should also be advised that he will be guided on the use of current exemptions which will help to reduce his taxable estate.

(d) In addition, Mr White apparently faces the problem of inadequate provision for retirement. There is no reference either in the branch records or in the profit and loss accounts of the company to pension plan provisions which, for a controlling director, can be written with particular tax advantages. Whilst it would not be within the branch manager's experience to explain the detailed workings of such a scheme, he should nevertheless mention that the premiums are fully allowable (subject to certain upper limits) against tax, thus reducing the corporation tax liability levied against his company.

Summary

Trust services, insurance and investment management all tend to be related. Any customer needing to make a will is likely to require insurance. So too is the customer who seeks to avoid inheritance tax or merely wishes to provide for a rainy day. Branch bankers need to understand the circumstances that provide opportunities to sell trust services, but having recognised the need the customer is often introduced to a specialist who provides the advice and recommendations.

Any adult married man or woman buying their own home should make a will. These people also need to plan for the protection of a family and the monetary requirements of retirement usually by the dexterous use of insurance. As such, married customers, especially those with families, offer the greatest opportunity to promote trust and insurance services. When these facilities are taken up by the customer, it helps to establish a closer relationship with the bank.

The matrix in Table 15.3 gives some examples of particular customer situations when trust and insurance services should be offered by a banker. The examples given are only a sample of the sort of sales opportunities that can arise and they also demonstrate that often more than one service is required.

Table 15.3

Situation	Will appointment	Investment management	Taxation	Insurance estate planning
Marriage	Make new wills and if necessary revoke old ones.		New tax situation	Life assurance as family protection/ saving, etc.
Addition to family	Revision of wills			Consider insurance scheme for school fees. Revise family protection cover. Policy in trust for child.
Moving house	Making wills if not previously executed.		Tax relief on mortgage interest claim (MIRAS).	Home risks cover. Insurance linked mortgages. Mortgage protection and other forms of family protection insurance.

Table 15.3 (*continued*)

Situation	Will appointment	Investment management	Taxation	Insurance estate planning
Foreign business travel and overseas employment	Will in order?	Expatriates service including off-shore account and investment management.	Tax advice repayments and claims.	Insurance review Expatriates services
Starting own business	Revision of will		Small business tax services.	Estate planning. Pension provision Key man cover. Business and personal risk insurances.
Redundancy	Is will required?	Lump sum investment advice and prospects for investment management.		Insurance bond investments. Pension provision.
Divorce or separation	Revision of will			Tax returns for ex-wife
Receipt of legacy. Premium Bond win. Maturity of life policy or large gift.	Is will arrangement adequate?	Scope for advice or investment management services. Consider unit trusts.	New tax case relieve problems of complex tax return or even higher rate tax.	Estate planning required. Scope for insurance bond investment.
Retirement		Revision of investments. Investment of commutation money.	Tax case to relieve customer of workload and worry.	Annuity or other contract to increase income. Insurance to protect against inheritance tax (depending on age and health).

Revision questions

1 A very wealthy customer has died and his will reveals that his chosen executor predeceased him. What services can the bank offer his widow?
2 Outline the main features and benefits to users of the bank's executor and trustee service.
3 Why should a customer use a bank's insurance subsidiary rather than a broker or insurance agent?

4 Personal Equity Plans were introduced in 1986. What are they, under what circumstances are they tax-efficient and how does your bank identify sales opportunities?

5 Using the life cycle concept, list the major changes in personal circumstances which give rise to the need for insurance and also indicate what type of insurance contract would be suitable.

Chapter 16
Small and Medium-sized Business Customers

Approximately ten per cent of a bank's customer profile are business accounts but despite this low percentage they are undoubtedly the most important sector. Their banking needs range from the simple requirement of clearing cheques to a lengthy list of complex services for the larger private and public companies.

In this chapter the business customer profile is segmented by size. Its needs are identified, and then cross-matched with the more popular services currently available from the major banks and allied financial institutions. Segmenting in this way is, as we have already stressed, an arbitrary process. It takes no account of the different types of trade, or special financial circumstances which are bound to arise in any business enterprise. Moreover, splitting the business sector by size and matching these segments to a particular group of services makes no allowance for the inevitable overlapping of each sub-segment's service requirements. There is no substitute for an appreciation of each business customer's circumstances and the identification of financial requirements based upon a thorough individual analysis and assessment.

Segmenting the market and services

Over 90 per cent of businesses are branded as 'small' and several attempts have been made to describe the word small which is a misnomer. Most definitions of 'small businesses' do seem to indicate that they have a turnover of less than £½ million per annum and employ less than 20 people.

However, the word 'small' denigrates the importance of a sector which produces 25 per cent of the nation's gross domestic product (GDP) and employs 20 per cent of the working population. Within the small business market you have virtually all the 'start-ups' – new enterprises which provide the best potential for banks to expand their market share of the corporate sector. Within the first five years, almost as many small businesses die quickly as those that start up. Picking the 'winners' requires a high degree of skill, but there are handsome rewards for a bank which successfully shepherds a business through three essential phases:

(1) starting-up;
(2) running the business successfully;
(3) profitable expansion.

Medium-sized businesses are generally those which have a turnover of £½ million–£35 million per annum. Again these criteria are arbitrary and if 'type of business' was also a factor in the decision on what is 'medium-sized' there could be an alternative range of services. By implication, large businesses are those with a turnover in excess of £5 million.

Accepting the difficulties and dangers of putting trading customers into broad categories such as these, the initial segmentation by size can be further analysed as in Table 16.1

The level of demand for financial services and their nature will also be influenced by the size of the trading organisation. But, as we saw in the personal market, the broad spectrum of need will be similar. For example, if a firm employs staff, no matter how many, they still have to be paid, and there is a variety of financial services which can be used for this purpose.

Having segmented the corporate market by size, and then highlighted the characteristics which might affect their requirement for financial services, the next step is to cross-match these groups with bank services that might be suitable. Table 16.2 (see page 338) is by no means exhaustive but is intended to demonstrate the logic of this type of segmentation process. What is important is the accurate matching of likely need with the services which have the right set of benefits to meet these needs. However, there is no substitute for an interview with the business customer to determine exactly what is required, for trading customers' needs, even within the segments we have defined here, will vary widely. Nevertheless, competition, and the importance of selling bank services more prolifically to generate revenue, now necessitates some pre-emptive action. Mass marketing campaigns in the corporate sector will raise levels of awareness of what is available from the bank and can be a useful forerunner for a calling programme. Furthermore, when preparing for visits to customers, an analysis of potential requirements and an appreciation of the trading characteristics is useful background information.

Linking services to these three segments must, of necessity, involve a fairly basic approach. In reality needs differ widely in each segment, especially the medium-sized segment, because it is the transitional phase between small and large.

Table 16.1

Group	Some likely business characteristics
SMALL (up to £½m turnover) Service, retail, manufacturing and market garden type, agricultural	Often 'family' businesses with limited financial resources Lack of administrative support staff, minimal business planning Localised business catchment area Heavy reliance on bank overdrafts and other short-term finance One or two key people's ability to work crucial to success Financial expertise limited to advice from bank or accountant
MEDIUM (£½m–£5m turnover) Service	Large number of employees Cashflow pressure creates need for longer-term finance to aid expansion
Retail	Large numbers of employees Heavy bookkeeping requirements with extensive cash handling and payment problems
Manufacturing	Depending on manufacture cycle cashflow problems Need for customised premises Sales staff required to promote goods
LARGE (£5m + turnover) Service and retail	Expansionist minded to gain economies of scale. Network of outlets creating need for organisation and control staff. Need for centralised administrative centre.
Manufacturing	Heavy investment requirement in plant and premises Very susceptible to competition and, therefore, need to be highly efficient Requirement to improve and introduce new products creating need for development and research facilities Constant search for new markets, especially abroad
Agriculture	Seasonal cash flow problems Considerable assets but often working on small return on investment High level of expertise and specialisation depending on type of farming

Table 16.2

Group	A few examples of potential services
SMALL (up to £½ m turnover) Service, retail, manufacturing, agriculture	Personal financial services and estate planning for busy proprietors Special 'start-up' loan schemes including Small Firms Loan Guarantee Scheme Hire purchase Key person insurance Bank money transmission services which reduce commitment to bookkeeping
MEDIUM (£½ m–£5m turnover) Service, retail, manufacturing, agriculture	Pay service and other computer based 'business support' financial facilities Credit cards for employee expenses or for retailers as a form of payment Leasing facilities, factoring Longer-term capital loans
LARGE (£5m + turnover) Service, retail, manufacturing, agriculture	Pay service Business advisory facilities Credit cards Importer/exporter services Registration facilities Equity finance Longer term lending support

Trading customers also have 'trigger points' – clearly identifiable changes in their circumstances which provide timely opportunities to promote particular services. The list in Table 16.3 identifies some of the main trigger point situations, but there are others. Moreover, the services indicated are merely a sample to assist in an understanding of the basic principles of matching needs of trading customers with the benefits of some of the banks' services.

Finally, one other aspect of the trading organisation should not be overlooked when assessing needs, namely that the self-employed directors, partners and sole traders have personal requirements just like employed people. So when assessing business development prospects this second 'personal' business opportunity should not be missed. Often personal financial needs are inextricably intertwined with the financial requirements of the trading concern itself.

Table 16.3

Trigger points	Potential for:
Forming a new business (start-up)	Government Enterprise Allowance Scheme Government Small Firms Loan Loan Guarantee Scheme Bank start-up loan schemes Business expansion scheme (BES)
Expanding network of distribution	Credit card retailer service Leasing of premises/vehicles
Expanding production	Loans for investment in plant and machinery
Altering product range	Business advisory service Franchising Plant and machinery loans
Entering export trade	Export/financial advice Loans Negotiations, collections, documentary credits
Taking on more staff	Conversion of unbanked workforce to bank-mandated pay Insurance/pensions
Moving to bigger premises or buying own premises	Business advisory service Business property loans Leasing on fixed plant
Acquisition of another business	Business advisory service Equity finance Registration services
Introducing employee enhancements – motorcars, pension schemes etc.	Trust services (pensions, employee insurance) Leasing for motorcars
Death of director or key man	Business advisory service 'Key man' insurance cover for remaining directors
Redundancy of employees	Investment potential among redundant employees – some may wish to go self-employed

The influence of cash flow

Before we look more closely at financial requirements of the small and medium segments, and the way in which bank services can meet the needs of these businesses, it is worth considering the importance of cash flow as the basis of success or failure of any trading enterprise.

It is not an accident that the key stages of cash control in any business can be matched with specific financial services tailored to appeal to the person(s) controlling the purse strings. All trading concerns must have cash or access to cash in order to trade. This is the 'pool' which will sustain life until it is allowed to run dry. The inflow and outflow of money from this pool is illustrated in Fig. 16.1.

The services available to sustain and even accelerate the working capital cash flow cycle are widely known and have three main functions:

(1) to finance the trading cycle;
(2) to assist administration and management of working capital funds;
(3) to reduce trading risks.

To finance the trading cycle and keep the process working smoothly overdrafts, loans, cheque books, cheque collections, status enquiries, factoring, invoice discounting and many other facilities indigenous to financial institutions are well known and well used by all businesses, whatever their size and the nature of the trade.

Once the trading cycle is complete, the pool will need to be kept at a prudent level. If losses have been incurred, further supplies of cash will need to be found to top up the reservoir. If profits surplus to normal trading and expansion requirements have been made, then this cash will need to be drained off. A comprehensive range of investment services exists to meet the needs of most businesses with surplus cash,

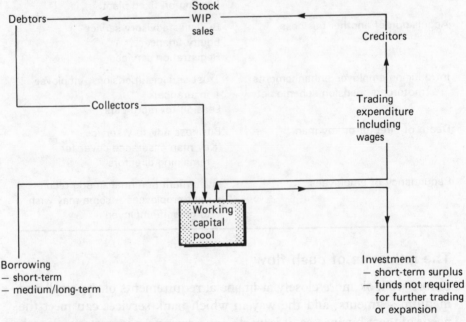

Fig. 16.1 The flow of cash

but the choice of investment and term will depend on the future plans of the business and any cyclical or seasonal factors which create abnormal waves in the pattern of trading. If losses have been sustained, bank services may provide a short-term answer, provided an end to adverse trading can be foreseen.

In summary, the overall financial management of business can be split into stages:

(1) gathering working capital;
(2) utilisation of funds in the trading process;
(3) control of trading activity at a level which matches cash resources;
(4) management of surplus funds.

Business requirements

There is no substitute for experience when dealing with business customers, but even a full understanding of a business and its problems will not, by itself, bring about solutions if a banker has a poor knowledge of the services that he can provide.

It is not possible or practicable here to include detailed product information. Space is limited and whatever is written today would rapidly become out of date. However, the point is made that a good understanding of the services available is an essential element in selecting the right one for the customer which will ensure satisfaction at a profit. Banks have always been the main source of finance for small and medium-sized businesses and this fact is unlikely to change. Now we need to consider more closely the marketing skills of correctly matching the features of services with the needs of the customer.

Earlier discussion of the segmentation of the business market and the influence of cash flow made it evident that a business needs financial assistance in three ways:

(1) administrative requirements;
(2) working capital requirements;
(3) capital requirements.

With small businesses and start-ups the need for a greater level of financial support (whether as capital or working capital) than the rest of industry is well known. These companies are not normally sophisticated, management resources are stretched and there is an overriding shortage of finance. Hence they offer a ready and often willing market for bank services.

Once the need has been identified, the banker's main objective will be to satisfy that requirement by selling the most appropriate service.

Matching the various types of finance with their intended use must be done well; if it is done badly it can spell disaster for the customer. As a demonstration of this point, financing business vehicles with an overdraft may seriously reduce the liquid funds available for trading, through failing to match longer-term financial requirements with a source of funds having a longer-term repayment programme.

Equally important is the need to match repayment criteria with cash flow features, if an imbalance in the cash flow cycle is to be avoided.

Bank services for small and medium-sized businesses can be segmented as shown in Table 16.4.

Administration and financial advisory services

(a) *Pay service* During the late 1960s, it became clear that the banks could use their considerable computer expertise to develop and launch a payroll service. At first the incentive for introducing this facility was to cement existing account relationships and foster connections with non-customers. Since the 1960s, pay service has become only one of a range of computer based facilities designed to assist businesses in improving efficiency and reducing the burden of administrative matters.

Pay service offers substantial benefits to employees, employers and to the bank administering the payroll.

(1) *Employee benefits* Having a bank account makes it simpler to budget, provides a safe place for money and gives easier access to cheap credit and convenient savings schemes.

(2) *Employer benefits* Employers probably benefit more than the employee or the provider of the service. There can be substantial cost savings, especially where the number on the payroll is considerable. Computerising the information speeds up the process and should

Table 16.4

Popular administration and financial advisory services	Popular sources of working capital cash flow	Popular sources of medium-term capital
Pay service	Factoring	Leasing
Barclaycard and Access company services	Invoice discounting	Small firms loan guarantees
	Overdrafts/loans	Term loans
Business advisory service	*Other sources*	*Other sources*
	Trade credit	Proprietor's stake
Insurance	Hire purchase	

release office staff for other work. Furthermore, the security costs associated with cash are minimised.

Other savings may well come from improved cash flow if employees can be switched from weekly to monthly pay. Stationery costs will also be reduced.

(3) *How the service works* Within the wide number of variations available the service can accommodate most employers' requirements. For instance, users can adopt one or any combination of four methods of paying their employees:

- payment direct to a bank account via BACS (Bankers Automated Clearing Services);
- preparation of individual cheques;
- payment by cash;
- payment by paper Bank Giro credits.

Whichever method of payment used, the pay service will calculate, prepare and distribute employees' pay. This distribution is supported by listings and summaries for the employer's record and accounting purposes. Additionally, end of tax year documents are supplied and budget alterations are dealt with immediately.

(4) *Market potential* Nearly half of all wages and salaries are still paid in cash – approximately to 10 million people. Although there is now a positive movement away from cash, for manual as well as non-manual workers, there are still some major obstacles to be overcome. These include opposition by workers who have no bank accounts and fear that their wives may discover their true earnings if they are paid by any other means than cash. Moreover, many employers do not appreciate that cost savings and improved security may well outweigh the cost of persuading employees and trade unions to accept a movement away from cash payment.

The market for pay service is enormous and for banks, who sell their service despite the problems, there are considerable benefits. Fee income, gaining new personal current accounts and the opportunity to sell other services to the employer are the major benefits. It should also be borne in mind that the pay service can be sold to non-customers as well as customers and, with the former, will come further opportunities to develop banking links.

(b) *Barclaycard and Access services* Both the major credit card companies offer schemes which enable employees to use a credit card to pay for expenditure incurred for business. Petrol purchase and business entertainment are the largest expenditure items charged in this way by employees.

Administration savings can be considerable, as cash floats are eliminated and release capital for other uses. There is also the ability of the
employer to exercise much greater control over expenses, as well as
settling payment by one single amount against itemised statements,
thus simplifying administration.

(1) *How the service works* A business requiring the company card
scheme will nominate employees to receive personal credit cards each
bearing an individual's name but carrying the Access/Barclaycard
account number that has been issued to the firm. Employees use the
cards as if they were their own but the expenditure is charged to the
firm. Total monthly expenditure by employees is shown on the statement which must be settled in full immediately; there are no extended
credit facilities available.

Neither Access nor Barclaycard place any restriction on the minimum
number of cards they are prepared to issue under one company card
service. It is also an easy matter to add and delete employees participa-
ting in the scheme at any time.

(2) *Market potential* Because firms using the service will enjoy credit
for one month up to an agreed limit, which is adequate to cover likely
employee expenditure, the potential users must be creditworthy. Apart
from this aspect, there is no other limitation. Any firm that has
employees travelling and entertaining must be a prime target.

Current take-up of the company card schemes provided by the credit
card organisations is low; there is considerable potential throughout the
corporate sector and especially among smaller businesses wishing to
save on administration costs and time.

(c) *Business advisory service (BAS)* Basically, the business advisory
service provided by the banks undertakes an assessment of past trading
performance, takes stock of the current financial strengths, weaknesses
and capabilities and weighs these aspects against future plans.

A business advisory representative visits the firm to examine and
evaluate the firm's financial affairs. This examination is conducted
against a backcloth of detailed discussions with the firm's management.
In this way, the financial appraisal and any projections are kept within
the context of special trading circumstances encountered and the firm's
objective views of their own future.

An analysis of past performance is usually based on previous years'
audited accounts. Trends are calculated of the main trading items in the
accounts, especially profit, expenses, debtors, creditors, stock, etc. By
this method, inherent trading capabilities can be established as these
are very relevant to an analysis of the current and future position.

When examining the present-day picture, the control of business assets (stock, debtors, cash, etc.) gives a clear indication of business efficiency and management ability. This aspect is emphasised even further when costing and pricing methods are examined. Probably the most important part of the business advisory examination is the assessment of future budgeting and forecasting. As we have seen already, the life-blood of any business is cash, and budgeting and forecasting skills are the basic needs of all businesses that are expanding in a controlled and profitable manner.

An examination of trading performance and the business generally will also reveal opportunities to give general advice on insurance, continuity and succession of proprietorships, estate planning including wills and pension provision. In fact, wherever a business and its management are financially vulnerable the business advisory representative should point out the problems and, if possible, suggest solutions.

Market potential This service can be offered to non-customers and customers alike. It is especially suitable for businesses which have only recently been established and those where rapid expansion is planned or taking place.

There are approximately three million firms in the United Kingdom and all businesses, whether large or small, need advice at one time or another. Merchant banks tend to advise the larger companies but the vast rump of businesses rely on banks and auditing accountants for financial guidance. The availability and quality of the advice that the smaller firm can call upon is limited. Thus the BAS offered by banks is helping to satisfy the needs for in-depth advice, based on a close examination of the financial picture in the small and medium size business sector. The BAS representatives, with their specialist training, can go much further than hard-pressed branch bankers and, where these representatives acquire an in-depth knowledge of a particular trade or industry through an examination of a number of similar businesses, the quality of the advice is further enhanced.

Where the advisory service is administered expertly there are obvious advantages to the firm prepared to listen to the advice. Banks also benefit from improved banker–customer relationships. There are usually opportunities to provide other financial services and with improved financial planning and control, banks can probably provide higher levels of financial support than would otherwise be considered prudent.

(d) *Insurance* Insurance is a highly complex subject, especially for the business customer. It is not the role of branch bankers to be specialists in insurance matters but they must appreciate the way in which insurance can be used to protect and provide for the business and the management which operates it. Having identified a need for insurance, it is then a specialist function to administer the advice and make recommendations.

For the sake of simplicity, insurance can be divided into the following broad areas:

(a) *General insurance* Banks can provide all the insurance cover requirements of a business, whether large or small. These range from insurance cover on premises, stock and other assets of the company to vehicle insurance, public liability, employee liability, travel and so on. In fact, almost everything and anything can be insured at a price. For most smaller businesses, a combined traders' policy can be drawn up which will cover most contingencies which could cause loss or damage to assets, employees and the public.

(b) *Life assurance* There are five major ways of protecting employees and the business by using life insurance.

1 Key man (or woman) assurance can be arranged to compensate a business for the financial loss it can suffer if a key employee dies during his/her working life. This is particularly relevant to the smaller firm manufacturing a specialist product, or providing a service where a high level of individual skill is required. Key employee cover can also be used to repay loans in the event of death of the individual who provided the financial support.

2 Partnership assurance, or share purchase assurance, can be provided to help overcome any problems arising when surviving partners or directors require to buy the shares of deceased partners or directors.

3 Temporary life cover can be used to protect families of employees engaged in extensive travel or hazardous jobs.

4 On a more permanent basis, life insurance can be arranged on employees' lives, not just as family protection but to augment pension provisions.

5 Last but not least, to ensure the survival of a business if the principal dies, personal life assurance can be effected to fund inheritance tax liabilities.

(3) *Pension schemes* Self-employed people, on retirement, will only receive the state pension benefit unless they make their own additional arrangements. There are a considerable number of pension schemes available to the self-employed; many are very tax-efficient and highly flexible. Some are based on single premiums which allow flexibility for those who may not be able to contribute regularly because business income fluctuates substantially every year. Annual premium policies on

the other hand allow regular contributions to be made and enable the business to budget for the cost in advance.

Retirement benefits for directors of certain types of company can also be arranged with the premium payable by the company as a tax-free expense. Directors can also contribute within certain limits on a tax-free basis.

Finally, the market for insurance-based pension schemes which can be arranged for the benefit of employees to add to the state benefit or on a 'contracted out' basis should not be overlooked.

Market opportunities and potential Suffice it to say that, as a nation, we are all under-insured and this service makes a major contribution to bank profits every year. Table 16.5 identifies the broad areas of opportunity which exist to sell insurance to business customers.

Some sources of working and start-up capital

(a) *Factoring* Factoring is really three distinct services which are closely integrated:

(1) sales accounting and collection;
(2) credit management, which includes protection against bad debts, credit control and chasing up slow payers;
(3) availability of finance against pledged sales invoices.

Table 16.5 Selling insurance to business customers

Type if insurance	Examples of use by businesses
Endowment assurance	To augment retirement provisions To fund loans
Pension assurance	To provide retirement income for proprietors and employees
Permanent health	To provide insurance replacement on disablement of proprietors and employees
Whole life or term assurance	To repay any loans in event of death of proprietors (assured) To provide key man cover To protect share purchase schemes
Business cover	To protect damage or loss of business assets To protect profits following losses from insurance risks To cover liabilities to employees and public To protect against theft, travel risks, legal expenses, etc.

The factoring company purchases the book debts on a continuing basis and in the process takes on the administration of the sales ledger of the client and looks after the credit control.

In this way, a business which is short of working capital can obtain additional finance as, at the commencement of a factoring arrangement, a down payment is made of a percentage of the book debts taken over. This service, therefore, appeals to the expanding company as it speeds up cash flow and also makes better use of management time and the money normally tied up in trade credit.

The service is operated by the client sending the factoring company sales invoices at periodic intervals. An initial payment can be made immediately based upon a pre-determined percentage of the invoices but if an advance is not required then payment will be made at a time based on the average maturity date of the invoices. Invoices are then mailed to the client's customers by the factor with instructions to remit payment direct to the factor. When payment is received, the difference between the percentage payment already made to the customer and the total of the invoice is then made available to the factor's client.

At the end of each month the factor's client will receive:

(1) copies of statements sent to customers;
(2) a statement of his account with the factor;
(3) an age analysis of outstanding sales invoices.

Costs incurred by users of factoring include interest on the advance payments made and a factoring fee or service charge which is normally between 1 and 2 per cent of turnover. There are also collection charges if extra credit control work is required on sales invoices which have not been paid within a reasonable period of time.

Benefits to customers using a factoring service include savings in the form of better purchase prices and discounts through having a strong cash flow and savings on administration costs and time. Protection against bad debts can also be included as this risk can be underwritten by the factors.

(b) *Invoice discounting* This facility is usually associated with factoring but differs from it in a number of ways. For instance, the purchase of the sales invoice is always with recourse and the fact that the debt has been assigned is not revealed to the client's customer. Moreover, the facility does not include any administrative support and it is possible to discount just one invoice or many invoices depending on what sum is required by way of an advance from the factoring company in anticipation of payment against sale(s) already invoiced.

(c) *Leasing* Instalment credit is not covered in this chapter as it is a well-understood method of obtaining finance over shorter periods, usually up to five years. Leasing, on the other hand, is a form of finance over the medium term, up to ten years or more. The leasing company buys the asset required by the business and then leases it at an agreed rental.

There are taxation benefits to both the lessee (the business renting the asset) and the lessor. For tax purposes, leasing companies can claim the same capital allowances as would be enjoyed by the business if it had purchased the asset. The benefit of savings gained by the leasing company is then passed on to the lessee in the form of lower rentals. Regional development grants can also be claimed by the leasing company and these too will be reflected in the final rental to be paid by the lessee.

Two types of lease are available:

(1) *A finance lease*, which is sometimes called a full pay out lease. This entails payment over an agreed period of amounts which are sufficient to cover the capital and financing costs of the leased asset. The rental period is usually less than or equal to the estimated life of the goods on lease.

(2) *An operating lease* involves an agreement whereby assets are leased for only a part of their estimated life, and so the rental covers only part of the capital cost. Firms using leased assets are generally responsible for insuring against fire, theft and other business risks, but the lessor is responsible for maintenance.

User benefits For the customer there are a number of benefits in leasing assets rather than purchasing them outright or through instalment credit:

(1) 100 per cent of the cost can be financed and leaves capital intact.
(2) A lease is a very flexible arrangement which can be tailored to suit most requirements.
(3) It is a longer-term arrangement than some financial alternatives so reducing periodic payments.
(4) Taxable allowances and regional development grants can be turned immediately into a cash advantage by way of reduced rentals at the outset of the lease.
(5) Budgeting advantages from a regular rental programme as capital costs are spread evenly over the years.

Leasing is yet another complex service calling for specialist knowledge. The branch banker should, nevertheless, be capable of identifying prospective users through an appreciation of the cash flow and taxation benefits that leasing offers. Moreover, it should not be forgotten that this service, like many others already mentioned, is widely sought and accepted by non-customers as well as customers. It is a strange phenomenon that firms will accept some services and yet not others from a bank where they have no account relationship.

Government and privately aided support schemes

(a) *Small Firms Loan Guarantee Scheme* This government-backed service to help finance small businesses is due to be revised shortly. Losses have mounted in what was supposed to be a self-financing scheme and it seems inevitable that criteria will be tightened and closer monitoring introduced. Nevertheless, approximately £100 million has been advanced to small businesses under the terms of the scheme.

First introduced in June 1981, the government Loan Guarantee Scheme has enabled the banks to lend up to £75 000 to individual businesses which for lack of security or proprietor's capital would otherwise have been declined. Money borrowed on a loan account under the scheme can be used for the purchase of fixed assets, business development generally or for working capital requirements. Up to 70 per cent of the lending is guaranteed by the Department of Trade.

Conditions for borrowing are flexible. The loan can be drawn in one amount or up to four tranches, each of which must be for a minimum of 25 per cent of the total loan. Term ranges from two to seven years and applicants can have more than one loan, provided total borrowing does not exceed £75 000. Even the repayment programme can be varied, with monthly or quarterly instalments and a capital repayment holiday of up to two years at the outset of the loan.

It can be readily appreciated that the market potential is large especially among the small businesses wishing to expand, and the start-up enterprises. One key factor is the viability of the lending proposition. When considering ability to repay, there is a 5 per cent annual premium on the guaranteed portion of the outstanding loan payable to the Department of Trade and Industry to take into account. This premium is in addition to the normal interest charges levied by the bank making the advance.

(b) *Enterprise Allowance Scheme* This scheme was introduced to help those people who are unemployed and want to start their own business. The Enterprise Allowance of £40 per week for up to 52 weeks compensates for the loss of unemployment benefit. This allowance is also designed to assist the small business until it becomes established.

Also provided under the Enterprise Allowance Scheme is free business counselling to help people overcome some of the problems associated with starting a small business.

To be eligible for the Enterprise Allowance an aspiring small businessman must satisfy the following conditions:

(1) Be receiving unemployment or supplementary benefit or receiving these benefits through a member of the family and be unemployed and actively seeking work for at least eight weeks.

(2) The applicant for the allowance must show that there is at least £1000 available to invest in the business during the first twelve months. This can be in the form of a loan or overdraft.

(3) People under the age of eighteen do not qualify.

(4) The type of business must be approved by the Manpower Services Commission. Broadly speaking, to gain approval from the MSC the business must be new, independent and not tied in any way to another business or third party; it must also be small and the nature of trade must be such as is not likely to bring the scheme into disrepute. Nightclubs, gaming clubs, drinking establishments, modelling agencies, etc. are unlikely to be suitable.

It is possible to form a partnership or limited company under the scheme. Partners will be limited to a maximum of ten and each will need to show that they have at least £1000 to invest in the business. In the case of a limited company the applicant should hold at least 50 per cent of the voting shares.

(c) *Franchising* Franchising is not new; it has been with us for many years. Early examples include the brewers who as long ago as the eighteenth century provided assistance to public houses in return for exclusive rights to provide beer.

More recently, 'business format franchising' has been developed where a trader buys a complete business system or way of trading. In this type of franchising, all businesses trade under a common name: Wimpy or Kentucky Fried Chicken are obvious examples. The franchisor, within a total business package, will provide training, ongoing research support, regular supervision and advertising coverage. In return he/she will be looking for a service fee from the franchisee and perhaps royalties, often in a form linked to turnover.

Business format franchising and other variations have grown tremendously in the late 1980s. The demise of old traditional industries coupled with large redundancy payments and a politically induced desire to be self-employed has encouraged growth to a level where most of the banks have a specialist management team devoted to the franchise market.

The basic principle behind franchising is supposedly that a well-known organisation, with a successful product or service and trading history, sells the right to trade in the same way to another. In the early stages, the franchisor will help the franchisee to set up the operation and administer it.

Clearly there are advantages in buying a franchise for a budding entrepreneur:

(1) Ostensibly it is his/her own business and he/she can assess the likelihood of success from an examination of other similar operations.
(2) Expertise is available to the franchisee especially training, bookkeeping, costing and other marketing skills.
(3) Often there are savings as the franchisor, by virtue of size, will be able to negotiate discounts and reductions when purchasing advertising and materials for sale.
(4) Often a good image or reputation has already been established.
(5) Operating or catchment areas are usually clearly identified and agreed between the franchisor and franchisee.

However, there are some downsides that should not be overlooked by somebody considering a franchise.

(1) A service fee is payable, and also in many cases royalties based on turnover, or restrictions whereby goods for resale must only be purchased from the franchisor.
(2) Franchisors will wish to inspect the books and the operation to ensure that their interests are safeguarded. The franchisee will also be expected to ensure that the trade of other operators is not jeopardised by their own actions.
(3) The franchisor may fail to provide the training, advertising and business support to a level or standard that is desirable.
(4) Often there are restrictions placed on the sale of the business by the franchisor. Moreover, on the renewal dates of the franchise contract there may be fresh conditions imposed.

A bank's duty will be to advise its customer who is considering taking up a franchise. Whether or not the customer wishes to borrow, the branch manager or bank's franchise expert will invariably advise and even assist the potential franchisee to consider the following:

(1) Assess how proven the franchising operation is. If it is a new

franchise, the bank would wish to see financial accounts for the pilot operation.

(2) Endeavour to measure the franchisor's management skill, track record and financial strength in order to assess whether the support for the new franchise will be forthcoming. Checking bank references, audited accounts and all marketing research sales forecasts will be pertinent. Estimating the nature and impact of competition in the area will also be necessary.

(3) Calculating start-up and running costs and the effect on profitability of borrowed money in the venture.

(4) Recommend a solicitor to check the agreement and an accountant to assess sales forecasts and profit projections.

There is no substitute for the experience and knowledge to be gained from talking to other franchisees in a network. However, for a new franchise venture this will not be possible, so the advice and help the customer gets from his banker, accountant and solicitor will be vital in deciding whether or not to take up the franchisor's offer.

Guiding a business on presenting its case

Because a bank's role should be more than lending money and selling its services, it is worth identifying which major aspects of a business should be covered when considering what needs to be done to survive or expand. Invariably bankers become more closely involved with business customers when they receive requests to lend money. At this point they will need to explore the historic and current performances of the business and assess the future growth before making a lending decision.

Few small business customers will prepare their presentation before this interview with the bank manager; if they did so their chances of a successful outcome would be enhanced. Therefore it falls to the banker to extract the relevant facts and figures by extensive questioning, which is both time-consuming and expensive. In an ideal world, the customer could be given a check-list prior to the interview, so that the most relevant information would be available to both parties in a format that can be quickly digested.

When making proposals to a bank, a presentation plan is required which might include some or all of the following:

Business objectives
– Brief details of objectives, how to achieve them and any time-scale within which this is expected to be done.

The product/service
- Detail the products or services that are supplied including, where necessary, a layman's explanation of any technical terms used.

The sales plan
- Markets for these products or services including specific names and response to any feelers.
- Principal competitors and what the applicant thinks they may do when he/she enters the market or expands his/her market share.
- Strategies for countering competitor activity.
- Sales literature and methods.

The operations plan
- Details of pricing, promotion, distribution facilities and requirements.

The facilities plan
- Borrowing requirements to cover buildings, equipment, transport, working capital, etc.

The people plan
- C.V.'s of all senior managers, emphasising their particular skills for the job.

The organisation plan
- Structure of who is responsible for what and whom.

The budget plan
- Estimate of the total of the project with details of how this and the working capital requirement will be financed.

The information and control plan
- Methods to be used to monitor and control the business.

Other relevant factors
- Anything else which would aid the discussions with the bank.

Naturally the extent of the information supplied will depend on the complexity of the situation being discussed with the bank. For a new business proposition, most of this information will be relevant. Where the bank already has a detailed knowledge of the business, some of the information can be left out of a proposal plan.

However, what this does demonstrate is the need to plan every important step, and this is as important for a small business customer as it is for a major high street bank. Many bank managers pre-plan interviews and calling programmes, setting out a list of key questions and objectives they want to achieve. Business customers should be encouraged to follow a similar line when dealing with a bank.

Case study I

AB Limited has banked with you for several years but over the last two has incurred trading losses of £60 000. The present limit is £150 000 secured by the factory which was recently valued at £200 000. Currently the borrowing is within the agreed arrangements but there have been excesses and there is evidence of pressure from suppliers, including the Inland Revenue. In the last six months, sales have increased to £700 000, the company is profitable, but debtors total £280 000.

As you are unwilling to increase the overdraft to placate pressing creditors, how can you advise the company?

The two services which could resolve the problem are factoring and invoice discounting.

The main features of factoring are:

(a) administration of the company's sales ledger to improve payment performance;
(b) credit protection; a 'with recourse' facility may only be offered in some cases;
(c) advances up to 80 per cent against the trade debts.

Invoice discounting differs from factoring in three ways:

(a) the whole of the sales ledger is not taken over;
(b) it can be a 'one-off' operation;
(c) the customer receives payment from the debtor and forwards it to the discounter.

Clearly there are factors to consider before these services are taken up by the customer, or indeed offered by the factor or discounter. Annual turnover must be above a certain level, the bad debt record will have a bearing and so will the costs of the service.

Case study II

Crabtree Manufacturing Limited have made reasonable profits over ten years and on 30 September 1983 the balance sheet showed a capital base of £100 000. Accounts are normally produced six months after the year-end and form the only financial summary. Last year, when reviewing the overdraft facility you suggested more regular financial information might be beneficial and now you see in the latest accounts to 30 September 1984 a loss of £15 000 even after the directors' salaries had been reduced.

The company borrowing has become solid, and additionally there have been bad debts of £10 000 and a resistance from customers to price increases. PAYE has not been paid and the Inland Revenue are pressing. The managing director feels he does not get sufficient advice from the accountants and wishes to re-open the discussion with you on financial control. How would you respond to his request for advice?

The areas of immediate concern are:

(a) cash management;
(b) control of debtors and creditors;
(c) profitability;
(d) profit and loss reporting on a regular basis.

Introductions to computer services and even factoring might be suggested but introducing the managing director to financial controls is the fundamental requirement, not least so that the bank can be in a position to fund the short-term cash difficulties. A business advisory service visit would be very helpful.

Case study III

At a recent meeting with Mr Smith, managing director of your valued customers AB Engineering Limited, during which you discussed the company's borrowing facilities, Mr Smith expressed his concern for the future. His worry was not the lack of work, but rather the competition for labour resulting from the movement of companies into the area. A substantial new office block has been completed in the town and a large United Kingdom insurance company has already announced its plans to move its main administrative workforce into these premises.

AB Engineering Limited has a turnover in excess of £5 million per annum, it employs 100 skilled and semi-skilled engineers and fitters, and a further 40 administrative staff dealing with invoicing, general bookkeeping, salaries and other clerical duties. The company also has a small accounting department dealing exclusively with preparation and monitoring of the company's cash flow projections and the costing of contracts.

Mr Smith feels that the higher office salary structure of the insurance company will entice some of his administrative staff, particularly as the insurance company's recruitment drive will start shortly. AB Engineering feels unable to raise the salaries and fringe benefits of its office staff because of the effects on the other sections of the workforce, and Mr Smith is resigned to disruption through loss of staff and the repercussions on the general efficiency of his company.

What opportunities do you see for introducing Mr Smith to specialised bank services which might be used to counterbalance the feared loss of staff and which at the same time will develop the bank's overall business? Having identified the appropriate services, show briefly why they are relevant to the company's needs.

In dealing with the expected shortage of administrative staff, the bank's factoring and/or computer divisions or subsidiaries would be able to offer services to mitigate the expected disruption through loss of staff.

(a) *Factoring subsidiary*   The subsidiary company would be able to take over the running of the company's sales ledger, including the preparation and submission of sales invoices to the company's debtors. Not only would this facility relieve the administrative staff of some of the workload, but it would have the added advantage of ensuring payment on set dates in respect of amounts due, and this in turn would be a useful aid to the accounting division in a more realistic preparation of cash flow projections. Also, the factoring service would be able to offer 100 per cent credit cover on all sales approved by that division. A further benefit is that this subsidiary or division will relieve the company of the burden of chasing slow-paying debtors, and this service is likely to prove particularly beneficial if and when the administrative staff section comes under pressure.

(b) *Computer division*   All the bank's computer divisions/subsidiaries offer a variety of facilities to meet various requirements. Among the many services available, the following would appear to be of interest to the company:

(1) Pay-roll preparation for both monthly and weekly-paid staff. Salary/wage advices would be either by bank giro or through the BACS magnetic tape system.

Whilst the company customer will undoubtedly have to provide the basic information required, nevertheless much time and effort can be saved by using the bank's payroll service. Whilst costs would vary between the banks, the outlay is nevertheless regarded as being small, particularly when it is compared with the saving on administration costs and time.

(2) Maintenance of the company's purchasing ledger, which would help effective paying and cash flow procedures as illustrated in factoring above.

If the factoring service was not used, the computer division would be able to handle and administer the sales ledger, producing the same benefits as for the purchasing ledger.

Summary

The small to medium business sector is vast, not just because of the number of firms involved but also because of its considerable potential. For the banks, this market is the main key to achieving profitable

Table 16.6 Summary of financial services widely used by small and medium-sized businesses

Small business (turnover up to £½m)	Medium sized businesses (turnover £½m–£5m)
General services	General services
Credit card company cards	Credit card company card and
Bankers Automated Clearing	retailer service
Services Limited (BACS)	BACS
BACS entries service	BACS entries service
Pay service	Business advisory service
	Treasury management services
Lending services	Collection accounts
Overdrafts and loans	Entry collection service
Capital and development loans	Pay service
Export finance (ECGD)	Unbanked workforce—
Factoring	conversion to bank mandated
Invoice discounting	pay
Leasing	
Small firms loan guarantee	Lending services
scheme	Overdrafts and loans
Other special loan services	Acceptance lines
	Capital and development loans
Overseas services	Equity finance
Collections	Factoring
Documentary credits	Invoice discounting
Foreign exchange	Leasing
Forward exchange	Small firms loans guarantee scheme
Guarantees, indemnities, bonds and	Special loan services
Associated Banks' Services	Term loans
Payments	Merchant bank services

Table 16.6   (*Continued*)

Small business (turnover up to £½m)	Medium sized businesses (turnover £½m–£5m)
Investment services	*Overseas services*
Interest bearing deposits	Collections
Money management service	Documentary credits
	Export finance (ECGD)
Trust services	Export finance – with recourse to
For the directors	the exporter
Estate planning	Foreign exchange
Tax	Forward exchange
Executor and trustee	Guarantees, indemnities, bonds
Investment management	Various payment facilities
For the business	
Corporate trusteeships	*Investment services*
Insurance	Interest bearing deposits
Pension fund management	Money management service
Money management service	Unit trust trusteeship
Unit trust trusteeship	
	Trust services
Franchising	For the directors
Advice, overdrafts and loans	Estate planning
	Tax
	Executors and trustees
	Investment management
	For the business
	Corporate trusteeships
	Insurance
	Pension fund management

growth. This sector is cash-hungry and yet, with some 40 per cent not borrowing also provides banks with valuable credit balances. In the main, these firms are not financially sophisticated and look to banks for advice. This, in turn, opens up opportunities to sell the types of specialist services mentioned in this chapter. However, it should not be forgotten that the banks have an extensive range of products for the business market – far too many to cover in detail. However, to aid the choice of further reading Table 16.6 gives a list of the services most widely used.

The need to consider the individual requirements of a firm in order to provide the right service or group of services is paramount. There is no substitute for having a sound appreciation of not just the customer's financial situation but also the nature of its trade and the market in which it operates.

Revision questions

1 Company X is considering trying to switch its cash weekly wages employees to a mandated scheme. What advice and support will be available from a bank?
2 As a training exercise for staff you have asked them to identify all the medium-sized company customers and suggest what services should be offered. Prepare a grid for your own use when cross-matching examples of a manufacturer, a wholesaler, an insurance broker and a farming customer.
3 How does the Small Firms Loan Guarantee Scheme work. For whom is it suitable?
4 What are the advantages and disadvantages of franchising. How would you advise a potential franchisee to proceed?
5 Your company customer is moving to larger premises and expanding his workforce. What financial considerations come to mind?

Chapter 17
Professional Customers

The professional market is an important one for the banks and merits special attention. Its members are high earners and, in the case of solicitors and accountants, can introduce their clients' business to banks. This special situation has led to a number of bank services being specially tailored to meet the professional customer's needs, and often some lending and investment services are promoted on very favourable interest terms. Most recently, special high interest-earning accounts for money which is held on behalf of clients have been introduced. These have a tiered interest structure – the higher the balance the better the interest paid on credit balances. A cheque book is also available to facilitate withdrawal.

Some bank services promoted to the professional sector are designed not just to generate revenue, but are favourably weighted to protect market share from other competitor predators. This relegates the profit motive which becomes of secondary importance where there is an obvious chance to gain new business from client introductions. Moreover, many professional firms are multibanked – especially solicitors and accountants – which also softens the banks' attitude towards such firms.

Profession	No. of persons	No. of firms (where known)
Solicitors	40 000	9 500
Accountants	110 000	14 000
Doctors	80 000	–
Dentists	17 000	–
Insurance brokers	7 500	–
Estate agents	20 000	7 000
Stockbrokers	4 000	200
Others (including architects, surveyors, vets, etc.)	65 000	–
Total	343 500	

Before looking more closely at the services that are of special relevance to the professional sector, it is worth spending a few moments examining the nature of this market both in terms of size and type of occupation.

In England and Wales the size of the professional market is approximately as shown on the previous page.

Segmenting services for the professional market

Once again it is necessary to embark on a degree of arbitrary segmentation of the market so that bank services can be grouped in a reasonably logical fashion. Indeed, some major banks actually package their services in this way, in order to strengthen the impact of their marketing activity on these important and influential groups of people.

Many of the needs of the subdivided professional segments are common, which is not surprising, when you consider similarities in their lifestyle. For instance, many are self-employed, generally affluent and, in the main, have higher than average disposable incomes. As an outcome of these characteristics, the broad financial needs of the professional market are as follows:

(a) Business needs
 (1) Business capital;
 (2) Administrative support;
 (3) Expansion and partnership support and protection.

(b) Personal needs
 (1) Pension and family protection;
 (2) Tax advice and estate planning;
 (3) Investment and advice.

(c) Client needs
 (1) Account for clients' funds;
 (2) Bank services generally.

This general marshalling of financial needs should not be allowed to disguise the fact that there are, nevertheless, distinct differences in some areas – not just between any given group of professions but even between the circumstances of two people in the same profession. For example, a doctor may welcome advice on tax and financial planning whereas invariably an accountant would not need or welcome it. A house doctor in a local hospital will have a modest lifestyle and not a particularly high disposable income. A Harley Street specialist may well have a different lifestyle, substantially more income and more business

Table 17.1 The professional market and examples of financial service requirements

Business needs	Solicitors	Medical practitioners	Other professionals including accountants, insurance brokers, stockbrokers and estate agents
Client considerations	Interest bearing current account for clients' money Bridging loans and estate advances		Interest bearing current account for clients' money
Business capital	Overdrafts/loans Leasing Term/mortgage lending	Overdraft/loans HP Leasing Term/mortgage lending	Overdraft/loans Leasing Term/mortgage lending
Administrative requirements	CHAPS Pay service Insurance	Pay service Access Insurance	CHAPS Pay service Access Insurance (except accountants)
Personal needs	Premier/Gold Card Investment facilities Personal pension loan scheme	Premier/Gold Card Investment facilities and management Executor and trustee services including tax Insurance Personal pension loan scheme	Premier/Gold Card Investment facilities and management Executor trustee services and tax (except accountants) Personal pension loan scheme Insurance (except accountants)

problems. His need for bank services will therefore be more varied, and he is likely to make greater use of them.

Bearing in mind that the professional market is complex, and that there will be anomalies when matching bank services to particular groups, Table 17.1 identifies the broad financial service requirements and the underlying reasons why they are needed.

Specialised services

Interest-bearing accounts for clients' funds

Keen competition for lodgements and other business introductions given by solicitors and accountants are the main reasons why banks have departed from their traditional policy of not offering interest on an account which can also be accessed by a cheque book.

Until recently, deposit accounts were used by professional firms who held clients' funds. But an interest rate which was not considered attractive, the need to give seven days' notice on withdrawals or pay a penalty, and the 'bureaucratic' system of making withdrawals inevitably led to the introduction of a bank service which redressed these defects. A 'high' interest current account, specifically to hold clients' funds, was introduced and has become widely available as each bank matched competition to protect its share of account relationships with professional customers.

The service and how it works Interest is paid on the clients' funds account and the rate usually increases in bands linked to the balance being maintained. For example, below £20 000 interest rates may be the same as the seven-day deposit rate. Over £20 000 the rate increases to a higher level with a further increase in interest payable on substantial sums held – say £50 000 or more. The interest is calculated on a daily basis and there is no maximum on the amount that can be deposited.

A cheque book is issued so that withdrawals can be made easily and without notice being given to the bank. Often there are other fringe benefits to the firm or individual with a 'clients' funds' account. For instance, service charges might be waived, and where inter-bank transfers are required (for example, between solicitors acting for a vendor or purchaser completing on a house purchase) any charge for this service might also be waived.

Not surprisingly, these interest-bearing current accounts have proved popular with the professions. It was inevitable that similar interest-bearing current accounts would be introduced for the rest of the business market where substantial surplus funds are available but which have to be kept readily accessible.

The disadvantage to the banks is that the customer is happy to move his money into this type of account from seven-day deposit, as a result of which banks merely pay more for funds which they already hold. Competition will ensure that cosmetic improvements continue to be made to these high-interest current accounts. Avid reading of the financial columns of the better quality newspapers will be necessary to keep abreast of changes as they occur.

Market potential is difficult to quantify. In this sector, one bank's marketing activity is quickly followed by others, and the professional market is in any case 100 per cent banked, so new business is hard to win. It is also a relatively small market with close links through the professions' own governing bodies, such as the Law Society. Hence, information about a new financial service which provides something special travels fast, and the facility is quickly taken up. When this happens, knowing the points of detail and competitive advantages of your own services, such as small differences in interest rates, becomes more significant in the quest for new business.

Clearing House Automated Payment System (CHAPS)

Within the professional sector, by far the biggest users of CHAPS are solicitors. The facility provides a fast and effective way of transferring funds by electronic means. Prior to the introduction of CHAPS in 1983, a variety of methods was used for making payments in the UK – bankers' payments, telephoned transfers, bank drafts and other transmission services. Some methods even involved messengers walking 'paper' around the City of London with attendant delays and additional risks.

CHAPS simplifies all this and even goes as far as promising same-day settlement for UK transfers, provided payment instructions are received into the CHAPS system before a certain time each day.

How the service works   An electronic network (illustrated in Fig. 17.1) has been established between the major English and Scottish clearing banks, including the Trustee Savings Bank and National Giro. Currently there are 13 banks involved and smaller banks can gain access to the service by forming an association with a member bank. Through this network between 9.30 a.m. and 3 p.m., payments will flow from the bank accounts of people wishing to transmit funds to those who are to receive the payments. (The payment process is illustrated in

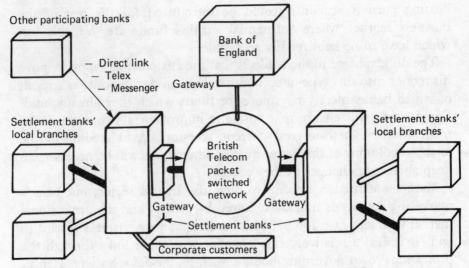

Fig. 17.1 Clearing House Automated Payment System (CHAPS)

Fig. 17.2.) Customers have the choice of accessing the CHAPS network through their own bank, either by their own terminal or by written instruction to the branch where their account is domiciled.

Because of the electronic nature of this facility, it is possible to add a number of special features which will be beneficial to those who make or receive several payments each day:

(a) *'Available funds' enquiries* At any time of the day customers with CHAPS terminal links in their offices can establish how much they have remitted against a pre-set limit which has been agreed with their bank as a daily CHAPS remitting facility. This limit arrangement is necessary

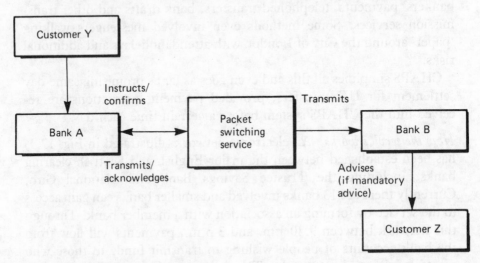

Fig. 17.2 The payment process

because of the same-day settlement. There is obviously a credit risk to the account holding bank where a customer is accessing the CHAPS network and only the customer would know the expected end of day position when all payments in and out have been made. Each user will negotiate a daily limit to cover CHAPS payments within which individual payments will not have to be authorised by the bank even if the account is overdrawn.

(b) *General enquiries* At any time of the day, details of the total value of payments made or received and full particulars of any individual payment or receipt can be obtained on the customer's terminal.

(c) *Payment instructions and receipts* are acknowledged through the terminal link. Where, for some reason, a payment cannot be made, this problem will also be notified to the sender.

(d) *Total security* All CHAPS payment messages are transmitted through British Telecom's 'packet switching' service (PSS). This is a relatively new data communications facility and gets its name from the fact that the message is broken down into small elements called 'packets'. Each packet is then sent to its destination by a different route from the others. Some settlement banks also insist on terminals with scramblers, thus, terminal messages from the customer through the branch on route for the CHAPS network are also coded. In these instances the transmissions are very secure as a coded instruction is then scrambled by PSS.

Benefits to the CHAPS users There are several major benefits of which speed, security and confidentiality are the main advantages.:

(a) Same-day payment can be guaranteed so that it is not necessary to send funds in advance and make allowance for postal delays. Customers can be advised of receipt of funds immediately on their terminals or by telephone.

(b) Security, as all payments have to be authorised by using a special codebook supplied to customers.

(c) Confidentiality through PSS and, in some cases, transmitting terminals with scramblers.

(d) Cost savings can be made as there is a reduction in paperwork and, as cash flow is much faster, CHAPS payments in are received more quickly and payments out can be delayed until the last moment.

(e) Reliability with standby arrangements agreed between the settlement banks in the event of network problems. Moreover, for customers experiencing difficulties with their own terminal facility, advice on what to do from the customer's bank is on hand via the telephone.

Market potential This service has been grouped with the accountant and solicitor segment but in reality the market is much wider. Solicitors will be the prime users, but stockbrokers, insurance companies, travel agencies, firms which are multinational, multibanked or just have a network of subsidiaries and associates will be prime sales targets.

Since the introduction of CHAPS in 1983, take-up of the service has been relatively slow. This stems largely from the fact that previous payment systems through the banks have proved reliable, reasonably quick, but above all very cheap. Indeed, the very popularity of the banks' 'steam driven' payments system has led it to become a major administrative burden. As the volume of transactions has grown so have the costs incurred in providing payment services which have a high level of paper processing. New, more profitable, means had to be found to cope with this growing demand.

Prestige charge cards

The benefits of possessing a charge card or credit card have already been outlined in a previous chapter. For the higher earner, usually those with an income of £30 000 or more, prestige or premier cards have been introduced. American Express, which joined forces in 1980 with Lloyds Bank to launch the American Express Gold Card package of services, produced and launched the first prestige card in the UK. Since that time, Midland, Barclays, and National Westminster have followed suit. Midland Bank announced the Midland Gold Master Card in 1982 closely followed by the Barclays alternative, both of which are backed by the VISA network. National Westminster has its own Gold Card.

What do prestige cards provide?   These links between clearing banks and the charge card organisations extend the convenience of using internationally accepted plastic cards for making payments by adding on a cheque book, and an overdraft facility at a special interest rate. In this way, the liaison of a charge card company and a bank gives ease of access to a complete range of financial services – a one-stop shopping concept.

An unsecured overdraft facility, currently £7500 to £10 000, at a preferential interest rate, enables users of the charge card to defer expenditure for an indefinite period. This is an important plus, for monthly accounts from a charge card organisation must be settled in full as soon as they are received. Thus, the overdraft facility provides a means of deferring expenditure which would otherwise be payable immediately. This overdraft can also be used for any other purpose and need not be exclusively reserved to pay monthly charge card accounts.

Moreover, the link between a charge card organisation and a major bank has other mutual benefits. The charge card organisation has an extensive and well-established network of bank branches providing sales outlets, support facilities to cardholders and a marketing team of bank staff to help obtain new cardholders, mainly from the bank's existing customers. On the other hand, the bank stands to gain new customers, all of whom are affluent and many are the captains of industry and commerce. This, in turn, may lead to further business acquisitions once a relationship with the new prestige card customer has been established.

Most prestige card schemes offer the following basic features:

(a) an unsecured overdraft at a preferential interest rate;
(b) the normal current account facilities including a cheque card and a cash dispenser card which often allows larger withdrawals than the normal card;
(c) special arrangements for cashing cheques worldwide using the charge card as sufficient authorisation and identification;
(d) automatic travel insurance cover of at least £100 000;
(e) a range of charge card 'convenience' services which include hotel reservation and travel ticket arrangements, discounts at service establishments, and emergency replacement card facilities if you lose money, travellers cheques or the card itself.

So what does it cost? Charge card organisations do not receive interest earnings like their credit card counterparts because the monthly accounts are supposed to be settled in full as soon as the cardholder receives his monthly statement. Therefore, they rely on annual subscriptions and the discounts payable to them by retailers when accepting a charge card in payment for goods and services. Currently, some prestige charge cards require once only 'joining' fees but all levy an annual subscription charge of approximately £40 and undoubtedly this subscription charge will increase in line with inflation.

Customer benefits and market potential Affluent customers do not usually want their expenditure restricted by the operation of credit limits associated with a credit card and will be attracted by the prestige card facilities. The worldwide representation and acceptance of institutions and organisations such as the major banks, American Express, MasterCard and Visa make the prestige card an ideal worldwide payments mechanism. It is particularly relevant for travel and entertainment expenditure, as the charge card links with these business sectors are long-established and extensive.

Market potential is more difficult to assess and various estimates of the number of people with an income in excess of £30 000 per annum range from half a million upwards. What is certain is that the market is not very large but it is potentially very profitable – not just from the interest and subscriptions earnings of cardholders but also from ancillary service sales. Although this service is included under the heading of the professional market, charge cards will be widely acceptable to anyone who travels and entertains for pleasure or as an important aspect of work.

Personal pension loan schemes

It used to be thought that putting money into a pension fund meant tying it up until retirement. But loan facilities linked to pension plans ('loanbacks' as they are sometimes called) have changed all that. However, this rather sweeping remark does not highlight the financially complex nature of a loanback facility and the severe restrictions on obtaining one and how it can be used.

How the service works A loanback facility is a lending scheme which enables the self-employed, particularly professional people and others in non-pensionable employment, to obtain a loan. The borrowing terms are based on an interest only basis with the capital repayment to come from the cash commutation portion of a personal pension policy written under Section 226 of the Income and Corporation Tax Act of 1970. It is worth stressing again that only those who have no pension provisions from at least one of their sources of earnings can write a policy under Section 226. Furthermore, the total policy cannot be surrendered to effect repayment, only the percentage which can be commuted – sometimes called the cash commutable value (CCV) – will be available to repay bank borrowing. The CCV is calculated for a prospective policyholder by the insurance company when a quotation is sought at the outset.

It is usual for loans to be repaid from commutation on retirement at age 65. Effectively, this means that for a young self-employed person, say aged 30, a loan term of 35 years is possible. Such a long term means there is the advantage of keeping policy premiums lower than would be the case for a loanback facility of shorter duration.

The amount which a bank would advance on the basis of repayment from a personal pension policy CCV is based on a scale of multipliers. There is also a further restriction of the amount of a loan based on a multiplier of annual earned income, usually a maximum loan of two and one half times the average of the last three years' earnings. Furthermore, loans are usually expected to be not less than £5000 and not greater than £75 000.

Thus the criteria for establishing how much can be borrowed are age- as well as income-related and based upon a multiple of the gross annual committed premiums payable on the policy. Where the policy has been in existence for a time, the cash value of premiums paid to date can also be included in calculating the maximum lending facility available.

This complex set of rules for determining the amount that can be borrowed is illustrated by a selection of examples from a typical bank personal pension loan scheme in Table 17.2. Borrowing arrangements using the pension policy will be supported by a facility letter which specifies the date when the borrower undertakes to clear the loan. This facility letter is especially important as the policy itself cannot be assigned to the bank as security. Because of this, it may well be necessary to seek alternative collateral.

Customer benefits Without doubt the major benefits include the longer-term nature of borrowing which is coupled with taxation savings and considerable flexibility. For these reasons, the service is very suitable to assist with the purchase of a practice or share in a professional partnership. Finance may also be provided for the purchase of the policy holder's matrimonial home or to finance or refinance home improvements. In cases where a house is being purchased or improvements are being made to property, it is likely that the bank will require the support of a mortgage over the property. In some situations,

Table 17.2 Amounts that can be borrowed under a personal pension loan scheme*

Present age	Maximum borrowing restricted to multiple of gross annual committed premium	Plus percentage of total premiums paid %
30–44	20	100
47	12	100
50	8	85
55	4	60
58	2.5	45
60	1.5 (but no more than $2\frac{1}{2}$ times earnings)	40

*This table assumes that applicants aged 40 or over will make repayment at age 65.

additional life cover may also be a condition of agreeing an advance under a personal pension loan scheme arrangement.

The taxation advantages are especially important to the higher income group and include:

(a) tax relief on premiums within certain limits at the highest rate being paid;
(b) part of the pension may be commuted for a tax-free cash sum;
(c) benefits payable on death may be written in trust normally without liability to inheritance tax.

Flexibility stems from the fact that retirement benefits can be taken at any time between the ages of 60 and 75. There is no need to actually retire from work before taking the benefits. This is particularly important to some father and son professional firms where fit elderly founders or senior partners continue to act in a consultancy capacity perhaps for several years after normal retirement age.

Last but not least many policies written under Section 226 allow for premiums to be varied each year (subject to any minimum requirements) to suit any fluctuating income features of the policy holder.

Insurance services

(a) *General insurance protection requirements* The way in which insurance can be used to protect the assets, income and family of a businessman have already been considered. Much of the information in Chapters 13 and 16 is also relevant to the self-employed professional customer. But as this is a market sector of particular importance to the banks, and to those professionals who are on the threshold of a career; it is worth expanding into the main areas of insurance that are relevant to their needs, especially those in partnership.

For a young man, it is usually more important to have adequate protection for himself and his dependants in the event of either permanent disablement or death, than to invest a substantial proportion of his personal income in endowment assurance or other investment contracts. Neither cover costs very much, and the level and type of cover will depend in part on the size of his family and also how much he can afford. Obviously, as the years go by, the insurance arrangements need to be reviewed at regular intervals taking into account the changes in family circumstances.

Insurance is a complex field and expert advice is usually necessary. Nevertheless the branch banker should have an adequate appreciation of the likely requirements of a young professional customer and know what type of insurance can be used to provide adequate protection.

Some of the more common forms of insurance for self-employed are discussed fully below.

(b) *Permanent disablement cover* Permanent disability of the bread-winner would, for many families, be a worse catastrophe than death. Normal outgoings would continue, such as mortgage payments and life insurance premiums. There would also be medical expenses, and in the case of the disablement of a husband, any chance of a wife taking up employment is unlikely.

Therefore, all self-employed, especially those in a partnership should have insurance against the eventuality of permanent disablement. Apart from the basic benefit of providing a continuing income through the insurance it is also possible to insure for pension contributions for any scheme maintained by the partnership.

(c) *Death before retirement cover* It is common sense for partnerships to lay down minimum levels of death in service protection so that the moral responsibility of surviving partners to support the deceased's family can be mitigated. There are several different types of life assurance available under the headings of temporary life assurance and various investment contracts.

(1) *Temporary life assurance* A fixed sum is payable in the event of death within a specified period but no actual return in the event of survival. This sort of policy was first introduced under Section 226A of the Income and Corporation Taxes Act 1970.

(2) *Level term assurance* A fixed sum is paid in the event of death before a certain date.

(3) *Convertible term assurance* This type of assurance is really a level term contract which includes an option whereby part or all of the sum assured may be converted at any time before the expiry of the policy into further types of life assurance – endowment or whole life contracts. This type of assurance is particularly useful to younger persons who wish to fix the ultimate cost of their insurance cover, whatever their state of health might be in the future, whilst keeping the initial cost low.

(4) *Family income benefit assurance* This type of assurance is very suitable for the man or woman with young children who want to protect their income and lifestyle whilst they remain dependent on parents.

(5) *Cross-insurance for partners* In order to provide funds for continuing partners to enable them to pay to the estate of a deceased partner the credit balance on his/her capital account, should he/she die before retirement, partnerships can take out policies on the life of each for the benefit of the others. It is also possible to extend this type of cover so that on retirement capital accounts can be repaid, and in this case an endowment policy would be used.

Summary

It is a fallacy to assume that because a customer is a practising professional he/she is financially aware of the dangers of being self-employed and the taxation advantages that can be enjoyed. Generally, customers seem to have little time to look after their own affairs, however conscientious they are about their clients'! This is an important market sector – affluent in the main with a need for, and a capability to purchase, many of the banks' more profitable services.

For lending services, it is a competitive arena and with high interest allowed on credit balances and fine rates quoted for loans, the profit from the sector must come from cross-selling other services. This will also engender greater loyalty to one particular bank among professional people and their firms in a sector which has a high incidence of multibanking.

The marketing policy should be to catch aspiring professionals at an early age – preferably by helping them through their studies with 'specially tailored' longer-term loan schemes. Once qualified, their needs and income should continue to grow throughout their working life, offering considerable profit potential to a banker.

Revision questions

1   Compared with five years ago, are solicitors' accounts more profitable or less profitable to a bank? Demonstrate how you arrive at your conclusions.
2   How could personal pension loan schemes be used by a solicitor partnership wishing to open an office in an adjoining town?
3   What insurance cover is appropriate for a self-employed person? Explain the reasons for suggesting each type of insurance contract.

Chapter 18
Importers and Exporters

Without doubt, compared with UK business opportunities, the marketing challenge for banks to sell 'overseas' services to importing and exporting customers takes on another dimension. Businesses which trade solely within the UK do not run the risks of loss through exchange fluctuations, or the associated difficulties of obtaining payment from overseas customers within an acceptable timespan. These special factors, and others, are now considered in conjunction with those bank services which help overcome such problems.

Despite the potential profit from selling services to importing and exporting customers, the major banks' marketing posture continues to be fairly passive. Business development activity tends to revolve around reacting to customer requests for information and services as opposed to aggressively seeking new business opportunities. Nevertheless, there is considerable expertise among employees with specialist knowledge in the international or 'overseas' departments and divisions of the major banks. When this expertise is promoted effectively by the branches in the high street, both customers and some staff are usually impressed with the service provided by 'overseas' specialists.

Following the now well-established pattern in previous chapters, the overseas services provided by the banks have been segmented into two groups – those that are particularly relevant to a potential importer or exporter, and services that are important to those who already trade regularly with overseas importers and exporters. Yet again this rather clinical approach ignores the overlapping requirements of the two market sectors. But, in mitigation, it enables the overseas services to be broadly marshalled into groups with similar functions and features in order to cross-match service benefits with customer requirements.

Range of overseas services available

There are far too many services to cover them all in detail, and in any case it is not the role of a branch banker to be an expert in all overseas services. However a good appreciation of what type of services are available and how these can be used to effect in given trading circumstances, is necessary in order to grasp opportunities to introduce business to the overseas department of the bank.

Table 18.1 Services available to importers/exporters

	Provided by UK bank	Provided through banks abroad
Deposit facilities	Various services Negotiations	Current and deposit accounts in local currency Night safe and safe custody Certified cheques
Lending facilities	Bill discounting/ negotiations Various schemes including supplier/ buyer credit with ECGD guarantees Produce loans Leasing Forfaiting Export factoring	Currency loans and bill discounting
Foreign business	Exchange of currencies Sales of travellers cheques Letters of credit Bills for collection (inwards and outwards) Credit cards and Eurocheque cards ECGD Currency accounts	Exchange of currencies Purchase/sale of travellers cheques Letters of credit Import/export bills for collection
Transfer facilities	Mail and telegraphic transfers Currency and sterling drafts	Mail and telegraphic transfers Currency drafts
Information and miscellaneous	Advice and information Status enquiries and reports Letters of introduction Guarantees, indemnities and bonds	Information Status enquiries and reports Letters of introduction Guarantees, indemnities and bonds

Some of the services shown in Table 18.1 are provided by associate and subsidiary companies or agents of the banks located worldwide. Knowing that they exist is all that is required. Other services are provided directly by UK banks and the most frequently used services among these will be considered in more depth in this chapter. There are other bank services available to importing and exporting customers but they are mainly the complex facilities for the larger company to be used in specialist trading situations. Additionally, the personal requirements of directors and representatives travelling abroad should not be overlooked – travel, insurance, cheque cashing arrangements and so on.

Services for potential importers/exporters

Advice and information

Because all the major banks have a network of connections worldwide, and monitor the political and economic climate of many countries very closely, they can often obtain and pass on substantial advice on almost every aspect that is likely to affect overseas trade. The advice and information available from a major bank can be summarised under the following headings.

(a) *Regulations of overseas countries* This information includes detail on foreign import licensing procedures and any overseas controls and formalities which have to be satisfied.

(b) *Status enquiries* The reputation and financial strength of overseas clients of firms importing or exporting can be assessed in a variety of ways. Measures include reports from overseas banks, special reports from agents abroad and, in some cases, even the balance sheets of the foreign business can be obtained.

(c) *Trade enquiries* Not to be confused with status enquiries, this service involves obtaining the names of prospective buyers and agents overseas. Before passing on the information to a customer in the United Kingdom, a status enquiry will be obtained as a necessary precaution. Conversely, overseas banks often seek openings for their customers in this country and will ask a bank to pass on details to firms which might be interested in doing business with their clients abroad.

(d) *Economic reports* There can be increased risks for businesses considering exporting or importing with countries where the political or economic conditions could create trading difficulties and could cause large fluctuations in rates of exchange. The major banks maintain information, especially on those countries which have a volatile history and this data is regularly updated. Some economic reports are very comprehensive and apart from the political and economic scene also consider the trading opportunities that exist for United Kingdom firms wishing to establish an import/export trade.

(e) *Other forms of advice* The banks will advise on most aspects of overseas trade from merely explaining how payments can be made or received, to actually making a direct investment in an overseas firm. The latter will require consultation on such problems as repatriation of profits, capital investment and other local regulations, legal and taxation matters.

Payment services

Terms of payment, and the method by which settlement will be made, are matters for negotiation between the parties importing and exporting. Nevertheless, a bank can advise its customers which payment system is likely to be the most secure and involve the minimum risk from exchange rate movements. There are five basic methods by which an exporter may receive payment for his goods and, conversely, can be used by importers to make payments. These are:

(a) open account;
(b) advance payment or payment with order;
(c) documentary and clean collection;
(d) documentary credits
(e) barter and countertrade.

Services for active importers/exporters

Apart from the likely need to borrow money to support import and export business, trading customers also require payment services both inwards and outwards which are safe, the means to reduce risks from exchange rate fluctuations and, finally, to facilitate trade, guarantees, tender bonds, performance bonds and export factoring among others.

(a) *Open account* Exporters with long-established links with overseas buyers who are first class companies, and exporters who do not wish, or are unable, to arrange other terms of trade, may be prepared to deal on an open account basis. Under such an arrangement, the exporter dispatches the goods and subsequently sends all the shipping documents to the overseas buyer or agent. On receipt of such documents, or after an agreed period of time, the consignee sends the exporter a cheque, banker's draft, international money transfer or an express money transfer.

Once the goods and documents have been dispatched the exporter has no further control over them and is dependent upon the consignee making payment at the appropriate time. The trading risks are obvious and, in all cases, exporters should be advised to seek status reports and review the financial standing of the overseas buyer or agent at regular intervals.

(b) *Advance payment*   This method of payment would only apply where the exporter is in a sufficiently strong bargaining position to insist on 'payment with order' or payment before the goods are actually exported. Clearly, the normal trading risks are removed, and any exporter able to insist on these payment terms has the ideal arrangement. However, it should be mentioned that in many overseas countries advance payments for imports are not permitted.

The bank's role with advance payment arrangements is basically to provide the means by which payments can be made. Usually overseas buyers will agree the arrangements with their own bank, which will then advise details through its UK banking correspondents for the benefit of the UK exporters.

(c) *Documentary collections*   Where the terms of settlement between the buyer and seller do not allow for advance payment, exporting customers may get some security of payment if they use the services of a third party in the importer's country who will hand the shipping documents to the importer against payment of the amount due, or against acceptance of a bill of exchange.

Under this arrangement the exporter does not lose possession of the documents (and thus the goods) until payment has been made or a bill of exchange, evidencing the debt, has been accepted. If no credit period is to be allowed a 'cash against document' system may be operated in trade with certain countries where the stamp duty on bills of exchange is high. The main problem with a documentary collection is to find a reputable agent in the importer's country, who will ensure that all the terms and conditions relating to the release of the documents are correctly fulfilled. This is where the UK banks can provide help through their network of agents and subsidiary or associate companies worldwide.

Documents for dispatch to the chosen agent of the UK bank in the importer's country are likely to include invoices, insurance policies, bills of lading, etc. These papers will be accompanied by a 'collection letter' setting out how the exporter wishes the release of the documents to be handled. This 'collection letter' will also deal with what must be done if the importers fail to meet their obligations. It may be necessary to warehouse goods and insure them against certain risks, or simply instruct the return of the goods to the UK.

(d) *Documentary credits* If exporters want better protection than the documentary collection system affords, they may ask the importers to arrange for the issue of a letter of credit in their favour. This is a very secure method of obtaining payment as it places reliance on the more trustworthy promise of payment given by a bank rather than the promise of an importer. However, importers also benefit because the bank will insist on the delivery of the correct documents before it will release payment, thereby also evidencing that the correct goods have been shipped.

Once overseas buyers have agreed to pay by documentary letter of credit, they make arrangements with their own bank whereby the latter will instruct a bank in the UK to make payment to the exporters against presentation of specified documents and subject to prescribed conditions. Alternatively, the UK bank may be instructed to accept a bill of exchange, drawn for a specified period and submitted with the required documents.

There are various forms of documentary letters of credit – they can be drawn to meet stipulations which call for the credit to be irrevocable and also require confirmation by a UK bank. If the credit is irrevocable, it contains the unalterable undertaking of the issuing bank and it cannot be cancelled or amended except with the consent of all parties thereto. If such a credit is merely 'advised' by a bank in the UK, it contains no commitment on the part of that bank. But if it is also confirmed by the advising bank, it also carries that bank's irrevocable undertaking to pay, accept or negotiate bills of exchange as the case may be.

Moreover, the exporter can also seek confirmation by a UK bank which in all probability will be the agent of the importer's bank overseas. Much of the business transacted against irrevocable credits of overseas banks of good standing is largely risk-free but a London confirmation provides an additional safeguard which in some cases may be considered desirable.

There are a number of customer benefits from the use of documentary credits for both buyers and sellers. For the *overseas buyers* who also arrange the documentary credit the benefits include:

(1) ability to stipulate which documents are required and the terms upon which payment for the goods will be made;
(2) assurance that they will not be required to pay for the goods unless all the terms of the credit have been fulfilled;
(3) possibility of financing imports by utilising a credit which provides for acceptance of a bill of exchange payable at some future date.

For the *exporters* the benefits are:

(1) absolute confidence that payment will be forthcoming where the credit is irrevocable and confirmed;

(2) quick payment after presentation of shipping documents which comply with the credit stipulations;

(3) opportunity to discount bills of exchange in the case of acceptance credits. Where the credit is confirmed, and the bill accepted by a London bank, fine discount rates will be applied.

(e) *Barter and countertrade* barter, as you would expect, is the direct exchange of one type of goods for another without money changing hands. This type of trading has been going on since time immemorial but in modern times is fairly rare.

In today's world there are 'hard' and 'soft' currencies. Hard currencies, including the dollar, sterling, Deutschemark and yen, are those used extensively for international trading by the major developed countries of the Western world. Less developed countries' currencies, sometimes described as 'soft' are not so readily acceptable as forms of payment. This problem, together with the desire of these less developed countries to retain their reserves of 'hard' currencies for essential purchases, are the main reasons for barter and countertrade continuing.

The main products bartered by some Eastern European countries and less developed countries are indigenous natural resources, such as oil and timber. These commodities are usually exchanged for consumer goods and capital equipment.

Countertrade differs from barter in that two separate trade contracts exist. One is for the import of goods by the less developed or Eastern European bloc. The other is for the export by these countries of the 'counter purchase' goods. The contracts are between unrelated parties and the money raised from the 'counter purchase' is utilised to settle the cost of the imports.

Barter and countertrade deals are complex and require specialist support. Branch staff responsibility is to recognise when their customers need the specialist advice which is available in all the clearing banks' international divisions or departments.

Bills for collection or negotiation Whether to collect or negotiate depends on whether or not exporters are prepared to wait for the proceeds of a bill drawn on an importer and collected by the bank to reach their account. If a bill is collected, the bank sends it to its agent in the foreign town where the importer lives and has the bill presented for payment. The proceeds are then sent back to the UK, converted into sterling, and credited to the customer's account after bank charges have been deducted.

The alternative is to negotiate the bill by selling it to the bank. If the bank agrees to buy the bill it will do so at a discount. However, to protect its position the bank only negotiates 'with recourse' which means that the customer pays the bank if the agent bank fails to obtain payment.

Collection and negotiation of bills and cheques are key services for exporters, especially negotiations which provide funds much sooner in the trading cycle to finance further trading.

Foreign exchange services to minimise exchange risks

UK exporters have five alternatives open to them when they know that they will receive foreign currency in payment of goods and services supplied:

(a) to convert the foreign currency into sterling on the date it is received at the prevailing 'spot' rate;

(b) to arrange with a bank a forward foreign exchange contract or option contract to sell the currency when received on a nominated date, or between two specified dates in the case of an option contract;

(c) to borrow from a bank an amount of foreign currency which, together with the interest payable on the borrowing, will equal the amount of the anticipated proceeds. The proceeds are then used to repay the loan when they are received;

(d) to have the proceeds paid into a foreign bank currency account;

(e) to arrange the right to sell currency against a base currency (e.g. US dollars or sterling) at a rate of exchange picked by the customer. This is a currency option and is covered in more detail later in this chapter.

UK importers also have five alternatives when they have to make payments in foreign currency for imported goods or services;

(a) to convert sterling to a foreign currency on the date of payment at the prevailing 'spot' rate;

(b) to arrange with a bank a forward foreign exchange contract to buy foreign currency on a nominated future date, or between two specified dates in the case of an option contract;

(c) to purchase foreign currency immediately and hold it until required.

(d) to make payment from a foreign currency bank account which already holds the currency funds;

(e) to arrange the right to buy currency against a base currency (e.g. US dollars or sterling) at a rate of exchange picked by the customer.

There is inevitably a delay between fixing a contract with an overseas buyer or seller and the date payment is made – an exchange risk is unavoidable. To minimise this risk, there are two types of forward exchange contract now described as 'fixed forward contracts' and 'option forward contracts'.

Fixed forward contracts A fixed forward contract is suitable when the precise payment date is known. By entering into a forward contract, the exporter or importer can plan on the amount to be paid or received and regulate his business cash flow accordingly.

Option forward contract If the date of receipt or payment of funds is uncertain then an option forward contract may be agreed with a bank. Under this arrangement, the customer undertakes to deliver or obtain currency from the bank at some time between two predetermined dates. The length of this option period can be measured in weeks or months. The total option forward contract can be utilised in several tranches known as 'part take up' or 'part delivery'. Forward rates for option contracts are calculated on the basis that, since delivery of the currency can be made at any time during the option period, the contract should be completed at the least favourable time from the bank's point of view. By using the forward contract service, customers can avoid possible risk of losses through adverse movements in spot rates over a period of time. Moreover, it enables the customers to price their purchase or sale accurately – this is particularly important for any trading organisation working on smaller profit margins.

Generally, forward contracts are arranged for periods up to six months but longer periods are possible where trading circumstances require it. If customers are unable to settle a forward contract when it is due, there are solutions to this problem. They can renegotiate the rate with their bank for a later delivery or purchase but probably an additional charge will be levied. Alternatively, the customers can simply take up the contract by buying or selling using the spot rates to close out the deal. A new forward currency contract can then be arranged for settlement at some future date. Funds could also be bought and stored on a currency account until required.

Borrowing foreign currency   Another way to avoid exchange exposure is to borrow currency now and repay the borrowing with the sale proceeds when these are received from the overseas buyer. Some of the ways in which the borrowed currency could be used are:

(a) to pay for any goods or services received that have been invoiced in that currency;
(b) to convert the borrowed currency into sterling at the prevailing spot rate of exchange in order to:

   (1) provide additional working capital;
   (2) reduce existing sterling borrowing;
   (3) place it on sterling deposit for the purpose of earning interest.

In most of the major currencies, borrowing can usually be arranged on an overdraft or on a fixed term loan basis. Because interest must be paid in the foreign currency concerned, an exporter would ideally choose to borrow less than the expected currency receipts, so that the interest as well as the principal will be repaid when the payment is received.

As long as currency receipts are certain, exporters are not involved in any foreign exchange exposure, since the currency borrowed will be repaid by the export proceeds. However, should the buyers default on their payment, the exporters would need to ask their bank to extend the borrowing until the proceeds were received, or to purchase sufficient currency, on a spot basis, to repay the borrowing.

Foreign currency accounts   Companies which frequently receive and pay out sums of the same foreign currency could find it beneficial to open foreign currency accounts. These are available in most of the major trading currencies and are generally maintained with banks in the UK. The advantage of a foreign currency account is that incomings and outgoings may be used to offset each other, thereby reducing the need to buy and sell the foreign currency concerned. In order to achieve the closest possible match between incomings and outgoings, a company may decide to change its invoicing policy. For example, if its US dollar payments exceed its US dollar receipts, a decision may be taken to switch more of its export invoicing into US dollars (if it is able to do so) in order to arrive at a better match between receipts and payments in US dollars.

Where a company borrows foreign currency on overdraft, interest is usually charged at a rate linked to the bank's base rate for that currency. Interest is not usually paid by the bank on foreign currency current account credit balances, but any excess funds may be transferred to call or fixed interest-bearing foreign currency deposit accounts. If these accounts are with banks in the UK, the interest payable will be based on the Eurocurrency deposit rate for the relevant period in that currency.

Currency options

Currency options should not be confused with option forward contracts. A currency option arranged with a bank gives the customer the opportunity, without any obligation, to buy or sell a currency against a base currency such as the US dollar or sterling at a rate of exchange selected by the customer.

There are two basic types of currency option. With the 'European' type option the currency is exchanged for a base currency on the actual expiry date of the option. The other is the 'American' type option, and here the customer can exercise an option to exchange at any time during the option period.

Because there are no obligations on customers the option can also be allowed to lapse. Banks charge fees for providing the currency option and these are payable when the option is arranged. These fees are higher for the 'American' type option as there is more flexibility than with a 'European' type option facility.

Currency options allow UK traders to know the precise sterling value of their contracts. There is also the added benefit that if rates move in their favour they can ignore the option and buy or sell in the spot market when settlement is due.

Currency options are very useful when a UK company is tendering in a foreign currency. By arranging a 'put' option at an agreed rate of exchange the company will be assured that if the tender is successful, the underwritten minimum sterling equivalent will be forthcoming eventually.

If, on the other hand, the tender fails, the UK company can simply ignore the option, buy currency and complete the option contract if there is a 'windfall' profit or, lastly, sell the option back to the bank. This would then offset some of the original premium costs which vary according to the length of the option and the perceived volatility of a particular currency.

The above details relate to UK exporters, but the option facility works in a similar fashion for UK importers having to pay in the overseas customers' currency.

Guarantees, tender bonds and performance bonds

From time to time customers may wish to arrange for bank guarantees or undertakings to be issued on their behalf in favour of overseas beneficiaries. These guarantees and bonds protect those overseas buyers against losses caused by the UK customers' failure to meet their commitments. This type of indemnity or bond is a valuable selling factor but, because of the size of the liability that can be incurred, support is only given to customers of high standing. The following are examples of the circumstances in which guarantees, etc. may be given:

(a) *Performance bonds* When large contracts for public works are being given by local authorities and government in the UK and abroad, it is a frequent requirement that a bond be entered into stating that the work will be completed to an agreed standard and by a certain date. Further, failure to meet these conditions usually incurs cash penalties which must be guaranteed by the contractor's bankers. Where bonds relate to UK contracts, a bank may be prepared to join in with the customer. However, in the case of overseas beneficiaries a bank can arrange for such bonds to be given in its own name, or by its correspondent in the appropriate country.

(b) *Tenders and advance payments* Tenders, particularly for overseas contracts, often have to be supported by guarantees, usually for a small percentage of the total tender price – generally 1 to 5 per cent. This sum is liable to be forfeited if, for example, the tender is withdrawn. Additionally, once signed, some contracts require advance payments to be made by the buyer, who may call for a guarantee of repayment if the contract is not completed.

(c) *Retention bonds* The contract may allow for the buyer to withhold up to say 10 per cent of the contract value for a specified length of time after the completion of the work. However, the purchaser may agree to release the retention money against a retention bond which secures the money if subsequently the terms of the warranty are not complied with.

(d) *Lost and irregular documents* The loss, overdue arrival or irregularity of bills of lading can seriously hinder clearance of goods. However, customers can arrange to provide an indemnity, joined in by the bank, to the carriers in order to obtain the release of goods without the production of the bill of lading. Guarantees or indemnities may also be requested by other banks where documents submitted in connection with documentary credits, or other formal collection agreements, are not in order.

(e) *Tax and customs payments* Payments to HM Customs and Excise need to be confirmed before the relative merchandise can be moved from port. This requirement can cause delays in shipments, but guarantees given by bankers are acceptable to this authority and allow merchandise to be transported more expeditiously. Additionally, guarantees can be arranged in favour of UK and most overseas customs authorities to permit the temporary import/export of samples or exhibits without payment of customs duty.

(f) *Guarantees on trade debts* Banks will also undertake in suitable cases to guarantee on behalf of their customers, payment of certain trade debts, the principal examples of which are to ministries and departments of governments, shipping companies and certain trade associations.

Export Credits Guarantee Department (ECGD)

(a) *Credit insurance* The Export Credits Guarantee Department (ECGD), which has existed since 1919, is a government department responsible to the Secretary of State for Trade. Its operations require the consent of the Treasury which has delegated authority to ECGD over a wide area, so that only a limited number of transactions require specific Treasury consent.

The purpose of ECGD is to provide exporters of both goods and services with protection, by means of export credit insurance, against the many risks encountered in trading overseas that are not covered by normal commercial insurance. It insures exporters against two broad classes of risk – the buyer's creditworthiness and the political and economic risks. As an extension of these services, ECGD also provides unconditional guarantees of repayment to banks against the security of which the banks provide finance to exporters at preferential interest rates. ECGD does not, itself, provide finance to exporters.

Some of the main types of insurance policies provided by ECGD are described below and it should be noted that they are not bank guarantees, nor do they guarantee the exporter in the event of default by the buyer, if the exporter fails to fulfil contractual obligations to the buyer.

(b) *The comprehensive short-term guarantee* This is the basic insurance policy available to exporters and accounts for by far the largest proportion of ECGD's total business. For a low premium, this type of guarantee provides a comprehensive insurance to exporters of consumer and light engineering goods when sales are of a continuous nature on credit terms of up to six months. Exporters undertake to insure their whole export turnover for a period of not less than twelve months, though in some cases ECGD will accept business on a range of markets provided there is a reasonable spread of risk. Cover runs either from date of shipment, or from date of contract if the exporters so require. In the latter case the 'pre-credit risk' cover must apply to the exporters' total insured export turnover, i.e. they cannot choose which contracts are to be included for this risk, and of course an additional premium is payable. Pre-credit risk cover is limited to contracts which provide for the goods to be exported within twelve months from the date of the contract. Under the 'comprehensive short-term guarantee' exporters do not have to inform ECGD of individual contracts, but there are credit limits on a revolving basis with individual buyers, and ECGD can vary or withdraw these limits.

The premium for each guarantee is payable in two stages. Firstly, a non-refundable premium is payable at the commencement of each year's insurance, based on export turnover and the degree of use made of ECGD's credit limit service. Secondly, a monthly premium at a predetermined rate is payable, based on a monthly declaration of exports. Premium for the additional pre-credit risk cover mentioned above is also payable monthly. The risks covered by comprehensive short-term guarantees are as follows:

(1) Insolvency of the buyer.
(2) The buyers' failure to pay within six months of due date for goods which they have accepted.
(3) The buyers' failure to take up goods which have been dispatched to them (where not caused or excused by the policy-holders' actions, and where ECGD decides that the institution or continuation of legal proceedings against the buyers would serve no useful purpose).
(4) A general moratorium on external debt decreed by the government of the buyers' country or of a third country through which payment must be made.
(5) Any other action by the government of the buyers' country which prevents performance of the contract in whole or in part.
(6) Political events, economic difficulties, legislative or administrative measures arising outside the UK which prevent or delay the transfer of payments or deposits made in respect of the contract.
(7) Legal discharge of a debt (not being legal discharge under the proper law of the contract) in a foreign currency, which results in a shortfall at the date of transfer.
(8) War and certain other events preventing performance of the contract provided that the event is not one normally insured with commercial insurers.
(9) Cancellation or non-renewal of a UK export licence or the prohibition or restriction on export of goods from the UK by law (this risk is covered only where the pre-credit risk section of the guarantee applies).

Exporters are required to retain a reasonable interest in the transaction, and the percentage of cover is as follows:

90 per cent for loss under risks (1) and (2);

72 per cent for loss under risk (3) (i.e., the first 20 per cent borne by the exporter, 90 per cent of the balance covered by ECGD);

95 per cent for the other risks, except for pre-credit risk (loss arising before dispatch of goods) where cover is restricted to 90 per cent.

Failure of the buyer to perform the contract may also be covered where the buyer is a public body, but this additional cause of loss is included in the guarantee only at the absolute discretion of ECGD.

Claims become payable at the following times:

For insolvency of the buyer: immediately on proof of insolvency.

For protracted defaults on goods accepted: six months after the due date of payment.

For failure to take up goods: one month after resale.

Where the cause is a delay in the transfer of payment or a shortfall arising from legal discharge of debt in local currency, claims become payable four months after the due date of payment, or four months after completion of the formalities for transfer, whichever is the later. For any other cause, they become payable four months after the event which causes loss, or immediately after loss is actually sustained whichever is the later.

With certain exceptions, the standard guarantee can also cover the re-export of goods imported into the UK, and contracts in foreign currency can be included if listed in a schedule to the guarantee. (It is advisable to consult the bank if in doubt as to the marketability of a particular currency on the London Foreign Exchange Market.)

Where exporters invoice in certain foreign currencies and protect themselves against adverse changes in the exchange rate by use of the forward exchange market or foreign currency borrowing, ECGD will, in the event of a valid claim by exporters with a foreign currency contract endorsement to their basic guarantee, cover up to 10 per cent more than they would otherwise be entitled to, provided the exporters have suffered the extra loss through participation in the forward exchange market or foreign currency borrowing. No extra premium is charged for this cover.

Cover can be extended for certain common trading arrangements including:

(1) Export contracts made with a UK merchant or confirming house.
(2) Sales made to an overseas subsidiary or associated company of the exporter.

(3) Sales made ex-stock of UK goods held overseas, following trials and demonstration or after exhibiting at an overseas trade fair.

(c) *The supplemental extended terms guarantee* Business of a repetitive kind involving semi-capital goods such as machine tools, commercial vehicles and production engineering goods is often transacted on terms in excess of six months' credit. This type of business can be covered by a 'supplemental extended terms guarantee' which, whilst a guarantee in its own right, is only available to exporters who already hold a comprehensive short-term guarantee. Such extended cover is also available for business where, although credit terms may not exceed six months, pre-credit risk cover is required and the delivery period does not exceed five years, and in approved cases a proportion of foreign goods sold under the contract may be included.

Premium is paid separately from that payable under the comprehensive short-term guarantee, being determined for each piece of business according to the period for which ECGD is at risk and the grading applied by ECGD to the buyer's country. In other respects the risks covered and the form of cover are similar to those provided for under the comprehensive short-term guarantee.

Where exporters invoice in foreign currencies and protect themselves against exchange risks by use of the forward exchange market or foreign currency borrowing, ECGD will, by endorsement of the guarantee, agree to pay claims at the rate of exchange ruling at the time of loss rather than at the time ECGD cover begins.

For each contract, the exporter chooses the amount of extra cover he requires for the possible additional loss that may be incurred. An additional premium is charged for this facility.

(d) *ECGD supplier and buyer credit cover* Thus it can be appreciated that the type of cover available from ECGD is comprehensive, relatively cheap and therefore attractive, especially to smaller importers.

Export trade falls into two broad categories. These is the trade which is repetitive and over the years conducted with more or less the same buyers. There are also larger capital transactions which are not repetitive and often involve substantial construction or installation. This necessitates local expenditure and extended credit terms for the UK company embarking on a major project of this type.

Large construction or installation contracts are not suitable for the normal ECGD cover and specific policies have to be negotiated for each contract. This business often involves accepting considerable liabilities for many years.

Cover is given in one of two ways, according to the manner in which credit is provided. For 'supplier credit' the manufacturer sells on deferred payment terms, borrowing from a UK bank to finance the period from shipment until payment is made. ECGD insures the exporter and in many cases also gives a guarantee direct to the exporter's bank. Buyer credit involves the overseas buyer drawing on a loan from a UK bank to provide prompt payment. ECGD will guarantee up to 85 per cent of the contract value of UK goods and services and this is the amount the bank will lend. The remaining 15 per cent is the responsibility of the buyer. This loan is repaid by instalments and ECGD provides guarantees to the bank against default by the overseas purchaser.

This type of 'buyer credit' is only available for larger capital projects and the sale of capital goods of £1 million or more, and for certain aircraft. It is rarely authorised for values of less than £2 million in the case of aircraft. ECGD cover for supplier and buyer credit with a UK bank provides a number of benefits to the exporter. As the sums are large there is protection against a loss which could put the company out of business. Moreover, the ECGD has a considerable knowledge of overseas companies and can confirm insurance on a buyer almost at once, leaving the exporter free to negotiate the sale with complete confidence. Finally, ECGD cover usually enables the insured to obtain bank borrowing at preferential rates.

Short-term finance schemes

The government has now phased out short-term finance schemes backed by ECGD direct guarantees. However, to fill this gap the banks have introduced various finance schemes of their own. They provide a combination of finance and ECGD-type credit insurance protection to ECGD-approved exporters for credit periods up to 180 days. Financial support up to 90 per cent of the amount of goods or services provided can be obtained against approved bills of exchange or invoices which are accompanied by correct shipping documents or similar evidence of export from the UK. In all cases a currency option would be required.

Exporters with their own ECGD policy can apply to join a bank's short-term finance scheme but it would be expected that an acceptable spread of business is passed through this bank arrangement. To qualify, businesses should have a minimum export turnover of £1 million and the minimum invoice value which would be accepted is £3000.

Export factoring

Many of the major banks, either through their international divisions or through subsidiary companies, provide an export factoring service.

Factoring generally is covered in Chapter 16. It relieves the exporting customer of the problems of handling the sales ledger for defined areas of overseas operations but is restricted to short-term credit contracts usually up to a maximum of 180 days. The service includes the dispatch of invoices, collection of monies and the provision of credit facilities if the exporter wishes to draw against the invoices before the funds are actually available, advances allowed are usually up to 80 per cent of the outstanding debts being collected by the factors.

Export factoring is more commonly used by companies selling to the USA, Canada or Europe but it is possible to obtain factoring support and finance for trade to almost anywhere in the world. The advantages of using export factoring include:

(a) saving of time and cost of operating a sales ledger;
(b) credit facilities available if required;
(c) the ability to predict cash flow with confidence and initially the speeding up of receipts through the advance available against invoices being collected by the factor;
(d) advice on local trading customs/systems and language;
(e) local representatives to appraise creditworthiness;
(f) possible exchange risk cover.

Leasing

This is medium-term finance for a company wishing to acquire the use of equipment without the initial burden of the cost of purchase. For exporters of capital equipment it may be advantageous to sell the equipment to a UK leasing company which would then arrange a leasing contract with the overseas user. The initial primary lease period would normally provide for the full recovery of the cost of the equipment, and the lessee would then have the option to continue the lease at a reduced rental or share in the sale proceeds.

If a country operates restrictions on this method of financing its equipment imports, then the UK exporter may be able to sell direct to a foreign leasing company. In either situation the exporter will receive immediate payment. To the importer of machinery and equipment the benefits of using leasing finance are that it leaves the company's capital and credit facilities unaffected, and the new equipment should improve its operating efficiency.

Forfaiting

Forfaiting uses 'free market' funds to provide fixed-rate medium-term supplier credit to exporters of capital goods. It enables the exporter to extend credit to the buyer and at the same time to discount the debt instrument for cash up front. This quick and simple method of non-recourse export finance has been widely used in continental Europe and is now becoming more popular in the UK where British companies have in the past traditionally relied on ECGD cover.

Gradually London has become an influential centre of the forfaiting market and this form of finance is now more widely used in the UK because of rising interest costs on government-backed schemes.

So how does forfaiting work? The forfaiter buys the debt instruments from the exporter at a discount. These can be letters of credit, bills of exchange or promissory notes. They must usually be guaranteed by a bank in or near the importer's country. The discount takes into account the cost of using the money, and a margin is added to cover commercial and political risk and the forfaiter's profit. Costs vary, depending on the level of interest rate for a particular currency at the time of the forfaiter's commitment and on the forfaiter's assessment of the credit risks on the importing country and guaranteeing bank. However, these charges can be calculated into the importer's payment if market conditions permit and when the forfaiter is consulted at the early stages of a deal. Finance can be provided up to 100 per cent with credit periods ranging from 90 days to five years.

The main advantages of forfaiting are that the simplicity of the transaction means that deals can be quickly agreed. There is no recourse to the exporter as the risk is transferred to the forfaiter. The main drawback is that it can be expensive, especially in difficult markets where the forfaiter's margin tends to be pushed up substantially.

Case study I

Worldwide Haulage Limited conducts a major proportion of its business with the USA as it specialises in moving military personnel and their possessions backwards and forwards across the Atlantic. It is contracted to US shipping and freight forwarding firms which, in turn, tender for this business from the US government.

Recently the dollar/sterling exchange rates have been very volatile. The finance director seeks the bank manager's views on how to protect the company's position, as although the tenders are in sterling the US freight forwarders convert these quotes into dollars as the basis of future payments. Moreover, it is impossible to predict with any certainty the inflow of dollar funds, or the specific amounts to be received at any one time.

This customer is very much at the mercy of currency fluctuations although there may probably be some margin in the fact that a pessimistic dollar/sterling exchange rate will have been used when originally quoting for the agency work. There is an added complication that often these quotations are supplied months in advance, as the US freight forwarders will require this information before tendering for the business. Clearly, if after the quote has been accepted the dollar weakens dramatically against sterling, Worldwide could make a heavy loss as its sterling quotes are converted into dollars in the USA as they are received, and not at the time payments fall due.

As trading is on 'open account' there are a number of risks to consider when coping with US dollar cheques. Equally, this type of trading reduces the number of ways exchange risk fluctuations can be minimised. If Worldwide pays its dollar cheques into the local branch for the credit of its account these are negotiated at the current rate of exchange. After the cheques have been negotiated there is no further exchange risk unless a cheque is subsequently returned from the USA unpaid. Moreover, Worldwide will receive the benefit of immediate funds, although there remains an outstanding recourse period liability which forms part of any agreed bank facilities. It is a liability to the bank if funds are not available on Worldwide's account to cover cheques subsequently returned unpaid, which would be the case if Worldwide were in overdraft.

Alternatively Worldwide can open an account in the USA as a collection facility, and this will ensure that dollar cheques are cleared more quickly and thus shorten the recourse liability period incurred if dollar cheques are negotiated in the UK. Against this benefit of a shortened recourse period there is the disadvantage of 'arm's length' banking, additional US bank charges and an accumulation of capital (still held in dollars) increasing any borrowing charges in the UK. The incidence of risk from exchange rate movements is also increased, as larger amounts will remain in dollars in the USA. However, Worldwide would be able to choose when to move the funds to the UK, and if the company had bills to pay in the USA it could use these dollar funds, so saving exchange conversion charges.

Whenever funds move from the USA to the UK an exchange risk will apply, and this can be dealt with as follows:

(a) If known sums are being transferred from a US-domiciled account, Worldwide can 'book' a rate with the local branch prior to receipt of these funds. This effectively guarantees the rate to be applied and is done at the bank's current spot buying rate for funds to be received within one week.

(b) For longer periods (say up to three months) the formal forward exchange contract will provide a guaranteed rate of exchange for delivery either on a fixed date in the future or between two agreed dates. The latter scheme enables Worldwide to choose the time for delivery but not to opt out altogether. If the precise amount in dollars is not available, any shortfall can be purchased at the top rate to make up the amount of the forward contract. At least this way the exchange risk element on the bulk of the dollars due to be received will be covered.

(c) A third alternative is for Worldwide to open a foreign currency account which can be maintained with the local branch of its bank. Dollar remittances from the USA are placed into this account. Worldwide can again choose when to convert to sterling but the company can also calculate its currency income in advance and draw down, by arrangement on overdraft or loan, the estimated amount it is expecting to receive. The borrowed money can then be sold immediately for sterling at the current exchange rate. The sterling proceeds would then be used to pay bills or reduce sterling borrowing and the currency borrowing will be repaid as and when the currency income is received.

It is unlikely that Worldwide's finance director can totally avoid taking a calculated view on exchange rate movements especially over the longer term. The measures described above will minimise exchange rate risks over the shorter term but in many instances, the negotiation of these types of freight forwarding contracts are completed many months in advance. It is the problem of not knowing what prudent price to quote when currency markets are volatile that is Worldwide's major headache.

Case study II

Mayes Engineering Limited is tendering for a large overseas contract to install replacement valves in an Australian pipeline. Because of the specialised nature of the contract, it was expected that finance would be required for a minimum period of eight years. The bank is now being asked what specialised services are available to help the company with negotiations for this contract which will be worth £3 million and payments will be made in sterling so no exchange risks are involved.

Mayes Engineering Limited is an excellent company with experience in export business and carries ECGD cover.

_____

The provision of bank guarantees or bonds and the possibility of 'buyer credit' will strengthen the company's negotiating arm.

Without seeing the terms of the contract it is difficult to be specific, but many large overseas contracts require the exporter to be able to provide:

(a) a bid or tender guarantee;
(b) a performance guarantee;
(c) a maintenance guarantee.

The manager would be able to explain that in its ability to provide a bank bid guarantee the company had the confidence of its bankers. This will be reassuring to the Australian importers. If the company was successful with its bid, a performance guarantee would replace the bid guarantee. Again the early offer of this support would give considerable comfort to the Australian buyers. Equally, the offer of a maintenance guarantee from the bank, as an extension of the performance guarantee, can only help the negotiating team with this valuable order.

Also in conjunction with ECGD it may be possible to make long-term buyer-finance available. It would be necessary to explain to the directors of Mayes Engineering that the Australian buyers would normally be expected to find between fifteen and twenty per cent of the contract price. However, for the remainder of the funding costs, the buyer would have access to long lines of credit, a guaranteed source of funds at competitive rates of interest.

Finally, the personal requirements of the officials travelling overseas should not be overlooked. They will require travellers cheques, charge cards, foreign currency, insurance cover, perhaps special cash drawing arrangements and account facilities in Australia.

Summary

When assisting an importer or exporter, specialist advice will invariably be necessary. The branch banker's role is to identify the need for a particular type of service or services through an appreciation of the difficulties or problems which could arise. This identification of needs will only occur if the benefits provided through a comprehensive range of overseas services are understood. This chapter has concentrated heavily on product appreciation and less on the identification of market opportunities. The reason for this is that importer/exporter problems and requirements vary widely, and there is no substitute for a clear appreciation of an individual customer's circumstances. Except in very general terms, the bank services for importers and exporters cannot be marketed on a 'blanket' basis.

Probably the two most important problems a bank will face are an exporter who has a liquidity problem because of the protracted payment schedule, which is a common feature of the export trade, and an exporter seeking support when negotiating a large contract overseas.

Revision questions

1 What are the main trading risks for an exporter accepting 'open account' terms and what ways can these risks be minimised?
2 Your customer is entering the export market for the first time and anticipates that giving a longer credit period could upset cash flow. What facilities could a bank suggest to help overcome the envisaged cash flow difficulties?
3 Explain in detail all the services available to an exporter wishing to finance the sale of capital goods to a customer in Canada.
4 What is forfaiting, how does it work, and what advantages can be derived from using this type of facility?
5 Explain ECGD buyer and supplier credit facilities.
6 You have been asked to give a brief presentation covering personal financial matters to a major company's sales force exploiting Third World markets. What subject areas and services would you cover?

Chapter 19
Meeting Some Needs of Larger Corporate Customers

Competition for the banking business of the larger concerns, especially the multinational companies, has increased dramatically in recent years with the influx of foreign banks into the UK.

To meet this challenge, some major banks have created specialist corporate divisions to harness the skills of associates or subsidiaries, such as merchant banks, hire purchase subsidiaries, overseas banks which are part of the group, the registrar's division and, not least, the company or department which buys and sells funds in the money markets. In this way, many diversified sections of the bank can be co-ordinated to provide a comprehensive range of services. These include:

(a) Corporate financial advice on such matters as stock exchange quotations, mergers, capital buyouts and capital raising through rights issues and placings.

(b) Merchant banking which also covers finance restructuring, raising funds for management buyouts and equity capital provision for development purposes.

(c) Leasing facilities both at home and overseas.

(d) Export finance through ECGD guarantees, tender and performance bonds and associated Eurocurrency lending services to cover down payments.

(e) Computer services which include pay service, bankers automated clearing services (BACS), clearing house automated payment facilities (CHAPS) and many others.

(f) Share registration services which include maintaining company records of shareholders, issuing certificates, paying dividends and a host of associated faciiities.

Some of these services have already been covered in previous chapters. Others are highly specialised and fall outside the syllabus for the Chartered Institute of Bankers' examination. However, it is worth looking a little more closely at the functions of the registrar's division, the specialist areas of interest to a merchant banking arm and finally the services available from the subsidiary which operates in the London money market.

Share registration

There are no accurate statistics of the size of the market for share registration business. However, it is estimated that there are 17 million shareholders of quoted companies and of this the major clearing banks look after approximately 45 per cent of all registration business.

The largest registrar's department in the United Kingdom is the Lloyds Bank Registrar's Department. It was founded in 1956 and now maintains the registers of well over 600 companies, local authorities and unit trusts involving more than 8 million shareholders.

The basic services

By law, companies must keep a register of the names and addresses of all their members (shareholders), the quantity of stock each member holds and the dates of purchase and sale of shares. Therefore, the registrar's role is to ensure that this legal obligation and others are met.

Registrar's services include the following:

(a) maintenance of register of members;
(b) preparation and issue of share certificates;
(c) handling enquiries from shareholders, stockbrokers and others;
(d) making dividend and interest payments;
(e) handling company circulars, notices, etc. addressed to share-holders;
(f) completing various statutory returns;
(g) assisting with company meetings including voting processes.

The basic registration service provided by the department consists of maintaining the register, registering transfers, issuing certificates, providing addressed envelopes and answering shareholders' queries. Approximately 60 per cent of a registrar's income is generated from this work. But this does not convey the full service – or the degree of expertise and advice provided in all situations in connection with the shareholders and the register.

A registrar's department also carries out all types of capital operations including rights issues, bonus issues, mergers, takeovers and offers for sale. Some of these operations can be enormous with individual issues involving sums in excess of £500 million and hundreds of thousands of letters. Share issues to the public are profitable, as a considerable amount of money may be held by the registrar's department for short periods. Income is also derived from compiling various types of analyses of registers for companies handling employee profit-sharing arrangements and savings-related share option schemes.

Seeking new business

An important source of new business remains the link with the domestic branches of the bank. Even though a branch may not have a suitable company customer, opportunities occur to introduce the services of the registrar's department to directors and secretaries or other officials of a company for whom these people work.

A company may seek the services of a bank's registrar's department for a variety of reasons:

(a) A new company requires help with a flotation on the Stock Exchange or the unlisted securities market.

(b) A company with in-house registration capacity finds its existing resources need replacing to accommodate volume or because key staff are retiring.

(c) A company seeks assistance with a capital operation and this is a prime opportunity to transfer its registration workloads. A bank's fee for maintaining a register for a small company would be less than a quarter of the cost of a person's salary and overhead expenses.

(d) A company may have been using a registrar who has ceased to operate. Small organisations sometimes use the services of a chartered accountant.

(e) A company may be looking for a new registration service because it is dissatisfied with the present arrangements, either because of costs or efficiency.

The potential benefits of using a bank's registration service can be considerable. Daily responsibility for register maintenance is eliminated with a saving of office space and staff. Nevertheless, the company retains full access to shareholder information and the basic detail can be supplemented by the registrar through reports and analyses. Undoubtedly, the efficiency of operations should be improved as the bank's registrars' departments are equipped with the latest computer and word processor technology. In turn, this high standard of service to shareholders should enhance the image of the company.

Merchant banking

Merchant banking has its origins in the trading methods of countries in the late 1800s when bills of exchange were drawn on merchanting loans. These merchanting houses enjoyed the confidence of traders and by agreeing with lesser-known importers to accept bills of exchange on their behalf the 'accepting house' was born. The accepting house would charge a commission for this service and so there grew up a business of accepting bills to finance trade, not just for themselves as major merchanting houses, but also for others.

Thus, acceptance credit became the main means of financing international trade and still is the alternative source to bank overdrafts for financing shorter-term transactions. Today, this business is supervised and regulated by the Accepting Houses Committee formed by representatives from the seventeen leading merchant banks.

However, acceptance business was not the only activity of the merchant houses. During the late 1800s and early 1900s, their standing in international circles also brought requests for them to raise money for foreign governments. This they did by floating loans in London, but during the First World War this business ceased with the failure of foreign currencies and the loss of international confidence.

From about 1930 onwards, British industry began to move forward through expansion and also by mergers. Raising capital and offering financial advice became another major activity for merchant banks from about this time. Today it is referred to as issuing business – issuing bonds and stock in the markets to raise capital for its corporate clients. This business is also regulated and supervised by the Issuing House Association with 56 members.

Therefore, merchant banks can be 'accepting' houses or 'issuing' houses but in fact usually provide both these services. More recently, the services offered by merchant banks have expanded into other areas of operation. Many conduct banking business both at home and abroad for their clients; they offer trustee services, registration facilities, are dealers in foreign exchange and bullion, sell insurance and so on. Some merchant banks also have specialist subsidiaries which operate in the commodity markets for timber, rubber and coffee, etc. Their role is, therefore, wide-ranging and merchant banks can now provide most of the financial services required by a major company.

Merchant banking by the clearing banks

It was a natural extension of banking business for clearing banks to create a merchant banking arm. Clearing banks have close links with company customers and vast resources which enable their merchant bank subsidiaries to back up financial advice with medium- and longer-term loans.

Range of services

A bank's merchant bank subsidiary can offer a wide range of services.

But as its target market is mainly the 1000 largest companies operating in the United Kingdom, it focuses most of its efforts on providing the following services:

(a) *General financial information* The need for independent advice from a merchant bank can arise when a company reaches a critical stage in development. For example, in the case of a private company, a group of shareholders may decide that they no longer wish to retain all their shareholdings, or the directors of a public or private company may decide that an injection of new capital is required. In such cases the merchant bank is able to provide advice based upon considerable experience of similar problems with other clients.

(b) *Mergers and acquisitions* A company may consider it appropriate to expand its business by acquiring another. This may occur when the international development of the existing business is not providing a rate of growth that is satisfactory, or when the directors want to enter a new field and consider acquiring an established business is the best way of doing so. The merchant bank can advise on the best means of effecting an acquisition, carry out financial appraisals on the potential acquisition and assist with carrying through all aspects of the acquisition or merger.

(c) *Sale of companies* Owners of companies may wish to sell out completely or just dispose of part of their operation. A merchant bank can assist in finding a potential buyer, act as a negotiator and co-ordinate the advice and support of other professional involvement such as accountants, solicitors and stockbrokers.

(d) *Raising long-term capital* When a company, whether quoted or unquoted, needs to raise long-term capital, or certain shareholders wish to realise the value of part of their investments, there are a variety of ways to meet these requirements. Possibilities include rights issues of equity, issue of sterling debentures or loan stock and the issue of preference shares. A merchant bank has the experience and contacts to help a client decide on a suitable course of action. Once the decision to proceed has been made, the timing of action and implementation can be arranged by the merchant bank.

(e) *Stock Exchange quotations* During the life of a large private company, a stage is often reached when the question of whether to obtain a Stock Exchange quotation arises. At such a time it is important for the shareholders and the directors to be able to obtain advice on the advantages and disadvantages of the different courses of action open to them. A merchant bank will analyse the company's financial needs as well as the individual objectives of the people concerned, since only then could a view be formed on whether the aims would best be achieved by obtaining a Stock Exchange listing.

The ways in which a Stock Exchange listing can be obtained are:

(1) *Offer for sale* An issuing house (which could be the bank) buys some or all of the shares in the company from existing shareholders and then sells them to the investing public and institutions.

(2) *Placing* For smaller companies it may be more appropriate for a quotation to be obtained for the shares by means of a placing. In this case the shares to be issued are placed by the issuing house with investment institutions. A placing will only be permitted when at least 25 per cent of the share capital is to be quoted and where the market value of the placing is less than £3 million.

(3) *Introduction* This is another possibility but is not often appropriate. It arises when the shares are already widely held and in such circumstances an introduction of the shares to the Stock Exchange may be permitted.

(4) *Other possibilities* It might be better if a company's shares are dealt with under the Stock Exchange Rule 163(2) or by obtaining a quotation on the new Unlisted Securities Market. These arrangements are less expensive and burdensome than in the case of a full listing.

Potential market

As we have seen, the merchant bank subsidiary provides a very specialist range of services each of which is tailored to individual client requirements.

Marketing these services, therefore, is also a specialist operation and the main role of the high street branches, and other divisions and departments, is to spot opportunities to effect introductions. For most merchant bank subsidiaries of the major clearing banks, the principal target customers will be companies or groups which fall within certain parameters:

(a) Smaller profitable companies or groups with a turnover of over £2.5 million and a net worth of over £1 million.
(b) Larger companies or groups with substantial pre-tax profits of around £5 million or less.
(c) Companies which are for sale.
(d) Companies which might wish to seek a Stock Exchange or unlisted securities listing sometime in the future.
(e) Public quoted companies with or without merchant bank connections.

It may take several years of fostering a connection between the merchant bank and a potential client, but when business is gained it is highly profitable. Moreover, the merchant bank facilities enable the branch manager to provide the customer with a complete range of corporate services and so compete effectively in this lucrative market segment.

Money market services

The finance directors of companies are becoming increasingly aware of the different lines of credit now available which are not linked with the bank's base rates.

The banks are large operators in the London market. As well as dealing on their own account to utilise their own surplus funds, they also service a growing number of customers who wish to deposit or borrow funds at rates of interest linked to LIBOR (London Interbank Offered Rate). Although banks operating in the London Interbank Money Market buy and sell deposits of not less than $£\frac{1}{2}$ million each, they will also buy and sell deposits of a lesser amount and link interest rates to LIBOR. These funds are often used by the banks themselves to balance their own statutory liquidity ratios, by their subsidiaries such as hire purchase companies or by their international arms. Rates of interest offered for funds obviously vary from day to day, but also depend upon the amount, size and the length of time the deposit will be available.

Deposits

Deposits can be 'at call' or for a 'fixed term'. Some customers with surplus funds which may be required at very short notice can deposit money 'on call'. Rates are quoted usually on sums in excess of £50 000 and reflect the prevailing market conditions for short-term funds on a day-to-day basis.

Fixed-term rates are quoted for sums as low as £2000 when funds can be deposited for an identifiable length of time. Rates vary with the amount of the deposit and the length of time of the investment. No withdrawals can be made until the maturity date, at which time the deposit can be renewed at the rate ruling then.

Loans and acceptance services

Money market loans are available to larger companies and are designed to assist with cash flow requirements for periods from overnight up to three months. Normally lines of less than $£\frac{1}{2}$ million will not be considered. If a deal is done, interest rates are fixed at that time and formalities are kept to a minimum. No facility letter is issued and invariably the customer will deal direct with the bank's money market division, so that arrangements are concluded instantly over the telephone.

Revolving loans for medium-sized companies can also be provided with interest rates linked to LIBOR. Unlike money market lines the facility is a definite commitment, and consequently a margin above LIBOR is negotiated before a loan is made available. Moreover, all loans necessitate the issue of a 'facility letter' (agreement for loan) and usually a commitment to provide the facility is stipulated for a minimum period of one year.

Finally, 'acceptance lines' are available through a bank's money market operation. These are committed facilities made available to corporate customers, whereby the bank will place its name on bills of exchange drawn by the customer. Once these bills have been 'accepted' by the bank, the customer can then discount them, either through a subsidiary company or elsewhere. As bills accepted by the banks are eligible for re-discount at the Bank of England, they command the finest rate for discount.

The mechanics of a bank providing an acceptance credit facility and discounting bills of exchange were outlined in Chapter 18.

Case study I

Jack Iron is the managing director of J. I. Engineers Limited, a machine tool company of long standing. The business is thriving and this year profits are expected to reach £$\frac{3}{4}$ million. As a result, substantial credit balances are being seen. In the past, money has been placed on deposit at seven days' notice and Mr Iron now seeks advice on how interest earnings can be improved. How can you help?

The question seems to imply that all Mr Iron wants is information on money market rates but there are other opportunities which can be explored.

There are essentially two separate investment considerations, the investment of short-term day-to-day funds and the possibility of funds being available for a longer period.

For the short-term investment the obvious thought is through the money market, with various terms from 'overnight' to say 12 months fixed or on notice. Funds should be 'cleared' before being invested in the money market.

For a longer-term investment there is an opportunity to introduce Mr Iron to a specialist department for advice and possibly estate planning and pensions. In general terms, there are various areas where investment could be made, including the gilt-edged market, certificates of deposit, yearling bonds, etc.

The key to a good answer here is a simple appreciation that with a company like this the principals will want to maximise and protect their own financial standing through financial planning, just as much as improving the return on funds surplus to company cash flow requirements.

Case study II

Stay Bright Holdings Limited is a holding company with six subsidiary companies involved in general engineering. By careful planning and control the group has continued to remain profitable. The record over the past three years has been as follows:

Year to 31 April	1980	1981	1982
	£	£	£
Sales	6.14 m	7.26 m	8.40 m
Net profit	200 000	175 000	225 000

The capital base of the business is now standing at £1.85 million.

The business has banked with you since it was incorporated in 1936 and the accounts of all the subsidiary companies have been transferred to you on acquisition. Overdraft facilities of $£\frac{1}{2}$ million have been agreed. However, in March 1981, as they were purchasing their last subsidiary company, the directors were introduced to an American bank, which agreed to provide a loan of $£\frac{1}{4}$ million at a better rate than you were prepared to offer. This offer was taken up.

The directors are John and Harold Bright, sons of the late founder, and Anthony Cash, management accountant, who was appointed seventeen years ago as the first subsidiary company was acquired. The shareholding is split as follows: 40 per cent to John Bright and his family; 40 per cent to Harold Bright and his family; 20 per cent to Anthony Cash.

The three men are now in their mid/late fifties. Other than their homes, all of their personal financial resources are in the business. They have become concerned at this and would prefer to correct this imbalance without, of course, losing control of the company.

They approach you at this early stage for general guidance on the options available to them. They explain that, in due course, they will need to discuss matters with their accountant and solicitor, and possibly with the American bank, but they feel that as their banker you are better able to help them.

When advice would you give them? How could your bank help them?

Stay Bright is looking for specialist advice, available from the merchant banking division and trust company. There are three main areas for general discussion.

(a) sale of the shares
(b) directors' personal financial position;
(c) succession in the company.

In (a) reference is expected to the Unlisted Securities Market – not the Stock Exchange – bank's equity involvement, perhaps ICFC, insurance company, and pension fund. Anther possibility could be a take-over by another company; the merchant bank is likely to be aware of a number of companies interested in such acquisitions and introductions could be effected.

In (b) the implications of CGT and inheritance tax, pension arrangements, and investment of the sale proceeds of the shares would feature.

Probably the most significant area is (c), where the decision could affect both (a) and (b). Serious discussions will need to be conducted between the directors.

Detailed knowledge is not expected but an examiner will expect candidates to be aware of topics that would be relevant to the directors of Stay Bright.

Summary

This chapter has only highlighted, in the broadest terms, the multitude of services available to larger corporate customers. It is also evident that there are overlapping areas of activity within the bank's divisions and subsidiaries, which can sometimes cause conflict and confusion within the bank and for customers.

To alleviate the problems of similar services being offered by more than one source within the bank's overall structure, there is usually a controlling department or division responsible for co-ordinating the following main areas of activity:

(a) Cash management services
(b) Term lending facilities
(c) Money market services
(d) Corporate financial advisory services
(e) Equity participation
(f) Leasing facilities at home and abroad
(g) Overseas services including export finance
(h) Confirming house facilities
(i) Computer services including BACS and pay services
(j) Share registration

This list is by no means exhaustive but does serve to emphasise that the range of bank services available can accommodate most, if not all of the needs of corporate customers from the smallest to the largest multi-national organisation.

Appendix
Approach to Examination Questions

Having reached this stage in a career there is probably little that can be said about examination technique which has not already been said many times over. Moreover, giving this type of advice on a management science, which is as much acquired with experience as it is learned from textbooks, is not easy. However, there are some readily identifiable pointers to achieving success in a marketing examination paper and there are also some general words of wisdom about simple examination procedures which may be worth restating.

Candidates taking the Financial Studies Diploma (FSD) examination 'Marketing of Financial Services' are the primary audience for this textbook. Therefore I hope that other readers, who have chosen to use this book in preparation for other examinations, will understand why these remarks are particularly aimed at candidates taking the FSD paper.

In the preceding chapters, the objective has been to provide a broad understanding of marketing as an attitude to business generally. Moreover, I have also tried to give an in-depth appreciation of corporate strategy and its relationship with branch planning in order to show how this systematic approach applies to the broad spectrum of marketing activity. There can be no 'rule of thumb' guideline for all questions, but candidates will be expected to have a sound knowledge of the following aspects of this wide-ranging syllabus which strives to maintain 'degree standards':

- An understanding of what marketing is, what it does and how it relates to other strategic management or corporate functions. In the total business structure, marketing has a key role which impacts on most other organisational requirements.

- The functions of the main elements of marketing within the overall planning process and how these elements influence the running of a financial institution.

- Commercial aspects of marketing within the total business philosophy. The reasons for 'loss leaders' and the importance of profit and the logic behind objectives.

- How to manage marketing in a changing business scenario. There are winners and losers in any competitive environment. To be a winner will require marketing skills. These include research, analysis and interpretation enforced with sound marketing and management judgement. Managing marketing also requires accurate blending of the marketing mix.

Although the philosophy of marketing, the strategic considerations, and the planning process form a major part of the syllabus, the marketing skills, including appreciation of opportunities and threats required to operate in a busy high street, are also important. Thus candidates will also be expected to demonstrate understanding of the following issues:

- Reasons for segmenting markets and how this activity relates to sales and promotional activity. A good understanding of the matching of needs and benefits of mainstream financial services.

- How to plan marketing activity in a high street environment, harnessing the strengths, yet recognising the constraints.

- Campaign selling, including the importance and use to be made of packaging, pricing, promotion and communication in all its forms.

- The appreciation of the cyclical and ongoing nature of marketing and business development activity. The constant refinement of knowledge and skill is paramount in building up the levels of experience and expertise required to meet the challenges of a fast-moving and competitive industry.

These are a few 'shoulder' headings but hopefully they highlight the breadth and depth of knowledge and management skill required to achieve a good examination pass in this very challenging subject. As has been said many times before, the only constant of the marketing of financial services is its propensity to change. The present pace of development is likely to continue for some time to come, and as changes in competition and the marketplace generally occur, answers to those questions beginning with Why? What? When? Where? and How? should be sought. In this way candidates will gain a full appreciation of all the underlying factors relating to marketing issues. Seeking the likely answers to these questions, which will establish the facts and suggest how changes are expected to influence results, is a crucial part of the marketing research process. Rest assured that future examination questions will arise to test candidates' perceptions of what is happening in their industry and their management skill in interpreting what should be done to meet internal and external forces of change.

Understanding questions

Correctly interpreting the scenario of the question is the key to formulating a good answer. 'Marketing of Financial Services' is a practical paper and many questions are set in a practical context. However, you are asked to adopt several different roles from chief executive to branch manager. Thinking like a chief executive or marketing manager is not easy unless you have been fortunate enough to work closely with these policy-makers. Equally, more junior staff may not have developed the self-assurance of a branch manager.

Nevertheless, it is important to identify with the role you are asked to play in order to get the right strategic emphasis and practical balance. As a chief executive or the bank's marketing manager, you will have a different type of responsibility and available support facilities compared with those of a branch manager. The policy-makers help to shape the bank as a whole, and to do this they can call on specialist research teams, advertising agencies and other departments or sections of the bank. Branch managers are usually expected to implement policy in their locality. Thus their role and responsibilities are different, and often there are limitations to the extent the branch manager can utilise the elements of the marketing mix in pursuit of local goals. A good example of the differing capabilities can be seen in the way 'price' can be used. Chief executives can select various pricing strategies to influence demand, more so now as many services have a 'managed rate' structure. Branch managers have less control over the price they charge, which is sensible as it would not be very helpful to have branches competing with one another.

Candidates must appreciate the mantle they are asked to adopt; otherwise they will fail to exercise the correct roles and responsibilities. Answers then become at best blurred, at worst irrelevant. Nobody can attain good marks if they fail to understand the implications of the chosen environment highlighted in the question.

Before spending a few moments on examination technique, it is worth stressing that there may be no one right answer to an examination question. Often there will be a choice of solutions and degrees of bias towards one or other route to a solution. What is important is the logic of the sequence of steps or general thinking which comes through in candidates' answers. As this textbook has highlighted many times, each bank chooses to develop and expand in different ways. One has an estate agency chain, others have their own stockbroker arm, some want to be the 'Marks and Spencer' in the high street with priority on quality rather than quantity growth. What a dull world it would be if all the banks chose the same strategies to achieve similar goals. Just as the banks have chosen to go in different directions, so too will candidates when answering marketing questions. Provided the reasons why are clearly stated, good marks will be awarded to any answer that contains well-reasoned and cogent arguments for the policy and action chosen. The examiner can only be sure that a candidate has reached the required level of marketing skill and judgement if statements made are also justified and suggestions of what needs to be done are reinforced with explanations of why, when where and how. After all, marketing activity can be expensive in both the use of scarce resources and money. Therefore suggested activity or changes must be supported with reasons in answers to examination questions just as, hopefully, they are in the real world at all levels of the bank.

Examination technique

Some of the following basic points will be reminders to some candidates, but others may help to ensure that the limited examination time is used in the most fruitful way.

- Think before rushing into an answer. Make sure you understand the scenario and the implications of the role you are asked to adopt.

- Remember question one currently carries double marks and is usually related to corporate strategies and planning issues. Allow sufficient time to answer this question fully.

- Make the answers fit the questions. Attempts to imply that a particular question has 'hidden' factors is a waste of time. So too is writing down all you know on a particular subject when only some aspects are really relevant.

- Always consider the practical nature of this examination. If you state what solution you feel is appropriate, also state why. Moreover, having decided on what and why, do not forget to explain how and when.

- Whenever possible, tabulate or use a note format. When considered appropriate also use diagrams. Marshal your comments under sub-headings. It helps the examiner and it also reduces repetition.

- Before taking the examination, read the examiners' reports. Apart from pleas for legible writing, care with spelling and the entreaty to use common sense there are other gems of information which will help to steer you in the right general direction. The Chartered Institute of Bankers also publishes answers to these examination papers – a service that is unique to this subject. They are well worth reading when the revision stage is reached.

Finally there is no substitute for following a carefully planned course of study. In today's climate, just relying on your current knowledge, even with common sense, will not be sufficient to gain a pass in an examination testing skill and judgement in a management science that is dynamic and constantly evolving.

Index